INFORMATION ACTIVISM

SIGN,

STORAGE,

TRANSMISSION

A series edited by

Jonathan Sterne

and Lisa Gitelman

INFORMATION ACTIVISM

A Queer History

of Lesbian Media

Technologies

CAIT MCKINNEY

DUKE UNIVERSITY PRESS DURHAM AND LONDON 2020

Printed in the United States of America on acid-free paper ∞
Designed by Aimee C. Harrison
Typeset in Minion Pro, Helvetica LT Std, and IBM Plex Mono
by Westchester Publishing Services

Library of Congress Cataloging-in-Publication Data

Names: McKinney, Cait, [date] author.
Title: Information activism : a queer history of lesbian media
    technologies / Cait McKinney.
Other titles: Sign, storage, transmission.
Description: Durham : Duke University Press, 2020. | Series: Sign,
    storage, transmission | Includes bibliographical references
    and index.
Identifiers: LCCN 2019046772 (print) | LCCN 2019046773 (ebook)
ISBN 9781478007821 (hardcover)
ISBN 9781478008286 (paperback)
ISBN 9781478009337 (ebook)
Subjects: LCSH: Lesbian Herstory Archives. | Lesbians—Archival
    resources. | Lesbian feminism—Archival resources. | Digital
    media—Social aspects. | Archives—Social aspects. | Archival
    materials—Digitization—Social aspects. | Queer theory.
Classification: LCC HQ75.5 .M44 2020 (print) | LCC HQ75.5 (ebook) |
    DDC 306.76/63—dc23
LC record available at https://lccn.loc.gov/2019046772
LC ebook record available at https://lccn.loc.gov/2019046773

Cover art: Based on the cover of a call log created by the Lesbian
Switchboard of New York City, 1980–81. Lesbian Switchboard
Records, box 2, folder 35, The LGBT Community Center National
History Archive.

for Hazel

CONTENTS

Acknowledgments

This is a book about activists, caregivers, infrastructure builders, archivists, newsletter authors, telephone operators, unrelenting amateurs, queers, dykes, gender troublemakers, and feminists who have given their spare time to movements bigger than themselves. I have been given the gift of their hours, energy, and commitment to building more homely worlds out of information. I am especially grateful to the activists who took the time to speak with me about their work, some of whom I cannot name here, and some of whom I can: Anthony Cocciolo, Rachel Corbman, Deb Edel, Beth Haskell, Erin Horanzy, Ronika McClain, Teddy Minucci, Colette Denali Montoya-Sloan, Clare Potter, Kaileigh Salstrand, Saskia Scheffer, and Maxine Wolfe.

This book started as a dissertation in the Communication and Culture Program at York University. I am grateful for support from my supervisor Susan Driver and committee members Kate Eichhorn and Bobby Noble. Allyson Mitchell and Victoria Hesford brought new energy at the defense stage. Kate and Vicky each took the time to map out for me in writing, how this project could become a book that other people might want to read when I could not see the bigger picture (an incredible gift to give a new PhD).

A handful of friends and colleagues read portions of the manuscript in progress over the years, and their words and thoughts are very present in these pages: Rachel Corbman, Jack Gieseking, Jessica Lapp, Dylan Mulvin, and Lisa Sloniowski. Rachel has read every draft without hesitation, and I know I'm not the only one in our tiny field who has benefited from her intellect, willingness to help others, and encyclopedic knowledge of lesbian history (even the gossipy parts). Dylan and I met fifteen years ago for reasons that had nothing to do with academia, and he has since become my most important collaborator, editor, idea guy, cheerleader, and friend.

Some of this work benefited from editing in preparation for other publications. I thank Daniel Marshall, Zeb Tortorici, and Kevin Murphy, editors of the 2015 *Radical History Review* issue on Queer Archives. MC MacPhee and Andrea Zeffiro at *No More Potlucks* stewarded the publication of parts of chapter 3, and Carrie Rentschler and Samantha Thrift gave generative notes on chapter 1 for a special issue of *Feminist Theory* they edited. I also workshopped these ideas at McGill University's Culture and Technology Discussion and Working Group and the Social Media Collective at Microsoft Research New England, each of which improved the project.

At Duke University Press, the two anonymous readers were supportive and generous and pushed me where I needed it. Courtney Berger walked me through every step of the book publishing process with patience and care and always made sure I felt capable and supported. Sandra Korn helped me navigate all the tricky aspects of manuscript preparation so they never felt daunting. Thanks to Susan Deeks for the copyediting and Celia Braves for the index. Ambria Dean, Emily Dorrel, and Meichen Waxer were wonderful research assistants who helped me prepare the manuscript for publication.

A number of archivists and archives assistants made this research possible at their institutions and directed my attention to materials I otherwise never would have found in their collections: Alan V. Miller, Don McLeod, Raegan Swanson, and Rebecka Sheffield at the ArQuives in Toronto (formerly the Canadian Lesbian and Gay Archives); the staff at York University's Nellie Langford Rowell Library; Rich Wadell and Caitlin McCarthy at the LGBT Community Center National History Archive in New York City; Jean Deken and Dorothy Leung at the SLAC National Accelerator Laboratory Archives at Stanford University; the reference archivists at the New York Public Library's Manuscripts and Archives Division, especially Tal Nadan; and Rachel Corbman, Saskia Scheffer, and Deb Edel at the Lesbian Herstory Archives. Thanks to Ginger Brooks Takahashi, A. L. Steiner, Tineke Graafland, the Lesbian Herstory Archives, the LGBT Community Center National History Archive, and the Rand Corporation for allowing me to reproduce images in these pages.

This research was funded by two grants from the Social Sciences and Humanities Research Council of Canada: a Joseph Bombardier Canada Graduate Scholarship and a Michael Smith Foreign Study grant, which funded my research in New York. My final year of writing was supported by a Susan Mann Dissertation Scholarship provided by York University. Postdoctoral fellowships from Media@McGill (via the Beaverbrook Foundation) and the Social Sciences and Humanities Research Council of Canada supported me as I wrote the book manuscript, and SFU's University Publications Fund provided financial support for the publication of this book.

A web of mentors helped me carry on in academia (despite the miseries of this job market) and finish this book, especially Elspeth Brown, Patrick Keilty, Carrie Rentschler, and Jonathan Sterne. They worked with me as a postdoctoral fellow at the University of Toronto and McGill University as I developed the manuscript, and each modeled the kind of feminist mentorship to which I aspire. Within a university system that leaves less and less time to take care of other people, they do the work in their own ways.

I have benefited from the friendship, intellectual engagement, writing support, and humor of the greatest colleagues across five institutions and beyond while working on this book. I especially thank Ellen Balka, Melissa Brough, Mary Bunch, Aleena Chia, Wendy Chun, Marika Cifor, Li Cornfeld, Natalie Coulter, T. L. Cowan, Karrmen Crey, Milena Droumeva, Zoë Druick, Sarah Ganter, Gina Giotta, Jade Huell, Jinah Kim, Joel Lemuel, Nicholas Matte, Svitlana Matviyenko, Anne MacLennan, Pavi Prasad, Jas Rault, Aimee Carrillo Rowe, Leslie Shade, Sarah Sharma, Rianka Singh, Kathryn Sorrells, and Melissa Tindage.

My family has been a steady source of support, laughs, and reminders not to take myself too seriously; thank you, Kim, David, Jessica, Devon, Brian, Thanos, Tamar, Jay, Bilee, and Cvjetka. I owe so many thanks to my friends: Mitchell Akiyama, Cecilia Berkovic, Alice Christensen, Aleesa Cohene, Sam Cotter, Eric Emery, Marty Fink, Joseph Flessa, Amy Fung, Jules Gaffney, Hannah Jickling, Zoe Kreye, Vanessa Kwan, Mason Leaver-Yap, Rachel Levitsky, Logan MacDonald, Stephanie Markowitz, Hedia Maron, Elaine Miller, Alexis Mitchell, Gabby Moser, Helen Reed, Elaisha Stokes, everyone at SQWISH (my queer and trans basketball league), Leila Timmins, cheyanne turions, and Brent Wadden.

My partner, Hazel Meyer, and my dog, Regie Concordia, fill every day with joy, even the lousy ones. Hazel taught me to notice how objects get made in ways that media studies never could. This project would not have taken the turns it did without her curiosity about material culture and reverence for little things like index cards.

Introduction

In the early 1980s, when computer networks felt new and their utility for feminist organizing was still unclear, the "Women's Information Exchange" began to advertise in lesbian-feminist newsletters. These women had witnessed the manipulation of computer databases by "enemies" to feminist causes such as the "anti-abortion Moral Majority" and thought it was time to form computerized information infrastructures of their own: "We recognize that many women are fearful about having their names on a computer. It is important to remember that most of us are already on any number of computerized mailing lists, none of which are voluntary nor oriented towards feminists. . . . Feminists, too, must come out of isolation and become part of a national communications network, made possible by computer technology."[1] Their lengthy announcements promoted a new, nonprofit "computerized databank" service: the National Women's Mailing List. Based in San Francisco, the project used database software to gather information about women's backgrounds and interests, and then connect them with corresponding publications and activist organizations they might not know about: "Formed by grassroots feminists, the Women's Information Exchange is dedicated to putting information technology to use in facilitating outreach, networking, and resource sharing among women. The goal of the organization is to use computer technology to support the efforts of women's projects throughout the country."[2]

To do this, the Women's Information Exchange gathered radical feminist resources from publications and community groups and added them to a computer database organized by "area of interest." Subscribers to the service mailed in surveys in which they chose fields for "the areas of interest that affect your working self, your political self, and your social self." This service allowed lesbians, often marginalized within mainstream feminist movements, to access information specific to their interests. Subscribers who worried about privacy could "select the level of access" others would have to their names and other personal information: "You can participate in larger information networks by choosing the highest level of access, or you can restrict your participation, for example, to women-only organizations." The service added information about each subscriber to the database, generating a rudimentary user profile, and subscribers received specialized mailings tailored to the data points they provided.

In many ways, the Women's Information Exchange was a typical 1980s computerized mailing list. It used a database to gather and deploy information about user demographics in ways that define online platforms decades later. This particular database matters because of the specific promises it made for lesbian feminism, including the autonomy and privacy offered to users regarding their data. The Women's Information Exchange explained to lesbians how computer databases could benefit their movements by connecting individuals with niche information about lesbian life that was otherwise difficult to access, even within feminist circles. Lesbian feminists evaluating their representation in 1980s computer databases raised unique privacy concerns, including fear of antifeminist backlash and wariness about the stigma that could result from personal information falling into homophobic hands. To address these concerns, the Women's Information Exchange promoted a burgeoning feminist data politics based on user control and transparency about how and why information about individuals would be collected and stored. This mailing list is one small part of a larger, community-generated information infrastructure behind lesbian-feminist movements and their transitions to digital technologies. Although it is much less exciting and less sweaty than the collective din of consciousness-raising circles and other embodied forms of activism, information has been just as critical to late twentieth-century feminism.

This book examines a series of social movement organizations and individuals in the United States and Canada whom I call *information activists*: women who responded to their frustrated desire for information about lesbian history and lesbian life by generating that information themselves.[3] Information activism describes a range of materials and processes constituting the collective, often unspectacular labor that sustains social movements.[4] This concept brings together people, their visions of justice, and the media they use to organize, store, and provide access to information, a relationship that is key to understanding feminism's role in histories of commonplace technologies such as computer databases.

Radical feminists have designed complex multimedia practices to circulate information that has been difficult, or even impossible, to come by otherwise—from basic wayfinding information about where to find a lesbian roommate, plumber, or therapist to historical information about earlier generations of lesbian activists from whom to draw essential inspiration. Information activism provides basic support and care that makes living a lesbian life possible. Oriented toward these goals, lesbian feminists practice technological resourcefulness and perform behind-the-scenes labor with new media technologies that constitutes a queer history of information.[5]

Feminist theory and politics develop alongside practical, technical skills; the specific media formats feminists choose; and the distribution methods they develop to reach a public.[6] Historicizing feminism means exploring these engagements with media as conditions of possibility. Media practices enact theory and politics, and technologies can enable and constrain relationships between feminists and the collectivities on which they rely. Lesbian feminists built or altered sociotechnical systems to carry out their work, and these systems materialize their imbrication in queer, antiracist, and feminist life-worlds. Information activism leverages the entanglement of politics with technologies to build infrastructures for lesbian feminism.

Theorizing a concept such as information infrastructure—and, more broadly, the turn *to* information and infrastructure within media studies— through lesbian feminism might seem like a non sequitur. I argue that groups marginalized because of gender, sexuality, and race have the most to tell us about how, when, and for whom information matters. As Susan Leigh Star put it, "Feminist, antiracist, and multicultural theory, and our collective experience in these domains is one of the richest places for which to understand these core problems in information systems design: how to preserve the integrity of information without *a priori* standardization and its attendant violence."[7] Lesbian feminists show us another way forward with information—a different set of questions to ask.

Late twentieth-century U.S. lesbian-feminist activists worked to collect and parse large amounts of information that would make marginal lives visible, adopting various information management and compression techniques to do so. They did this work within conditions of exclusion from access to reliable, high-quality information about lesbian life and from the margins of social structures and even mainstream feminism. Their tactics often created anxiety over the effects rationalization procedures might have on information meant to represent messy, sexually and politically complex lives. To address these tensions, activists reworked existing standards in information management through the design of unique subject-classification schemes; the use of alternative communication networks; and the appropriation of tools such as telephones, filing systems, early computer databases, and, more recently, digital archives.

Lesbian-feminist activism's transition from paper-based methods to computing and other digital technologies spans a period from the early 1970s to the late 2010s. Following historiographic methods that consider media through emergence, negotiation, transition, and struggles over meaning and use, I zero in on a series of moments "before the material means and the conceptual modes of new media have become fixed, when such media are not yet accepted as natural, when their own meanings are in flux."[8] Through analysis of social movement archives that gather the records information activists leave behind, and interviews with activists about their technological work, I examine how lesbian feminists shaped developing understandings of digital media when it was new.

This story begins in the Women in Print Movement of the 1970s and '80s, when feminist publishing houses, periodicals, and bookstores began feverishly producing printed matter for a growing popular movement. Within their niche corner of this print revolution, lesbian feminists wanted to organize, describe, distribute, and archive newsletters and other gray literature *as information* that present and future generations could use.

Scholars have generally approached the Women in Print Movement's history through the rubric of print culture studies. The affordances of new, low-cost publishing technologies drew lesbians toward what Barbara Sjoholm so elegantly calls "the sheer butch glamour of printing."[9] This "print" movement took shape during the emergence and wide adoption of computing and accessible database technologies. Digital understandings of information shaped how print-newsletter makers understood their publications as building communication networks. Housed today in LGBTQ community archives, this print activism's paper trail continues to search out digital avenues for wider access. Lesbian history accounts on platforms such as Instagram provide online engagement with the past as they reproduce a wide range of print ephemera generated by this movement, scanned and recirculated for an intergenerational audience eager to connect with, critique, and reimagine queer history.[10]

But present-day online collections are not where this paper movement first entered digital spaces; rather, ways of thinking digitally about information were embedded in lesbian-feminist work with paper, in the ways lesbian feminists learned computing and imagined and built networks and databases for storing and sharing information. Tracing the digital life of a paper movement responds to Lisa Gitelman's critique of "print culture's" conceptual paucity—specifically, its inability to account for the specificities of media and the messy work people do across forms.[11] Rather than rely on "print" and "digital" as stable categories that represent a temporal progression—paper is scanned and "put online"—this book takes a more archaeological approach, considering complex transitions between media and listening for the unexpected echoes of the digital in the past: how, for example, lesbian-feminist indexers sifted through mountains of paper index cards while dreaming of computer databases.[12]

Echoes are not always easy to hear, and the historical aspects of this work were not always obvious to me. This research began as a contemporary study of digital archives that enliven lesbian-feminist histories. More specifically, it began in the basement of the Lesbian Herstory Archives (LHA), where I found myself at the end of a tour on the first of what would prove to be many visits over the coming years. The LHA is an unusual space to begin with; a volunteer-run, community archive housed in a brownstone in Brooklyn, it's part cultural heritage organization and part domestic space.[13] Researchers visit the archives from around the world in search of records that document lesbian life and activism, most of which have been donated by individual women, or grassroots social movement groups.

Working in the archives, you feel as if you're in someone's home. There is a couch and a kitchen where coffee is often brewing, but there are also vertical files, worktables, computers, scanners, an audio digitizing station and acid-free boxes filled with special collections. The basement similarly straddles the domestic and archival spheres. Like the basements in many homes, it is crammed with things that don't quite belong upstairs but are impossible to throw out. But these particular objects aren't old Halloween costumes or discarded sports equipment. They're the remnants of twentieth-century lesbian history. Audiocassette tapes, posters, records, and other ephemera crowd the partially finished basement. Despite occasional moisture problems, the materials are generally safe but take on an undeniable quality of "overflow" when situated in relation to what is upstairs.

I found myself standing in this overcrowded basement, staring at a wall of shelving filled with three thousand audiotapes (the archives' spoken word collection), thinking about the twentieth-century archive as a space presented with a very twenty-first-century problem of transition: what to do with all this stuff—box after box filled with magnetic tape, paper documents, and other precarious formats? This was 2013, and the archives was beginning to implement digitization projects they hoped would improve and expand access to collections, address the problem of preservation, and ameliorate a physical space crunch. As I learned over the coming years, they were doing digitization their own way, bringing a feminist critique of technological accessibility and a resourceful, "good-enough" approach to bear on established archival standards. The archives' intervention with digital media became the focus of my work. I wanted to learn how these women were approaching digitization as an extension of their broader lesbian-feminist activist practice, and I wanted to learn what their work could tell us about the politics of digital media more generally.

Like basement storage, the edges of this project slowly expanded as more objects in need of care arrived. What began as a contemporary study of these particular archives in transition expanded into a media history of U.S. lesbian-feminist information activism; it couldn't have been any other way. Thinking about digital archives in the present proved impossible without understanding a longer history of how lesbian feminists appropriate commonplace media technologies toward the goal of better, more accessible information that might sustain feminism, and the everyday lives of lesbians. While watching archives volunteers create records using a desktop computer and the simple database software program DB/TextWorks, I found myself asking when the archives got its first computer (1984); what the first mailing database looked like (pretty rudimentary); and how volunteers learned how to use the new system (one computer-savvy woman was responsible for teaching everyone else). I searched for ways to connect the archives' choice of open-source audio-capture software today to the organization's founding principles of accessibility, written in 1978: "Archival skills shall be taught, one generation of Lesbians to another, breaking the elitism of traditional archives."[14] Understanding how feminist histories live on in digital archives means engaging deeply with the information infrastructures out of which these digital histories emerged.

Lesbian Infrastructures

In addition to looking both backward and forward in time, information activism bridges a range of media technologies that lesbian-feminist organizations used to create actionable information that could *do something* for their movements. Information activism works across multiple media toward accessibility and social transformation. Technologies are combined to form the larger information infrastructure that allowed lesbian feminism, as a social movement, to cohere.

At the core of this infrastructure are print newsletters, which became a common lesbian feminist activist technology in the early 1970s and were important for telling women about events, issues, and resources. Newsletters used information to facilitate everyday connections among readers, who might live in different places but share interests and political commitments. Information activists created indexes and bibliographies to make the content in these newsletters searchable and actionable. These resource guides categorized information drawn from print newsletters by subject so that those in need of information on a given topic—Censorship, Chicana Lesbians, Pornography, or Softball, to name a few—could find it at their fingertips. Indexes to lesbian materials became definitive "guides to the literature," assembled by capable lesbian-feminist hands that parsed raw information using paper index cards and, later, computer databases. Circulated in the form of books or smaller, self-published documents, these indexes were often advertised or excerpted in newsletters.

Telephone hotlines provided yet another avenue for accessing this information. Lesbian-identified telephone operators thumbed through reference books or drew from file cabinets full of print resources to provide callers, some in crisis, with the information they asked for, which was also the care many needed to survive the day. Today, the work archives do to organize and open access to collections through digitization evokes many of the management and pathfinding techniques practiced by earlier newsletters, telephone hotlines, and indexes. These technologies are entangled across time in ways that become apparent through a longer history of lesbian feminist information-management as activism.[15] Through historiographic methods, a wide range of media technologies become interconnected in a larger activist information infrastructure.

The term "infrastructure" describes technical systems in which resources operate in complex combination to make communication or knowledge work possible.[16] Infrastructures operate in the background and thus are often taken for granted, until they break, fail, or otherwise frustrate users.[17] Infrastructure failures and breakages are not equally shared. Lesbian-feminist activists came up against these failures often, like many groups marginalized from mainstream information sources. For example, indexers created their own sets of terms to classify information because existing schema, such as the Library of Congress's standard subject headings, failed to describe lesbian materials in sufficient detail or in affirmative, subculturally meaningful terms.[18]

Activism is most often written into history as big events and public spectacles, which renders quieter infrastructures invisible. A recent turn in feminist historiography seeks to address the basic methodological problem of how to write about a monolithic social movement—twentieth-century feminism—that is in fact made up of many tiny, unevenly connected groups.[19] My attention to information infrastructure is most specifically in dialogue with alternative feminist historiographies grounded in the study of activist mediation.[20] Activist infrastructures are where the messy, grinding, generally invisible labor of "doing feminism" takes places. As Samantha Thrift and Carrie Rentschler argue, "Feminists build technological, affective and cultural infrastructures through which they produce, disseminate and share resources, ideas and knowledge."[21] This everyday work provides crucial support for the high-stakes goals that drive social movements in the first place. It's work feminists do together in collaboration, conflict, or something in between. As Star and Karen Ruhleder discuss, infrastructure is a "fundamentally relational concept" wherein processes, technologies, standards, systems, and work become infrastructures only in relation to particular organized practices and cultural contexts.[22] Although Star and Ruhleder are not writing about activism specifically, their emphasis on praxis is instructive: "Infrastructure is something that emerges for people in practice, connected to activities and structures."[23] The history of feminism is also a history of media and the infrastructural work activists do.

Researching information activism means paying attention to a lot of run-of-the-mill, often overlooked work with common media technologies. Rentschler takes an infrastructural approach to the study of feminist social movements and their media practices, arguing that much feminist activism is "communicative labor" that takes place out of sight of its final representational forms. Rentschler makes a methodological argument for studying feminist social movements at "the midlevel scale of their communication," through documentary research among memos, reports, newsletters, and other movement texts.[24] These papers form "rich documentary evidence" of a movement's communication networks.[25] Focusing on these document genres and work processes, and their entanglements with people and politics, is an entry to understanding how activist infrastructures develop across time. Reading closely and for relationships across texts, I examine a range of documents that include newsletters, meeting minutes, telephone call logs, internal memos, letters and other correspondence, online archival interfaces, photographs, catalog records, log books, subject thesauruses, instruction manuals, handbooks, bibliographies, and actual index cards.

The LHA is an unusual institution, and other research has emphasized its eccentric physical space.[26] While a thick description of the basement is part of understanding this archives' media practices, an infrastructural approach also considers the invisible, interstitial processes that make archives tick, such as batches of index cards that are written on, edited, and sorted with care. The work of writing this book began in a basement full of audiotapes and ended sorting through boxes of telephone hotline call logs. The differences between these materials—the often-invisible, strange paths taken to get from one to the other—are precisely the project's point. Studying information activism means following information as it moves—the logistics of information—to see the infrastructures that quietly get it where it needs to go: across space, across different forms of media, and through time.

As a method, following information lends itself to studying process over product. Lesbian-feminist *media practices* are the everyday, amateur work activists perform with technologies to build grassroots information infrastructure. My research objects tend to be less glamorous records: I explore how books are assembled instead of the words they convey and investigate how archives are run at the cost of paying close attention to the unique materials and rich histories they house. This approach is foremost about the project's grounding in media and infrastructure studies, a field that considers the systems, technologies, standards, and routines through which knowledge is produced. A media studies approach to process investigates the conditions of mediation through which identities such as lesbian are relegated, rationalized, and ordered retrospectively. Information activists do work "about" sex and sexuality but spend most of their time on the not-very-sexy shuffling of documents—paperwork that is crucial and urgent even when it cannot capture the vitality or erotic energy represented by what is printed on these papers.

In archival documents, interviews, and second-wave publishing, the term "information" is often used in subtle ways that foreground its interstitial role in making collaboration among feminists possible. "Information" is a slippery term, pinned down most notably by the Data-Information-Knowledge-Wisdom (DIKW) hierarchy prominent in information science. The DIKW model constructs information as a stage in between "raw" data and actionable knowledge, where information is parsed to some extent so that it might be readily used by human actors. Information also requires additional work, and critical analysis, by these actors, to advance knowledge. Scholars in information studies have questioned the methodological usefulness of these divisions, which are often arbitrary in practice or based on dated philosophical assumptions. Similarly, the media studies scholars

Lisa Gitelman and Virginia Jackson have outlined the troubling cultural work that the "raw data" myth performs.[27]

Information's essential properties are elusive, so the term is best characterized through its forms and transmission processes. As "knowledge that is communicated," information achieves its status as "information" through the act of being imparted and the forms that this movement takes.[28] Information must be "capable of being stored in, transmitted by, and communicated to inanimate things" ("information, *n*."). For example, genetic information becomes information, as it were, when it is transmitted through biological matter. This book understands information primarily through the material work processes that organize and transmit information so that it might be useful to marginalized publics who otherwise lack easy access to these resources. Distinguishing information from data, or knowledge, is less important than the category's emphasis on creating infrastructures and interfaces that open up worlds.

I approach information as the object that moves through the application of specific media practices—practices that form nascent publics and shape their demands. Information is articulated to political visions of what might be, the kind of worlds and lives that strong lesbian-feminist infrastructure might sustain. The ability to access information is always about much more than the simple fulfillment of a query. In its movement and use, information makes promises that are much greater than "finding things out."

Activists are at information activism's center: the people who publish newsletters, answer telephones, and maintain archival collections. They are actors in bold sexual subcultures who have taken great personal and professional risks by working to make and distribute information about sexuality. To supplement my documentary methods, I have interviewed these activists whenever possible. During three months of research at the LHA, I interviewed a number of the archives' volunteers about digitization, online media, and the future of the archives. These interviews involved a lot of talking, but also showing: I asked volunteers to walk me through the work they were doing, whether it was scanning photos of Dyke Marches from the 1980s and putting them online, "cleaning up" metadata in the archives' catalog, or digitizing a tape-recorded speech by Audre Lorde.

How these volunteers described their work was important, but I learned just as much from watching them do digitization, especially about how commitments to technological accessibility take form in practice. This show-and-tell was also an education in how community archives work; these volunteers, not all of them professional librarians or archivists, taught me what my own training in the humanities and media studies had not. They patiently explained terms such as "Dublin Core" (a metadata standard), "original order" (a contentious approach to records arrangement), and "OPAC" (online public access catalog, or the public's interface with a library database), equipping me with the education I needed to do this work. As I listened to, watched, and worked alongside these volunteers, the interviews became opportunities to learn how information activists transgress standards in information management though everyday technological decisions.[29]

The information activists whose work is considered here—archivists, newsletter makers, telephone operators, and indexers—engage with new media technologies in ways that are critical for establishing more expansive, comparative media histories of information. For example, these activists brought grounded commitments to self-determination to the decisions they made about database design, resulting in systems whose flexibilities around classification are informed by lesbian feminism.[30] Put another way, these activists needed to be able to easily revise how they were describing political and identity-laden materials in databases in order to be sensitive to shifting community values. Lesbian feminists thought computers would offer this flexibility, even though these machines were otherwise difficult to access. The LHA and the Circle of Lesbian Indexers are two organizations whose attempts to "go electronic," chronicled in this book, offer feminist interventions with common understandings of computerized information management when it was new. Hesitant computing practices interrupt histories of the "user-friendly" computer in the 1980s as an inexorable and accessible time-saving device, placing lesbian feminist values in the way of computing's promise as a new technology for managing information.

Feminist media studies often draws on archival research to account for the contributions of apparently "minor figures" in media and technological history. Jennifer Light's study of mid-twentieth-century women computer programmers "hidden during this stage of computer history," Lisa Nakamura's work on the Navajo women who assembled early microchips in the late 1960s and early 1970s using hands practiced at weaving, and Patrick Keilty's account of the women librarians who tediously developed machine-readable cataloging standards in the 1960s are three examples.[31] These feminist media histories argue that gendered labor is easy to overlook because it takes place behind the scenes, as programming, manufacturing, or data input. However, this work constitutes inventive sites where new media technologies are tested and adapted, building a cultural infrastructure for twentieth-century information management.[32]

The invisibility of women's work in histories of media and technology is perhaps most acute when this work takes the form of service, care, or emotional labor, categories that include activist projects understood as labors of love. By centering "minor players" in media histories we become attuned to how sexuality and emotion make technological systems work smoothly. Dylan Mulvin's history of the Lena test image, a torn-out *Playboy* centerfold used to develop image compression algorithms, shows how women's sexualities became a form of communicative exchange in computer engineering labs.[33] Similarly, Alana Cattapan and Quinn DuPont's history of "Alice and Bob," characters used as standard prototypes in computer engineering problems, uncovers the heteronormative relationship dynamics at the heart of how students who go on to develop new computing technologies are trained.[34] Even as prototypes, stand-ins, or what Mulvin calls "proxies," women such as Lena and Alice do deeply cultural, communicative work that matters in how technological systems are established.[35]

Women's affective work with media and technology sits stubbornly at the heart of communication studies. A "Telegram Girl" is central to Claude Shannon and Warren Weaver's foundational theory of transmission, the postwar communication model still taught in introductory communication studies course today. Shannon and Weaver argue that the content of a message does not matter to its successful transmission by describing the "very proper and discreet girl accepting your telegram [who] pays no attention to the meaning, whether it be sad, or joyous, or embarrassing."[36] Women performed telegraph and telephone operations and other low-level communications tasks in the post–World War II period, and these workers were expected not to remark on the sensitive information they relayed. The choice to read and then not act on the content of hundreds of messages each day would take an emotional toll on workers that complicates how we understand the so-called neutrality of information delivered by telephone operators. These women surely took subtle, subversive maneuvers with whatever agential opportunities they found.[37]

This telegram girl's labor, attention, or refusal is central to transmitting information. As I explore in chapter 2, lesbian-feminist telephone operators responded in creative ways to the information hotline's expectations that they "be neutral" on the phone, practicing forms of affective management, active listening, and commitments to "meeting women where they are at," even when they disagreed with a caller's position. Attention to this careful telephone comportment centers affective labor and everyday information technologies in how social movements are built.

Information activism describes how movement-related information is stored, sorted, searched for, and retrieved by lesbian-feminist activists serving communities they care about. Archives figure prominently in the lesbian-feminist information infrastructure to which this book is attuned. Information activists draw on archives for research when they create resources and use these archives to store their finished work so that it can continue to serve in the future. Lesbian-feminist archivists are themselves information activists, building and maintaining community archives to document the everyday work social movements do with information. These archives, especially in their digital manifestations, emphasize access and community accountability over preserving documents in boxes kept "safe" from use. Preservation and access are inextricable aspects of collections management that ideally should be complementary but often are in tension in archives.[38] The LHA has an open access policy, and even one-of-a-kind special collections are stored on open shelves so visitors can take down boxes and peruse at will. This policy materializes a unique feminist access politics that shapes the archives' overall preservation strategy: visitors who handle these materials share an unusual level of responsibility for their care.

Digitization offers no easy solutions for problems of preservation, as it introduces a host of concerns about managing digital objects over time. Archivists migrate data across formats as they become obsolete and confront the pressures of ongoing user demand for access to original records.[39] Bracketing many of these concerns, the LHA's digitization initiatives seek improved access for community members and researchers, practicing a "good-enough" approach to creating and managing digital collections. This approach to digitization puts into practice what Lucas Hilderbrand has described as an "aesthetics of access" with media technologies.[40] When the archives uploads photographs from their collection to an online database, they want to get great scans and write useful, consistent metadata, but they are not intimidated by elusive technical standards or best practices. The archives will not wait to acquire better technology or settle on a perfect, controlled vocabulary for metadata; those photos of lesbian history need to be online because queer communities need access to them now.

Digital archives have democratized historical research but long after information activists sought to do this democratizing work with paper and "analog" electronic tools.[41] Newsletters, telephone hotlines, and indexing projects share with community archives the goal of mediating between a public and various kinds of information; they give users access to primary sources or published materials, someone kind and knowledgeable to talk to, or connection to a network of other lesbians they did not know about. Digitization introduces new ways of thinking about media and access but ultimately builds on the movement's longer work with media and information technologies.

Approaching archives through the rubric of information, infrastructure, and access reconsiders the status of the "archive" and what a media studies approach might offer to queer and feminist archive theory. Feminist media studies scholarship considers the archival logics and material timescales of particular technologies, as well as how those technologies underpin actually existing archives, broadly conceived.[42] Community archives are built, managed, and encountered within specific mediated conditions that shape social movements' histories. Some feminist media practices are more, or less, "archivable." The dominance of print culture in second-wave feminist historiography ought to inspire us toward more speculative methods that can account for the kinds of feminist media practices that resist documentation: the actual telephone calls made to information hotlines or the connections with embodied others facilitated by newsletter networks. In the archive, call log sheets filled out by volunteers and classified ads placed in newsletters gesture to these mediated encounters, even as actual connections resist capture. These are the aspects of social movement infrastructure that we can only *sort of know* via actually existing archives.

In *The Archaeology of Knowledge*, Michel Foucault describes the archive as a discursive system, or a kind of infrastructure.[43] For Foucault, an archive is made up of statements, units of speech that have meaning only in relation to the communicative web in which they are situated. Archives organize statements in such a way as to produce a notion of "history," grouping together what is thinkable and sayable in a given social context, such as Lesbian Feminism (capital L, capital F). For Foucault, the archive is a living constellation in which the relationships among statements are always under negotiation. Some contemporary scholars of archive theory have bridged these ideas with actual archival collections. Ann Stoler's work on colonial archives and her methodological incitement to read along the archival grain imagines archives as systems that have particular organizing logics and governing effects, shoring up power over colonial subjects over the long term.[44] Jarrett Drake, a digital archivist and scholar, argues that the foundational principles structuring archival science (ownership, authorship) "valorize and venerate white western masculinity."[45] Kate Eichhorn's work on feminist print archives of the recent past positions archival collections as technologies that order feminist social movements in retrospect, where archives make forms of feminist activism appear discrete at the cost of preserving their complex heterogeneity.[46]

Community archives attempt to ground their work in different logics. Created by minority groups, these archives respond to what Michelle Caswell terms "symbolic annihilation" performed by mainstream archival institutions, which "has far-reaching consequences for both how communities see themselves and how history is written for decades to come."[47] Caswell and other scholars emphasize archiving from below as a form of protest communities use to imagine other kinds of histories and futures, including by opening up archival processes to critique and revision.[48] Community archives are interfaces with history and discursive systems that have epistemological, ontological, and social consequences.[49]

As Jamie A. Lee explains, recognizing and understanding the intricacies of how community archives work differently is necessary for opening up the archives and its methodologies, and experimenting with queer approaches to the digital mediation of stories about the past.[50] Similarly, Tonia Sutherland and Drake each argue that community-based approaches to archiving can alter the terms through which marginalized people's histories are narrated by building alternative systems that make visible the role archives have played in sustaining anti-Black racism.[51] Community archives organized around gender and sexuality do not always offer these alternatives, and can be complicit in sustaining cis-normative and racist practices within the field, framing queerness as a unifying experience of historical erasure at the cost of attending meaningfully to other axes of difference. Syrus Marcus Ware and Rio Rodriguez, each working on activist archives by and for queer and trans Black, Indigenous, and People of Color, have theorized some LGBTQ community archives as tools of white supremacy, oriented toward understandings of events, spaces, and documentary practices that systematically erase queer and trans people of color from the historical record.[52]

Each of these scholars understands archives as constructed interfaces with history and discursive systems caught up in larger operations of power. Their work frames archives as epistemological technologies that structure how the past is encountered. Basic information-management techniques play a role in these encounters, where various media practices central to archival processes facilitate historical ordering. The archive is indistinguishable from its conditions of mediation, including the kinds of activism that gets documented, kept, or digitized one day and the practical decisions archives make about the technologies they will and will not use to do this work.

Information studies scholars, along with practicing librarians and archives scholars, have helped me consider how everyday choices such as the assignment of a particular subject classification to materials mediate access to information in ways that matter.[53] Queer and feminist indexers, librarians, and archivists examine the digital present with an eye to a longer history of queer, trans, and feminist information activism.[54]

In the early 1970s, at the height of the women's liberation movement, Dee Garrison published "The Tender Technicians," a significant feminist information studies text that identified a need for historians of information science and women's work to recover the history of gender's influence on information.[55] Since then, theory and historiography by feminist information studies scholars has sought to fill this gap.[56] Focusing on ruptures with standards in libraries, archives, and other information contexts, this work considers such sites as the feminization of information work; the careful, gendered labor of description; the queerness of cataloging practices; and the trans-ing of archival systems.[57] Improving access to information within archives and databases is bound up with digital understandings of interface design, search retrieval, networks, disability, and ethical questions about minoritarian users and their digital records.[58] Historicizing these ways of thinking digitally shows how queer digital media practices emerge out of long-established activist information work.

Lesbian Counterpublics and Information Precarity

Information brings a public into existence by giving shape to networks, framing common interests, and acting as a shared resource for activists. Reading, researching, writing, publishing, communicating, and archiving are all tactics marginalized users adopt to imagine and enact transformative modes of counterpublic address.[59] They are discursive and self-organizing processes for circulating information, through which strangers with something in common come into relation, working out the terms of shared (or divergent) political visions. The terms "social movement" and "counterpublic" are distinct but related here. Social movements bring together activists who may or may not have common identities to work toward a shared vision of social justice and transformation external to the groups themselves. Counterpublics describe groups with shared identities who gather for mutual support and world making that can include, but is not limited to, outward-facing transformation.

Nancy Fraser's construction of counterpublics emphasizes their distinction from social movements, where counterpublics "function as spaces of withdrawal and regroupment" and "as bases and training grounds for agitation activities directed toward wider publics."[60] In Fraser's model, marginalized groups require spaces in which to do identity work, in part because gender and sexuality are perceived as "private issues" that are often excluded from legitimate public contestation in wider discourse.[61] Second-wave feminism's commitments to "the personal as political" explicitly worked against this public-private bifurcation, and lesbian-feminism in particular understood that dismantling compulsory heterosexuality would liberate all women—straight, gay, and otherwise—from oppressive socio-economic structures.

Lesbian feminism created places of respite from mainstream feminism and the gay liberation movement. It also looked outward, toward critiquing patriarchy and building a more inhabitable world for lesbians. Information brought lesbians together for support and acted as a catalyst for a broader critique of standards. My focus is on information's role in lesbian feminist counterpublic formation and expression, even as "social movement" is most often the shorthand through which lesbian feminism is categorized. Approaches to lesbian feminism as a social movement varied, because of ties to discrete counterpublics formed around race, ethnicity, class, and disability, which mattered even as women came together in activism.

"Lesbian Feminism" here describes both a historical social movement active in the United States and Canada in the 1970s and '80s and an on-going politics in the present. Historically, lesbian feminism is the branch of women's liberation-era feminist activism that set itself apart from the mainstream feminist movement through the political and emotional ideals of lesbianism and the bond among women. The ideological underpinnings of the movement involved envisioning a life lived without a primary relationship to men as a choice made in service of emancipation rather than "merely" sexual gratification.[62] Lesbian feminists were also leaders in the pro-pornography and s/m debates that characterized much internal conflict within feminist movements in the 1980s. While lesbian feminists took different stances toward porn and censorship issues, their readiness to center sexual expression as a ground for politics speaks to the broader conceptual work lesbians did, and do, within feminism. Lesbian feminists often referred to themselves just as "feminists," and my language follows this practice while marking lesbian feminism as a distinct set of commitments, publics, and practices when this distinction is most relevant.

Sexual identification with other women fueled lesbian-feminist counterpublic formation, but this sexuality was entwined with political action. The "Woman-Identified Woman" the activist group Radicalesbians described in its much-cited 1970s manifesto "may not be fully conscious of the political implications of what for her began as personal necessity, but on some level, she has not been able to accept the limitations and oppression laid on her by the most basic role of her society—the female role."[63] As "the rage of all women condensed to the point of explosion," lesbians energetically organized with others out of anger at exclusions within an increasingly moderate and strategically heterosexual women's movement.[64] By the mid-1970s, lesbian feminists who had worked tirelessly to sustain women's movements were frustrated by a lack of reciprocal attention to lesbian issues and invigorated by developing lesbian activist methodologies.[65] Similarly, lesbians worked in the gay liberation movement but wanted to carve out alternative spaces for organizing around sexuality that centered feminist concerns about gender, race, class, and other forms of difference that were often sidelined by gay men's issues.[66] Still, forming coalitions with men remained crucial to women of color, especially Black lesbians, who needed "solidarity around the fact of race."[67]

Lesbian-feminist counterpublics have never been monolithic, in part because attention to the ways in which women are different from one another informs consciousness-raising as a communications method and guides how embodied, structurally informed experience can be a ground for politics.[68] Despite these commitments, SaraEllen Strongman argues that interracial organizing among lesbians depended on deep investments in exploring the intimacies and erotics of racial difference, consciousness that white women often failed to develop.[69] Aware that a singular lesbian-feminist counterpublic was neither realistic nor desirable, the information activists featured in the book—many of whom are white—tried to create useful resources that would speak about and across difference.

Communications media are critical for counterpublic formation, particularly for marginalized groups, because they allow members of an emerging public to work through internal issues, recruit new members, and do outreach. Catherine Squires's work on the Black public sphere compels scholars to focus on a given counterpublic's safety and access to communicative resources and institutional supports. "Enclaved" groups working together within hidden spaces to "create discursive strategies and gather oppositional resources" emerge into more outward-reaching counterpublic formation "in response to a decrease in oppression or an increase in resources."[70] In other words, counterpublics form at the point where marginalized groups begin to experience slightly less precarity and fewer threats to safety and security and gain access to self-determined communications media.

Lesbian-feminist counterpublic formation has been intimately entwined with burgeoning access to communication technologies. Lesbians' growing ability to express their sexual identities in public, and in print, in the late twentieth century came along with diminishing fear of obscenity charges, employment discrimination, physical violence, and losing custody of children in a homophobic court system. Information activists took advantage of access to low-cost print methods, private telephone lines, and other communication technologies to support lesbian-feminist counterpublic formation, even as censorship of lesbian materials and expression persisted, particularly in Canada.[71]

Lesbian-feminist counterpublic communication reaches its apex in the Women in Print Movement. Within this broad second-wave feminist publishing movement, lesbians created their own newsletters, pamphlets, resource guides, reading lists, and small-press books. These publications facilitated communication, circulated information, and ultimately performed outreach that would bring more women into lesbian communities. Niche publications recognized the diversity of lesbian experience, targeting rural women, women of color, and other groups.

Agatha Beins and Trysh Travis each emphasize how feminist theory and politics defined the Women in Print Movement's drive to build communication networks outside patriarchy.[72] Evoking the inside-outside counterpublic model, Travis writes, "Participants believed they would not only create a space of freedom for women, but would also and ultimately change the dominant world outside that space."[73] Creating alternative communication methods responds to conditions in which many women lacked access to other lesbians and were desperate to find connection. While women's movements had entered wide popular consciousness by the early 1970s, that did not mean that interested women knew how to find these organizations and spaces in their local contexts.[74] In this respect, lesbian print activism shared strategies with the midcentury homophile movement's "sexual communication networks," which used print resources such as bibliographies, magazines, and travel guides to show isolated gay men and lesbians that they were not alone.[75] Information acts as a homing beacon, bringing the uninitiated into proximity with queer worlds they had only imagined.

Building on, but also departing from, this emphasis on communication networks, I study information activists who worked alongside burgeoning lesbian feminist publishing movements to create not just networks, but a broader information infrastructure undergirding lesbian-feminist social movements. Information matters differently to precarious populations, for whom reliable access is never guaranteed. For sexual and gender minorities, access to good information helps to determine a life that is livable. Think, for example, of trans communities finding support on Usenet in the 1990s, people living with HIV seeking out accurate health information via online Bulletin Board Systems in the 1980s, or men who have sex with men in the 1960s sharing countersurveillance knowledge via wallet cards that taught others how to avoid arrest for cruising.[76] In each of these cases, marginalized users facing various stigmas and threats to safety access vital information resources generated carefully and clandestinely by activists.

Information activism is part of this much larger twentieth-century infrastructure for sustaining LGBTQ+ life. Lesbian feminists have leveraged multimedia strategies to share otherwise precarious information about lesbian life through the telephone and online interfaces. They have drawn on indexing technologies, computer databases, and community-generated classifications to organize information gleaned from print materials. Thinking into the future, they have built archives to ensure this information has ongoing utility and digital reach. This movement-based topology shows how information-based communities work within scarce conditions to design knowledge-production methods consistent with their constituents' social and political orientations. Information's ethical aspects and vital, world-making potential become clearest within these high-stakes contexts. Beyond lesbian history, these activists have much to teach all of us about why, when, and for whom information comes to matter.

The Erotics of Information

Queer and feminist theorizations of archives and affect seek to account for information's emotional currencies. Archives provide present and future generations with access to information as an affective encounter with the past. Ann Cvetkovich's framing of queer cultural texts as "archives" that become unlikely "repositories of feelings and emotions" has laid tremendous groundwork for understanding "lesbian" as a shared horizon felt in relation to others.[77] Working across affect theory and information studies, Marika Cifor argues that LGBTQ archives are in constant flux because their appraisal processes, spatial configurations, and reasons for being in the first place are guided by queer affects, including felt, material attachments to histories in which users might find themselves.[78] While scholarship on archives and affect has guided much of my thinking about how archives order or make sense of shared emotion, reading women of color feminism has helped me to think about the relationship between archives and the emotional register of accessing social movement information.

Information activism is motivated by desires for shared history and an erotics of being in proximity to a past organized by sexuality—a history built and occupied by others. The Black lesbian writer and theorist Audre Lorde uses "the erotic" to describe material, affective forms of power that emerge from creating vulnerable connection with others across difference.[79] Lorde's erotic is a way of knowing and being that thrives in the face of exploitative structures.[80] A range of everyday experiences offer erotic connection, "whether it is dancing, building a bookcase, writing a poem, examining an idea."[81] The erotic "is a source of power *and information*" through which women can know the world differently in intimate collaboration.[82] Lorde's use of the term "information" is not generally remarked on in turns to her theory of the erotic. Information implies that the erotic is in part a communication practice: the erotic transmits actionable knowledge between a scene and a woman who has opened herself to this kind of knowledge. This use of "information," combined with Lorde's list of everyday activities, points to the erotic as a transformative, affective practice built out of seemingly unremarkable sites shared with others (information, a bookcase).

Recently, several scholars working at the intersection of critical race and queer studies have taken up Lorde's erotic in relation to affect theory in ways that have influenced my thinking about information and counterpublics.[83] Amber Jamilla Musser argues that Lorde's erotic provides a model for understanding what drives community formation: "Talking about affect helps displace identity as the basis for community formation and opens political possibilities. Lorde's discussion of the erotic touches on this potential because the most central component of the erotic, after all, is its creation of an affective community. . . . This formation of community through affective flows is one of the hallmarks of the plural subject."[84] Guided by the erotic, lesbian feminism's plural subject recognizes others and their distinct histories, joys, and struggles as openings to difference as a ground for knowledge. As an erotic practice, providing access to information is more than just helping divergent publics find what they are looking for; it is a world-making gesture constructed by specific media interfaces and technologies to which users might open themselves. The plural subject brought into lesbian-feminist community often arrives by finding the information she was looking for: where to go, who to talk to, and how. As she arrives to this information, she also learns that others in community came with entirely different questions, histories, interests, and needs.

In media history, information technologies are often constructed as seductive, overwhelming, and powerful, especially when these technologies are new and their introduction promises to deliver new intensities and proximities via communication or information.[85] Brenton J. Malin explains that the "emotional power of communication technologies" is felt most acutely with "*developing* media that seem to be transforming a culture's abilities to connect in ways that can only be imagined."[86] As an active stance generating these kinds of erotic but also identity-based communities, information activism is affective labor that produces collectivity, or the spaces and contexts in which individuals might feel part of something.[87] Information work gives ground to nascent counterpublics by establishing new terms of reference and building shared infrastructures for encountering information.

Affective labor is intrinsically gendered. It is associated most often with domestic and care work's construction as women's work and with digital economies that celebrate the "flexibility" of working from home.[88] Feminist activist labor and volunteer work present another kind of "second shift," often done on the fly or in the margins of one's "spare time." Worked on within these temporalities, information technologies become sites of infiltration, appropriation, and resourcefulness for marginalized users. These are the tactics through which feminists usurp or appropriate technology toward collective ways of doing politics, out of urgency and love.

While affective labor is often understood as immaterial, particularly in its digital manifestations, information activists emphasize the hypermaterial aspects of activism performed with media technologies as they work across digital and "analog" forms.[89] Lesbian feminists who made print resources or sat at desks night after night, working the hotline phones, carved pathways through information that others without prior access might follow. Indexing is a material form of affective labor, whether it is performed with paper cards or computers, because the practice assembles people, information, and technologies toward social goals.[90] Information activism brings together people marginalized from access to these resources, pushing on the divisions that can bifurcate information and emotion in the first place.

When finding information means finding deeply needed forms of support, the experience can offer transformative invitation to community. But lesbian feminism has also promoted and practiced painful exclusions, leaving behind legacies of white supremacy and trans exclusion that live on in the present. These conflicts in late twentieth-century lesbian-feminist organizing have been well documented by scholars studying histories of feminist theory, the institutionalization of women's studies, transgender organizing, and women of color feminism.[91] Unpacking these acrimonious histories matters because of how they persist in contemporary "LGBTQ" or queer women's activist spaces centered on whiteness and cis-normativity, or committed to homogenizing difference through an additive framework that simply invites more people to the same lousy table.[92]

This book asks how conflicts over difference are worked out through everyday decisions lesbian feminists make when they design and work within information infrastructures. Activist work with information can shore up what kind of lesbian life counts as a life worth serving on the phone or preserving in an archive. Work with information can put into practice antiracism, for example, through the *Black Lesbians* (1981) bibliographic project I examine in chapter 3. This text built an information infrastructure that centered Black women in lesbian history, making their leadership undeniable. As the Black writer Barbara Smith put it in her foreword, the bibliography generated "the excitement of finally having a substantial body of information on Black lesbians."[93] "From the bibliography it is historically verifiable that it was Black feminist/lesbian women who consistently and courageously raised the issue of racism from the beginning of the women's movement, finally pushing white women to make anti-racist work a priority in the late 1970s."[94] By organizing this history into a quick reference list of resources women could use for future research, *Black Lesbians* showed users another way forward, beyond whiteness as an unacknowledged center for lesbian history.

Smith wrote that the bibliography can "inspire us Black lesbians to write about and to manifest our lives in every way possible."[95] Sara Ahmed has described a "lesbian feminism of color" that recognizes "the struggle to put ourselves back together because within lesbian shelters too our being was not always accommodated."[96] Some information infrastructures have constructed uninhabitable shelters that ought to be torn down and rebuilt, while others have offered lesbians of color these tools of assembly.

Studying late twentieth-century lesbian-feminist social movement archives often means confronting transphobia and transmisogyny at the level of organizational policy or as regular speech acts made between activists. At their best, these movement archives also document the mundane ways lesbian feminists carved out spaces for trans people with the choices they make about information. As Susan Stryker has argued, "There was nothing monolithic about second wave feminist attitudes toward trans issues. The feminist second wave simultaneously espoused some of the most reactionary attitudes toward trans people to be found anywhere while also offering a vision of transgender inclusion in progressive feminist movements for social change."[97] Recent transfeminist histories have developed less polarizing, multivalent studies about trans participation in "second-wave" feminist movements.[98] Finn Enke asks why stories of trans exclusion and abjection have been so "magnetic" and implores feminist historians to think about the cultural work these narratives perform and the "generations of scholars and activists who need more than easy critiques of exclusion."[99] Sometimes trans exclusion or solidarity happens in uneven, everyday ways, through seemingly minor choices about information design.

These choices include how to describe materials or people in a database or whether or not to help a trans woman in need who calls a telephone hotline. The purpose of accounting for trans people's places on the margins of lesbian feminist history is not to search out ways in which trans people might become politically aligned with lesbian community, a "habitual assumption" in social movement studies critiqued by Viviane Namaste.[100] Rather, I argue that understanding how radical feminist movements regard trans people through the design and provision of information can show us how particular ideas about gender inform infrastructure design and determine how care is provisioned at a technological level. Historicizing these decisions matters because the complex lineages between lesbian and transfeminist ideas still need to be fleshed out and because lesbian groups and spaces that want to do better must continue to learn from these histories at the level of their information design.

As Ahmed writes, "It is transfeminism today that most recalls the militant spirit of lesbian feminism in part because of the insistence that crafting a life is political work."[101] Ahmed's words insist that lesbian feminism has some kind of present-day urgency despite this movement's apparent untimeliness—what Elizabeth Freeman has called the feeling of "temporal drag" lesbians elicit in the present. Lesbian feminism is out of fashion, yet it's being revived through critical projects that include Instagram history accounts, contemporary throwback clothing, museum shows, and scholarly research. Information precarity motivated past generations of information activists but does not define these new projects in the same ways. In response to the threat of complete erasure, 1970s and '80s information activists produced abundant archival conditions that facilitate enlivenments of lesbian feminist history via digital networks today. Put simply, young people are sifting through digital collections to discover and recirculate lesbian feminist iconography. While lesbian information is no longer so precarious, the fervor of these digital "archives" materializes an ongoing, urgent drive to imagine, critique, and repurpose information from the past.

Lesbian feminism is not a visible social movement with a firm set of aesthetic and actionable commitments anymore, yet it continues to guide these projects and the principles of organizations such as the LHA. Founded in 1974, this archives is staffed not only by women in their sixties and seventies who came to activism during the civil rights and women's liberation movements, but also by a growing contingent of young folks in their twenties born under the sign of queerness. This younger generation often brings commitments to transfeminism or queer politics, even as they revel in "deep-lez" desires to understand and embody butch-femme dynamics and terminologies or wear labrys necklaces without irony.[102] They are motivated by lesbian activist history even as they do not quite occupy its terms. Women who have worked at the archives for decades have their own, evolving relationships to lesbian politics and do not think about gender today the way they did forty years ago. As a queer history of information, this book shares with these volunteers a comfort with the messiness among feminist, queer, transfeminist, and lesbian-feminist histories and their surprising temporalities.[103]

How these ideals shape the organization's archiving practices is one example of lesbian feminism's ongoing effects on information infrastructures. This "historical" movement continues to exert affective pull on the present and on "queer" subjects.[104] This pull has been mediated, past and present, through lesbian-feminist work with technology as it shapes the ongoing stakes of access to information. An exciting body of literature has worked to historicize late twentieth-century feminist history from the present through the rubric of affect theory.[105] Put broadly, this scholarship asks what historical feminisms *do* in the present when we remember, study, or otherwise enliven them. Here, ambivalent feelings about feminisms of the past are held open: accusations of essentialism, normativity, single-issue politics, and racism leveled at lesbian feminism become potentially productive obstacles because of their continued relevance and pressure in the present.[106] As Victoria Hesford explores, it is precisely these antagonisms and the ambivalence they engender that give the women's liberation movement boundaries and contours, making it nameable as a phenomenon both during its operation and from the present.[107] This work challenges the celebration of queer as inherently progressive and unmarred by these concerns and questions queer studies' search for only those historical objects that serve the field's political goals.[108]

I foreground ambivalence because to some extent my ambivalent identifications with lesbian feminism are at the center of this media history. As a researching subject bringing together a particular set of objects toward historiographic ends, I have tried to foreground my desiring attachments to this work, these women, and this political movement. Beginning in the LHA basement, I include my "archive stories" about coming to and moving among the objects and actors that make up my archive here.[109] Doing this work has asked me to reckon with my own attachments to lesbian feminism and even to the category "lesbian." I have moved through this research and the spaces it has brought me to with frequent uncertainty about how my nonbinary gender identity and commitments to transfeminist practice might fit—all this despite wanting to occupy some relation to lesbian and caring deeply about lesbian feminism's ongoing place in digital archives of the ever-unfolding present.

Chapter Outlines

Although the chapters that follow cover a range of media and a span of decades, they consider to some extent a relatively small—or, at least, overlapping—group of women based in the United States and, to a lesser extent, Canada, primarily on the coasts. These activists worked across lesbian-feminist archives, service provision, and publishing, and their paths sometimes crossed: for example, call logs documenting labor at the Lesbian Switchboard of New York show that sometimes callers sought information about the LHA. Figures whose work represents the subject of one chapter make cameos in others. Julia Penelope Stanley, who started the newsletter *Matrices* in 1977—the subject of chapter 1—for example, also helped to found the LHA three years earlier. When I spoke to these people during interviews, they often knew or knew *of* one another and seemed to enjoy telling me about what they remembered.

Similarly, when I have presented this work at conferences, there generally have been a few folks in the audience who came because they remembered being there: they subscribed to "that newsletter" or used "that index." This book's theoretical underpinnings are intertwined with the book's archival objects. For example, Susan Leigh Star's scholarly information studies work has deeply influenced how this book understands infrastructure and the embeddedness of technology in practice. Star's earlier writing on lesbian-feminist activism is also present in this book on another level: Star was one of the founding editors of *Matrices*. With *Matrices*, Star helped build a newsletter *network* grounded in her larger intellectual project, which was committed to understanding how information systems work at a deep level so that communities might build better ones together.

Information activism is often guided by feminist theory, just as feminist writers draw on activist-built information infrastructures to research, write, and share their work. While writing this book, I have sometimes found myself thinking about the technical aspects of digitizing cassette tapes that record the very materials—feminist thought—that inform my theoretical approach. Feminist media histories form complex webs that are difficult to pull apart: this book's argument about the entanglement of information, media technologies, and feminist social movements depends, to some extent, on leaving them tangled up. I hope that guiding the reader through these entanglements allows a picture of the larger infrastructure to emerge.

The book begins with newsletters as print-based movement infrastructure. Chapter 1 approaches newsletters as networked technologies that supported the lesbian-feminist history and archives movement and the scholarly field known as lesbian studies, focusing primarily on *Matrices: A Lesbian Feminist Research Newsletter*, published from 1977 until 1996. Using a range of communications media including photocopiers and letter mail, *Matrices* figured itself explicitly as a network that would facilitate what the editors called "interconnections" among anyone doing research related to lesbian feminism. *Matrices*' network operation was fairly typical of what feminist newsletter culture sought to do during this "pre-internet" era, so the chapter situates this publication among others, including the LHA's newsletter.

Matrices is approached through network theory rather than simply as a proper object of "print culture" to argue that networks have been critical to the construction of feminist histories. A feminist mode of network thinking can be traced through small-scale print newsletters that draw on the language and function of networks, including circulating models from computer engineering. Publications such as *Matrices* emerged into wide production and circulation in the early 1970s and had all but disappeared by the mid-1990s, an era that spans the nascent women's liberation movement and Women in Print Movements on one end and the emergence of the World Wide Web on the other.[110] Newsletters, archives, and network models work together as interconnected social movement technologies. Newsletters enabled activist-researchers writing feminist histories to share difficult-to-access information, resources, and primary sources via photocopying and other modes of print reproduction. Network thinking has been a feature of feminist activism and knowledge production since before the consumer internet. Lesbian feminist also offered predigital feminist critiques of networks as egalitarian ideals that can conceal functional hierarchies and threaten the privacy of participants. Publications such as *Matrices* are part of a longer history of networked communications media in feminist contexts.

Chapter 2 builds on the book's engagement with how lesbian-feminist print cultures are enlivened through their entanglements with other information technologies, turning to lesbian telephone hotlines. Like newsletters, telephone hotlines connected lesbians at a distance using information. Hotlines sprang up in the 1970s to provide alternatives to generic crisis lines and gay switchboards staffed primarily by men. Run by volunteers and generally open in the evenings, these hotlines handled a wide range of calls, from suicide interventions, relationship advice, and emotional support for women who were coming out to requests for bar listings, roommate matching, and referrals to lesbian doctors, lawyers, carpenters and plumbers. Callers to these hotlines often felt isolated from access to basic information about how to live a lesbian life—how to meet other people "like them." Volunteer operators gathered and organized a wide range of print resources into filing systems they could use to give callers the information they needed, often desperately. Telephone information services drew on a combination of print and electronic technologies, troubling the telephone's position as a quintessentially "electronic" medium.

The chapter focuses most closely on New York City's Lesbian Switchboard (1972–97), a counseling and referral hotline that operated in the evenings out of Manhattan's Women's Liberation Center and, later, the Gay and Lesbian Center. The switchboard combined detailed, journal-like call logs, a paper database of referral information, and the telephone itself to connect individual callers with the wider communities they sought. To account for the switchboard's work, I rely primarily on the abundant collection of meticulous call logs volunteers kept to document each and every call made to the hotline over twenty-five years of operation. This paper logging practice describes how operators provided care to callers but fails to capture the actual audio of these calls, offering in their place short texts that elide the voices and embodied vulnerabilities of callers.

My reading of these call logs dwells in the tension between what they offer and what they withhold. I consider, for example, how operators blew off steam from handling angry or sad callers or managed the boredom that came from waiting for the phone to ring on a slow night by doodling and leaving notes in the logbook's margins for other volunteers to read. Some media practices are more readily archivable than others, and doing feminist media history means understanding that these affordances shape how activist labor is understood in retrospect. The switchboard's call logs attempt to document the intense tone and content of calls to record the emotional needs of callers and the economies of care that formed an emerging lesbian public. Telephone hotlines form a primal scene of information as care within lesbian feminist movements. Call logs point to the importance of studying media practices in theorizing the affective dimensions of feminism's archive.

Ultimately lesbian hotlines did not make the transition to online counseling and information referral evident in LGBTQ "hotlines" that operate today. By 1997, calls had mostly stopped coming in to the switchboard, and the organization closed. The switchboard never used a computer, even in the 1990s, though it wanted one and remarked often in meeting minutes about what a switch to electronic information management might offer the service. Chapter 3 turns to an organization that did attempt to transition its information activism to a computer program in order to frame a lesbian-feminist critique of "accessible" computing as it emerged widely in homes and workplaces in the 1980s. The chapter examines indexing projects, which share with telephone hotlines an ethos of using media to put actionable information at users' fingertips. The index is a genre that includes bibliographies, subject-based guides to whole runs of periodicals, and the familiar form of a topic listing by page found in the back of nonfiction books. Indexes gather and organize marginalized lesbian information to make it useful.

The chapter considers two lesbian feminist indexing projects: the Circle of Lesbian Indexers (1979–86) and its *Lesbian Periodicals Index* (1986), and JR Roberts's *Black Lesbians: An Annotated Bibliography* (1981). I focus on how these indexes were produced, working with paper records that document work processes and circulation strategies. These "behind-the-scenes" objects and procedures—everyday paper records such as letters, memos, and notes—are far removed in tone from the vibrant sexual subcultures they exist to serve. While published subject indexes and bibliographies look like simple lists of resources organized by theme, they start out as collections of paper index cards stored in shoeboxes and edited and reordered as the "database" grows. Feminist indexers worked with thousands of little paper slips to manage material databases that became life-changing tools women used to find pathways through lesbian-feminist publishing. Indexers did this often-cumbersome work with paper when they could have been using computers, and this moment of computational emergence is key to developing a queer history of digital media in emergence.

Feminist indexing in the 1980s took place just as database computing and online search retrieval became standard in institutional information contexts. This lesbian-feminist history of database computing analyzes how indexers imagined and attempted to use new information management programs that were just becoming accessible to amateurs. Enticed by the promise of computing but critical of technological accessibility for their communities, feminist indexers practiced what I call "capable amateurism" in the computer lab: a fearless approach to learning and implementing new media technologies that emerges out of feminist commitments to craft techniques, collectively organized work, and figuring things out on the fly.[III] Capable amateurism rejects the negative associations "amateur" can carry; these activists benefit from a lack of professional baggage, including firm ideas about protocols, standards, and what we might call "best practices" today. They bring flexibility to how technologies ought to be used and confidence in their capacity to get things done.

The chapter also explores how activists manage the boredom and isolation that often accompanies organizing information. The routine, meticulous task of sorting cards or entering data is made meaningful by a larger political vision of what might be achieved through better access to information in an affective economy that characterizes feminist information activism. This queer history of indexing and emergent computing examines indexes as "predigital" interfaces facilitating access to marginalized information about sexuality through search and retrieval.

While the previous chapters both rely on feminist media archives and analyze their construction, chapter 4 turns explicitly to archiving processes through a study of the LHA's digitization work. The previous chapters are concerned with how lesbian feminist print cultures imagined and anticipated digital information technologies, putting pressure on the apparent distinctions between "analog" and "digital" media. The study of the LHA takes place in what is more clearly a digital moment, exploring these archives' ongoing digitization practices, which began in the early 2010s.

Complex technological politics emerge when information activists convert analog materials to digital environments. Through interviews, observation, and documentary research in organizational records at these grassroots archives the chapter connects lesbian-feminist politics to the design and implementation of accessible digitization projects that sometimes counter archival standards. For example, the archives digitizes their audiocassette tapes using a commercial-grade analog-to-digital converter and the open-source software Audacity, creating files that are, above all, good enough, even though they might not meet the fidelity or digital preservation standards in place at many large institutions. These capable amateurs are guided by feminist values of resourcefulness in how they manage information. The LHA's approach to digitization is improvisational, self-reflexive, and willfully imperfect in its technological choices.

I situate close analysis of digitization practices within a longer media history of the archives to understand the deeper activist commitments that shape the organization's multiple digitization projects. They include digitizing oral histories tapes and other audiovisual materials and streaming them online; scanning photographs and offering public access through an online image database; and updating the archives' text-based catalog for eventual online access. The digitization protocols accommodate the unusual, queer cultural material and ephemera that constitute the LHA's unique collections. Digitization presents the archives with the opportunity to consider the ways their unfolding technological choices might challenge the normative imperatives that often accompany digital media practices, including the ways that lesbian-feminist lives, and diverse gendered ways of being, scramble the categorical logics of structured databases.

The archives must "clean up" their computer catalog by standardizing descriptive terms, but they resist framing this data-hygiene project in terms of "progress" and carefully maintain records of imperfect, volunteer-driven metadata. My analysis of how lesbian feminists write data also considers the status of archival records in transition. I consider how trans subjects within the archives' holdings are described in online databases, framing digitization as a process through which lesbian-feminist social movement organizations build trans-inclusive systems. Digitization presents the archives with the opportunity to consider how the historical representations of gender and sexuality they house challenge the normative imperatives that can accompany digital media practices, including sexuality and gender's difficult fit with structured databases.

The epilogue turns to images of information abundance. Whether it is talk of stacks of cards managed by indexers, the countless networked connections the newsletter facilitates, or the mountains of old lesbian stuff trying to find its way from the shelves of the archives to the internet, there always appears to be too much information to manage. Information activism exists to address precarious access to information, yet it produces an economy of abundance where it is normal to feel overwhelmed and to keep working despite the fear that you might drown in paper cards. Beginning with Lauren Berlant's turn to cruel optimism, where the goal that is sought is precisely the obstacle in the way of its achievement, the conclusion examines the economies of information within which these projects take place.[112]

Lesbian history is always being made, and we are always catching up, working to document and provide ongoing access in a project that is paradoxically uncompletable. The impulse to archive, what Jacques Derrida called "archive fever," extends to a feminist practice of carrying on with the everyday work of managing information, despite the odds.[113] Here, the digital, with its promise of limitless management through compression, instantaneous access, immateriality, and Big Data rhetorics, might be made into fodder for the lesbian-feminist killjoy. She does digital media with the same kind of care, skepticism, and attention to the deep political implications of information she brought to all those decades of paperwork.

Information activists built life-sustaining infrastructures for themselves and their communities out of simple information technologies. They did this work, and do this work, because they must find standing where none has been offered.[114] Through imaginative, improvisational, careful work with information, lesbian feminists make a world, a movement, and a life lived in networks with others.

ONE

The Internet
That Lesbians Built

Newsletter Networks

Julia Penelope, a professor of English at the University of Nebraska, described herself as a "white, working-class, fat butch dyke who never passed."[1] She challenged universities and their conservative structures. Before landing at Lincoln, she was kicked out of two different graduate schools and fired from one academic appointment because of homophobia.[2] A political lesbian separatist, Penelope edited several collected volumes of writings on lesbianism, but one of her greatest contributions to lesbian-feminist politics begins with a modest, mimeographed letter sent to other researchers in the Spring of 1977. Addressed "Dear Sister," the letter proposes a newsletter to be circulated to academics, activists, artists, and community researchers across the United States working on lesbian-feminist topics, mostly historical in focus. The letter begins,

> Several wimmin across the U.S. have been corresponding back and forth, exchanging papers, and we've been considering starting a Lesbian/Feminist Research Newsletter that would facilitate communication among the members of what we perceive to be a growing network of wimmin doing exciting research on issues and problems that touch on all of our lives. Right now, our communication is haphazard, and we don't always know who's doing what research. A newsletter would help to keep us in touch with each other, and inform us of recent papers and publications and ongoing research.[3]

That fall, Penelope collaborated with four other women spread across the country—Libby Bouvier, Sarah Hoagland, JR Roberts, and Susan Leigh

Star—to found *Matrices: A Lesbian/Feminist Research Newsletter*. In a classic feminist move toward diverting institutional resources, Penelope asked her department chair, John Robinson, whether the department would fund the newsletter, and he agreed. It was produced using the department's photocopier and distributed free of charge until 1982, when a modest subscription fee was instituted. Circulation had increased to "800 womyn in nearly every state and seven countries" by the newsletter's fourth year of publication.[4] *Matrices* bridged the worlds of academic lesbian studies and community research, attuned to a lesbian-feminist politics of class-consciousness and institutional critique. Subscribers and contributors included artists and academics who made major interventions in queer and feminist scholarship, from Jonathan Katz, the gay and lesbian historian and founder of OutHistory.org, to the fiction writer Sarah Schulman and lesbian-feminist filmmaker Barbara Hammer.

Matrices supported each of these people's work; the publication functioned explicitly as a network designed for sharing information and resources with anyone doing research related to lesbian feminism. A communications network uses technology to create interconnections among people or groups at a distance. Using various media and communications technologies—photocopiers, telephones, letter mail, and the newsletter itself—the *Matrices* network facilitated collaboration across space with people who were otherwise difficult to know about, let alone reach. *Matrices* offered an information and communications infrastructure that made it possible to do lesbian research within unsupported and sometimes openly hostile conditions.

Although *Matrices* is the object of my focus in this chapter, its operation is not at all unusual situated in the larger context of lesbian-feminist newsletters during its time, which drew on do-it-yourself (DIY) publishing methods to provide marginalized readers with otherwise unavailable information. *Matrices* is one of at least one hundred periodicals in the United States and Canada that specifically targeted lesbians in the 1970s and '80s (figures 1.1–1.3).[5] The story of *Matrices* offers an entry into a general history of networks as one part of an information activist topology.

Newsletters predate online communications media but also used networked communication to circulate information to geographically dispersed but politically organized individuals and groups. Distributed primarily by letter mail, issues of these newsletters acted as slower, print communication infrastructures. They published a range of materials designed to be useful for movement building: requests for information and resources, updates on the activities of others, surveys, phone trees, listings of archi-

FIGURES 1.1–1.3
A selection
of mastheads
from the
Matrices
newsletter,
representing
the 1970s–90s.

val holdings and primary source materials at community and institutional archives, mailing lists, and bibliographies. Newsletters were a kind of connective tissue that made readers aware of the larger information infrastructure lesbian feminists were building; newsletters published reviews, listings, and calendars that told communities about new archives, books, or events. They were one of the main places telephone hotlines advertised their services to would-be callers, generally as classified-style "ads" in the backs of these newsletters. As a communications genre, the newsletter network brought grassroots materials produced by information activist into a larger movement constellation.[6]

Each newsletter issue's publication was an initial moment of communication facilitating a range of subsequent connections among recipients, generally taking the form of further, task-oriented correspondence among individuals and institutions. The first *Matrices* exemplifies how the network idea animated the newsletter's communicative functions; announcing the first issue, the editors write, "We open what we hope will become a continuous dialogue and exchange of information, a network of Lesbian/Feminist researchers working in the community and academia. . . . *Matrices* hopes to facilitate interconnectedness among us, so that we can work together, sharing information and resources."[7] These interconnections promised to transcend class difference and uneven resource limitations through information sharing.

This chapter illustrates how a lesbian-feminist mode of network thinking animates small-scale newsletters that draw on the language and practice of networking. These newsletters were published between the early 1970s and the mid 1990s, bracketed by the Women in Print Movement and the popular adoption of online communication.[8] Feminists took political advantage of new access to communications media and printing technologies, including less expensive offset printing presses, and the normalization of copying machines in workplaces, used covertly by women workers.[9] Networks have been critical to the construction of lesbian histories. This chapter examines the relationship between networked print cultures and the U.S. lesbian-feminist history and archives movement to highlight the critical role networks play in information activism. Archives and newsletters as interconnected technologies that enable activists to share difficult-to-access information, resources, and primary sources via photocopying and other modes of print reproduction. Today, the archival collections that have grown out of these networked print cultures redress the relative invisibility of essential media practices that have built lesbian history.

The first part of this chapter considers how the *Matrices* network operated at two levels: first, as a unique conceptual model in which the idea of networked communication is articulated to lesbian-feminist political goals; and second, as an actually functioning schematic for uniting a community of researchers and activists through decentralized forms of communication, such as the newsletter's maintenance of a shared subscriber profile system. The chapter then considers the role this Lesbian-Feminist Research Network had in building early lesbian history. I situate the publication in a larger constellation of primary-source research, publishing, and the beginnings of women's and lesbian community archives, including the *Lesbian Herstory Archives Newsletter*. Finally, I highlight moments when the network failed to live up to its egalitarian communicative promises, framing lesbian-feminist disappointment in relation to the structure's outsize idealization in communication theory. I argue that feminist historiography is built collaboratively, in and through print networks such as

Matrices. Understanding what networks have meant to lesbian feminism reveals the counterpublic and sexual politics behind this everyday communications structure and its mediated promises.

Newsletters as Information Activism

Matrices is one among several newsletters that provided communicative support for grassroots lesbian historical research. Often called simply "lesbian studies," this field grew in the 1980s out of the more established women's history movement and the nascent gay and lesbian history field.[10] Other newsletters that had a similar focus include the *Lesbian/Gay History Researchers Network Newsletter* (1980–81) and the annual newsletter of the Lesbian Herstory Archives (1975–2004). A loosely organized community of academics, noninstitutional researchers, and activists working to redress the elision of gay and lesbian experience from the historical record established community archives across the United States and Canada and conducted primary source research and publication.[11]

Several intersecting politics form the movement's ideological roots: the post-Stonewall gay liberation movement is key, as is the longer legacy of the midcentury Homophile Movement, particularly its middle-class, assimilationist investment in the free circulation of gay and lesbian literature depicting "accurate" information about homosexuality. Lesbian-feminist historical organizations also emerged out of the women's liberation movement in the 1970s, as did new university women's studies departments and feminist oral history methods. Organizations such as the Lesbian Herstory Archives (LHA) straddled both worlds. Run by feminist activists who came of age in the women's liberation era, the archives also found an uneasy home in the larger world of gay and lesbian community archives noted for emphasizing white gay men's histories.

Community archives such as the LHA constructed and maintained mailing lists to extend the reach of their work beyond the physical building and those women able to visit New York. The archives bought their first computer and database software in 1984 to manage this growing mailing list. The LHA understood the transition to computerized information management as networked outreach even as the computer itself was not, in technical terms, "networked."[12] Mailed newsletters performed outreach that was critical to fledgling gay and lesbian archives for a few reasons. First, newsletters sought funding from the community to run archives. Fundraising helped to pay rent and utilities, buy supplies, and reduce the financial burden shouldered by volunteers, who paid for many archives activities out of pocket. Second, newsletters reported research findings and alerted readers to publication of this research. Third, and key to my analysis here, newsletters told potential researchers what was available in archives, providing the information infrastructure needed to use collections. The resulting publications served the historical movement's ultimately pedagogical goal: connecting marginalized counterpublics with the histories they craved but could not find.[13]

I found *Matrices*—or maybe it found me—during my research period at the LHA studying the archives' digitization practices. I was at the archives on a Saturday afternoon in my capacity as a volunteer, sorting through a stack of donor agreement forms. I was creating a spreadsheet to identify which collections of personal and organizational papers had the go-ahead to be listed online. On Saturdays, the archives is staffed by founder Deb Edel, and her partner, Teddy Minucci.

Edel and I were sitting at the large, shared worktable in the archives' main-floor library, talking about how my research was going. I told her I had begun to think that I needed a longer history of lesbians and technology at the archives if I was going to really understand the politics behind their current digitization projects. We talked more generally about my interest in print newsletters and the communicative work the archives performed. Edel told me how feminist social movement organizations, including the LHA, relied on networks of their own, albeit predigital ones. All of a sudden, a light seemed to go off in her head. There was a publication she wanted to show me. The name was on the tip of her tongue. Edel led me up the stairs to the periodicals room and went straight to the Hollinger box that contained nearly every issue of *Matrices*. She didn't need to check a computer to find out where the box was; she just knew from decades spent organizing these shelves.

I spent some time with the newsletter that day and found myself returning to it each time I was in New York during that research year. Meanwhile, *Matrices* and the people who used the publication to communicate kept surfacing as I continued my research on lesbian-feminist information activism. For example, when the LHA launched its digital audio site, the first tapes made available as streaming audio were drawn from Madeline Davis and Elizabeth Kennedy's Buffalo Women's Oral History Project.[14] From reading *Matrices*, I knew that Davis and Kennedy had used the newsletter to tell others about their project and find similar oral history projects focused on lesbians. The Circle of Lesbian Indexers and *Black Lesbians:*

An Annotated Bibliography both appear as works in progress in the pages of *Matrices* and the *Lesbian Herstory Archives Newsletter*. Later I learned that Julia Penelope—that "white, working-class, fat butch dyke who never passed"—was a member of the five-woman collective who founded the LHA, four years before she wrote the letter that launched *Matrices*.

I realized gradually through my immersion in the worlds of these intertwined media technologies, people, and events that *Matrices* exemplified how lesbian-feminist information infrastructures are built and sustained through networks that facilitate collaboration and resource-sharing amid precarious conditions. *Matrices* became a way to consider some of the more interstitial media that made lesbian-feminist organizing possible. Although it was not affiliated with any single archives, *Matrices* supported emerging community archives, publishing requests for donations of funds and primary source materials and making potential researchers aware of collections they could access. *Matrices* is one outlet in a complex web of print-based communications that allowed these archives to operate and that, by extension, allowed researchers to find information about lesbian history.

Matrices was published three times a year from 1977 until the mid-1980s and then infrequently until 1996. In the early 1990s, many print newsletters lost relevance as web browsing developed and email listservs became key networks for sharing information in both feminist social movement organizing and humanities and social science research communities.[15] While studying *Matrices* I closely analyzed a total of twenty-four issues gathered from partial collections at two different periodicals collections. My method of close reading across issues emphasizes the people, projects, spaces, and conversations that transcend individual issues rather than focusing on any of the publication's singular moments. For example, the New Alexandria Lesbian Library in western Massachusetts appears in the pages of the publication beginning in 1978. Updates chronicle New Alexandria's initial conception and fundraising drive to its move from Chicago and search for new volunteer staff. The library's short listings in *Matrices*—generally a few paragraphs in length—updated readers (who were also potential donors, volunteers, and researchers) on the project's status and told them about the sources available at the library. These listings also solicited input on the collection's direction from the *Matrices* community.

Today New Alexandria has evolved into the Sexual Minorities Archives, run by Ben Power Alwin, a trans man who inherited the collection when the original lesbian collective dissolved in 1978. As the transgender archives scholar K. J. Rawson notes, Alwin transitioned the collection to an "all-inclusive" LGBTQI archives alongside his own transition in the early 1990s.[16] For Rawson, this shift reflects broader movements away from gay and lesbian toward LGBTQ+, but more interestingly, it shows that archival collections, like the people stewarding them, have individual identities that are adaptable. The Lesbian Herstory Archives' ongoing grounding in the lesbian community and collective organizational structure maintain the focus on *lesbian* materials, even as the meaning of this category changes. Following New Alexandria's activities through *Matrices* over a period of years illustrates the publication's ongoing entanglement with a larger, evolving activist movement and its instrumental role in facilitating outreach. But as Alwin's work reminds us, these networks also extend into the present and can depart from their lesbian-feminist entanglements.

In addition to reading across the *Matrices* archive, my method situates the publication in a larger constellation of feminist and lesbian-feminist periodicals by following citation practices across other newsletters.[17] Reading *Matrices* as a network is necessarily retrospective, requiring a larger view of how various efforts at making history drew on one another in a united movement. Seeing this network from the present also depends on feminist libraries and archives with open-access policies that allow me to bring these publications into conversation with one another. I am literally describing the ability of a researcher at the LHA or York University's tiny Women and Gender Studies Library to sort through open stacks of rare feminist printed matter—newsletters that would be gated behind rare books desks and doled out one box at a time at most institutions. At these collections I could bring issues from a few different publications over to a table and look at them together. I could let the pages touch. Open access to periodicals collections allows feminist researchers to follow a citation by pulling out more than one publication at the same time. Policies that open the stacks allow for material entanglements among texts, scenes, people, and geographies. For Kate Eichhorn, this methodological proximity is rooted in a feminist, open-access archival politics that makes collaborative, network-based feminist histories possible.[18] Libraries and archives practice access and classification strategies that are critical to the preservation of feminist networks, which might not otherwise survive the isolating disciplinary technologies of archival accumulation.[19] In other words, activist archives require activist archival methods to maintain the intelligibility of the larger relationships they made possible.

Matrices drew on cultural ideas of how networks could facilitate communication and action, reworking network thinking in the specific context of lesbian feminism. *Matrices* took form in relation to circulating network models from computing cultures and exemplifies the "network thinking" germane to feminist print cultures. Networks animate the design of *Matrices* at two distinct but interconnected levels: one high-level and ideational; the other pragmatic and operational.[20] In other words, networks allowed *Matrices* to imagine a robust communications infrastructure suited to high-level movement goals and facilitated the practical, regular work of sharing information with others across distance.

Feminist communication networks reflected the popular understanding of networks illustrated by computer engineering models developed as early as the mid-twentieth century. Paul Baran's diagram for the Rand Corporation is the most widely circulated, and ARPANET developers took it up to develop the packet-switching protocols that became the internet's backbone.[21] This model, from 1964, compares centralized, decentralized, and distributed network structures to explain how systems design can redistribute vulnerability and support alternative ways to share power (figure 1.4).[22] "Print" media such as newsletters typically created networks that would be described as centralized, represented by the diagram at the left in Baran's model. Here, a publication is the central hub and each line or connection disperses from or gathers into this hub, in what the media theorist Alexander Galloway calls a "strategic massing of power and control."[23] The diagram at the far right in the model represents a "distributed" network and is used to explain how the internet works, distributing power "into small, autonomous enclaves."[24] Counterpublic and network scholarship share attention to "enclaves" and the tactical advantages offered by autonomous access to communicative resources.

Distributed networks are less vulnerable because the destruction of one hub does not critically affect the network, while centralized networks crumble when the main hub fails (e.g., when a publication goes out of print).[25] *Matrices*' connections transcended the limits of the centralized network model (left diagram) typically associated with a print publication or broadcast media, which center a single creator. Each individual *Matrices* researcher or organization is a "node" or "dot" that received the publication. *Matrices* built a decentralized network (middle diagram) by publishing subscribers' contact information, interests, and details about

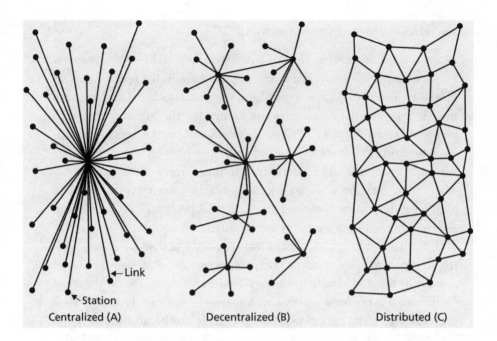

←Link

↖Station

Centralized (A)   Decentralized (B)   Distributed (C)

FIGURE 1.4 Centralized, decentralized, and distributed network models. From Paul Baran, "On Distributed Communications: I. Introduction to Distributed Communications Networks," memorandum RM-3420-PR prepared for the U.S. Air Force Project Rand, RAND Corporation, Santa Monica, CA, August 1964, 2. Image Courtesy RAND Corporation.

the kind of information they were looking for. These subscribers could use subsequent *Matrices* issues, or adjacent organizations like an archives, to communicate, following a decentralized structure. Or they could continue their communication independently of the publication's pages, forming a distributed model (right diagram).

Network imagery and language was prevalent across a range of gay liberation, feminist, and lesbian-feminist periodicals and newsletters in the 1970s.[26] These publications' names and purpose statements give a sense of the role mediated communication played in imagining a movement that would, above all, bring into the fold women who were *not yet* enfranchised as feminists. Some publications featured the word "network" in their titles, such as western Michigan's *Network News* (founded in 1988), while others drew on more colloquial network concepts, such as the *Grapevine* (1983), of New Brunswick, New Jersey. Grapevine models illustrate how information moves through a larger community from person to person, branching out with each act of communication. The *Grapevine* newsletter announced itself as "a communication network that exists in order to insure that women have access to relevant social and political information. . . . The *Grapevine* is a two-way communication process: members both receive information from it and feed information into it."[27] Reciprocal information exchange would secure new connections among lesbians and support movement building.

Toward this end, San Francisco's *Telewoman* (1977–86) attached the Greek prefix *tele-* (over a distance)—*tele*phone, *tele*vision, *tele*graph—to the newsletter form and to the idea of a lesbian network. *Telewoman's* masthead reads: "We provide networking services for lesbians who live anywhere through this newsletter. . . . We connect lesbian mothers. We make referrals to women's service organizations, lesbian-feminist therapists, and give job/housing information. We connect city lesbians and country lesbians. We serve isolated lesbians and integrate them into the local and larger women's communities."[28] *Telewoman* thought about connecting its subscribers over a distance to service their need for information and their need for other emotional forms of care that would, among other things, ameliorate isolation or provide access to mental health services. Newsletter networks promised subscribers the possibility of feeling less alone against a world hostile to women's liberation and especially cruel to the figure of the lesbian feminist.[29]

The network is a conceptual model for imagining a kind of utopian feminist politic. "Network" stands in for an idea of what a large, organized feminist movement could do. As Elisabeth Jay Friedman has argued, queer feminist counterpublic organizing through online interfaces such as listservs extends and remediates existing feminist communications networks and their strategies.[30] Similarly, Cassius Adair and Lisa Nakamura's research on the publication history of *This Bridge Called My Back* (1981) connects the networked pedagogies of 1980s women of color feminism to digital archival work by feminists of color on social media sites such as Tumblr.[31] This scholarship on the long history of feminist networks argues that network imaginaries are bound up with feminist ideals about communication, capacity building, and the power of alternative structures for organizing people and ideas.

Feminists might participate in communication networks to find the kind of support for their work that was denied in their "offline" lives. For example, lesbian-feminist academics such as Penelope were often the only women—let alone the only out lesbians—in their departments and were further marginalized within their broader disciplines for doing work that was "too narrow" in focus.[32] Imagined and accessed from these marginal spaces, the network represents an ideal and a respite. Newsletter producers drew on this vision to describe how their publications could facilitate other kinds of collectivities in which to work collaboratively. *Matrices* emerges out of, and contributes to, the political possibilities that networked communication offered the lesbian feminist imagination. These possibilities include the "recovery" of women's history lost to the gendered biases of researchers and institutions and the creation of sustainable libraries and archives to support this research. Using the network, scholars might also circulate papers on lesbian topics outside the mainstream publication venues that failed to support this work, so that this information could reach the wider community. These achievements all fall under the broader, social-justice oriented goal of improving lesbian lives with information.

Far from merely political, these possibilities represent relief from the injustices of invisibility, marginalization, and diminished career chances, which are injustices felt as frustration, shame, and isolation, among other embodied affects. While a goal such as "Help Build the New Alexandria Library's Collection" is practical and measurable, and aimed at developing one part of a larger information infrastructure, this mission also fulfills needs that highlight the emotional dimensions of networks. Making this infrastructure together, bit by bit, materializes a desire for history and gives life to lesbian feminism. These possibilities give the network form its pull on the feminist imagination. Information circulated through a newsletter network is always more than just informative and always greater than the sum of its parts.

Theorizing the roles of newsletters in feminist information economies, Agatha Beins and Martin Meeker each argue that newsletter culture's ability to circulate information to wide-reaching groups of people was understood as a condition of possibility for feminist organizing.[33] In the early 1970s, newsletters animated the idea that the women's liberation movement might become a singular, unified national and international undertaking. Newsletters promised informational support for the pedagogical drive to "recruit" women into feminism via consciousness-raising. This desire for proximity is about more than just achieving a critical mass, couched as it was in the language of "sisterhood" and "survival." Meeker argues that the "politics of communication [was placed] squarely at the center of the emerging movement for homosexual civil rights," reaching "its most forceful articulation in the context of lesbian feminism."[34] Lesbian-feminist information activists approached the formal, material aspects of movement communication as key activist work. Functional networks promised the communicative support needed for lesbian-feminist information infrastructures.

Chapter One

For Meeker, the actual integration or connection offered by publications such as *Telewoman* mattered less than the awareness that such communication was possible. He writes, "Lesbian-feminist networks . . . were the ideological basis of the social movement in which they originated; they were the raison dếtre of the movement itself," unlike homophile networks, which he describes as "largely instrumental and nonideological."[35] Meeker asserts that simply having an operational network was one of lesbian-feminist newsletters' goals and that "the network" thus is fundamentally "ideological." Networks promised to support feminist investments in connection, collaboration, and equity, as the descriptions from *Grapevine* and *Telewoman* illustrate. However, bracketing the network's ideological operation from its "instrumental" role in facilitating everyday information sharing is inadequate to the ways in which feminist politics entangles the practical and affective spheres.

Feminist organizing balances an ambitious vision of the world as it might be with the "instrumental" micropolitics of stuffing envelopes or providing childcare; the women's liberation movement strategically insisted that these "practices of everyday life" were significant symbolic sites for much larger struggles over gender justice.[36] Putting out a newsletter takes a great deal of work—work that is messy, physical, repetitive, and less than glamorous, even more so in the days before desktop publishing software. The work of small-scale publishing—typesetting, gluing pasteups, printing, fighting with photocopiers, making address labels, folding, gluing stamps—is nothing if not instrumental. This labor's entanglement with the affective and ideological promises of newsletters is what makes it bearable, even fun. Meeting other women who might become friends, lovers, or coconspirators of some kind turned the promise of an "envelope stuffing party" into a tenable method for recruiting volunteers. The LHA has used this technique since the beginning, hosting regular "workdays" during which volunteers can drop in to organize, file, or do data entry (figure 1.5).

Feminist theory that considers the relationship between affects such as optimism or hope and the ability of feminist activists to carry on with their difficult, everyday work helps to explain a newsletter network's generative effects.[37] A future orientation guides the work of making, circulating, reading, and recirculating communicative materials. Newsletters materialize political desires with the information they deliver and the connections they promise (figure 1.6). These horizons are then chased through the network itself, as users reach out to others and follow up on leads. Newsletters facilitate networked communication that guides hopeful, politicized investments in lesbian feminism and its continuation.

FIGURE 1.5 Volunteers sort newsletters at a Lesbian Herstory Archives work party, late 1980s. Pictured are Joan Nestle, Polly Thistlethwaite, and others. Image courtesy Lesbian Herstory Educational Foundation.

Newsletters have effects that transcend the expectations of a singular publication, related to the network forms they generate and the social movement work they facilitate. As Anna Feigenbaum argues, "More than instrumental tools, rituals or resources for mobilization," feminist newsletters are discursive communicative practices that *form* social movements— "the very means by which their politics garnered shape and meaning."[38] A newsletter network promised to circulate information that was hard to find, but it also promised that feminism itself might carry on through dispersed but networked communities united by shared interests and goals. Securing a future for feminism is a massive undertaking guided by the much smaller communicative endeavors information activists can achieve. Networks embody how feminist social movements connect utopic visions with the modest pragmatism symbolized by ink, newsprint, and stamps.

The *Matrices* network operated through an affective register in which the newsletter's generative promise exceeds pragmatic, individual moments of information exchange. The ways in which *Matrices* described the

LESBIAN HERSTORY ARCHIVES NEWSLETTER 6
LESBIAN HERSTORY SOURCES

JULY, 1980

FIGURE 1.6 Cover of *Lesbian Herstory Archives Newsletter*, no. 6, July 1980. Photograph by Morgan Gwenwald. Image courtesy Lesbian Herstory Educational Foundation.

service it *hoped* to offer point to the charge information could carry. A 1980 editorial explains:

> We need to share our knowledge and resources, including contacts, jobs, how and where to publish our work, exchanges about how we survive in academia or outside of it, offer support to each other, mobilize to help Lesbian/Feminists who are fired, or to know other Lesbian/Feminist researchers we can turn to when we are having specific research problems. Other possibilities: to serve as a liaison between researchers in academia (who have access to libraries, laboratories, meeting places) and those working without such support; to share information about our experiences in institutions—the courses we can offer, departmental colloquia we might be giving, which libraries have what kinds of information.[39]

Some of these proposals seem only tangential to the actual work of "doing research." "Instrumental" supports are entangled with the community-based care that the network valued as critical to lesbian-feminist organizing: supporting one another, sharing information about how we survive institutional harm, amplifying the work of those without institutional support.

Beyond these stated aims, other instances of communication through the network provide examples of subscribers connecting to one another as more than just information-distribution hubs. In a 1980 letter placed on the publication's cover, the historian of sexuality Gayle Rubin solicits small financial donations from subscribers to pay for Jeannette Foster's nursing home care. Foster wrote *Sex Variant Women in Literature* (1956), the first comprehensive bibliographic study of lesbianism in literature.[40] Rubin's invitation to care for Foster, whom she calls "a national treasure of the Lesbian Community," points to what circulated through the network beyond the proper object of information. Community care circles are based in alternative kinship structures that understand inheritance and accountability outside autonomist, accumulative models. Put simply, these circles use communication networks to care for activists as they age, in recognition that activism serves the public but doesn't pay. Networked care for queer and trans activist elders including Barbara Smith and Miss Major Griffin-Gracy continues forty years after Foster's campaign using social media and crowdfunding tools.[41]

This appeal for Foster exemplifies how *Matrices* subscribers connected with one another to form a larger economy of care, following desires for networked intimacy that was perhaps unachievable through individual practices of *reading* information in print materials. The idea that Foster might be cared for in her old age by other lesbian-feminist historians points to "sisterhood" as an affective constellation guiding women's liberation-era organizing. Networked sisterhood promised belonging to some and threatened a persistent outsider status to those whose political desires, sex practices, or others ways of being in relation to feminism contravened the ideal. Although *Matrices* ultimately sought to democratize history and researching processes, the publication still had a tenuous "cannon" to deal with.

When Rubin invokes the language of "nation," "treasure," and "lesbian community," she describes an economy of attention that suggests all nodes in the network were not necessarily equal in terms of access, participation, and perceived importance to research. These are just some of the network's gatekeeping functions. The language of connection, care, and "sisterhood" articulated to feminist newsletter networks obscured boundaries and hierarchies intrinsic to any collective, particularly one self-consciously grappling with knowledge production's gendered, classed, and racialized biases. Even my own focus on this letter over other examples of care in the *Matrices* archive points to a retrospective economy of attention determined by Rubin's outsize status in the field of sexuality studies.

So far I have described how *Matrices* used the network as a conceptual model that was both ideological and affective for lesbian-feminist researchers. The newsletter was also a network in its "actual operation," or how *Matrices* facilitated decentralized and distributed communication among lesbian researchers. *Matrices* asked each subscriber to complete a profile with contact information; a short biography; research interests; titles of papers written and published and information on how offprints could be acquired from other subscribers; current projects; and support they needed from other subscribers. Published in each issue, these subscriber profiles facilitated a distributed network in which connections were initiated by *Matrices* but did not necessarily rely on its pages to proliferate. Subscribers communicated directly with other lesbian-feminist researchers who offered or requested information that might be of value.

Matrices used a decentralized network model to assemble the "Notes and Queries" section, which housed these subscriber profiles. Five regional editors spread across the United States collected completed profiles and other subscriber-submitted information, sending it on to the managing and general editors for publication. While it served to distribute labor, this purposeful spread of editors across the country also points to a conscientious use of the network form to transcend the geography that made collaboration difficult. The Circle of Lesbian Indexers, featured in chapter 3, also recruited indexers from across the country in what was perhaps a broader equity-based effort to amplify lesbian-feminist activism away from the coastal cities that dominated gay and lesbian imaginaries. This work conscientiously mapped a decentralized schematic onto physical geography, ensuring that competent nodes could be found across the map. A 1985–86 *Matrices* callout for new regional editors to serve Canada and Europe demonstrates the newsletter's international outlook.[42]

The geographical distribution of editors materialized the desire for a dispersed network by placing powerful nodes in strategic locations. This logistic practice could expedite communication across space by establishing a clear workflow; however, the distance between regional editors, who communicated using the postal service, also presented significant difficulties. Miscommunication occurred, and editors reverted to the de facto centralization of control in moments when it was easier to just *make a decision already* instead of building consensus by letter mail. Print specificity set the rhythm and speed of *Matrices*.

Issues of *Matrices* included sections that will be familiar to readers of any specialized academic listserv. They include "Conferences and Calls for Papers," "Book Reviews/Articles," and a listing of lesbian and feminist periodicals and their subscription information. "Notes and Queries" also included more general calls for information and assistance from the network. The third issue, published in spring 1978, includes this request from Madeline Davis at the Buffalo Women's Oral History Project: "Madeline Davis wants to hear from other oral history projects currently being undertaken in lesbian communities—she is part of a group working on such a project in Buffalo, NY. Also, she has been teaching a course on lesbianism, an historical, political, and personal view, at State University NY at Buffalo. She would be grateful for any suggestions from women who are teaching or formulating courses on any aspect of the topic."[43]

With Elizabeth Kennedy, Davis used this research to write the first comprehensive history of working-class lesbian subculture in the United States, drawing in part on modest support from networks such as *Matrices*. Some requests made via "Notes and Queries" are much simpler and more general than Davis's. The same issue features this notice: "Mary C. Peterson wants to know what women/lesbians are doing in athletics."[44] While some information requests solicited practical support for concrete works in progress, more formless requests reflect how hard it was to find good information on lesbian topics in scarce conditions.

By design, *Matrices* used the distributed and decentralized network forms to circulate information in ways that would support movement building. A community archive that published a request for funds or materials in *Matrices* might become a small hub with lines emanating out to individual readers. Those who began to communicate independently of the publication might forge new activist alliances or collaborative research projects. By creating and maintaining these structures for sharing information, *Matrices* imagined how a network could facilitate collaboration among lesbians who were otherwise isolated from these opportunities. Everyday "instrumental" information exchanges among researchers, activists, and archives made the larger project of doing lesbian feminism possible, transcending the limitations of time and space.[45] The editors quipped about *Matrices* facilitating a utopian project in their third editorial: "As we sat around talking one evening, it occurred to us that, barring patriarchal conceptions of time and space, LFU [Lesbian Feminist University] existed."[46] This university would have no football team and would feature a Love Department and a faculty association called The Union of Feminist Utopian Futurists.

The editors of *Matrices* deploy "network" as a purposeful mode of description that imagines a strong, distributed web as a critical infrastructure for lesbian-feminist information activism. My retrospective exploration of the network metaphor from the present necessarily associates *Matrices* with online communication technologies. As Friedman argues, historicizing media technologies through queer and feminist activism can concretize how there is no singular "internet," only many internets shaped through specific interpretive practices.[47] As part of a longer and wider cultural history of networked communication, these newsletters add a distinctly lesbian-feminist interpretation of network technologies and their affordances.

Speculative Network Histories, or Did Lesbians Invent the Internet?

Julia Penelope and the other editors at *Matrices* did not invent the internet (and would probably call internet history's emphasis on invention patriarchal foolishness). But this provocation is an entry to a speculative history of networks written through older forms of feminist print culture. Such a proposition takes up Roy Rosenzweig's description of the internet as a "meta-medium" in need of many histories that consider the multiple contexts of its conceptual and technical beginnings.[48] Kevin Driscoll, Elisabeth Jay Friedman, Eden Medina, Benjamin Peters, and Fred Turner offer histories of network or cybernetic *thinking*, as a condition of possibility for the web.[49] These histories attend to practices of dreaming about and working with network technologies, sometimes by amateurs, instead of emphasizing the research, design and market uptake of network technologies. Like sociomaterial science and technology studies, this approach emphasizes an artefact's use, negotiation, and meaning–in–practice, over its initial design.[50] Though it is not historical in focus, Marisa Elena Duarte's study of Indigenous broadband development also emphasizes how communities incorporate hard-won network technologies into existing practices as an exercise of sovereignty and self-determination.[51] Building on these and other comparative studies of network communication, I argue that situated, minoritarian investments in networked communication are critical for understanding the political possibilities associated with emerging media technologies.

Feminist media studies has considered multiple trajectories of "networks" across a range of media, documenting both the cultural politics of newsletters and the relationship between feminist social movements and other mediated network forms, such as zine distribution networks, VHS "chain letters," and contemporary social media and GIS mapping.[52] Online communication does not present a turning point for feminist social movements; rather, it extends existing media infrastructures of networked communication. In this kind of history, consistencies and divergences in the politics of feminist networked communication across time take precedence over formal network development. Lucas Hilderbrand's history of Riot Grrl VHS chain letter distributions networks illustrates this approach; despite being "analog" and "specifically nondigital" in their formal properties, they share a feminist model for "social networking."[53] Here, the impetus to mediate one's relationship to distant others who share politics characterizes feminism's "networkness."

Feminist networks are communicative infrastructures that extend across emerging forms of media, and across time, particularly in the case of a network that is "historical" in a double sense: *Matrices* is of the past as I write this book, but was also of the past during its years of publication, as the network facilitated *historical* research. Networked communication and feminist historiography are interdependent. Feminist historiography is a heterogeneous set of practices and desires built through networks, and is difficult to map onto more conventional understandings of information created by a single, authoritative source. As the editors of *Matrices* put it, "Lesbian/Feminist research is significantly different from what we have been taught to regard as 'research,' because it arises out of our lives and the community we are creating."[54] In other words, lesbian histories are assembled from multiple nodes of information and are difficult to isolate to singular sources or authors. Among these nodes are archives and other spaces for doing historical research, which are themselves mediated through networks and network thinking. Feminist organizations emerging out of the 1970s—artist-run centers, cooperative women's buildings, bookstores, academic networks, journals, etc.—were informed by values of non-hierarchy, direct participation by members, and an investment in decentralized processes.[55] Commitments to collaboration and sharing power inform how and why social movement organizations imaginatively invest in decentralized and distributed communication networks to create and circulate information. Feminist archives and archival sensibilities share these traits.[56]

Matrices' support for archives shows how a working communications network was vital for circulating information about the kinds of primary source materials available for research. Lesbian community libraries and archives called upon the network to help build their fledgling collections, so that these nascent institutions could remain independent and community-run. In a March 1984 issue callout, the new Archives Lesbiennes in Paris declared that they "do not want to depend on any external powers: they will continue to exist and develop with the support and contributions of lesbians. In order to realize our projects and plans, we have to believe in our collective power. Please send documents, information, or financial support."[57] Here the Archives Lesbiennes imagines network support as intrinsic to its non-hierarchical operation. This communication structure undergirds collective economic models.

Every issue of *Matrices* contains some listing of archival holdings or an archive's request for materials. Other major contributors include the LHA and the Canadian Lesbian and Gay Archives (CLGA, now the ArQuives). By the early 1980s, *Matrices* featured a distinct archives section to accommodate these listings. The 1982 Archives and History Projects insert, reprinted from the CLGA's newsletter, explains the importance of communication networks for building these precarious institutions: "An intimate relationship should exist between history groups and archives. . . . To help groups to contact one another and allow others to do likewise we list here various archives and history groups. We encourage you to contact these people, offer your help and see what they can do for you."[58] Feminist and queer histories emerge from collaborative processes that mirror the network mode of collective feminist organizing and of noninstitutional "community archives."

These collaborative processes extend beyond *Matrices* to a larger network of feminist periodicals through content sharing and cross-citation. *Matrices* published individual researchers' requests for assistance with projects that went on to become significant texts in the gay and lesbian historical movement, such as Katz's 1982 request for information to support a proposed second volume of *Gay American History* (volume 1 was published in 1978). Requests were often submitted directly by the author, but *Matrices* also borrowed content from other newsletters. Some examples include the Archives and History Projects insert originally produced by the Canadian archives; a detailed partial listing of primary source holdings at the LHA in a 1979 issue; and short entries in the *Matrices* "Notes and Queries" section gathered by editors from other lesbian-feminist periodicals, with their provenance noted through citation. This exchange was reciprocal. The 1978 issue of the *Lesbian Herstory Archives Newsletter* announced the launch of *Matrices* to its readers. By reproducing content across periodicals, lesbian-feminist newsletters ensured that requests for participation reached a wide range of publics, a clever tactic given that these publications often served niche communities such as lesbian mothers, rural women, "Third World women," or specific regions.

Larger practices of citation can be read across these publications through what Eichhorn calls "archival proximity," the way in which archival documents make a certain kind of sense insofar as they are ordered in relation to one another.[59] By tracing citations across publications, classified-style "ads" for archives that might otherwise seem unremarkable construct norms about the kind of work thought to be worthy of attention as they are recirculated through wider networks.[60] Community archives had to make choices about what collections to highlight in these generally short announcements, anticipating what would be of widest "research value." This cross-citational economy of attention inevitably affected the kinds of materials accessed by researchers and, perhaps, potential donors' perceptions of what these archives wanted to collect.

While the *Matrices* network supported the construction and use of community archives, it is this very network form that renders the publication's effects difficult to archive. Women's print cultures of the late twentieth century are ephemeral in the sense that they have not been collected widely and evenly and rarely have been preserved well.[61] Even when full print runs of past publications find their way into archives, these collections fall short of mapping the ongoing, networked connections among readers. The *Matrices* network is to some extent ephemeral. *Matrices* editorials often comment with frustration on a lack of feedback from subscribers about how they were using the network. Michelle Meagher argues that feminist newsletter editorials provided space for reflection on a periodical's broad mandate and frank, confessional commentary on how an issue was made.[62] *Matrices* editorials follow this pattern. The October 1979 issue laments: "For two years, we have published *Matrices* as a source of networking, but have little indication if it is serving this function. We assume it is, because the mailing list has grown to over 600 and new subscriptions arrive regularly. So, if you have had any positive experiences through *Matrices*, we'd like to hear about them."[63] The publication's reach is extended beyond those subscribers accounted for though profiles via the "after-market" circulation of newsletters through photocopying, further demonstrating the decentralized operation of these networks.

Matrices initiated communications that were fleeting, a problem identified by the newsletter's editors during its period of publication and a methodological challenge for my study of the network from the present.[64] Soliciting evidentiary feedback through editorials was a belabored practice that reflects the burnout characteristic of much feminist activism and academic service work. Assembling issues of *Matrices* was labor-intensive, time-consuming, unremunerated, and aimed at long-term, structural changes that were difficult to measure except in the abstract. Research conducted through the network depended on the interplay of the newsletter, archives, and the quite concrete form of books and articles that this research left behind. Newsletter networks ask us to reckon with feminist historiography's conditions of mediation as a formative subject of these very histories. As one aspect of lesbian-feminist information activism, newsletter networks gesture toward the existence of a rich infrastructure that is difficult to capture retrospectively. Publications such as *Matrices* must be historicized through methods that attend to their dispersed forms, chasing the "interconnections" hoped for by editorial staff through cross-citational research in the same archival collections *Matrices* helped to build.

Newsletter Networks and Outreach at the Lesbian Herstory Archives

In the 1970s, newsletters were a primary form of information outreach for lesbian-feminist organizations housed in physical spaces, including community archives. These DIY publications could be printed cheaply and easily on an informal schedule, and they could be sent through regular mail, all of which suited cash and labor-strapped grassroots organizations. The *Lesbian Herstory Archives Newsletter* was a significant communications and fundraising device for the archives in its early days, and provides a foreword to chapter 4's longer history of digitization at these archives. The newsletter's importance to the early operation of the LHA points to the archives' role as more than just a repository for records; wide-reaching activities, events, and other forms of outreach promoted through the newsletter evidence a broader, pedagogical information strategy. The newsletter was a technology for transforming the archives from a repository bound geographically to New York into a site of information activism.

The archives' 1979 newsletter announced the incorporation of the LHA as the Lesbian Herstory Educational Foundation, Inc., a move that "broadens our scope to be an information service that publishes a newsletter, does public speaking and in as many ways as possible gathers and shares information about the Lesbian Experience."[65] The physical archives would function as the "resource room" and "cultural center" for this expansive mandate.[66] As a printed document that mediates between the archives and its public, the newsletter speaks to the Lesbian Herstory Archives' goals of outreach and access, rather than just preservation and research. While *Matrices* demonstrates the interstitial role of newsletters in a larger, dispersed lesbian-feminist history and archives movement, the archives' use of newsletters shows how community archives, far from just storehouses grounding this movement, are dynamic networks in their own rights.

The *Lesbian Herstory Archives Newsletter* was published from June 1975 until spring 2004, generally once a year, with occasional extended breaks between issues, for a total of nineteen issues (figures 1.6–1.8).[67] This newsletter was also typewritten, pasted together, photocopied, and circulated by letter mail. Content updated members of the archives' community about the archives' work, future goals, and how they could help. Early issues published in the 1970s featured an "Archives Needs" section, which listed specific books and newsletter issues sought for the collection, along with skills like foreign language translation that the archives lacked in its existing volunteer base. A short "Research Queries" section included reader requests for help with specific research projects, much like *Matrices'* "Notes and Queries" section. These early issues always included bibliographies, often of materials that could be accessed through the archives. Among them, an index of short stories about or by lesbians, a list of "Serial Media with Lesbian Content", and even a bibliography of other lesbian bibliographies.[68] Later issues published in the late 1980s and '90s moved away from these listings toward longer, informative articles that updated readers on financial statements, and activities and events related to the archives.

FIGURE 1.7 Lesbian Herstory Archives founder Deborah Edel typing the newsletter, 1979. Image courtesy Lesbian Herstory Educational Foundation.

FIGURE 1.8 Deborah Edel making pasteups for the *Lesbian Herstory Archives Newsletter*, 1979. Image courtesy Lesbian Herstory Educational Foundation.

Julia Penelope was one of the founding collective members of the LHA, three years before she sent the letter that would spark *Matrices*. Her sense of a network's vitality to lesbian historiography is clear in a note she contributed to the *Lesbian Herstory Archives Newsletter*'s first issue, published in 1975. She imagined a national mailing list of lesbians illustrated by a map: "One of the projects of the Archives Collective will be a large map of the United States on which we will represent the Lesbian network by marking the small towns and villages where Lesbians are establishing themselves on farms and in communes. We would also like to maintain a mailing list of rural lesbians. This project is an effort to keep all of us in touch with each other and to provide records of our lives."[69] Though I found no records of this map's realization, Penelope's vision points to the idea of lesbian networks as a spatial imaginary that could meaningfully connect city dwellers with the rural lesbian lands movement that began in the 1970s.[70]

These tactics reached beyond urban enclaves, expanding the range of materials that donors might send, and providing knowledge of the archives' work to a growing network of lesbians. De-centralized regionalism was also behind a "A Plea for Regional Clippers," which asked readers to clip articles of relevance about lesbians in their local press and mail them to the archives for incorporation into subject files.[71] This workflow further demonstrates the network's reliance on a range of print technologies for sharing information. The newsletter supported regional outreach, and also reported on other efforts the archives made to circulate lesbian history beyond New York City, including a traveling slideshow, and a one-woman, six month, thirty-four-city motorcycle tour.[72] All of these networked outreach strategies were based in the idea that information infrastructure could be purposefully designed to unite diverse groups of lesbians.

The LHA imagined a functioning network as crucial to building an archives that above all was inclusive of as many lesbian lives as possible. Outreach through the newsletter could develop a collection reflective of the archives' intersectional, lesbian-feminist mandate, which recognized that minoritized women faced extra barriers to archiving. Working class women, rural women, women of color, women who were young or old, were encouraged to think of the archives as part of a larger infrastructure they could participate in, and make their own.

Building a collection means materializing a mostly unwritten history through group effort in which the newsletter formally assigned specific tasks to readers: send money, send clippings, send photos of your life. The newsletter also informally fostered a shared responsibility for this infrastructure.

Issue five describes the need for a "grassroots network" to sustain the archives' work: "To all lesbians who read this newsletter. The Archives grows in fullness only when you take the time to send us a contribution—a photo, a tape, a letter, something of your lives. We cannot personally attend every Lesbian event, go to every organizational meeting, *but a grassroots network can*. Please make tapes of events in your area, clip articles, write your impressions and send them to the Archives. We need all your voices!"[73] This request imagines the archives serving a dispersed public capable of capture within one network map—the kind of model Penelope proposed, but never drew.

As a political and affective strategy for imagining shared lesbian space outside actually existing conditions, an archives network echoes Jack Gieseking's description of the "constellations" through which lesbians imagine their embodied and spatial relations to community.[74] The archives' newsletter assumes that lesbians living far from New York City—a monolith in LGBTQ cultural geography—created precious information that was key to establishing a diverse historical record. The New York-based archives identified precarious access to lesbian history as a problem that might be differentially felt by those living without ready access to lesbian information infrastructures. The archives was precisely *for these women*, whose information might resist capture without outreach strategies that drew carefully on networked capacities.

The *Lesbian Herstory Archives Newsletter* often articulates the responsibility for history and for the archives to the community constituted in and through the publication and its participatory cultures. The archives actively democratized its collection by insisting that readers take responsibility for documenting their lives and communities, their personal and political experiences. The newsletter's pedagogical strategy tried to convince readers of this responsibility, which meant convincing them that their seemingly unremarkable lives mattered: "Our legacy will be realized only through the efforts of every lesbian. . . . [I]t is through our collective rejoicing, reclaiming and renewing that our survival as a Lesbian community will be determined."[75] This three-fold strategy (1) gave lesbians a concrete reason to believe that evidence of their lives was important; (2) taught them how to document their lives by making and gathering records; (3) implored them to donate the materials created through this process. Readers who followed these instructions became information activists by carrying out self and community archiving affiliated with a larger network.

Through these instructions to readers, the archives' newsletter became entangled with other forms of mediation individuals could use to create their own information about lesbian life. Women were encouraged to become active makers by taking photographs, gathering print media (the materials of "clipping" culture), and audio-recording interviews, conferences, radio shows, musical events, and talks. Inspired by the oral history movement, issues from the late 1970s and early 1980s encouraged readers to make audio, film, and later video to document aspects of their lives. Women were encouraged to use these recording technologies to "Talk about important memories . . . people, places, experiences, things that touched you deeply or angered you. Don't lose your own history in the rush of daily life."[76] Through notices in the newsletter, the LHA offered to lend eager contributors recording equipment, and supply blank tapes, to make this activity accessible to women with limited resources. A 3,000-tape spoken-word collection emerged partly out of these calls for recordings, and as I outline in chapter 4, this same collection became the archives' earliest comprehensive digitization project.

Situated among the tapes, buttons, yellowing magazine clippings and Polaroids, email blasts and streaming audio of the present, the newsletter's print specificity both does and does not matter to the network it facilitated. Networks are a cultural logic for mediation, rather than a singular format consistent with a specific moment in media history. A more expansive media history of feminist social movements understands the idea of networks as paradoxically bound to, but also independent of, particular technologies. In other words, communication networks are one topology of lesbian-feminist information activism, and also a broader ideal guiding how feminists imagine working together.

Newsletter networks share some characteristics with online networks: for example, they connect distant others to support counterpublic work, non-hierarchical collaboration, and high levels of engagement. Lisa Gitelman centers *genres* to understand these kinds of connections. Genres "resist any but local and contrastive logics for media; better to look for meanings that arise, shift, and persist according to the uses that media—emergent, dominant, and residual—familiarly have. Better, indeed, to admit that no medium has a single, particular logic, while every genre does and is."[77] As a genre, newsletters represent a set of formal expectations about how organizations will communicate with their publics. These expectations include how documents are produced (on the cheap, on the fly) and circulated (toward specific movement goals). As a genre, newsletters also transcend specific printing techniques: *Matrices* and the *Lesbian Herstory Archives Newsletter* were both mimeographed, photocopied, pasteboarded, and desktop published at various points in their lifespans.

The importance of genre notwithstanding, print specificity does matter to lesbian-feminist information infrastructure because these paper newsletters have a particular rhythm and pace. They are a slow, messy, deliberate, labor-intensive, and sometimes cumbersome format that seemed to frustrate the archives' coordinators at times: "It took countless hours to do each mailing."[78] Computers allowed the LHA to finally print mailing labels and more easily update subscribers' addresses. The newsletter proudly announced, "In 1983, on one of the hottest September weekends on record, about 20 Archives volunteers and 2 borrowed Kaypro computers got together in an un-air-conditioned apartment in Brooklyn and put the archives mailing list on a database."[79] This presented a major improvement over "the original list," of 3,632 subscribers' addresses, which had been "handwritten onto envelopes and sorted by hand into [Z]ip code order for each mailing."[80] The new distribution database was followed by a shift to desktop publishing in 1986. The first issue made with a computer looks different;[81] it looks neater, is easier to read, and it includes a description of how the newsletter would be changing, becoming more "streamlined" in both form and content.[82]

The archives' newsletter did not facilitate the kind of person-to-person, distributed networking *Matrices* sought out, favoring a centralized model that positioned the institution as the network's hub. Although early issues published requests from readers for help with specific projects, this kind of communication was not the focus. Most women stayed in touch with the archives through the newsletter and worried when issues were not timely. The newsletter often reassured readers not to worry about breaks in contact: "Putting out the newsletter is a time consuming and costly project. Please do not give up on us if there is a long pause between Newsletters. Be assured that our daily functioning is ongoing."[83] The pace of print and the network's centralized structure required faith from readers that the larger lesbian-feminist history project they believed in carried on.[84]

Elusive Remnants of Lesbian Networks

The *Lesbian Herstory Archives Newsletter*'s effects are visible in the archive's collections development. For example, requests for regional clippers published in the newsletter led to the development of subject files so unusual and comprehensive that they were licensed for microfilming by Gale as part of its Gay Rights Movement series. The newsletter's centralized design made communication through the network more palpable because engagement from readers went directly back to the archives. *Matrices* leaves less of a trace. Its network is difficult to historicize precisely because of its dispersed form. The editors of *Matrices* wanted "interconnections" among readers to proliferate independently of the newsletter, because this would strengthen historical research on lesbian topics. The editors saw the newsletter's printed form as an invitation to begin, invoked through their choice of name: "Because we believe that our work is a beginning, we decided to call this newsletter '*Matrices*,' 'a situation or surrounding substance within which something originates.' . . . Our research is the material of our lives. *Matrices* seemed to capture all of our meanings for the newsletter, the interconnections we wish to establish and maintain, the intersections of research interests, our woman-identification."[85] Ephemeral "interconnections" are precisely this network's mission, but they are also incommensurate with the editorial staff's and subscribers list's desire to establish concrete social movement history. *Matrices* could not keep track of its own influence as the network proliferated.

Returning to Baran's models, connections facilitated by a distributed network are strong because they no longer rely on the publication as the central hub; they are semiautonomous from the printed newsletter and have effects that exceed its pages. Distributed networks offer futurity because they can carry on beyond the life of *Matrices* itself. This relationship to feminist futurity differs from working to sustain publications, institutions, social movement organizations, and even archives at all costs. Grassroots feminist spaces always seem so precarious. They are perpetually on the verge of collapse, and we expect to lament their demise sometime soon. *Matrices* promised a future by promising a past in the form of history built collaboratively through the network. This past could carry on into the future if information circulated freely among the researchers producing this work. The "failure" of *Matrices* to fully document the network's reach is also a critique of unattainable, toxic metrics, including the idea that the "best" social movement organizations last the longest and leave robust archives behind.[86]

Lesbian feminism idealized communications networks, but conflicts specific to network relations also occurred. As Wendy Hui Kyong Chun and Galloway have argued, communication networks make egalitarian promises that conceal the power structures, protocols, and control mechanisms they actually exert.[87] Information circulated through the network according to the tacit ethics and expectations of subscribers. Conflicts emerged when centralized control undermined investments in the antihierarchical, decentralized model *Matrices* imagined as its infrastructure. Examples of these conflicts are plentiful and tend to galvanize around privacy, self-determination, and the ad hoc development of organizational hierarchies.

JR Roberts, eastern coordinator of *Matrices*, resigned her post in 1984, explaining in a published resignation letter that she could no longer tolerate the publication's movement toward centralized control. "The present structure, in which a decision is made by one woman and then presented in print as a 'group decision' supposedly made by *all* the editors, is not a structure I feel comfortable with," Roberts wrote. "It just goes against my grain of how things need to work in the world. . . . It is difficult because we are all so busy and our geographical separation and distance is not conducive to group activity."[88] Roberts argues that the *Matrices* network did not always operate according to its egalitarian, distributed "network" ideal, as power clustered around centralized nodes within the publication's editorial leadership. Making subscribers aware of this incongruity, and of the network's failure to meaningfully surmount geography, seemed an urgent project for Roberts as she resigned her post.

Roberts, a white woman, also compiled *Black Lesbians: An Annotated Bibliography* and worked as a member of the Circle of Lesbian Indexers. She abandoned *Matrices* because the realities of collective organizing through a print network were sometimes incommensurate with a lesbian-feminist desire for "sisterhood" built on shared values and equal footing. Ultimately, networks, no matter how purposefully built, cannot overcome what ultimately are interpersonal and structural factors that delimit lesbian feminism's ability to be the umbrella it claimed to be for all women.

Privacy and self-determination became heated issues when *Penthouse* magazine salaciously excerpted the lesbian activist and "lavender menace" Karla Jay's book *The Gay Report* (1979), which drew on survey work about lesbian sexuality.[89] Jay relied on the lesbian-feminist print movement to circulate her survey, and she promoted her research in the "Notes and Queries" section of *Matrices*. In a letter of complaint printed in the June 1979 issue, a reader named Amethyst wrote that she was "shocked/angered/infuriated by this exploitative, anti-feminist, misogynist act/use of Lesbian/'Feminist' research!"[90] Amethyst listed the lesbian periodicals that distributed the survey—*Lesbian Connection, Lesbian Tide*, etc.—and then wrote, "We remember how we were urged by Karla Jay's many ads to fill in her questionnaire and send it to her. It was beneficial to the Lesbian Feminist movement. I/We were suspicious at the time of how this could benefit us."[91] Seeing Jay's research represented in *Penthouse* angered survey participants because of lesbian feminists' concerns about pornography, but also because of the magazine's male audience, voyeuristically consuming data about lesbian sexuality that participants had contributed in good faith. This choice of venue did not benefit the lesbian community whose labor and data made the study possible, and it violated tacit community values around how data ought to be gathered and shared. Jay explained in a follow-up letter that her publisher had provided the excerpt to *Penthouse* without her permission. While lesbian-feminist values guided how *Matrices* circulated information, interventions from outsiders contravened network norms. Here, a network's open structure and lack of oversight is too promiscuous for a sexual public with real concerns about the privacy and safety of its members.

While the *Matrices* network aimed to do away with centralized control, it was also caught up in larger operations of power that put it in conflict with lesbian-feminist ideas about who could rightfully represent women's sexuality. Responding to another subscriber's query was a choice underwritten by an implicit trust that became tenuous in the case of Jay's *Penthouse* excerpt. This trust was built on shared beliefs about how information ought to be gathered, kept, and used. Jay's publishing company worked outside these community values when it chose *Penthouse* as an ideal publicity mechanism for *The Gay Report*. In an internet age in which information's proliferation and promiscuity seem inevitable, this incident from *Matrices* is a reminder that networks establish and maintain shared practices that allow participants to feel safe communicating through them.[92] Violating these formal rules or informal beliefs damages the network as participants lose trust and drop out.

It is worth considering for whom privacy mattered most among the readers of *Matrices*, given the gradations of financial autonomy and cultural and intellectual capital in a network that served both tenured professors and "nonprofessional" researchers who would call themselves writers, artists, activists, or simply feminists before they would take up the label "historian." *Matrices* wanted to democratize history and dismantle the hierarchies among researchers, but it also wanted to stay bound to institutional models of knowledge production, where "productive" research leads to an article or book celebrated in the newsletters' pages. Who felt at home in the network, comfortable enough to become an active, named participant, and who remained silent in the background, "lurking" by reading but never contributing information? Did these hesitant users take advantage of the network's decentralized and distributed affordances by forming sidelined enclaves of their own? These questions are unanswerable because of the kinds of archives print cultures leave behind.

Given the kind of knowledge the network valued most, some forms of historical research were not recognizable to *Matrices*. For example, antiracist interventions in the history of sexuality have shown how the life and activist worlds of queer and trans Black, Indigenous, and and people of color resist documentation through forms of knowledge production structured by whiteness, including universities and publishing companies.[93] Barbara Smith explains in the foreword to *Black Lesbians*, "It is still frustrating to think that there are probably three or four times as many resources [on Black lesbians] as are listed here, and that the very nature of our multiple oppression makes them impossible to identity and obtain."[94] *Matrices* served lesbian-feminist researchers, the majority of whom were white. Some members of the network shared information about new work focused on the histories of lesbians of color. For example, issue three, published in 1978, includes a request for contributions to Roberts and Smith's *Black Lesbians* project in progress and listings for several publications, including Eleanor Hunter's "Double Indemnity: The Negro Lesbian in the Straight White World" (1969), an unpublished paper on file at several archives for which readers could send away, and Ethel Sawyer's "unpublished thesis focusing on mid 1960s Black Lesbian bar group in St. Louis," available through interlibrary loan from Washington University.[95] Similarly, the LHA, which celebrates leadership by women of color, used the newsletter to amplify their contributions to the collections.[96] The archives thought the newsletter could be used to highlight "international" materials in the collection, along with "multi-ethnic material" on "Asian-American, Afro-American, Native American, Latina and Chicana Lesbians."[97] These efforts hoped that reaching out to wider networks could reshape the field but remained bound to the bibliographic structures Smith critiqued.

Matrices often represented "the network" as an ideal political structure, yet this form emerged from multiple communities with visions that overlapped as much as they conflicted: from debates over sexual politics to class tensions between activist and academic communities and the whiteness of bibliographic logics. The *Matrices* community sometimes sought centralized characteristics such as privacy and control while eschewing them more generally in pursuit of the network's distributed promise.

Conclusion

Just as the *Lesbian Herstory Archives Newsletter* was phased out in the mid-2000s, mostly replaced by online communications, *Matrices* stopped publishing in 1996. This happened after several years of infrequent publication, marked by a shift in tone toward more editorial content and away from subscriber participation. Notably, the last two issues include a new column on "Lesbian Cyberspace" and an announcement of *Matrices'* new website. These issues explained the internet to *Matrices* readers, going through "URL," "HTML," and other basic terminology; described how readers could access the web; and made a case for the new network technology's value to lesbian researchers by listing and annotating existing "Lesbian Resources on the Web."[98] These final issues signal what Barbara Sjoholm marks as the end of the Women in Print Movement in the 1990s—replaced, ostensibly by the "digital universe" of "Amazon," "the internet," and "digital publishing."[99] And yet, zine culture in the 1990s reinvigorated feminist print cultures, and young queers on Instagram circulate remnants of lesbian print cultures today.[100] Rather than replacing earlier forms of feminist publishing, online networks link print "texts"—including their forms of distribution and the connections they engender—with contemporary platforms.[101] Given this continuum, the end of the *Matrices* newsletter did not foreclose its effects; rather, *Matrices'* remnants can be located in this ongoing networked "print" culture, as well as in community archives' digital outreach. We need more expansive, intergenerational models for understanding the feminist "networks" powering information activism.

More modestly, the network's remnants are available on the Lesbian Herstory Archives' website. After publishing *Boots of Leather, Slippers of Gold* in 1993, Davis and Kennedy donated all of their audiotapes to the LHA, where they have been digitized and are offered as streaming MP3s.[102] This is one of the archives' first comprehensive online projects and represents a decades-long entanglement among *Boots of Leather*, *Matrices*, the LHA, and the larger community upholding this work. Networks provide the conditions of possibility for lesbian-feminist history across decades, formats, and technological change.

TWO

Calling to Talk
and Listening Well

Information as Care
at Telephone Hotlines

THE LESBIAN SWITCHBOARD CALL LOG, AUGUST 1, 1973. ♀: "How do you lead in slow dances?" But she was really talking about roles and feeling incompetent. She's seeing a woman now who she says is "fem" who likes to dance and who leads because this woman can't. She sees herself as butch and wants to please this other woman by learning how to dance better and being able to lead.[1]

The phone rings and the caller asks for information about dancing. Jackie, who is staffing the hotline tonight, could walk her through the box step but knows better. They talk it through.[2] In her log, Jackie records what the caller was *really* asking for: to talk with another lesbian about vulnerability, gender, and care. To figure this out, Jackie drew on one of the *Switchboard Handbook*'s main tenets: "Try to figure out the problem behind the problem," or "What is the caller really calling about?" The *real* problem with not knowing how to dance is feeling inadequate navigating a form of masculinity derided in most spaces and encounters. As Ann Cvetkovich writes, "Representations of butch feeling convey a sense that vulnerability is not a sign of disempowerment but a privilege that is often unavailable and harder to achieve than the conventional stereotype of women as sentimental would have it."[3] By explaining the problem behind the problem, this call log becomes metadata about butch-femme relationships that speak through the archive to the economies of care available by calling lesbian feminist telephone hotlines. Jackie's log records butch vulnerability in motion. Hotline call logs show how asking for information was often a way to seek and receive care.

This log is one of thousands that document labor at the Lesbian Switchboard of New York City from 1972 to 1997. For four to five hours each night, a single volunteer like Jackie sat at a desk in the switchboard's small rented office in the West Village, waiting for the telephone to ring. The volunteer was surrounded by ready-to-hand information technologies she used to assist callers: a filing cabinet full of referral information, including pamphlets for other social services; a bulletin board crammed with notes about local events and flyers for upcoming bar nights; a Rolodex of contact cards for gay-friendly business, tradespeople, therapists, and other care workers; stacks of current newsletters and periodicals containing community listings; a ledger of women seeking roommates; and a shelf of reference guides "to finding nearly everything lesbian oriented anywhere in the country."[4] The volunteer spent her night fielding between ten and twenty calls from women in need—callers who saw the switchboard advertised in a newsletter or on a bulletin board or heard about it from a friend. Callers asked for help finding something fun to do that night, for information about support groups or help with coming out, for referrals to lesbian doctors and plumbers, for relationship advice, or for crisis intervention. Or they asked just to "rap" (code for heavier talk about the personal as political).

The logs suggest that many callers expressed despair, loneliness, or confusion. These callers didn't need anything in particular—they usually asked "just to talk" while someone listened on the other end of the line. When a ringing telephone is answered, it connects two people at a distance who may have little in common beyond a sometimes tenuously shared sexual identification. As one switchboard staff member explained in an article about the organization, "I used the Switchboard a couple of times before I joined the staff. Once my mother was there and I called up and heard 'Lesbian Switchboard' and hung up. It was enough to hear that there was a living, *breathing* lesbian somewhere. I thought I was the only one."[5] Saying something supportive, knowing when to be quiet, asking the right questions of someone who is upset, just being another body that breathes—all of this takes place through a receiver, between strangers, in a context in which silence can be uncomfortable. The caring practices that transpire when a phone is answered are singular, even minor in a larger struggle, but they make social movement participation and service work matter in the everyday lives of individuals. Hotline operators feel like their labor makes a difference, and callers become part of something larger when they dial a hotline to ask for help.

Several intertwined media practices, not just the telephone, are necessary to run a hotline and provide information as care. Guidebooks, pamphlets, referral cards, and other reference materials drawn from broader feminist print cultures were sorted and filed for easy access by capable operators trained in using these tools. A volunteer used her hands to do this work.[6] Operators shuffled through paper records and spoke on the telephone to make lesbian life more livable for hotline callers. Hotlines promised assisted information retrieval. The "information" operators provided also connected isolated or unsupported callers with others, including movement-based services they did not know about. Telephone hotlines were connective infrastructure in which practical, communicative work was also emotional support because it brought callers into the fold of a larger lesbian movement and its services.

This chapter explores the information economies that lesbian telephone hotlines facilitated to expand understandings of what information does within feminist activism. As communication technologies, telephone hotlines are not just about telephones. Rather, telephone work is a multimedia practice that troubles the emphasis on print cultures within second-wave feminist historiography. The switchboard combined detailed, journal-like call logs; an indexed database of print referral information; and the telephone itself to connect individual callers with the wider communities they sought. While the Lesbian Switchboard never used a computer, the organization thought about providing access to information in ways that echo digital culture's emphasis on search retrieval as user empowerment. Operators were trained to retrieve and deliver meaningful results from a collection of resources selected and organized to be searchable and useful.

A secondary focus of this chapter is to consider *why* late twentieth-century feminist activism is so often remembered through its print practices and to pursue this question as a media problem. While working in the switchboard's organizational papers I found it necessary to ask what kinds of media practices are remembered, or *rememberable*, within feminist archives. I focus primarily on New York's Lesbian Switchboard because of its unusually rich and detailed archive of call logs. For comparison, I also devote some attention to the archives of Toronto's Lesbian Phone Line (1976–80). This chapter presents an interpretive rather than systematic study of lesbian telephone hotlines, reading the Lesbian Switchboard's call logs and other organizational records from my place in the present for what they reveal, and what they withhold, about hotline work. As the research for this chapter developed, I continuously tried and failed to find former hotline volunteers to interview. Anonymity is built into the design of hotlines: volunteers leave only their first names in records, and twenty years have passed since the Lesbian Switchboard shut down. Through word of mouth I was able to locate and interview one switchboard volunteer. I found one other, but she did not want to participate in the project. Firsthand accounts of hotline work published by volunteers during the switchboard's years of operation helped a little, as did an oral history interview conducted by a researcher in the 1980s with two volunteers at the Toronto hotline. But all of this amounted to a tiny, partial firsthand perspective on what hotline work was actually like. Yet the call logs were so resolutely abundant.

The resulting chapter is precisely about this imbalance and how we study feminist media histories through social movement archives. It is a partial, interpretive history of call logs that does not claim to offer a systematic account of what hotline work was like—only how it reads, to me, through this archive. The chapter puts forward suggestions for how, and why, feminist activism might be historicized beyond the oral history and print culture strategies that have been indispensable to scholarly work in this field thus far. While the chapter is *about* telephone hotlines, it also theorizes documents, memory, and the textures of doing feminist archival research on media technologies that seem to resist capture in print or have a complicated relationship to documentation. The chapter begins to frame this book's contribution to queer and feminist archive theory, which forms chapter 4's focus. I argue that the switchboard's call logs attempt to capture the intense tone and subjects of calls to record the emotional needs of callers and the economies of care that formed an emerging lesbian public. The logs point to the importance of studying entangled media practices and of thinking speculatively about gaps in documentation when theorizing feminist archives and affect.

Reading Call Logs

Today, the Lesbian Switchboard's records are held by a community archives located in the same LBGT Community Center in Manhattan's West Village that once housed the switchboard's office. The building has been renovated in the way that heritage buildings with institutional functions often are: airy, open spaces where walls and doors used to be but the building's original bones show through. I walk the halls on breaks from reading in the archives, wondering which nondescript room once housed the hotline. The switchboard is so present in this space but also feels very far away when I return to my desk in the frigid reading room and crack open another call log. Call logs make up about half of the switchboard's collection, filling one bankers' box. Dozens of spiral-bound notebooks filled with entries like Jackie's are filed in chronological order. The notebook covers are all different—some are brightly colored; others are drab manila. The books are worn from being handled each night by volunteers as they logged their work (figure 2.1). Each book is a treasure trove of doodles, jokes, idiosyncratic handwriting, and notes passed among volunteers. This is marginalia to the notebook's substance and purpose: to provide nightly logs of every call made to the switchboard.

Volunteers used very different styles for recounting phone calls. Lana's log (figure 2.2) represents a middle-of-the-road style in terms of length and willingness to interpret callers' feelings. The previous night's volunteer left a note for Lana at the top of the page, telling her to expect a follow-up call: "Barbara [last name redacted] from Maryland will call about a place to crash. I said I'd check on the Staten Island Commune. I'll call in the info to the switchboard." Volunteers used these logs to communicate with one another outside monthly coordinating meetings and establish consistency for callers. Once her shift starts, Lana provides callers with bathhouse and event information and counsels a young caller whose parents are kicking her out of the house. In my read across decades of nightly logs, Lana's record for January 18, 1973, represents a pretty typical evening at the switchboard: a balance of simple information requests, calls from people in trouble, crank calls, and an hour-long conversation with a lesbian from Westchester who wanted to talk about "lesbian life." Lana deals with a lesbian caller (signaled in the logs by a "♀" with an extra line through it, or sometimes "♀♀") who masturbates on the phone and another who calls to talk about "fantasies"; Lana doesn't want to and, we assume, ends the call. Finally, a man calls and asks to kiss her, a repetitive act of harassment volunteers logged almost nightly. By making themselves available to help any lesbian in need, hotline volunteers also made themselves vulnerable to crank callers, early trolls of feminist information activism.

Lana's log raises some of the mysteries involved in interpreting the politics of lesbian feminist organizations from the present. Entries such as "♂ Transvestite, gave him address of [STAR]" might signal a helpful referral to a more appropriate information source for the caller or a denial of service to a transgender caller who seeks identification with lesbian

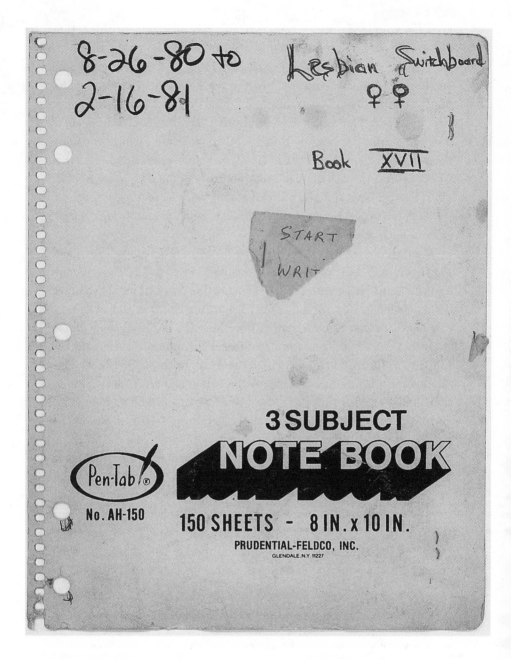

FIGURE 2.1 Cover of a call log created by the Lesbian Switchboard of New York City, 1980–81. The switchboard used various brands of spiral-bound notebook. The metal spirals were removed by the archives as a preservation measure. The Lesbian Switchboard of New York City, Inc. Records, Box 2, Folder 35, The LGBT Community Center National History Archive.

THURSDAY. 18.

BARBARA ▨▨▨ FROM MARYLAND WILL
CALL ABOUT A PLACE TO CRASH. I
SAID I'D CHECK ON THE STATEN
ISLAND COMMUNE. I'LL CALL IN THE
INFO TO THE SWITCHBOARD

Thursday

6:00 bars in Long Island
6:02 young ♀ parents found out she's a lesbian +
are throwing her out of the house. She had to
hang up.

6:10 P.O. box (woman wanted to use switcbd for
phone calls. told her no

6:15 baths
6:10 ♀ from westchester. Talked to her for 1 hr.
about ♀ life etc.
6:30 ♀ wanted to talk about fantasies. I didn't
want to
6:45 ♀ masturbating on phone. told her goodby.
7:b Sue ▨▨▨ called for Orri's #
7:15 ♀ whats happening this weekend
7:20 ♀♂ transvestite. Gave him address of S.T.A.R.
8:00 places in NYC to go
7:55 ♂ can I give you a kiss

feminism. Lana offers this caller—whom she may misgender in the log—a referral to New York's Street Transvestite Action Revolutionaries (STAR), the activist organization founded by two trans women of color, Sylvia Rivera and Marsha P. Johnson, in 1970.[7] Reading this exchange in the present, I am left to make sense of a symbol, five words, and an acronym to sketch out the complex politics of trans service provision practiced at the Lesbian Switchboard.

How can one use this log in all its willful incompleteness? There are many incitements for the researcher here. How did volunteers feel talking to sad teenagers? What kinds of strategies did they use to do this talking? What kinds of resources were available to recommend (the Staten Island Commune, contact information for lesbian social spaces, event listings, the STAR referral), and how did volunteers choose them? How did Lana and women like her keep coming back to volunteer when it meant facing regular unwanted propositions and harassment from some callers? What was the rhythm of an evening working the phones? What happened during all the minutes that are not logged?

To answer these questions I read the logs in the aggregate—there are thousands of them—looking for patterns and rhythms, along with anomalies. In this chapter I sketch out answers to these questions about the hotline by reading logs alongside the organization's other documents. As Kate Eichhorn has shown, archival collections have structuring epistemologies that shape how feminist social movements of the past are ordered from the present.[8] Because logs are shared documents, meant to communicate with other volunteers through a common genre, they reflect an organization's "order": how policies, conflicts, relationships with other organizations, and ideas about lesbian feminism influenced volunteers as they answered calls and then wrote about them. These logs also span twenty-five years of social transition and reflect the ways in which lesbian feminism, as a dynamic political orientation, ordered service provision differently over time.

For the duration of the switchboard's twenty-five operating years, each and every call was logged by volunteers such as Lana. The switchboard kept logs to improve communication among volunteers, storing the books in a lockbox to maintain confidentiality.[9] Call logs record in writing the sound of asking for and receiving help; of building community and capacity through simple, routine exchanges between two strangers made over telephone wire. They log the rhythm of a night spent on the phones, making oneself available to others in need, and the longer-term mediated rhythm of a social movement organization that no one can call anymore. The logs chart the organization's decline. It is clear from the logs that the phones were ringing less often by the late 1990s, until there are no more logs to read. Ultimately, the call logs are print documents that attempt to represent sound—more specifically, the rhythm of conversation. These documents fall far short of what an audio recording would offer, but they provide another kind of archive instead. Logs are entries to thinking about feminist research methods in media history. How might the sound of silence, of breathing on the other end of a phone, be accounted for through print documentary practices? How can we use paper archives—the dominant form of twentieth-century records—to understand multimedia practices used by activists once hotlines and their actual phone calls are long gone?

This book, like much historiography focused on twentieth-century LBGTQ histories, draws primarily on print culture archives.[10] Paper shapes research methods in the field for a number of reasons. As the previous chapter argued, the Women in Print Movement's infrastructural role in facilitating communication among lesbian feminists was one of these reasons. Paper is also a stable format that lends itself to archiving and use by researchers: you don't need to find a working reel-to-reel player to "listen" to a call log. Finally, paper remains dominant in archives because of the way organizations do "paperwork" and hold on to this paper. Paperwork is designed to be kept, as files that can be ordered and stored away for future access, without taking up too much space.[11] From the early to mid-twentieth century, paperwork proliferated within businesses and institutions, including social movement groups. By the 1970s, inexpensive new paper stock and more readily accessible photocopying technologies led organizations to imagine tasks such as coordinating people, ideas, and events and keeping records through the medium of paper. [12] New lesbian feminist organizations developed their work processes within these conditions.

Archives adjusted to this paper glut. Beginning in the midcentury, the archives field developed a new emphasis on appraisal: the systematic assessment of which records to keep or discard. Theodore Schellenberg's influential theories of archival appraisal argued that archivists ought to appraise the potential future "research value" of records to decide which documents to keep or discard. Shellenberg proposed a theoretical response to a practical, media problem: too much paper.[13] His theories have been influential in the United States and Canadian archives world, but as Luciana Duranti argues, they are flawed precisely because of their practical grounding, which runs counter to how the field ought to understand records—their organic emergence and profound relational character.[14] Community archives, where the papers of lesbian organizations generally end up, tend to base appraisal decisions in grounded community needs rather than archivists' judgments about what researchers might want.[15] Community archives err on the side of keeping any papers that are not duplicates and privilege the emotional resonances records might have.[16]

When an organization eventually shutters and volunteers look to donate records to an archive, this process often looks like transferring file cabinet contents into banker's boxes.[17] Most LBGTQ community archives emphasize social movement records but often lack the resources to do more than minimally process collections. The Lesbian Switchboard of New York City's papers, however, have been meticulously kept, filed, and organized into logical series. A clear picture of how the organization imagined its work, and talked to callers, emerges. Toronto's Lesbian Phone Line, by contrast, has partial, disorganized records that document the hotline's high-level policies and procedures but reference no actual calls. At some point in 2017, during my work on this book, an entire box from the Toronto collection disappeared during a shelf relocation project at Canada's LBGTQ+ community archives. As a volunteer at those archives I was able to spend hours searching for the box, which I had previously worked with, in the basement and off-site storage, but I turned up nothing. The archives' computer database had no record of this box, but I swear I had held it and read through its contents just months before. Paper can also be precarious media in volunteer-run community archives.

As Cornelia Vismann has shown, paper files do not merely document. They also mediate how we understand systems and their role in knowledge formation. Studying activist organizations requires a methodologically reflexive approach to considering paperwork, filing logics, community archiving, and their relationship to what eventually becomes an organization's "archives." Paper tends to stick around, but we must also ask about media activism that paper cannot capture. Print culture fueled the hotlines' work distributing information, but talk between volunteers and callers on the phone exceeds capture in print.

Hotlines kept files about calls because recording calls would have been impractical, at odds with the anonymity most callers sought, and ultimately unnecessary for the hotline to function. A written log was sufficient for keeping basic records and communicating among volunteers. Telephone calls are abundantly present in call logs, just not *as calls*. These logs point clearly to the audio that escapes the organization's filing practices. Telephone information services drew on a combination of print and electronic technologies, troubling the telephone's position as a quintessentially "electronic" medium and the feminist archive's emphasis on paper remains. Calls are made into logs, which are made into files, which are made into archives, where they become something else: records, or documents.

The epistemic power of documents lies in what Lisa Gitelman describes as their "know-show" function.[18] Knowledge is produced through the acts of showing, copying, and circulating documents, a list of acts to which I add "archiving." These media practices, all of which are forms of "paperwork," produce the document *as document* rather than as "piece of paper." Documents mediate between users and the information they seek. Because documents *carry* information, they are "the object of knowledge rather than knowledge itself."[19] Craig Robertson argues that paper documents make information into an object that can be handled; this concretization produces the sense of objectivity we assign to some kinds of documents.[20] Thus, documents are "worth keeping" but also narrow and temporary in their utility. Once their usefulness ends, they remain important enough to file away rather than discard. Think, for example, of a passport that has expired. You might keep the document not only as a record of where you have traveled and of what you once looked like, but also because throwing it out would be a weird thing to do—a profound divestment in its former status as evidence.

The information value of documents changes over time. As John Guillory explains, "The document . . . aspires only to a moment of interest, the moment of its transmission; once transmitted, its interest falls off potentially to a zero degree, and it suffers the indignity of being filed away."[21] The switchboard kept call logs to improve communication among volunteers from night to night. The log's immediate value as information lasted a week or two, as volunteers caught up on calls to the hotline since their last shift. And yet the switchboard kept all of these spiral-bound notebooks for posterity, as a record of the hotline's everyday labor. In the archive, these logs transmit information on a time scale that extends beyond everyday communication between volunteers, or even the organization's lifetime. Working within the bourgeoning feminist history and archives movement, the switchboard likely had a sense of its own work as worth keeping.

In the archive, documents are interpreted and ordered in boxes by archivists for future researchers who will parse those documents for information. Like passports, archival documents have a kind of "original" aura in the Benjaminian sense: we show credentials to look at them and handle some with gloves; we place folders on a flat surface to avoid creasing the paper. We take these precautions even when, in practice, late twentieth-century social movement archives are often filled with photocopies that *could* easily be reproduced. The photocopies that fill these archives are valuable, but their precious status is not intrinsic; rather, it comes from what this paper might show us about the feminisms we inherit and the everyday rhythms of working at a feminist organization. Researching in feminist social movement papers requires orientating to activism's *eventful-ness*. Samantha Thrift describes eventfulness through minor, even repetitive moments of struggle rather than the singular events that constitute most historical methodologies: "The parallel history delineated by the archived minutiae" of feminist organizing ultimately challenges normative temporal logics of eruption or revolution.[22] Writes Thrift, "A feminist approach to eventfulness means adopting a more flexible and attentive vantage point from which to view history in order to discern that which is unexpect-edly transformative and significant."[23] This approach can mean thinking about documents differently—how to bring together the minutia of meet-ing minutes, call logs, and training manuals to understand the complex scriptural economies of feminist service provision *as activism*.

Hotline volunteers do not necessarily identify this service work as ac-tivism. The former Lesbian Switchboard volunteer I interviewed is a Black woman who worked at the switchboard for "five or six years," from the late 1980s to the early 1990s.[24] She told me, "I know the women that I worked with were not politically active for the most part. The one woman I know worked for the Girl Scouts; another owned an antiques business. Every-body had the usual 9–5 jobs. I don't remember anybody speaking out as politically active for the most part. We just gave out the information that we could find." Although these women may not have identified readily as activists, their service-provision work is certainly political in an expanded sense. Deborah Gould, Jennifer Brier, Cindy Patton, and Marty Fink have each provided distinct treatments of service provision and care work *as ac-tivism* within the context of queer and transfeminist HIV/AIDS activism.[25] Distinctions between activism and service work are often racialized and gendered, shoring up the riskiest forms of demonstration as valuable and archivable instead of attending to the "basic," life-sustaining work most often performed by women, people of color, and trans people.[26] Caring for others using information is vital service work that builds basic move-ment infrastructures. Feminist social movement archives are shaped by the media practices attendant to providing service and care, which are bound up in "eventful" forms of paperwork.

The methodological adjustments involved in doing feminist media histories become especially apparent when paper documents reference the emotional register of telephone calls. Because hotline callers often sought emotional support or crisis intervention, many charged exchanges took place over the phone. These exchanges are documented in call logs, but only partially. For example, quick summaries of calls such as, "So lonely Black woman. She will go to the CR [consciousness-raising] group at firehouse [the Women's Liberation Center]," reference isolation, racial identity, and the need to find in-person forms of support from others in whom you recognize yourself.[27] But they do so with only a few words. Operators used shorthand that referenced shared, subcultural understandings of consciousness-raising as a methodology for antiracist lesbian organizing across differences. They also drew on local geographic lexicon ("firehouse" referred to the Women's Liberation Center, located in a city-owned former firehouse).[28] While reading these call logs in the present, in the aggregate, this shorthand coalesces into a picture of everyday feminist labor aimed at providing care.

Lesbian shorthand is also used to log calls about coming out, an experience fundamental to lesbian-feminist and gay liberation visibility politics. Log notes such as "Just out—scared stiff," "Having trouble 'coming out'—nice rap," and "♀ very heavy coming out trip"—are brief but reference so much more for operators who had both "been there" in their own lives and were used to the rhythm of supporting these frequent calls, night after night.[29] Sometimes operators would remark on a caller's tone as part of this shorthand. For example, "Woman confused, lonely, doesn't know if she's a lesbian or not—stammered profusely. Gave ID House [Identity House, an LBGT counseling service], SAGE [social service for older LBGT adults], NYC Women's Exchange [nonprofit store and community space]."[30] The stammering here describes an anxious sound in print. "Stammered profusely" evokes what it feels like to struggle to find the words you want to say to someone else as they tumble haltingly out of your mouth. Noting a caller's stammer is shorthand for listening with patience to someone who is lost but starting to find their way. Stammering on the phone rather than face to face also meant that this operator and this caller could not rely on body language or facial expressions when interpreting anxiety or showing patience. Silence, false starts, and words that arrive with difficulty are all the more raw when there is only sound to go on. By noting a caller's situational stammer, this volunteer references what it felt like to be on the line—listening to this call was difficult, but we got through it together, and now she has resources in hand.

Hotline shorthand often relied on a shared horizon of expectation about what support offered and how callers ought to feel about receiving it. Coming-out calls share investments in coming out as a hard but liberating experience that callers ought to move through willingly, with support from the hotline. Two coming-out calls handled by the same operator on the same night in 1990 demonstrate how this horizon of expectation was communicated through logs and may have saturated the tone of these calls themselves. The calls took place at the beginning of a decade in which gay and lesbian investments in coming out as an identity politics was linked to media representation and the achievement of equal rights under the law.[31] In other words, coming out in the early 1990s (and today) is an imperative that exerts pressure on queer people, with little regard for the differential vulnerabilities that make coming out impossible or undesirable for some:

> **CALL 1, 7:12 PM:** Rap call. A woman who was uncertain about her sexual identity wanted to talk about her confusion. She was very hung-up and couldn't even bring herself to say the word "lesbian." After we talked for a while, I told her about Identity House. I explained about the Saturday afternoon rap sessions, the walk-in counseling and the coming-out workshops. I strongly encouraged her to call but she was pretty hostile and I rather doubt she will.

The next call came in just two minutes after this "pretty hostile" caller hung up:

> **CALL 2:** Information call. A woman wanted to know about coming-out groups. I told her about Identity House and she sounded pretty positive, I think she (unlike the woman described above) will call.[32]

The first caller reacts to "helpful" information and emotional support in the wrong way, orienting away from the hope this ought to offer.[33] Her anger and despair could not be ameliorated by information about a community counseling service. The second caller is "unlike the woman described above"; she receives information from the hotline and feels better, hopeful, "pretty positive."

Queer media studies scholars working on youth cultures have been critical about how horizons of expectation around coming out held by adults or social movements can overdetermine understandings of media.[34] Similarly, volunteers' expectations about the positive effects their labor on the telephone ought to have influenced how they evaluated a good or bad call. Callers struggling to come out should hang up feeling better than they did when they first dialed the hotline. These callers are "positive," while those who resist advice or strike an angry tone are logged as "hostile."

At other times, logs for coming-out calls document the operator's frustration with hotline policies and procedures that limited their ability to help others in need. Jess, training a new volunteer named Leila in 1979, logged her disappointment at the end of a call as a critique of the telephone's limited proximities:

> 18-yr. old ♀, isolated. Doesn't have any lesbian friends. No connection with lesbian community. In Bklyn. Living with family. Still in high school. Has been to Gay and Young—too male. Referred her to Hiking Dykes, Bklyn. College ♀'s Center, ♀♀ Pride dance and march. She sounded so lonely. Very quiet. Frustrating sometimes that we can't do more. She said if she called again she wouldn't get me again. I told her there were other ♀ at the switchboard, etc. Is our policy of not telling ♀ when we staff firm?[35]

Jess is unable to form close bonds with individual callers because of the switchboard's policies. The switchboard was not a long-term counseling service, and these policies were designed to set boundaries with repeat callers by keeping staff schedules private so callers could not reach the same volunteer consistently. Jess's log suggests that she ended this call feeling deflated by administrative limitations.

Telephone work created mediated distance from callers that was part of a hotline's point: callers could maintain anonymity and reach out for help without joining a group or even leaving their homes. This distance is the hotline's media specificity. However, the distance limited a volunteer's ability to bring women in trouble into the fold of counterpublic care. When calls ended badly or without callers articulating that they felt better, hotline volunteers such as Jess were left to question the value of their labor on the phone.

Feeling bad is part of doing social movement work. Volunteers often leave an organization or struggle because of "burnout," the point at which "bad feelings" such as anger no longer motivate but overwhelm.[36] Hotline volunteers knew they needed to keep their bad feelings private from callers, who were often struggling with enough bad feelings of their own. In *Depression: A Public Feeling*, Ann Cvetkovich critiques depression's role as the antecedent to hope in understanding how people are motivated to act. Cvetkovich's project is in part to "depathologize negative feelings so that they can be seen as a possible resource for political action rather than as its antithesis."[37] Cvetkovich builds on queer and feminist theory's turn to "negative" emotions and what they might do for politics.[38] Feeling terrible might bring us to new political scenes as we commiserate with others.

The switchboard existed to sit with callers in their sadness, but also to provide information that would make sad callers *feel better*. Volunteers were often required to muffle their own bad feelings so they could hold the bad feelings of another. The *Switchboard Handbook* instructed operators to be aware of how affect could be shared over the phone: "Don't become flustered by the caller's anxiety or urgency. One of the most important things is to remain calm in a crisis. Your anxiety can easily be transmitted over the phone."[39] Volunteers managed their affect and its potential transmission as a habitual part of working the phones.[40]

By descriptively logging emotionally challenging calls, volunteers might imagine others on subsequent shifts helping them to hold these difficult conversations. Reading in the margins of call-log sheets, it seems that volunteers needed places to put all the bad feelings they weren't going to reveal to callers. While reading the logs I often came across marginalia that seemed like "venting" and wondered about the incidents that inspired them. For example, what led Amber-Dawn to scrawl, "One woman cannot work the board alone during heavy conversations!!!" across the top of a notebook page?[41] Her red ink, all-caps handwriting signals exasperation and a plea for attention from other volunteers. These are perhaps generative notes for discussion at the next staff meeting (*we really need another phone line and more volunteers*), but they are also ways to expend frustrated feelings for others to read, recognize, and hold. Notes in the margins might remind volunteers that working the phone is draining and hard and that feeling that burn is OK.

Reading emotion into call logs is a partial process based in interpreting how operators described their own feelings, articulated callers' needs, and perceived the tone of each exchange. By design, the log format withholds callers' feelings in their own terms. Logs are overly, even obsessively, documentary; they are an abundant record of hotline work that I was surprised to find in the archives. Yet so much is missing from these documents. Emotionally charged scenes are indexed by just a few words of description, which can mean reconstructing what silence might have felt like and signified: "Lots of silence—♀ Said she was depressed—hard to talk—she talked about being depressed."[42] Imagining in and through these silences and absences maps affective encounters over the phone, where a stammer, a too-long pause, or stops and starts in conversation are the unhappy rhythms of lesbian feminism's larger care economy.

What Makes a Telephone Hotline "Lesbian Feminist"?

The Lesbian Switchboard was among several telephone hotlines that specifically operated from a lesbian-feminist perspective. Among them, Toronto's Lesbian Phone Line offered lesbian-focused peer counseling and information referrals. Lesbian-feminist telephone hotlines can be defined by several high-level principles and practical approaches. Both the New York and Toronto hotlines

1. Were staffed by volunteers recruited from within the lesbian community and strove to be broadly inclusive in who volunteered, seeking women from diverse class backgrounds, races, and ethnicities (although this effort often failed).
2. Grounded administrative models in consciousness-raising and anti-oppression frameworks. Volunteers met regularly in a fairly horizontal power structure, and decisions were made using a consensus model.
3. Tried to gather and circulate "high-quality" information that was either produced by other lesbian organizations or solicited through questionnaires and evaluated by volunteers or trusted community members.[43]
4. Made active listening political by describing "talking on the phone" with other women as a unique form of care and capacity building, for both individual callers in trouble and for the lesbian-feminist movement.

These principles are based in the belief that telephone technology could sustain mediated but intimate exchange and support the unique needs a lesbian-feminist public had for connection with community.

Telephone hotlines were significant information technologies within lesbian-feminist social movements, performing on-demand outreach that informed callers about print resources, services, businesses, and social spaces they could access. These specialized hotlines modeled but also departed from the crisis intervention and information referral model developed by U.S. hospitals in the mid-1960s as a form of public-health provision. Community psychology literature dominates scholarly investigation of telephone hotlines. While this literature traces the first hotline to the hospital-initiated Los Angeles Suicide Prevention program, the media historian Hannah Zeavin offers an alternative lineage via psychoreligious suicide hotlines run by U.S.-based Christian organizations beginning in the 1950s.[44] Zeavin's research highlights how hotlines were always ideological in their operation, bound up with outreach models that combined service provision with religious organizing. Hotlines claimed to serve neutral purposes such as "just listening" or providing referrals to "high-quality" services. However, hotlines were often organized and staffed by volunteers working within specific religious or social movement contexts.

By 1974, more than one thousand crisis hotlines were operating across the United States.[45] The explosion of these hotlines during the 1970s related to the rise of organized social movements engaged in building mediated outreach and service provision.[46] These hotlines also took advantage of changes in the technology and political economy of telephone communication. Between 1960 and 1980, the percentage of Americans with access to a telephone increased substantially.[47] The use of shared party lines was widely replaced with private phone lines as telecommunications companies developed switching technologies and the cost of copper wire decreased. The telephone saturated domestic spaces and became a tool people could access in private to reach out to others over a distance.

Like social movements, hotlines responded to conditions of discontent and the unmet needs of "those who felt alienated by established helping agencies," including sexual minorities.[48] Gay and lesbian hotlines emerged out of the gay liberation movement in the 1970s to address isolation from social services, fear of judgment by homophobic hotline operators, and resistance to a counseling psychology that pathologized same-sex desire as mental illness. These hotlines expanded widely in the 1980s as a technological measure for circulating information on HIV/AIDS and doing antiviolence work in the context of growing social response to hate crimes.[49] The switchboard took up this challenge in the 1980s by providing women with HIV-transmission information related to lesbian sex. As in other areas of gay and lesbian social movement organizing, lesbian hotlines formed to address a lack of resources focused on womens' needs and committed to situating callers' problems within an intersectional understanding of gender, sexuality, race, and class. The National Association of Gay and Lesbian Switchboards formed in 1997 and generated the first database registry of hotlines across the United States, listing 150 organizations, the oldest of which were founded in 1966.[50] Hotlines were major components of an emerging grassroots gay and lesbian social-services infrastructure built for collecting, organizing, and providing access to information and community using media technologies.

Gay and lesbian hotlines connected information-seeking callers with basic services taken for granted within heteronormative frameworks, such as bars and restaurants, housing, health information, and organized social groups where callers might meet others like them. Autoethnographic reflections on these services written by volunteers reveal a great deal about *why* people chose to work at hotlines and, more specifically, how they understood the political and emotional investments of doing this work. Volunteers write about this work as rewarding, crucial, and sometimes fun, but also draining and a source of burnout that was often boring, especially when the phones didn't ring. Listening to their written and recorded stories forms a significant secondary method of this research, helping to supplement my study of the paper documents these hotlines left behind.

Lisa Power, a long-time volunteer at the London Gay and Lesbian Switchboard, explained in 1988 that while hotlines were grounded in a gay liberation framework that sought to unite a perceived constituency of sexual minorities, working at the hotline revealed to her that, "in reality, there is no united lesbian and gay community with a common set of needs."[51] For Power, "The challenging history of Switchboard is in many ways the history of changing needs of lesbians and gay men and reflection of a growing understanding of our diversity."[52] This growing attention to diversity was often inadequate; according to Power's account, all but two women volunteers left the London switchboard in 1977–78 to form a separate Lesbian Line, an exodus she attributes to the growing frustration of women marginalized within "gay" activism. Lesbian-feminist telephone hotlines brought explicit commitments to feminist forms of consciousness-raising, such as "rapping" with callers, an active listening strategy grounded in shared investments in the personal as political. Rapping is one among several tactics that drew on the expertise telephone operators brought from their grounding in lesbian-feminist social structures.

I use the term "gay and lesbian" to describe hotlines during the late twentieth century because those were the terms the hotlines used most often to name themselves, their volunteer base, and the communities they most wanted to serve. "Gay and lesbian"—or, as Bobby Noble aptly spells it, "gayandlesbian"—resists the erasure that the term "LBGT" applied in retrospect would perform here.[53] Hotline services for sexual and gender minorities continue to operate in the twenty-first century and even gained users in the 2010s. Today's hotlines serve callers within the umbrella of "LBGTQ+" and, in response to the particular vulnerabilities young trans people face, often provide separate services for transgender youth staffed by specially trained volunteers.

Contemporary hotlines also reach youth via text message and online chat.[54] Still, the phones continue to ring with callers seeking an immediate, voice-to-voice connection. The ongoing use of hotlines by young LBGTQ+ people foregrounds how being seen on YouTube or Instagram, or finding community online, do not replace the need for more direct mediated experiences of community facilitated by talking on the phone. As intimate, one-to-one communication, hotlines contradict the visibility politics that undergirds popular understandings of LBGTQ media practices today. [55] The desire to connect on the phone through information referral has both a long history and a likely future.

Lesbian-feminist uses of the telephone are one part of the medium's longer gendered history. From the telephone industry's outset in the late nineteenth and early twentieth centuries, operators were women. [56] Talking on the phone remains gendered in contemporary call-center cultures, where operators (often women of color) are trained to manage their affect and be pleasant while serving irritable callers who probably don't deserve their patience. [57] Telephone talk is also a pastime associated with gendered domestic space in the second half of the twentieth century; the telephone allowed women confined by housework and childcare responsibilities to reach out to others. Feminist media studies from the 1970s to the 1990s frames the telephone (along with soap operas) as its proper object: the telephone is understood as a prime site for women's communicative labor.

Lana Rakow's *Gender On the Line: Women, the Telephone, and Community Life* (1991) remains the most significant feminist media studies work on telephones. Rakow's study is a model for examining how gender minorities draw on everyday telecommunications practices to sustain alterative networks of support. She writes, "If we are genuinely interested in learning how gender differences are carried out in and through communication technologies, clearly we must investigate the uses of the telephone." [58] Women talk to each other on the telephone to socialize and exchange care while living in isolation. These uses of the telephone are not explicitly politicized in any way, and Rakow is careful to separate this work from "feminism" proper. But telephone talk engages in gendered economies of care that are key to feminist praxis. Telephone talk sustains women's unique social structures: "Even more than other technologies, the telephone must be examined in relationship to the network of people it holds together." [59] Like newsletter networks, the telephone does infrastructural work for feminist movements by organizing information and making it accessible. Calling a hotline connects distant others with shared political and emotional investments through intimate forms of exchange—speaking, even conspiring, right into another person's ear. An expanded understanding of information through affect is needed to make sense of this intimate work and the network of people it held together.

Providing Service

Decisions about who the hotline would serve and how reflect larger tensions around identity and inclusion within lesbian communities. Lesbian organizations in the 1970s and '80s debated and worked through who belonged within the constellation of lesbian identity, practicing gatekeeping that was often painful for those excluded from spaces, services, or groups in which they wanted to participate. Some lesbian organizations defined themselves in part through exclusion—for example, many lesbians defined their identities through staunch separation from men, leaving bisexual women on the fringes of movements to which they wanted to belong. The Lesbian Switchboard's call logs show that the organization served many trans callers and bisexual callers, as well as callers whose gender identifications or sexual practices did not fit neatly within the often strident category "lesbian." These callers took risks phoning hotlines that did not claim to serve them with either their names or mandates.

Hotline volunteers promised to "work within the switchboard ideology" when they joined the organization, but the bounds of this ideology were not always spelled out. The switchboard had no policy on trans women's place within lesbian feminism. Its approach to trans callers shifted over time, along with lesbian politics, and varied from operator to operator. In the late 1970s, transphobia in lesbian organizations was a prominent and polarizing issue, most often remembered through spectacular TERF (Trans Exclusive Radical Feminist) actions. They include protests against the leadership position of Beth Elliott, a trans woman, at the West Coast Lesbian Conference in 1973 and death threats made to Olivia Records' sound engineer, Sandy Stone, also a trans woman, in 1977. The trans historian Cristan Williams argues that these events overdetermine feminist history, foreclosing understandings of much radical feminist work led by lesbian-identified trans women.[60] These events, and others like them, were widely covered in feminist print culture and constituted an issue volunteers at lesbian-focused service organizations had to address.

Volunteers at the switchboard discussed their positions on trans inclusion at staff meetings. At a 1977 meeting, one volunteer said she was uncomfortable and wouldn't talk to trans callers, while another shared this discomfort but "would handle it" and take calls. Two others expressed trans-exclusionary ideas about lesbian feminism and the category "woman." One volunteer said simply that she "talks to everyone," while the last volunteer to participate in the discussion said she would write to other organizations to learn about their approach.[61] This lack of clarity put trans callers in the 1970s at risk as they made themselves vulnerable to an identity-based hotline staffed by volunteers with very different ideas about the place of trans people—and, in particular, trans women—within lesbian spaces. However, these minutes indicate recognition by some volunteers that serving trans callers in need was more important than their own positions.

These minutes suggest that on any given night a trans caller committed in some way to the category "lesbian" might call and find a sympathetic ear or a volunteer who refused them. Explicit, negative responses to trans callers do appear in 1970s logs but are very rare. More ambiguous notes in logs leave open the question of whether these callers were served. For example, the note "♀ transvestite (genital male)," without the usual description of how the volunteer handled the call, *could* indicate refusal of service, or not.[62] The term "transvestite" on its own reflects common usage in queer and trans communities in 1973 to identify transgender people who were not "transsexual" because they did not pursue medical forms of transition (this was before common usage of the term "transgender").[63] The emphasis here on "genital male" might imply a trans-exclusive rejection of trans women and their bodies (or it might not). What is most clearly suggestive about this note in the log is that the operator does not include what she and the caller spoke about (all the other calls from that night are logged in more detail). I am left wondering if the call ended abruptly, and speculating as to the tacit values in which merely noting the caller's gender identity was considered sufficient communication for this log.

Despite occasional ambiguities in the logs, in most instances, even in the 1970s, trans callers were simply served by the hotline. Descriptions such as "♂ transsexual called wanting to know how to stimulate other women and where to meet them. Gave him phone numbers of transsexual referral services and bisexual bars" misgender this trans woman but also matter-of-factly provide the best information referrals available to serve her needs.[64] By the mid-1980s, positive, unremarkable responses to trans hotline callers had become routine, and operators' precision with language had improved along with shifting vocabularies in queer and trans communities. For example, "♀ → ♂ transsexual looking for a G.P. Gave listings" acknowledged trans men's unique health-care needs and the switchboard's responsibility for providing that information.[65] The switchboard kept a transgender information file, which included positive print resources and clippings, some drawn from the Reed Erickson Foundation. By the early 1990s, few trans callers were trying to access the switchboard, likely because trans-specific social services had grown significantly and trans people with the means could take advantage of sizable online BBS and USENET communities.[66]

The Lesbian Switchboard's ambivalent position toward trans callers reflects the nuance that transfeminist histories have brought to understandings of feminism's "second wave."[67] As Susan Stryker has shown, second-wave attitudes toward trans issues varied widely and played out in the form of dialogue and debate, via painful, spectacular print-culture showdowns among well-known women such as Sandy Stone, Jeanne Córdova, Shulamith Firestone, Mary Daly, and Janice Raymond.[68] Attention to the everyday practices of a telephone hotline enriches this history of second-wave feminist attitudes toward trans issues through attention to everyday service provision and the words of regular feminists, who were not writing manifestos and might not even have identified their hotline work as activism. Hotline logs provide more modest records of how trans people were addressed in movement-based economies of care.

While the hotline's approach to trans callers was uneven, particularly in its early days, the organization conscientiously built other kinds of intersectional care, including capacity for providing peer support to women of color that understood the location of their experiences at the axis of gender, race, and sexuality. Some lesbian organizations developed antiracism by ensuring that leadership roles were filled by women of color who could direct an organization's resources and attention to the needs of their communities.[69] The switchboard was mostly staffed by white women and worked to recruit, train, and retain volunteers of color.[70] Staff came and went over the years, but in 1990 volunteers were "20% women of color, 6% differently abled women, 26% Jewish and 48% white, non-Jewish." These volunteers came from all five boroughs of New York and were "ethnically, sexually, physically and age diverse."[71] New volunteers were evaluated after their initial training shifts on whether they "promote or exhibit racism, classism, ageism, heterosexism, anti-Semitism and/or discrimination against women on the basis of physical ability and/or appearance."[72] Women of color calling the switchboard were most likely to have their call "peer counseled" by a white volunteer, but these volunteers were careful to recognize the importance of race and difference in selecting information to relay to callers.[73]

The volunteer I interviewed explained why racially sensitive information referrals mattered in relation to the codified knowledge she brought to the switchboard as a Black lesbian: "There were places where if you were Black you weren't going to be welcome there, and there were places if you were white you weren't going to be welcome, and there were places where everyone was welcome."[74] Sending a Black lesbian who felt isolated to a predominantly white lesbian space could do more harm than good. A hotline volunteer recorded in a 1977 log that a caller interested in lesbian-friendly resorts in New York State was "concerned about whether a Black woman would feel comfortable there (as her lover is Black). We talked about that for a while and I turned her on to Salsa Soul, which she was very excited about."[75] Salsa Soul Sisters was a social and consciousness-raising group founded in New York in 1976 by a group of primarily Black lesbians to serve all queer women of color, including Latina, Asian American, and Indigenous women.[76]

To ensure a variety of experiences and identity formations across its volunteer pool, the switchboard also attempted to make its training program more accessible to volunteers with disabilities. Training records from 1989 include a lengthy reflection from a new volunteer on finding ways to adapt the organization's systems to her limited vision. The volunteer describes memorizing important referral numbers and addresses. She suggests working in collaboration with another volunteer on her shifts so that she might contribute her skills with crisis counseling while deferring calls that required research in the organization's inaccessible print resources to the other operator:

> I know that you have been talking about installing a second phone line and this I see as an enormous advantage for me in particular. Naturally, it would benefit our callers to have a greater chance of getting through on the first try but also having another person in the office with me would decrease my inability to service the callers. That is, if a request for information came in, I could simply refer the call to the other staffer. I honestly think that this logistical problem is quite minor and can be worked around without too much effort. Thanks for giving me the chance to try.[77]

The switchboard's efforts to alter its systems, and this volunteer's work to resourcefully adapt those systems to her needs, are emblematic of lesbian feminism's broader connections to disability activism in the 1980s.[78] For example, Mara Mills's research on Womyn's Braille Press shows how lesbian service organizations in the 1970s and '80s approached the accessibility of information via media technologies as a feminist issue.[79] Telephone operators with disabilities might help hotlines better understand

and serve the needs of callers with disabilities. These callers made requests for accessible information about lesbian life, and they did so using the telephone, a media technology that figures prominently in U.S. disability activist history.[80] Callers looking for support related to disability ran the gamut from "a couple of blind people wondering if there is someone who would read feminist literature to them, possibly on tape?" to more general calls for "disabled lesbian info."[81] To improve referral information for these callers, the switchboard reached out to other organizations that focused on disability, requesting literature and other information.[82] The switchboard approached lesbian sexuality and disability as a critical intersection to be supported through its services.[83] A lesbian-feminist critique of ableism extends here to understandings of the telephone as a media technology that might be adapted to include lesbians with disabilities in the information and care networks it could provide.

The switchboard cared deeply about who was answering the phones and saw staffing as a reflection of organizational principles. The *Switchboard Handbook* lists twelve "Requirements for Membership," which remained consistent over the years. Item one reads, "Staffers must be a lesbian and at least 18 years old." A marked-up draft of this list from the organization's archives, dated 1982, includes a handwritten insertion of "(not bisexual)" after "lesbian."[84] The parenthetical "not bisexual" never made it into any final, typed version of the handbook. This marginalia may have been a talking point for members working on these requirements, who wished to clarify that the lesbian category did not, in their minds, include bisexual women, who maintained relationships to men that were incommensurate with lesbian separatist perspectives. Operators routinely served bisexual callers with thoughtfulness and care, according to the organization's logs. Attending to the minutia of call logs, organizational gray literature, and unpublished marginalia shows that debates over who fit within lesbian communities are often subtle, ongoing, ambivalent, and inconsistent. Information work happens at everyday registers that make this complexity apparent, offering counters to more resolute movement histories.

Information Intimacies

Like lesbian newsletters, telephone hotlines worked to organize and provide access to information, but the telephone's immediacy—its communicative synchronicity—differs from print technologies. One of the Lesbian Switchboard's challenges was simply keeping the phone line open—ensuring that a volunteer was available, as many nights a week as possible, to be there answering calls. A warm body needed to show up, wait for the phone to ring, and then sort through and deliver the information each caller requested. The switchboard kept a desk calendar where volunteer's names were penciled in to particular shifts, and organizational documents re-iterate that showing up for shifts or finding a replacement were serious commitments volunteers made when they joined the organization. Each collective meeting included a report on the number of nights the switch-board managed to be open that month. When the hotline failed to answer the phone because a volunteer didn't show up to work, or because no one signed up for a shift in the first place, the switchboard risked disappointing callers who depended on the service for basic, life-sustaining information.

The switchboard's volunteers answered many calls from women and trans people living in isolated conditions, looking for advice and informa-tion about coming out or just wanting to talk to someone like them. As its "Requirements for Membership" outline, "Staffers must be able to deal with women in process, whatever that process may be." Callers were free to be messy when they called the hotline because volunteers committed to listen to them *wherever they were at*. Toronto's Lesbian Phone Line, an organization very similar in structure to the Lesbian Switchboard of New York City, outlined a similar policy in more explicit terms:

> All sorts of women call the phone-line. Some know they're gay and have known it since they were three. Some are just thinking about a lesbian identity for themselves. Some make a terrific effort of courage to call us and some call because they're passing through town and want to say "hi." Some are married, some single, women of all ages. Mostly they want to talk over what it's like to be a lesbian with someone who is going to take them seriously. Some call up once in a while, some come along to the drop-in to meet other women, talk, make friends. We have this in common: that we recognize our feelings for other women; that we want to express our feelings of love for women without being hassled; that we want to live our own lives the way we want.[85]

Finding a lesbian-feminist hotline meant learning that someone else was "out there," mediating access to information. Knowing that was perhaps as important as the quality of information a volunteer offered. Just as dial-ing the hotline was a significant demonstration of vulnerability, picking up the ringing phone was a profound gesture of availability as care: I am here for you in your process, whatever that process may be. The telephone's synchronicity—callers and operators talk to each other in "real time"—makes these practices possible and is part of the reason the telephone feels more immediate and personal than other media.[86] *Dial-Ring-Response* is an embodied technical process that connects strangers in need with others who have care to give in a relation based in some kind of shared attachment to "lesbian."

Presence on the other end of the line mitigates the ongoing vulnerabilities presented by living with limited or stigmatized access to information about lesbian lives. Hotlines fulfilled simple, individual needs for information and care from callers whose resources and connections to lesbian community were usually very limited. Hotline work reflected movement-based values, but without any expectation that callers ought to share these values. Support was anonymous, often messy, incoherent, and purposefully basic. While lesbian-feminist hotlines did not directly seek political coherence, they provided the kind of fundamental support of life that is the precondition for counterpublic organizing. You must know where to go to meet the other lesbians if you are going to join them in build divergent community unrecognized within the wider "public sphere." Hotline operators built basic communications infrastructure and emotional support that is fundamental to producing conditions in which more obviously transformative movement action becomes possible. This is service provision as activist work.

As women of color feminism has shown, the personal and erotic dimensions of political life are key to a feminist practice. Referring a Friday-night caller to a women's bar or dance, helping her find housing, or listening to her talk about her personal problems matter as movement labor. These acts provide the kind of life-sustaining and even erotic connections with others that make living a feminist life not only possible but desirable.[87] In an oral history interview, Sue Cook, a long-time operator at Toronto's Lesbian Phone Line, describes phone lines as bringing young women into the fold of an intimate but also politically active community: "It took me about a year before I really wanted to act on my lesbianism and I wanted to call a phone line or someone and talk about it. I didn't want to clear up a problem, I just wanted to know where I could meet women and where I could get involved. Before I found a phone line to call, somebody I worked with came out to me and that gave me an opportunity to come out to a lesbian for the first time."[88] Cook came out and, in so doing, *came into* a world of women with whom she could "get involved" and make politics happen. She insists on the phone line's life-building significance for callers in need. Cook worked at the telephone hotline so she could provide others with the kind of intimate exchange that brought her into lesbian feminism, community, and intimacies in the first place.

Telephone hotline work is intensely interpersonal, where voices exchange information or care at a distance through microphone and speaker. This intimate exchange exemplifies the telephone's status as a communication technology providing person-to-person communication at a distance, often from within private or domestic space. In her study of phone sex hotlines, Amy Flowers describes telephone talk as a form of "disembodied intimacy" callers choose because it provides both "some intimacy" and "some security" from the "riskiness of direct sexual and emotional contact."[89] Flowers argues that sex on the phone is not *less* intimate than sex between bodies sharing physical space but, rather, a different kind of intimacy—one that takes advantage of the telephone's formal qualities to extend intimate practices into different terrain. Flowers writes, "People find creative ways to use the very aspects of communication that have been assumed to be alienating. They use technological innovation to reinvent intimacy in an environment that often hides and distorts intimacy as it has been traditionally understood."[90] Understanding mediated intimacy requires scholars to ask after the telephone's intimate affordances and why it is chosen, or not, in specific circumstances. Nancy Baym has shown that speaking on the telephone is often preferred to texting or online communications by users seeking intimacy. A phone call roots the other caller in a particular place, is immediate, and therefore is more personal than text-based communication.[91]

The voice is an indispensable component of telephone intimacy and, perhaps, the aspect of telephone talk most conspicuously absent from hotline archives. Aside from talking on the phone, we rarely hear another person's voice speaking right into our ear, comportment reserved for whispering lovers, conspiring best friends, or children playing telephone. Rotary phones in the 1970s and '80s vibrated slightly against the ear with the cadence of a caller's voice, in a haptic rendering of embodied proximity at a distance. David Suisman's research on early twentieth-century phonographs theorizes listening to another person's voice at a distance as part of the intimate novelty presented by new recording technologies for the home. He writes, "Both despite this technological mediation and because of it, countless anonymous listeners could cultivate relationships with performers that approximated real intimacy: knowing the rhythms of another human being's breath, registering the grain of another's voice in one's own body, and perhaps experiencing genuine feelings of exaltation or ecstasy."[92] Hearing a disembodied but emotive voice at a distance, through a speaker, engenders affective ties to the person speaking, but the pleasure of this intimacy depends on hearing a voice one expects.

Operators practiced listening tactics aimed at identifying hotline "imposters" by voice. Take, for example, this note from a 1972 switchboard log: "♂ saying he was woman wanted to know where to go. Told him just in case it really was a ♀ with a very low voice."[93] Notes like this one occur sporadically in call logs and generally either explain why an operator was suspicious or justify a reason to hang up. The operator in this case is concerned about other women's safety—worried that a potential misogynist or homophobic male caller is trying to obtain information about meetings and events he might disrupt. It is also possible that this caller was a trans woman under suspicion because of the sound of her voice. Essential ideas about gendered embodiment manifested in the everyday surveillance of lesbian-identified trans women and the denial of their access to basic information. For transgender callers seeking to access services over the phone, having one's voice heard in the wrong way was, and is, a precursor to rejection. Hostile telephone tactics persist for trans people, especially trans women, in the present, with very material consequences—for example, phone operators at a major Canadian bank shutting down trans women's accounts for wrongfully suspected identity fraud.[94] The intimacy of voice-to-voice exchange is not universal; rather, it depends on having a voice that the person on the other end of the line recognizes in the right ways.

Vocal intimacy can also be an intimidating barrier to seeking information. Countless "hang-up" calls in the switchboard's logs represent requests for information that were never uttered aloud because callers lost their nerve once a real, breathing voice materialized on the other end of the line. Given the telephone's associations with intimacy, the perceived decline of voice-over telephone use in the twenty-first century is often attributed to "phone-phobia": being "on the phone" with someone else presents an uncomfortable and undesirable intimacy.[95] Why be this vulnerable to another person when sending a text will do? The functionalist argument that there is an overall preference for "less intimate" forms of synchronous communication such as texting signals, if nothing else, talking on the phone's *perceived* intensity over other available communications media.

Departing from this trend, LBGTQ+ information hotlines continue to receive many telephone calls, even as these hotlines offer and actively promote text and online messaging options.[96] In other words, contemporary hotline callers want the very intimacy with queer or trans community they are supposed to fear, according to digital "phone-phobia" narratives. This persistent seeking out of supposedly outmoded opportunities to talk on the phone presents a problem for the stories we tell about telephone media histories. Queer social movements used to rely on the telephone, but they also *continue to use the telephone*. Today's hotlines might be best understood within a longer genealogy that does not turn around digital networks as a fundamental transition in queer, community-based communication strategies.

Feminist Hotline Infrastructure

Answering the phone for other women in need does not build anything concrete or lasting, like a newsletter or an archive; instead, hotlines are ephemeral technologies that make living a feminist life endurable, even joyful, within the often-daunting present.[97] Commitments to consciousness-raising, meeting women where they are at, and understanding the personal as political saturated the hotline's practices with information. Telephone hotlines have been critical to forming queer and feminist support networks, doing the kind of background work with information that social movements and the human activists behind them need. The switchboard's organizational strategies purposefully built information infrastructure for lesbian community. This section analyzes how the hotline understood the kind of infrastructure it was building by analyzing the hotline's administrative documents, training program, and relationship to the larger constellation called "lesbian-feminism."

Providing basic access to information along with peer support made lesbian a more inhabitable category. As Kristen Hogan's history of the feminist bookstore movement shows, second-wave feminists used print resources such as the print periodical *Feminist Bookstore News* to unite disparate women's publishing efforts into an intelligible, organized movement. For Hogan, this work to build infrastructure was about creating a feminist book industry that would support lesbians, and especially women of color, as working writers. But it was also equally about "time-intensive movement and relational infrastructure work."[98] In other words, building lesbian-feminist information infrastructure is a preliminary condition of possibility for doing feminism, including by sustaining the kinds of relationships that make movement work meaningful.

Information infrastructures operate in the background: under ideal conditions, they *appear* invisible because they are doing "what they are supposed to do."[99] As Geoffrey Bowker and Susan Leigh Star's work demonstrates, infrastructures sort, classify, and apply standards and frameworks that reflect the particular values of the actors who build and maintain them.[100] In a queer and trans context, information's "neutrality" is apparent only to those for whom a given infrastructure's organizing logics are common sense. Those who can go with the flow of information as it is made available see a more neutral interface, while those who experience a lack of fit with that information are pushed to ask hard questions about how resources are chosen, described, or left off the table altogether.[101]

A lesbian telephone hotline appears most neutral for callers whom the service anticipates—those who fit within what counts as a "lesbian" and who ask for the kind of help the hotline is willing and ready to provide. The *Switchboard Handbook* states that the organization "functions as an informational, referral and telephone support system for the lesbian community. We do not advertise, endorse or support any political viewpoint aside from our *basic support of lesbianism*."[102] The former switchboard volunteer I interviewed echoed this position when asked about the organization's politics: "I don't remember people calling for political reasons. People called for information for the most part. Nobody had computers. It wasn't like you could go on the internet and find stuff. Everything we had was in a book or a magazine or a flyer that came out."[103] Sharing basic, previously published information, evaluated for accuracy and quality, is disarticulated from lesbian feminist politics in both the *Switchboard Handbook* and this volunteer's memory. "It wasn't a political thing at all," she said. "It was basically giving people information. What are the good bars? Where is a restaurant I can take my girlfriend to? What's a hotel where I won't be harassed?"[104] The term "basic" in "basic support of lesbianism" and in "basically giving people information" does a tremendous amount of work, promising to separate lesbian from the "political viewpoints" weighing it down. This disarticulation work happens through the rubric of neutrality, working against a context in which lesbianism did not just mean "women who have sex with other women" but was (and is) a politicized identity that transcends mere sexual object choice.[105]

The switchboard's call logs employed a distinct terminology for calls that purposefully exceeded "neutral" information exchange. Nightly "rap sessions" between callers and operators based active listening and advice giving in shared or divisive political orientations to lesbianism. Sometimes volunteers would disagree with callers or try to bring them around to the values they held about lesbian identity, gently or otherwise. Far from "basic," these rap calls ground dialogue in attachments to "lesbian" as a category worth arguing about with others. Returning to Rakow's terms, the telephone holds together a network woven in part through strained conversations that test out different visions for what lesbian might mean and how it might be lived. Telephone hotline records show that the terms "lesbian" and "lesbian feminist" were worked out not just within the expected locales of feminist theory or political organizing, but also within information infrastructures, by the people who built, operated, and accessed them in all their purported "basicness." Lesbian is a point of information as much as an experienced identity, talked through, and collectively held.

As infrastructure providing basic support for lesbian community, the hotline wanted to be both politically neutral *and attached* to feminism ideals—a potentially paradoxical combination. Sustaining this position meant leaving "lesbian" open to volunteers' and callers' interpretation rather than pinning down its meaning at an administrative level. The hotline also encouraged operators to rap with willing callers. A range of guidelines outlined in administrative documents gave shape to these practices for volunteers. As the handbook put it, "No caller's problem should be condemned or condoned. Regardless of the volunteer's personal biases, the caller needs to be handled with kindness and concern for the well-being of the caller, not the evangelical needs of the volunteer. This attempt at some form of neutrality is difficult but functional and beneficial."[106] "Evangelical needs of the volunteer" is hyperbole meant to playfully poke fun at the energy it might take for an earnest hotline operator to swallow her opinions on the phone. This is a gentle jab at the stereotype of "man-hating, chainsaw wielding, separatist lesbians" described by Jack Halberstam, or the slightly kinder "gentle angry people" employed by Heather Love.[107]

Good hotline volunteers would keep their emotions in check at all times. Even callers seeking only information could expect to receive referrals without qualification: "All information in resource books is informational and not intended as a recommendation. Staffers are advised to give callers as many referrals as possible. Personal recommendations are not encouraged, and must be acknowledged as such."[108] The hotline delivered "good" information that was accurate, up to date, and verified by trusted community members, but did so either without communicating judgment or while making their bias explicit. Here the hotline's infrastructural thinking about its work is bound up with a belief that information could be neutral—that it was simply *out there*, and an operator could be proximate to particular feminism ideas without betraying a strong viewpoint on the phone. Volunteers were trained to parse the hotline's filing system, which gathered wide-ranging information about lesbian-focused services and issues, ostensibly reflecting many perspectives. Information, unlike advice or counseling, was easier to simply thumb through, select, and pass on.

New volunteers received training in these practices, learning from more established volunteers in a peer-mentorship model. Trainers and new recruits evaluated each other across a series of points based on working together during training shifts. Is a potential volunteer "sensitive and accepting? Does she have a good attitude toward lesbianism?" Does she "listen well" and "have patience with callers?" "Does she force her own ideas on the caller? Is she supportive of the caller? Is she able to handle a crisis situation"?[109] And new volunteers assessed whether the trainer "had a good attitude" and was able to "assist or encourage you to take calls."[110] New volunteers were also asked to evaluate the switchboard's information resources and make suggestions for what they could add. Complete evaluation forms in the archive show that most new volunteers quickly learned how to talk to women in need of support without judgment but struggled to use the organization's resource files seamlessly. The former task depended on lived experienced and intuition, while the latter required clerical skills, practice, and strong institutional knowledge of the organization's files. Volunteers were learning how to bring what they knew as lesbians living in the world into conversation with information and a complicated system for delivering that information to others.

Volunteers had to stay neutral about politics on the phone, but they also needed a place to vent off the phone. Paying rent on the office, organizing supplies, and getting along with one another were all part of the behind-the-scenes labor sustaining the organization's basic operations. Volunteers often used meetings and call logs to hash out conflicts and administrative frustrations. One long note, scrawled in the margins of a call log during the switchboard's early days, lays out some of these concerns:

> Where is the schedule for women staffing phones? When are we moving to the ♀'s building? Who is working on this LSB [Lesbian Switchboard]? When are we going to have a Wednesday night meeting where ♀♀♀ [multiple women] come? ♀♀♀ who work our phones! Let's call a meeting to pull our heads together. Our keys have been ripped off. There are obvious conflicts going on here that are being ignored—overlooked. Let's talk—we're good at asking for money—but are we good at asking each other for support. Do we feel like a collective?[111]

None of these complaints is remarkable for anyone who has been involved in grassroots feminist organizing, but together they show how managing conflict and working through emotion behind the scenes was necessary for maintaining a neutral hotline on the surface. Sometimes volunteers blew up in planning meetings in ways that would never fly on the phone with a caller. Take, for example, this note of apology from a 1977 call log: "To all the wimmin who attended Wednesdays meeting: I'm very sorry for my poor, uncontrolled behaviour before, during and after the meeting. I was feeling flipped out and couldn't stop. Please clamp the muzzle next time! Love, [name redacted]."[112] Hotline work meant managing one's emotions for the benefit of others, both on and off the phone.

Although volunteers tried to keep their opinions hidden—or, at least, in the background of their interactions with callers—telephone calls and call logging practices were also moments to work on high-stakes issues. As the anecdote that opened this chapter suggests, by the 1970s, butch-femme dynamics popularized in midcentury working-class lesbian communities were still joyful, life-sustaining forms of relationality to some. To others steeped in 1970s lesbian-feminist rejections of all masculine expression, butch-femme became a reprehensible reproduction of heteronormativity. Lesbians fought about being butch, femme, or resolutely opposed to this framework, and the debate was always caught up in how class and race met gender presentation within lesbian life-worlds.[113]

Two very differently logged calls show how this issue was handled by volunteers. The first was logged by an operator named Nancy:

> MAY 4, 1977, 10:05 PM. ♀ called into HEAVY BUTCH ROLE (REALLY?)
> Anyway, this ♀ is very insecure about herself, example "Why do
> I always want to be stronger or the strongest, the MASTER(?) in my rela-
> tionships?" Master? Who wants to be master (owner) of another woman?
> We rapped for 40 mins. At the end she said "you sound so down to earth."
> Peace and Love, Nancy.

Nancy's views about the relationship of butch identity, s/M dynamics, and what we might call "toxic masculinity" today shape how she logged this call. Nancy indicates that she and the caller "rapped" about the issue: they talked through the woman's problems in ways that were informed by their unique perspectives on gender, power, and desire. The log leaves us guessing about the specifics, but it is clear that butch-femme dynamics as a larger political orientation shaped the call and its documentation.

Grace, another operator, applied a more nuanced understanding of lesbian subculture, gendered play, and "the social and cultural experiences they come out of" to a different call about butch-femme made to the switchboard eight months later:

JANUARY 15, 1978. ♀ called and just came out. Hates "butches" and wants bars with "femmes." Talked to her about understanding roles and what kinds of social and cultural experiences they come out of. Also gave her names of a shit-load of bars and told her to get over her prejudice. Said she was turned on to girls and faggots. I gave her info on gay youth and told her that when you first come out you only see stereotypes and as you are out longer you see all types and varieties of dykes and it will get easier for her to accept "Butches" with more exposure to the community.

Grace's ideas about butch-femme are far apart from Nancy's, but both women have a role to fill at the hotline. They each find ways to balance the organization's preferred "neutral" approach with their own commitments to lesbian life-worlds. Ongoing talking through of feminist politics was possible at a phone line, and this talk could be brought home to the singular, emotional struggles articulated by each caller. At home is where these issues hurt the most and where they needed the generosity that comes from holding open an ambivalent position in dialogue.

Lesbian service organizations negotiate the personal as political every day. This rhythm is part of the cultural infrastructure necessary to sustain more obviously transformational social movement work. "Cultural infrastructure" is Fred Turner's term for how commonly held beliefs practiced by collectives of people in delineated shared spaces make new forms of work with technology possible. Turner writes about the relationship between the countercultural Burning Man festival and Silicon Valley's tech world. In Turner's analysis, Burning Man seemed "somehow like the internet" to technologists, so they came out to the festival in droves.[114] There they experimented, worked through fantasies about creativity and new media, and brought these experiments back to their work at companies such as Google. In short, Burning Man provides cultural infrastructure for the tech industry, for better or worse.

Turner's context is *very, very far* from lesbian telephone hotlines in the late twentieth century. But the cultural infrastructure model illustrates how lesbian work with specific information technologies offered proxies women could use to explore broader communicative techniques—rapping, listening, staying neutral, explaining one's position. Hotlines were also a *cultural infrastructure* because lesbians used them to work on problems that mattered to the larger movement, in dialogue with others. Calling a hotline might help you feel less lonely or give you an outlet to rap through a problem or simply pass on a new bar's location, or a lesbian plumber's phone number. All of these registers matter for living a lesbian life in proximity to others. Put simply, talking things through on the phone is cultural infrastructure for lesbian feminism. Hotlines create intimate exchanges with strangers that help to hold this network of people together, using information and care as glue. As one hotline volunteer put it, "The switchboard is a desk, a chair, a phone and the wall-sized bulletin board plastered with notices," but it is also so much more.[115]

Conclusion: Waiting for the Phone to Ring

In the switchboard's call logs, volunteers often document long breaks between phone calls with the word "Quiet." This is a description of the phone not ringing—a way to mark what it feels like to wait to do your job or worry that your time is being wasted. "Quiet" scrawled in a notebook does not account for whatever else the switchboard operator did to fill the time while she waited for the phone to ring again. Sometimes volunteers doodled in the call logs to pass this time.

This tall, muscular, naked figure (figure 2.3) drawn on the back cover of a log book has long, untamed hair and strokes her left nipple distractedly, ostensibly because she's bored. As the volunteer's caption explains, she enjoys answering the phones but doesn't know what to do with herself when they don't ring. Volunteers' boredom punctuates logs throughout the switchboard's nearly three decades of operation, with doodles, "quiet" notations, and shifts cut short when a volunteer couldn't stand a slow night for one more minute. This note appears in the log for November 9, 1972, 10:45 PM: "I'm leaving—it is too much to sit here alone for 5 hours." On December 2, 1972, at 11:38 PM, the operator wrote, "It's too boring here—I'm leaving. Good-night!"

Boredom, repetition, and isolation are intrinsic to much practical, activist work with information. These feelings and actions are part of the less-than-glamorous media praxis propping up transformative feminist movements. At telephone hotlines, time spent waiting for the phone to ring is mitigated by volunteers' belief that when they do answer the phone, they might save a caller's life—or, at least, make her Saturday night out in New

FIGURE 2.3 "I enjoy answering the phones, but don't know what do with myself when they don't ring!!!" doodle on the back cover of a switchboard call log, 1973. The Lesbian Switchboard of New York City, Inc. Records, Box 2, Folder 25, The LGBT Community Center National History Archive.

York a lot more fun by recommending the right party. Lesbian information activists find imaginative ways to manage boredom, frustration, and repetition when working with information. Like volunteers working the phones, indexers in the next chapter were often frustrated as they struggled to wrangle a daunting mass of data into reference information other lesbians could use. The people who created and maintained hotlines, indexes, and other information services often sat alone in front of a telephone, computer, or another kind of information technology, sometimes for hours on end. This work generated transformative encounters with information that could make information activism's more tedious qualities feel worthwhile.

"Quiet" punctuates the call logs more and more as they approach 1997, the year the switchboard closed. Grassroots feminist organizations eventually shut down. Their demise can be the explosive end result of drawn-out conflict, but more often organizations close because a space is lost, or because someone gets sick, or because other organizations move in. The switchboard lost the space it was renting in the Gay and Lesbian Center. In the years leading up to the closure, the switchboard also lost many callers to bigger hotlines, such as the Gay and Lesbian Switchboard of New York. By the early 1990s, the phone was only ringing five or six times a night, and some of the calls were hang-ups or pranks. The desk calendar for 1997 is sparsely populated with volunteers who signed up for shifts, and staff meetings that year took place every three months instead of monthly.

Then there just aren't any more call logs to read. The archive is finished, and I am finished with the archive. The collapse of an entire service organization and the information infrastructure it sustained is represented through the gradual tapering off of calls. As the rhythm of the ringing phone slows, so do the documentary practices that surround hotline work.

The Indexers

Dreaming of Computers
while Shuffling Paper Cards

The boom in small-scale lesbian periodicals publishing during the Women in Print Movement of the 1970s and '80s created a mass of paper with the potential to document a wide range of feminist thought and action. This ephemeral "gray literature" presented information activists with urgent challenges: how to collect and store all this paper for future generations, and how to organize and classify the information so that it could be used. Periodical publishing offered a comprehensive authority on lesbian issues—art, literature, sexuality, politics—but it was not searchable or, by extension, accessible in any systematic way. Purposeful infrastructures could activate and mobilize this information in the long term so that present and future researchers could use it.

Imagine a new lesbian parent in the 1980s confronting homophobia in health care or juridical contexts. She might need legal, medical, and emotional support. Or she might want to be reassured by stories of others who struggled in the same ways. This woman might find the information she seeks by calling a hotline or visiting a support group, if there was one in her area. But "lesbian mother" was not yet a search term she could bring to the public library catalog to find resources. Lesbian information was marginalized from mainstream libraries and databases and needed to be gathered and indexed by eager lesbian hands to serve the community.

Indexers armed with paper cards and a facility for sorting, filing, and describing lesbian materials stepped in to address these access problems by building community-based subject guides. The Circle of Lesbian Indexers

(1979–86) was one group that took up this challenge, using thousands of paper cards and a frustrating computer program named WYLBUR to design feminist indexing protocols on the cusp of popular database computing. The circle was a small group of lesbian-feminist information activists scattered across the United States who worked collaboratively to index hundreds of periodical issues. Their work culminated in *The Lesbian Periodicals Index* (1986 [figure 3.1]), a comprehensive subject guide to lesbian publishing still used by researchers and community archives today.[1]

Clare Potter, a white lesbian and trained librarian based in Boston and then San Francisco, led the Circle of Lesbian Indexers, a shifting group of four to six other women. The circle's goal was to create a complete, "usable" subject-based index of lesbian-focused newsletters and small-scale magazines. Publications produced using low-cost printing methods such as mimeograph and Xerox machines were circulated through feminist bookstores, sent under cover to small subscriber lists through the post, or photocopied and shared among friends. These distribution networks lacked stability, institutional support, and formal cataloging practices. Lesbian feminist indexers worked outside of formal institutions, often at night or on weekends after their day jobs.

The Circle of Lesbian Indexers' story exemplifies how lesbian-feminist information activism improved access to published materials by creating "predigital" interfaces people could use. Published indexes offered search-retrieval functions for counterpublics otherwise marginalized from consistent, long-term access to their own print cultures. In the circle's manual *How-to-Index in the Circle of Lesbian Indexers*, Potter explains the problem clearly: "Identifying a research problem commonplace in lesbian herstory, that is, of finding lesbian women in the past, we began to feel that we were guilty of falling into the trap that a lesbian-hating society had laid for us—of losing ourselves and the lives we had lived by a careless disregard and offhand destruction of the records of organizations and projects that we ourselves had been part of and cared about deeply."[2] Mediating access to lesbian periodicals through indexing could protect these publications from the indignity and irrelevance of being filed away in a dusty box or stashed in a mildewy basement. The circle consulted old periodicals at community archives and acquired personal collections from individual subscribers. They designed systems for their work, built out of deep community knowledge and a lesbian-feminist understanding of classification as a material, social, and ethical process that ought to be more transparent.[3] The circle debated and revised their contentious descriptive terms and protocols with care, know-

FIGURE 3.1 *The Lesbian Periodicals Index*, compiled and edited by Clare Potter and published by Naiad Press (1986).

ing that their classification practices would shape the finished book's user interface and the ways future generations made sense of lesbian feminism.

Seen through a lesbian feminist lens, the index is a resolutely political and willfully constructed interface between users and information. Whether they are built from paper cards or code, the fantasy of indexes is routed in a digital imaginary of unencumbered mediation—stripped-down interfaces that create clear, effective paths between users and materials.[4] Writing long before online databases, Potter describes indexing's social role in the circle's manual:

> In your library jargon an index is a link between the user who wants
> information and the actual source of that information, functioning like a
> library card catalog. An index pulls together people, events and concepts
> and is a *medium for the delineation of culture*. This is the reason our efforts
> to bring into being a lesbian periodicals index are profoundly cultural
> because we are documenting lesbian experience and thought, and, most
> importantly, organizing this experience when we assign subject headings.[5]

Aware of its work as generating a "medium" that would pull together people, events, and concepts, the circle made critical choices about the tools its indexers would use and the classification schemes they assigned to "lesbian experience." The finished index represents a lengthy and deliberate process of classification and compression, which usually describes digital processes that make data smaller to improve the efficiency of storage and movement.[6] The circle worked with paper on a compression-related media problem; this index sought to capture the breadth and complexity of "lesbian experience and thought" within a rationalized, hierarchical classification system aimed at fast access and efficient usability for lesbian feminists and their movements.[7]

This chapter begins with an overview of lesbian-feminist indexing culture as it engaged broader critiques of description, evidence, and historiography in the 1980s. Specifically, I consider how white lesbian feminist activists used indexing toward antiracism through the case of *Black Lesbians: An Annotated Bibliography* (1981).[8] I situate lesbian-feminist indexing in broader indexing culture by analyzing popular manuals that the Circle of Lesbian Indexers drew on to design their work. Next, the chapter considers indexes as media—paper documents that operated as interfaces between published materials and counterpublics on the verge of coherence. Here, indexing is theorized as another site for understanding the relationship between information infrastructure and lesbian-feminist counterpublic formation. I then turn closely to the circle's work processes to show that their labor was gendered information work focused on accessible tools and collaboration. Finally, the chapter considers Potter's abandoned attempt at "going electronic" by converting the circle's paper index card system into a computer database. The circle's work between paper and computers offers a feminist critique of technological accessibility in the early 1980s, when ease of use and inexorable ubiquity were the predominant values associated with computing.

Information activists rethought standard information management practices through a lesbian feminist critique of classification's ethical complexity. They brought these concerns to database computing, shaping a unique perspective on computers in the 1980s. By attending to processes of making and distributing indexes, this chapter offers a general history of amateur, activist indexing and a queer and feminist critique of emerging popular computing, written through the circle. Lesbian indexing matters to our information histories because this work shows how marginalized users build other kinds of technical infrastructures: systems that understand classification as a form of attention, reciprocity, and care.

Indexing Pathways

An index shows the way; it is an object that points someone else in the direction of a path that might not have been obvious to them before. In semiotics, the index's sign function is to point out an object, whether real or imaginary, in time or space or in relation to other objects.[9] One of the tool's most "digital" manifestations is a pointing index finger, a gesture that shows others where to go in space or where to focus their attention. Deployed as the cursor in some early graphic user interfaces, this pointing *white* hand is a racialized representation of the default user in control of their machine.[10] By pointing at some things over others, indexes engage in a symbolic economy as they make choices about what is most valuable or important to denote. A pointing finger also makes accusations or adds emphasis—"You did this" or "An injustice is happening *right here.*" Similarly, an index can point to evidence to correct an unjust omission or denial. An index that points to a body of marginalized "evidence" becomes an activist tool: "X" is true, X matters, because all of these "Ys" I have collected and synthesized say so.

Indexes and bibliographies are an everyday document genre; they are a common place reference tool for learning, research, and scholarship, and a professional expectation that is easy to take for granted. Academics make bibliographies—the most common type of "index"—at the beginning of a new research project. We write bibliographies to accompany grant applications in order to demonstrate expertise, breadth and depth, and the rootedness of our projects in a field. Undergraduate students make and annotate bibliographies as one step in learning how to perform the sometimes nebulous task called "humanities research." Overall, indexes and bibliographies are used to create a sense of a field and relate that overall sense to others, providing pathways through large, obscure, or otherwise difficult-to-navigate bodies of literature.

Subject indexes such as *The Lesbian Periodicals Index* similarly provide pathways, but do so by organizing materials through the attribution of categorical meanings through which users can find information on a very specific topic. There are many different kinds of subject indexes, but the most common is found in the backs of books. These indexes call out topics and sections of the volume that the indexer anticipates will be of greatest quick-reference importance to an imagined readership. (This book's index was made by Celia Braves, a professional indexer.) If I want to quickly find Raymond Williams's thoughts on "structures of feeling," I search out this term in the index to *Marxism and Literature* and then flip to page 132; that familiar passage, "not feeling against thought, but thought as felt and feeling," is ready to hand.[11]

Online indexes and databases to journals and primary source materials similarly index printed matter by subject, partly through the attribution of keywords. These digital indexes are algorithmic infrastructures whose inner workings are generally invisible to us.[12] Google is an index that "crawls" the web to render information findable through online search retrieval. It is faster to Google "structure of feeling Williams" than pull down *Marxism and Literature* from the shelf. Crawling is, of course, a metaphor for what bots do; far from arbitrary, "crawling" evokes the kind of careful, thorough, and tiring process any decent indexing job requires. Search algorithms index materials according to instructions from the engineers who design them, and their indexing methods reflect human cultural biases, just like paper indexes.[13] Although computing is imagined to be objective and nearly instantaneous, the use of slow and cumbersome imagery with the term "crawling" references indexing's paper roots and hints at the fact that computer databases aren't always so expedient or neutral, either.

Index and bibliography making by feminist information activists collected disparate resources into print guides that self-consciously constructed lesbian history. These indexes are collections of statements in the Foucauldian sense: they determine what is thinkable and sayable on a particular topic by framing that topic within a larger scaffold of information.[14] In this way, indexes make lesbian feminism coherent and intelligible for insiders and outsiders. Indexes are tools for what Joan Scott calls "the evidence of experience"; they aspire toward correcting histories that exclude marginalized subjects but do not necessarily alter the broader historical norms and formats that marginalize in the first place—for example, history's colonial drive to recognize coherent subjects and consistent evidence.[15] Lesbian-feminist indexers worked toward this additional critical step by searching out alternative, flexible means of classification, taking care in their work because they understood indexing's field-forming role.

The Circle of Lesbian Indexers was not merely "documenting" experience but necessarily "organizing it," a process that required ongoing choices about what to include and exclude, what words to assign to subjects and their politics, and ultimately what mattered enough to constitute a high-level subject heading for the lesbian public this index imagined. These were deeply political choices caught up in broader lesbian-feminist critiques of language, self-representation, and movement making.

Working independently in their corners of the country, each member of the circle would index her materials using standard index cards, drawing on the fledgling periodicals collections of organizations such as the Lesbian Herstory Archives (LHA). Complete cards were mailed in batches to Potter, the project coordinator, who processed the work. Potter was also the primary indexer on the project, particularly in its final years, when long-distance collaboration by letter mail proved to be more time consuming and cumbersome for her than just doing the work on her own. When I interviewed Potter thirty years after she made *The Lesbian Periodicals Index*, she explained that what began as a work process designed to put into practice feminist commitments to "community, cooperation, women loving women, we'll all work together" was, in the end, "idealistic." She said, "In theory it was a good idea, but it didn't work out."[16] Circle members struggled to learn and apply the same protocols and standards to materials, and new recruits' initial excitement often waned when they confronted the endless paper cards required to do this work. Potter estimates that she completed 85–90 percent of the indexing herself, as other women came and went and it became too difficult to recruit, train, and manage new indexers.[17]

Although the circle's collaborative work process failed, the finished *Lesbian Periodicals Index* works exactly as Potter planned. The circle organized every article published in selected lesbian periodicals under descriptive subject headings. The book functions like a typical subject index. Readers can look up a topic in the alphabetized index—for example, "Class and Classism"—and find a definitive list of thirty-eight images, letters, and articles published on lesbian class-consciousness. This reader can then seek out back issues of these newsletters, or mail away to archives such as the LHA for photocopies. Subject headings were unconventional, generated by the circle out of the materials themselves, with the goal of representing lesbian "realities" and "every aspect of experience."[18] A representative sampling of headings gives a sense of what these community-generated terms looked like:

Black Lesbians
Coming Out
Demonstrations, Marches, and Other Fight Back Actions
Disabled Lesbians
Film Festivals
Home Remedies
Hotlines
Isolation and Loneliness
Menstruation
Michigan Women's Music Festival
Native American Lesbians
Pornography
Prisoners
Racism
Rural Living
Sisterhood
Softball
Third World Lesbians
Transpeople
Women's Studies
Zionism

These headings shaped a user interface entrenched in lesbian subcultural worlds, from obviously politicized concepts to recreation and leisure.

The index operated within conditions of scarce and precarious access. The indexers addressed a context in which information about lesbian subcultural worlds existed but was hard to find, keep, and use. Materials were produced using low-cost, quick-and-dirty strategies such as self-publishing, small print runs, DIY periodicals and pamphlets, and other kinds of gray literature inclined toward ephemerality. Lesbians who lived in cities with women's bookstores, or who could afford subscriptions to periodicals (and had a private place to receive them), found these publications more easily. But lesbian-feminist gray literature was difficult to know about, let alone gain access to, for those who were not out or already keyed in to lesbian feminist culture. As Potter explained it to me, "There was no library you could go to, except, of course, the work that the Lesbian Herstory Archives were doing. We were faceless. I saw this as one opening to the contemporary history of lesbians before we lost it. . . . [L]et's seize the time. Of course, I didn't know how much work was going to be involved."[19]

The Lesbian Periodicals Index was not just a subject index; it was also *the* definitive list of lesbian periodicals from the women's liberation era. Potter explained, "In terms of doing lesbian history, we had none of the bibliographies. We just had a few: Barbara Grier's *The Lesbian in Literature* and Jeanette Foster's bibliography, but we really didn't have periodical indexes."[20] Potter imagined that the circle's index would provide a substantive map to this dispersed, unevenly preserved body of work: "We really didn't have anything that opened up the literature. . . . [W]hen I saw the value of indexing and preserving these publications, it became my life's work."[21] Potter and JR Roberts each wrote essays for Margaret Cruikshanks's significant collection *Lesbian Studies* (1982).[22] Potter laid out this research community's central problem: "We are aware of the dire need that exists for indexes and bibliographies in lesbian studies. Without their facilitating role, the researcher of contemporary lesbian history has recourse only to reference supplied by word of mouth, or to scanning footnotes and bibliographies in published books, or to the painstaking labor of individual searches in the periodical literature itself."[23]

The circle wanted to activate all of the newsletter back issues lying dormant in women's basements, garages, and closets. A lot of its work was caught up with simply gaining access to complete collections of periodicals or taking inventory of what was out there. Potter placed ads in periodicals soliciting tips on where to find back issues. She wrote to people, drew on word of mouth, and visited the women's library at Radcliffe College in Cambridge, Massachusetts, where she lived for the first few years of the project. Potter "remember[ed] going to Madison, Wisconsin, and tracking [issues] down in a woman's basement. She was very active in the lesbian community there."[24] Her collaborator JR Roberts had a small periodicals collection of her own to draw on. "JR was an incredibly smart woman, very talented, and she's a historical thinker, if you know what I mean," Potter said. "She could envision lesbian history before it existed. She had collected things."[25] Once published, the index became critical for lesbian community archives and lesbian studies scholars and was purchased by many institutional libraries seeking to expand gay and lesbian reference offerings. In other words, the index succeeded in making it possible for researchers to readily use lesbian periodicals as primary sources.

Sara Ahmed's work on tools and their pathfinding effects helps illustrate how an index points users down potentially generative paths. "Desire lines" is an architectural concept that describes those unofficial paths marking how travelers deviate from the paths they are supposed to follow.[26] Imagine an urban park whose paved paths do not lead to the less popular destinations some users seek. Over time, the deviations of this small group will wear marks into the grass that become paths of their own. (Desire lines often mark cruising grounds in parks and ravines where people, primarily men, go to have sex.) For Ahmed, these "traces of desire" are generative: they shape a new landscape that others might follow.[27] Indexes to materials marginalized from the historical record or from institutions such as public libraries break paths for users, wearing lines in the grass where no one has walked before. Their published forms—the subject guide or bibliography— take on this pathfinding quality; they are print objects that orient or point, encouraging readers to turn in certain directions as they emerge out of their encounter with the index.

Ahmed extends her discussion of desire lines to books as objects that point readers via the rubric of scholarship.[28] Books insist on getting their way, turning wanderings and digressions into lines worn in the ground that others might follow. Books present willful deviations "premised on hope: the hope that those who wander away from the paths they are supposed to follow leave their footprints behind."[29] The celebrated Black lesbian writer and activist Barbara Smith expressed just such a point in her foreword to *Black Lesbians: An Annotated Bibliography* (1981), compiled by Roberts: "This book encourages and strengthens us to keep on living as fully as possible *against the grain*."[30] Smith's wood-grain metaphor and Ahmed's trodden path both describe information as a hard-won life support for queer women, especially women of color.

Desire lines form because city-built paths were not put in the "right" place for a critical mass of pedestrians who protest with their feet by wearing down the natural habitat. The habitus of many people trumps the landscape design of those in power. *The Lesbian Periodicals Index* began as a deviation from the unhomely paths carved out by homophobia and misogyny in universities. Potter decided to form the Circle of Lesbian Indexers after her committee at George Washington University rejected her dissertation proposal on the midcentury lesbian group the Daughters of Bilitis. She told me,

> This was before people like you can now go to school and say, "Hey, I want to do some research on lesbians," and they're all for it. No, they rejected my dissertation. . . . I had proposed that I wanted to do this work on the Daughters, and they made all kinds of excuses: "Well, it's not really valid. Who are these people?" They just put it down. And also, contemporary history was still kind of a push in some universities at that time. I decided that I was going to do this index. I had started working on it and had become really fascinated with what I could see and where I thought it could go and what it would reveal about lesbians.[31]

Like Julia Penelope at *Matrices*, Potter was one among many women who turned off the straightening, disciplinary paths paved by universities to wear down more supportive paths for others to follow.

Indexes to social movements are worlding technologies that produce alternative pathways to knowledge production. They testify to a public whose existence and informational needs have been ignored by mainstream libraries, indexes, and databases. Activists serve this public by building indexes to relevant information they know about, use, and find worthy of wider attention. Indexes can also enforce movement norms, laying out what kinds of literature, topics, political investments, and lesbian lives are recognizable enough to include and name through subject headings. Because indexes and bibliographies select, organize, and rationalize information, the paths they generate are inevitably normative to some extent. These tools stake out a lesbian-feminist field: its major actors, texts, and themes. An index's path is generative but leaves others untaken, by design. Far from inconsequential, the minutia of the circle's work process points to one information pathway through which lesbian feminism cohered as a movement and field.

My path to working on these indexes was about finding my way through research, encountering one object only to be surprised by an adjacent one in ways that are never anticipated at a project's foggy beginning. The story of how I came to appreciate the index's relevance to this book is a story of wayfinding—of using the tool to find something I thought I needed, and then finding something else instead. I was at the LHA on a hot day in early September, working with their collection of the *Matrices* newsletter. The catalog entry for *Matrices* didn't say whether the archives held a complete or partial run (it is often hard to find definitive issue lists for lesbian periodicals). The volunteer that day told me to cross-reference the archives' holdings with *The Lesbian Periodicals Index*, pointing to a book at the top of a narrow, dusty reference shelf in the entryway to the building. It turned out that the circle did not index *Matrices*, but the index's existence intrigued me, so I asked more questions and learned that the archives also held the Circle of Lesbian Indexers' papers. Familiarizing myself with the circle's work process, I moved through their papers on a hunch that indexes and bibliographies formed another important, though perhaps less glamorous, aspect of the story about lesbian-feminist information activism I was piecing together.

Through the archive and the newsletter I found my path to the index, a sort of reverse order of what *The Lesbian Periodicals Index* promised to do for its users. This "outdated" index finds its way into the present through service as a tool for historical research. My encounter with the index felt specific to the kinds of relationships among texts and generations of researchers that community archives can facilitate at their best. The archives' open collections policy, longtime staff with specialized community knowledge, and serious treatment of feelings such as a hunch all coalesced, and my research became something else altogether. Information infrastructures built by lesbian feminists decades ago facilitate serendipitous explorations of lesbian history today.

Indexing and White Antiracism

Potter's collaborator JR Roberts (a pseudonym), also a white woman and trained librarian, became a member of the Circle of Lesbian Indexers after sharpening her indexing skills on the earlier lesbian indexing project *Black Lesbians: An Annotated Bibliography* (figure 3.2), published in 1981, also by Naiad. Roberts lived in Virginia at the time but previously lived in Massachusetts, where Potter was also based before she moved to California. *Black Lesbians* is exemplary of the indexing and bibliographic culture that supported the Women in Print Movement and used information work to address whiteness's centrality in movement histories. *Black Lesbians* indexes published and primary source materials by and about Black, mostly U.S.-based lesbians. The bibliography is comprehensive of every reference

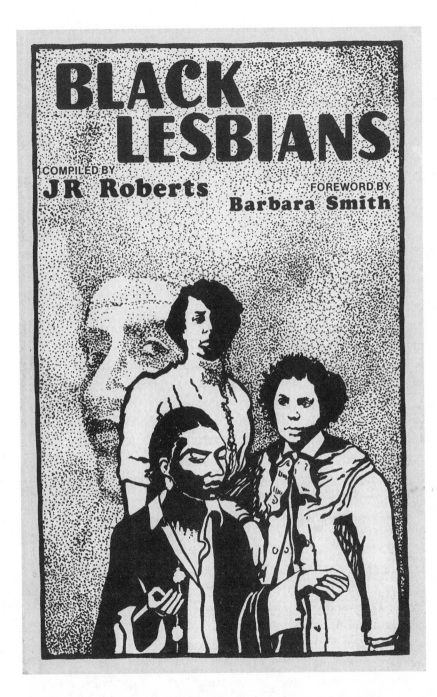

FIGURE 3.2 *Black Lesbians: An Annotated Bibliography*, compiled by JR Roberts with a foreword by Barbara Smith, published by Naiad Press (1981).

to Black lesbians Roberts was able to find through her work in archives, special collections, periodicals, and literature.[32] It features 341 detailed annotations on a range of media, including books, magazines, photography, and recorded oral histories. *Black Lesbians* demonstrates the strategies of historical revision, evidence gathering, and lesbian world making that indexing projects delivered.

By the time she came to the Circle of Lesbian Indexers, Roberts was an experienced activist indexer. In addition to *Black Lesbians*, she had produced a batch of cards called the "Master List of Lesbian Serials Published in the United States since 1947." These cards identified publication titles, print runs, and leads on where issues could be acquired, including the names and contact information for women in the movement known to collect a particular publication.[33] *Black Lesbians* emerged out of Roberts's frustration with the perception that historical materials by and about Black lesbians existed but were rendered invisible within cultural understandings of lesbian identity defined through a white, middle-class framework. Roberts explained in the book's introduction, "The concept of the bibliography gradually emerged out of my own growing political awareness of Black lesbian life and culture. . . . 'Lesbian' for the most part has connoted 'white, middle class lesbian' to the exclusion of other realities and perspectives."[34]

Black Lesbians exemplifies how information activism was implicated in larger antiracist lesbian feminist struggles. Lesbian antiracism in the early 1980s developed out of multiracial conversations among lesbians prepared to understand difference along multiple axes—gender, sexuality, race, class, and ability—and build coalitions out of these differences.[35] For Kristen Hogan, lesbian antiracism describes how queerness, through its strategies of working from difference in coalition, can become "a call to antiracist practice."[36] In the early 1980s, when *Black Lesbians* was published and the circle began its work, leading Black feminists such as Hazel Carby, bell hooks, Audre Lorde, and Bernice Johnson Reagon published several notable calls to decenter the white, middle-class subject from women's history and the women's liberation movement.[37] This work was urgent to repair the divisions between white women and women of color in academic and movement feminisms. Developing better information infrastructures was part of this work.

Indexes and bibliographies could alter lesbian history and theory by providing schematics for working differently. Women of color were deeply engaged in doing their own historical, bibliographic, and movement publishing work during the 1970s and '80s.[38] *Black Lesbians'* primary goal was to serve women of color doing historical research, which was key not only to supporting autonomous Black lesbian feminism but also to developing a meaningfully *coalitional* women's movement.[39] As Carby put it,

> The herstory of black women is interwoven with that of white women but this does not mean they are the same story. Nor do we need white feminists to write our herstory for us; we can and are doing that for ourselves. However, when they write their herstory and call it the story of women but ignore our lives and deny their relation to us, that is the moment in which they are acting within the relations of racism and writing history.[40]

As a white lesbian indexer, Roberts joined others within the movement working to build accountability to lesbians of color through historical projects, and better research support.[41]

Antiracist information activists understood that information was not neutral but, rather, a mechanism built out of movements that might be constructed differently, in cross-racial collaboration. In the book's introduction, Roberts explains that

> as a white lesbian I have chosen to work on this project because it needed to be done, and I have had the time, political commitment, skills, and interest. As a librarian and a lesbian I have long had a commitment to making lesbian materials and information more accessible generally, and particularly I have strong concerns about the lack of opportunity for the voices of Black, Third World, poor white, and working class lesbians to be heard. Hopefully this bibliography is one way to help change this situation.[42]

Black Lesbians was designed for Black women to use, but the book was also for white women to witness.[43]

The volume's dual purpose speaks to its potential as an infrastructure for what Aimee Carrillo Rowe calls transracial feminist alliance: the expansive "shared experiences and meaning from which we are excluded if we stay within our own racial ranks."[44] White lesbians might develop a better understanding of Black lesbian life and consider their role in the economy of attention in which Black lesbian materials are "obscured by the bulk of white lesbian information."[45] A bibliography of Black lesbians in history organized information as an intervention into how lesbian culture and identity was imagined and represented. *Black Lesbians* is a record of how information activists understood the discursive operations they performed by framing the public-facing identity of "lesbian" in historical terms. Information activists assumed responsibility for this framing through commonplace information management tools, including indexes.

Although a white bibliographer compiled *Black Lesbians*, the volume emphasizes Black women's voices in the authors and historical figures it features. The well-known Black lesbian writer and activist Barbara Smith wrote the book's foreword, which predicts that the bibliography's effects will be monumental for Black feminist scholarship, historical visibility, and, by extension, social justice. Smith asserts that a bibliography of Black lesbian scholarship and primary source materials will make ridiculous the frequent "claim that there are no Black lesbians and other lesbians of color."[46] Smith is unequivocal on the project's potential, asserting, "This bibliography puts that lie to rest."[47] That lie is buried under the weight of information gathered, sorted, and arranged by indexers working to open pathways through which others might reconstruct a field.

Black Lesbians responded to precarious and paradoxical conditions: the Black Lesbian subject positioned as the solution to making movement histories less racist, was also unimaginable within dominant movement frameworks. The white lesbian-feminist economy privileged middle-class ideals of sisterhood without difference, rejected patriarchy without distinguishing between white and racialized men, and understood sexual identity as an experience isolated from race.[48] Women of color were excluded, or rendered entirely invisible, by this framework. *Black Lesbians* did the basic recovery work of locating a Black lesbian subject in history as information that might be activated by others: Black queer women researchers who could turn down new paths through lesbian feminist history.

In addition to addressing lesbian feminism's whiteness, the bibliography challenged Black feminism to celebrate lesbian sexuality. As Amber Musser argues, Black women during second-wave feminism "became *the* sign of marginalization . . . invoked as a trope to consider the multiplicity of marginalization." Yet "the category's own multitudes were seldom interrogated."[49] Audre Lorde's essay "I Am Your Sister: Black Women Organizing across Sexualities" (1985) outlines how and why Black lesbians were often feared or made invisible within Black feminist struggles.[50] As lesbians committed first and foremost to antiracist activism, Smith and her collaborators at the Combahee River Collective and, later, Kitchen Table: Women of Color Press led efforts to define the political relationship among lesbian feminism, Black feminism, and women of color feminism in ways that provided important antecedents to queer theory's expansive approach to identity.[51] In the early 1980s, these and other lesbians of color were at

Chapter Three

work publishing knowledge that centered race, class, and ethnicity in explorations of sexuality.[52] Smith's endorsement of *Black Lesbians* speaks to the project's alignment with these goals.

A Black lesbian bibliography is an activist-intellectual project guided by an intersectional erotic of gender, sexuality, and race that might be advanced through stable access to information. Information was not a solution, on its own, to the exclusions practiced by white lesbian feminism or Black feminism, but it provided a resource users could draw on to build these insurgent, counterpublic capacities. Writing on the history of the Black public sphere, Catherine Squires argues that scholars must attend to the specific resources that counterpublics can leverage in their discursive interventions, including media and institutional supports.[53] Indexes and bibliographies were resources Black lesbians could use to redefine lesbian studies.

Because this field was built from predominantly white tools and institutions, the Black lesbian bibliography presented a crucial site for antiracist intervention.[54] For Roberts, lesbian studies' white "bibliographic situation mirrors the denial and invalidation of Black lesbian experience and uniqueness by a homophobic, white racist society and a lesbian-fearing Black culture."[55] But, as Roberts put it, "Black lesbian materials *do* exist."[56] The bibliography critiqued knowledge production, including the whiteness of gay and lesbian community history work, through awareness of indexes as fabricated tools that could change and be changed.

The antiracist techniques Roberts practiced with *Black Lesbians* were also deployed in the circle's work on *The Lesbian Periodicals Index*, although they were not the focus of the index. The circle wanted its indexing work to "reflect the diversity of the lesbian experience and be representative of our political, racial, class, and cultural differences."[57] This politics influenced the circle members' title selection—they indexed *Azalea: A Magazine by Third World Lesbians* published by the Salsa Soul Sisters collective (New York) and the *Lesbians of Color Caucus Quarterly* (Seattle), two of the limited 1970s lesbian feminist periodicals by and for queer women of color. The circle classified materials by subject headings that would provide pathways for researchers to explore how lesbians of color had written about specific experiences of race and ethnicity within movement print cultures. For example, the heading "Latina Lesbians" gathers articles from the circle's whole corpus. From this heading, a user learns that *Out and About* (Seattle) published many articles about Cuban lesbians. The circle's strategies reflected lesbian feminism's concern for difference within its ranks and understood that a subject index could remediate lesbian as an identity category.

With *Black Lesbians*, Roberts's index built something new by gathering hundreds of disparate resources by and about Black lesbians into a usable quick-reference document. The document's primary aim was access, purposefully mediated by Roberts's techniques. Skillfully challenging these conditions, Roberts describes her always-interpretive, sleuthing method of turning raw information into a usable index. In the bibliography's introduction, she describes searching under "cloaked" euphemisms for same-sex desire in Black literature and drawing on "grassroots communication networks and newsletters" to find newspapers, journals, and magazines about Black lesbians that had never been systematically collected or indexed and were "inaccessible" as a result.[58] Lesbian indexers worked as benevolent infiltrators within conditions of gendered, racialized, and technological exclusion from control over information. Their guides were designed not just to be read, but also to be used, toward the development of rich new histories that would shift the very terms of lesbian identity and politics. Forty years later, this work is ongoing through projects such as Cite Black Women, a transmedial information activist campaign created by Christen A. Smith and led by women of color.[59] Twitter users draw on the hashtag #citeblackwomen to ask for and share work by Black women scholars across disciplines.

Potter and Roberts described their indexes and bibliographies as pathbreaking, as guides that would point researchers—scholars and amateurs alike—in new directions for discovering and synthesizing information so they might create materials that would point others down subsequent paths of their own. Information organized through the index becomes an invitation to explore a path that seemed unpassable before. Imagining these paths, Roberts ends her bibliography with a two-page bulleted list titled "Some Suggested Activities for Black Lesbian Research." The list encouraged bibliography users to "create oral histories of older Black lesbians," "collect Black lesbian poetry, both published and unpublished," and "write your life story."[60] These generative activities might turn casual users into agents of history making who could create new materials for archives and fresh entries for future Black lesbian bibliographies. Given that lesbian-feminist indexers were aware of their work as a form of cultural media making—"a medium for the delineation of culture," in Potters' terms— these provocations serve as statements about historical knowledge production as a contingent process involving a range of actors: researchers, indexers, and critical users of reference tools. Black lesbian history would be written by community researchers with the will to do this work. *Black Lesbians* offered these researchers guidance down formerly invisible pathways, marked by urgent desire for a coalitional movement.

Lesbians Infiltrate Indexing Culture

Lesbian indexers infiltrated an existing indexing and information management culture, taking up some techniques while dismantling others. Potter wrote, "Both JR and I have used indexes, but never gave their creation two thoughts. We have, since starting to work through lesbian periodicals, given them a lot of thought and have tried to look critically at some standard indexes and some not so standard."[61] Index culture imagines index making through shared understandings of information and classification and investments in specific approaches both established and new. I describe indexing as a culture, first, because indexing is a set of techniques, semi-professional standards, physical equipment, best practices, and folk wisdom for making an index; and second, it is a set of qualities, traits, and habits that the ideal indexer—one who is ready to roll up their sleeves and do this meticulous work—ought to possess. In addition, "index culture" refers to a set of expectations about what indexes could do for a public with vested stakes in a given subject matter. In these cases, lesbian feminist and Black lesbian publics were marginalized by their exclusion from information in the first place. This horizon guides indexing culture and the indexer's work.

Indexing culture reflects common understandings amateur indexers had about their work. Gay and lesbian indexing projects straddled activist worldviews and standard indexing practices, working from the margins of library science's normative techniques and expectations. Indexing from the midcentury through the 1980s also traded in computational metaphors and early ideas about electronic databases. Paper index cards and other simple materials promised data management, search retrieval, and cross-referencing possibilities refracted through emerging understandings of digital databases. Lesbian indexing culture built these capacities with paper tools while imagining "electronic" indexing's future efficiencies, offering a queer antecedent to digital cultures.

Indexing manuals published between the late 1950s and the early 1970s supported amateur and semiprofessional indexers (those trained in library fields but not as indexers proper). The British and American societies for indexers published a range of guides to manual indexing.[62] The manual I examine most closely is Robert Collison's *Indexes and Indexing* (1959), because Potter and Roberts identify the text as the "background reading" that they "found most helpful" when learning how to index.[63] General guides to manual, paper indexing circulated alongside a range of manuals to computational indexing published in the 1970s and '80s. Computing corporations released these manuals to accompany indexing programs they designed and marketed primarily to large businesses, universities, and government agencies. Organizations that produced computerized indexing guides include the RAND Corporation and Stanford University's Computer Center, which created the WYLBUR program that Potter tried to use. RAND and Stanford both played formative roles in developing early computing and database management systems in the United States, and indexing projects represent some of the most practical, user-oriented instances of their work. Indexing guides provide practical instructions and set the stakes for what indexes could do, including what computers could do for people who wanted to manage information.

Both manual and computerized indexing guides describe how indexers could build processual filing systems: early examples of what Lisa Gitelman and Virginia Jackson call "relational databases" for information retrieval on a given subject.[64] Relational databases could bring publics together by organizing data to draw connections among materials and users and across subject matter. Because guides to manual, paper indexing were informed by the emergence of "business machines" in bureaucratic settings, they often drew on computational metaphors to describe how and why users might want to classify data. For example, G. Norman Knight's *Indexing, The Art of* recommends that indexers use a card and shoebox system over a bound notebook as a way to imagine autonomous files that can be edited, sorted, and deleted without consequence to the larger system.[65] Collison's book concludes with a chapter on "mechanized indexing" that speculates on how indexers can prepare for the inevitable application of new computers to their indexing work.

Amateur indexers who worked with these paper tools made very material databases during a period in which computing was new and unsettled in its meanings and applications. Indexing guides emphasize that indexing "tools" are accessible, and that making an index is easy, provided you are inclined to fastidiousness. Guides construct a common typology of ideal, nonexpert "indexers" and the information systems they might build with their capable hands.[66] Handmade indexes could mediate between a confusing mass of "data" and a public with search queries, provided that careful indexers with deep subcultural knowledge produced them.[67]

Feminist, lesbian feminist, and gay liberation indexes and bibliographies were made of paper and circulated in their finished form as photocopied documents or small-press books. These energetic social movements generated a great deal of vital yet disorganized printed matter to which indexers hoped to provide easy access.[68] They made up a distinct "print culture"; however, their status as information management tools designed to be used rather than read foregrounds the index as a document *in process*.

In *Indexes and Indexing*, the instruction manual referenced by the Circle of Lesbian Indexers, Collison describes the twentieth century as "the great age of indexing," in which "heroic efforts" are needed "to provide a key to the growing mass of information which is accumulating so rapidly that no-one can grasp its immensity."[69] Collison's effusive description of indexes and their social importance contrasts with the modest dedication at the beginning of the manual, in which he thanks his family for bearing "the sight of many little slips being shuffled and reshuffled without any apparent result."[70] Collison's gendered epigraph positions his wife and children as unnamed witnesses to technical paperwork they could not possibly understand. The index's information management promise is set against the simple materials used to make it. "Little [paper] slips" suited amateurs (implicitly men), who could work at home using everyday materials: cut-up paper, index cards, old shoeboxes, hole punches, glue, and sorting needles.

For indexers, these tools matter in their specificity. Index cards allowed indexers to imagine autonomous files that can be altered without consequence to the bigger system.[71] They were precomputational but materially entangled with early electronic punch-card systems, which also relied on paper cards. Indexers preferred cards over other possible ways to manage paper indexes for reasons that were similar to the appeal of computer files. Knight makes this clear in *Indexing, The Art of* when he describes a notebook's limited effectiveness for indexing projects because it was not modular:

> The use of a notebook—preferably loose-leaf—is one of the earliest methods of recording the entries for an index. Indeed it has been described as "primitive." I used it in some of my early indexes and found it completely satisfactory for a short, simple index of, say, six to eight pages. But the consensus of opinion among experienced indexers is that it lacks the flexibility of cards or slips and that it could not be expected to work well for a larger index, or one involving many sub-subheadings.[72]

Throughout his manual, Knight makes many different suggestions for card size, thickness, and the everyday materials that might be repurposed to sort them (such as an old shoebox). Bigger cards allowed indexers to write more; thickness made cards more durable to the wear and tear of sorting; shoeboxes kept everything together, could be put away when not in use so indexers (or their wives) could have their kitchen tables back, and allowed for easy rifling through a collection of cards. Cards are always described advantageously in indexing guides because they are easy to manipulate and revise.

Indexing guides such as Knight's and Collison's encourage would-be indexers to use modest and manageable means to address a historically specific information management problem: the twentieth century's massive proliferation of printed information in workplaces, libraries, institutions, and other contexts. This paper glut ushered in an era of bureaucratic, scientific management, and emerging computational understandings of how information might be organized and used.[73] Gitelman traces the emergence of a contemporary indexing sensibility to the rapid expansion of scholarly publishing in the United States that began in the 1930s. She attributes the emerging "scriptural economy" to changes in printing methods, the availability of cheap paper, and scholarly subspecialization.[74] For Gitelman, indexes and bibliographies represent a new genre of midcentury document, constituting "materials that inventory, describe, catalog, or otherwise facilitate control over other materials."[75] Lesbian feminism generated its own scriptural economy: a desperately needed print culture made up of newsletters and other gray literature that activists needed to manage because institutions did not care. As tools for managing lesbian feminism's scriptural economy, indexes were important movement technologies in their own right.

The midcentury index ushered in a modern, nearly electronic era of indexing but is part of modernity's longer appeal to human mastery over information, born out of eighteenth- and nineteenth-century celebrations of rationalism, classification, professionalization, formal education, and general knowledge.[76] The late nineteenth century saw the beginning of international maneuvers to produce bibliographic systems, an organized effort described by Gitelman as a "bibliographic movement."[77] The nineteenth-century index was imagined by, and in turn helped to shore up, a new sort of specialist learner who was after the efficiency of what we call "search retrieval" today rather than a more romantic ideal of generalized knowledge or well-roundedness.[78] The nineteenth-century turn to indexes and the random access they provide represents a shift to learning conceived as the search for information rather than the development of knowledge.[79] As Sasha Archibald describes, "An index adds usability, accessibility, and efficiency—practical, important values indeed, but values not dear to the heart of literature."[80] The age of the specialist welcomed a narrowing and professionalization of knowledge made possible by tools such as indexes.[81] As an indexing sensibility saturated documentary practices in the twentieth century, indexing fundamentally shaped emergent understandings of the user, data, and the infrastructures governing information.[82]

Indexing capitalizes on the belief that people can wrangle information. Information becomes a standing reserve waiting for sorting and interpretation by a human actor who can mediate access for others. This human actor is stirred by a feeling common to those who work closely with information: frustration. Writes Collison, "No person who is engaged in the work of extracting information from printed sources—be he librarian, information officer, journalist, secretary, scientist, or research worker, etc.—can fail to be aware of the frustration constantly presented by knowing that the information exists, without knowing where it exists."[83] This frustration took on a different kind of urgency for lesbians confronting the erasure of their materials from mainstream reference tools and from the public imagination.

Expressing frustration, Roberts's introduction to *Black Lesbians* describes the project's origins in 1977 while she was at graduate school in Massachusetts: "On the surface not a great deal was readily available, and a frequent refrain of those in search of these materials was, 'But there just *isn't* anything!' Yet many materials do exist, although as a result of racist, sexist, and heterosexist politics, there is a lack."[84] In the case of lesbian indexing projects, frustration at a lack of access to materials that are surely "out there" is further affected by the marginalization of this information from institutional contexts such as book publishing and public libraries.[85] Antiracist indexing responded to frustration at white lesbian feminism's relegation of race to the periphery. Indexes assembled information that could be used not only to build "Lesbian History" but also to legitimize the place of lesbian materials in popular culture. The index might ultimately persuade libraries to acquire lesbian materials by demonstrating the breadth and scope of lesbian contributions to literature.

Indexing, Distanciation, and Lesbian Counterpublics

Collison's frustration at not being able to locate what he knew was "out there" describes desire to close distance. Indexing culture responds to a feeling that information is out there, and the right tools might bring it closer. In media studies, this feeling of distance and attendant desire for proximity is called "distanciation," a concept John Guillory develops to describe how the pull to communicate using media is motivated by affects such as pleasure, attachment, and anxiousness. Guillory writes, "Distanciation creates the possibility of media, which become both means and ends in themselves—not the default substitute for an absent object. If this were not the case, we would be unable to explain the pleasure of talking on the telephone, reading novels, or even accumulating money as the medium of exchange."[86]

Creating mediated encounters with information imagines a counter-public made up of others who want but can't find the same information and who will *share* that information once they find it. For Guillory, "Pleasure in mediation may have grown out of the need to relieve the anxiety attached to the dispersion of persons in social space."[87] For lesbians in the 1980s, indexes addressed fears about the precarity of lesbian spaces and lesbian community, even in hubs such as New York City.[88] Barbara Gittings, editor of the early lesbian periodical *The Ladder* and creator of *A Gay Bibliography* (1971–80), describes how gay and lesbian index culture touched on this raw need for mediated encounter with others: "For thousands of gay people who aren't active in our movement, information is more than finding gay books and newspapers—it means finding other gay people."[89] The index creates proximity through an interface that is in itself a shared printed resource, and it imagines a field of users collectively accessing the same materials it lists—perhaps, in the case of library or reference copies, even touching the same book.

Indexes create proximity to others that is part of queer investments in libraries more generally. Think of the singular check-out card tucked into the back cover of a library book, replaced in the twenty-first century by a disposable "date due" slip printed on flimsy receipt paper or an email reminder that your books are due. Check-out cards, which are also index cards, document who borrowed the book before you and when, with a signature written in each library user's unique hand in the column "Borrower's Name." The card becomes an index to a user public with shared stakes in the book's content, who might also have taken risks in coming to the library to check out lesbian materials. Making an index creates proximities that are much greater than simple information retrieval: the index makes promises about what information might do for emerging lesbian feminist publics, including bringing eager users closer to the materials they desired and the communities represented by those materials.

Indexers were not unlike the women who worked at newsletters and hotlines in their drive to mediate access to lesbian materials. Indexers perhaps best exemplify the term "information activist" because they work most explicitly with "raw" information that awaits processing to be meaningful.[90] The writing these women did to introduce their projects to readers frames the indexes they worked on as indispensable interfaces that would mediate between a public and the information they both desired and couldn't do without. Dispersed users needed this information to be intelligible as a "public" in the first place. Potter explains that lesbian newsletters needed systematic indexing because "They provided a means of expression for a community *in the process of creating itself.*"[91]

The Circle of Lesbian Indexers built its index at a time when lesbian publics did not have any access to information interfaces that reflected the terms through which this community described itself; during this period, most libraries followed the standard subject headings of the Library of Congress (LOC) to classify all lesbian materials, no matter their specialization, under "Lesbian," with a cross reference to "Sexual Perversion."[92] Creating a subject index to lesbian materials meant starting from scratch to design a "medium for the delineation of culture" that would impose an interpretive framework that reflected "lesbian experience and thought."[93] *The Lesbian Periodicals Index* was a willfully constructed lesbian-feminist interface: the "front-end" experience through which users encounter information. The forms interfaces take matter—they "classify, frame, and link" users to information in ways that are caught up in larger gendered and racialized operations of power.[94] As Lisa Nakamura explains, the interface can withhold, foreclose, and distribute, or provide ways of "negotiating, navigating, and situating oneself."[95] The interface metaphor emphasizes how libraries, archives, indexes, and bibliographies act as intermediaries between "documentary evidence and its readers."[96] Interfaces are "neither natural nor neutral." They are tools that impose "an interpretive framework."[97]

For information activists, information was out there but in need of work. A dedicated hand needed to corral this information into something meaningful and usable for a nascent political movement. This indexer needed specialized knowledge to (1) find materials; (2) parse their meaning through the attribution of subject descriptions carefully selected to reflect movement values; (3) design an index or bibliography that was easy for laypeople to use; and (4) circulate the completed index through activist networks via specialized women's presses. This work was an invested labor of love, far removed from the neutral classification schemes professional catalogers and indexers applied. As Potter explains in the circle's how-to guide, "Making author entries is a straightforward and blithe process. However, subject entries are problematic for several reasons. In the first instance, it involves constantly making judgements—hopefully informed but nonetheless individual judgements—about what an article is actually about."[98] The circle did not efface the index maker from the center of interface design and maintenance; rather, it acknowledged her responsibility for shaping lesbian public formation by creating mediated conditions accountable to movement values.

Indexes imagine and delineate a public through the selection of entries, the organization of information into headings, and the circulation of the finished index. These techniques carve out a textual community already caught up in the cultural politics of gay and lesbian, and women's, liberation. Index counterpublics take shape in relation to shared materials and marginal reading practices. These materials gained legitimacy and context through their inclusion in indexes and bibliographies, gatekeeping technologies that queer librarians could use to justify new acquisitions. Indexes are reference documents that support the development of what Michael Warner calls "agency in relation to the state."[99]

For Warner, counterpublics are discursive and self-organizing imaginaries whose terms of existence are not pre-public but are formed and transformed through participation on the margins of a wider public.[100] Counterpublics are poetic and "world making," bringing together strangers in new modes of sociality that are outside the critical-rational discourse of publics proper.[101] Indexes give readers opportunities to locate and engage in counterpublic discourse; they also facilitate efficient, categorical, and, one might say, "rational" forms of knowledge production through search retrieval. Straddling this tension, *The Lesbian Periodicals Index* and *Black Lesbians* address lesbian counterpublics who had been excluded from reading practices and left to "mumble" or "fantasize" their way through an opaque field of texts.[102] However, bibliographies and indexes might offer lesbians legitimacy and respectability by facilitating entry to research and publishing's "critical-rational discourse." The potential for institutional recognition presents a political direction at odds with lesbian feminism's more radical leanings.

Indexes and bibliographies affirmed the existence of past lesbian publics once marginalized from historical records in implied chains of continuity with lesbian users in the 1980s, and in the present. The index reaches backward in time to establish a public retrospectively but does so to secure a public in the future—one that is unthreatening to the present because it is recognizable and anticipated. Potter explains, "I think we are trying to imaginatively connect with the next generation of lesbian women, to speak to them, and so this work we are doing, I think of metaphorically, as a long letter to our lesbian daughters, a work of our hands for them."[103] Here Potter invokes the matriarchal trope of inheritance and recognition—"this is my daughter"—that can smooth over acrimony in feminist histories.[104] Joan Scott critiques the "fantasy of feminist history" as a process of writing the self into a coherent narrative category ("woman") that moves developmentally across eras.[105] The safety of lesbian feminism's perceived stability across time periods, racial formations, and gendered ways of being can either blot out or preserve productive discontinuities, depending on the indexer's approach to difference. The index writes a coherent lesbian across time, becoming an affective tool in its generative guarantee of feminist futurity.

Liberation and futurity attach to indexes because of their role in manifesting and sustaining publics; however, the best indexes disappear from view, becoming merely tools. The index should point, but it should do so as an apparently neutral interface accessed by an agential user. Writes Archibald, "A good index does not advertise, promote, or flaunt itself, but crisply details a series of perfect routes, from heading to subheading to page number to morsel of information. The less time spent considering the index [by the user], the better the index."[106] A "good index" evokes fantasies of pure mediation, transcending the distance between users and the information they desire through easy information retrieval that feels virtually seamless.

In the circle's how-to guide, Potter quotes Elda Dunham and Beverly Miller's introduction to their *WomanSpirit* index (a lesbian feminist quarterly): "I see an index as a tool (the primary purpose of which is to be functional), and the indexer as a craftsperson who produces the tool. The job of the indexer, like that of the jeweler, is to highlight the facets of the already-existing creation."[107] Because their work emerged from lesbian-feminist commitments to accountability and subjectivity, information activists knew indexes were never neutral. Instead of neutrality, they aspired to index materials through reciprocity, using the language and worldview used to create those materials in the first place. To the circle, categorizing materials was an inevitably value-laden process. As members of the counterpublics they served, these indexers tried to use accurate, community-specific language and be transparent about their own motivations and choices. Lesbian indexes are infrastructures for counterpublic history and research, designed with care for others to enliven.

Simple, handmade databases such as the Circle of Lesbian Indexers' card collection used gendered construction methods, including accessible materials, tools, and design. A hands-on DIY sensibility familiar to feminist activism—and, more generally, to "women's work"—made creating an index to published materials at home, in one's spare time, seem manageable.[108] Working with paper index cards is a gendered style of routine, meticulous, and very material labor. Paper cards are relics of women's information work as professional catalogers in libraries, but also in the home, via recipe cards.[109] Historically, information work, especially librarianship, has attracted a high rate of LGBTQ workers, who felt that they could be more visible in these workplaces than others.[110] As librarians, Potter and Roberts had some knowledge of indexing from library school, but they were not trained or practiced indexers. They were not amateurs but, rather, capable semiprofessionals who drew on a combination of adjacent specialized training, experience with lesbian activism and publishing, and belief in their own capacities to figure out a technical and intellectual process in service of the movement.

Other members of the circle had no experience with librarianship or indexing but were still invited to join, said Potter, who explained her recruitment process to me: "I understood that there's a theory and practice around [indexing]; that it's not just something you could do. But I thought that if there was a love of the idea of the project and wanting to do this that anybody could be trained. I didn't say you have to have a master's in library science or information technology. It was just, would you want to do this?"[111] The circle's capable amateur ethos believed excitement, commitment, and care were more important indexing qualities than preexisting technical skill. Potter learned that holding space for amateur indexers in the circle created a lot of extra work for her: "I didn't feel like you had to have the background in it, but in actual fact, it helps, because otherwise you spend so much time educating people in how to do it. If I ever did it again I would say, yes, you should have a background. JR did, of course."[112] The circle's belief in indexing's potential accessibility to nonspecialists reflects a gendered belief in the capacity of amateurs to work hard at acquiring new skills when larger movement goals are at stake.

Ideas about gendered labor also shaped larger indexing culture. Indexing's approachability by nonprofessionals is often explained through gendered, domestic metaphors. Collison compares indexing to "setting one's house in order."[113] Collison's construction of the domestic sphere as an illustration of how indexing is easy also has the effect of diminishing indexing work: *if a woman can index, anyone can.*[114] Potter and Roberts turn this logic on its head, describing feminist resourcefulness and willingness to try as the impetus for going forward with *The Lesbian Periodicals Index*, even though they didn't really know what they were doing, having each "glossed over" that part of library school.[115] The "genesis of the idea of creating a Lesbian Periodicals Index" was a simple connection between two women both enmeshed in lesbian feminist politics and activism: Potter was motivated by "the many hours of conversation between JR and myself concerning just about everything—from recipes and families, to our dreams of lesbian books and archives, and of communities of women."[116] (I imagine that the recipe boxes Potter and Roberts brought to these exchanges were meticulously organized).

Indexing culture diminishes women's work to relay its approachability, but lesbian indexers draw on gendered labor as powerful and unique. Take, for example, the willingness of women such as Potter and Roberts to take on a "second shift," indexing at night after their day jobs and domestic responsibilities had been fulfilled, or their readiness to implement a collective work model that was often frustrating to maintain.[117] Activists in the Women in Print Movement imagined the acquisition and application of technical skills, especially those related to the management and reproduction of paper documents, as a way to materialize feminist theory.[118] As Trysh Travis explains, doing and thinking were intertwined: "The simultaneous development of women's heads and hands was necessary to prevent a divisive split between radical theory and practice. Without a conscious blurring of the lines between manual and mental labor, feminists risked recreating among themselves the hierarchies of class, intellect, power, and so forth, that they were committed to eradicating."[119] Doing information activism across difference and across lesbian communities of struggle meant working collaboratively with a mess of cards. It also meant grounding this practical work in dialogue and intimate friendship. As Potter wrote, "I am quite pleased to have been able to talk with JR over these past months and know that this primary connection and 'sparking' is what makes us move, it is the seedbed of our culture."[120]

Lesbian-feminist activism structures how the circle organized its workflow. It also informs the choices these indexers make about how to describe materials. Potter evokes consciousness-raising, lived experience, self-determination, and the personal as political—characteristic movement philosophies—when she describes the subjective, interpretive act performed by attributing subject headings in indexing:[121]

But "subjects" is a term that encompasses events, emotions, concepts, images, places—every aspect of experience. In fact the term is so broad that the imagination stretches to consider all the possible meanings adhering to such an innocuous looking word. We must keep in mind that lesbian realities reflected in our periodicals are just as vast, as all-encompassing as the word subjects implies. The task we have set for ourselves is to try to name this vast, fluid, and changing experience. . . . [T]he subject headings in [*The Lesbian Periodicals Index*] were going to reflect internal realities—our life and times in the lesbian community—and external realities—our life and times interacting with the mainstream society.[122]

This approach reflects some of the central commitments of any feminist epistemology. If such a thing can be said to exist in any kind of coherence in the first place, it might be summarized, according to Scott, by such axioms as, "There is no inclusiveness without exclusion, no universal without a rejected particular, no neutrality that doesn't privilege an interested point of view; and power is always an issue in the articulation of these relationships."[123] In this ethical critique of classification's effects, Scott evokes a question that is also prevalent in media and information studies' critiques of technologies and infrastructures that sort and standardize, with human implications.[124]

Bringing these concerns together, indexing by subject is the ultimate, systematic act of categorization and classification that attributes set meanings to another person's words and records those meanings as information pathways for others to use. Thus, for Potter, classification necessarily "violates any sense that reality is process, flux, and change, that it defies categorization, and that each event, idea, or person is perceived differently by different people in different circumstances."[125] The circle's feminist indexing method is based in an acknowledgment of these limitations by an indexer who then proceeds with care and is willing to revise, even if it means having to discard or redo an entry or two.[126] Writes Potter, "With the recognition that at some level, indexing is delusive, we can, I think, try to make the best judgments and the most informed decisions that we can about the subject(s) of the material we're indexing."[127] Lesbian indexers draw on movement values to determine what counts as good, informed judgment.

Information activists approached the index as a "woman-centered" form of mediation, staging critical interventions with the default rationales and thesaurus terms for subject description. Dismantling masculine language structures and etymologies was a popular 1980s feminist tactic, deployed in activists' spellings of "womyn," for example, or in French feminist critiques of language that were beginning to find U.S. audiences through English translation during this period. A notable example of feminist language politics applied to the index is Dale Spender's unorthodox index to her book *Women of Ideas and What Men Have Done to Them* (1982), which includes subject headings such as "reasoning, male limitations of."[128] Spender enacts her book's argument—that women's perspectives have been erased from literary history—through the form of the index, a primary interface for interpreting and rationalizing a field. Spender calls out this ubiquitous tool and the vocabulary it relies on as gendered and in need of revision.

While the circle was indexing, the American Library Association's Task Force on Gay Liberation advocated for the redevelopment of Library of Congress subject headings to reflect the terms sexual minorities used to describe themselves rather than the standard practice of classifying all materials under blanket headings such as "homosexuality."[129] The circle consulted the LOC's standard headings not for their content, but to understand how hierarchical and relational structures work.[130] The circle's guide to indexing cites a range of standard indexing resources, such as the LOC's subject headings, alongside many earlier feminist and lesbian feminist indexing projects—for example, Joan Marshall's *On Equal Terms: A Thesaurus for Nonsexist Indexing and Cataloging* (1977) and the index to the first five years of the feminist antipornography magazine *Off Our Backs*.[131] The circle developed its classification tactics within this broader critique of language and classification, familiarizing themselves with standard practices and existing feminist interventions with those practices.

Although feminist information workers brought an insurgent energy to language reforms, they learned cataloging and indexing at library schools under the auspices of being trainable, complacent, and amicable to the status quo. Librarianship and other midlevel forms of information work are historically feminized professions (and continue to be). The proliferation of women library workers in the late nineteenth and early twentieth centuries—in 1910, more than three-quarters of U.S. librarians were women—met little social resistance from male librarians, in part because library work "appeared similar to the work of the home."[132] Organizing information was gentle work that didn't threaten women's constitutions or jeopardize their suitability for domestic roles. In other words, women information workers seemed to shore up the existing social order. Women workers were preferred for the "tedious job" of cataloging, in particular, because of their "stored great reserves of patience," which allowed them to perform "the most monotonous tasks without boredom."[133] These sexist understandings of information work identify technological labor as routine maintenance rather than inventive practice. At the same time, this willingness to perform the small, routine tasks necessary to achieve a larger vision is precisely the kind of scrappiness that makes lesbian-feminist activism so effective. Doing unglamorous work with paper or indexing software is how lesbian-feminist information infrastructures get built, one card at a time.

From early on, index cards were gendered materials in their form and use, reflected by the standard script expected for writing on them. "Library hand" is a rounded style of standardized script for writing on index cards (not unlike schoolteachers' printing) developed by Melvil Dewey (of the Dewey Decimal System) when he ran the library school at Columbia University in the late nineteenth century.[134] Whether because of Dewey's particular aesthetic choices or his investment in the feminization of librarianship, or merely because most catalogers were women, library hand has a "feminized" look and feel, characterized by a neat, compact, looping script and the occasional serif.[135] All this is to say that the handwriting on index cards matters; its cultural politics is steeped in a gendered history. Actual index cards in the circle's archives feature handwriting by members that matters for understanding their collaborative, revision-centered work.

The average index card is a work in progress, returned to and edited over the years as information about an entry changes. Members of the circle sent their cards to Potter for feedback on their work—she would photocopy the cards on 8½ by 11 sheets, mark up the sheets with a pen, and mail them back to the indexers so they might improve their work. This is the arduous training and coordination work Potter remembers as vital to the circle's collaborative values but an impediment to actually completing the index. Potter's marginalia do not just instruct; they also reflect a collective revision process: there are scribbles of "Make sense?" and "What do you think?" and "Sounds like a good article—was it?" (figure 3.3).[136] Cards offer material remnants of gendered information management. The replacement of card catalogs with networked databases and digital interfaces effaces a history of women's hands in information management as the physical product of this work is discarded. As the next chapter argues, the LHA resists this erasure by keeping records of previous volunteer-generated subject classifications for materials, even when they are replaced with "better" description.

The circle's index cards reveal far more than just the indexer's hand or each text's bibliographic details. They offer contextual information about the project, its reach across lesbian and feminist communities, and the

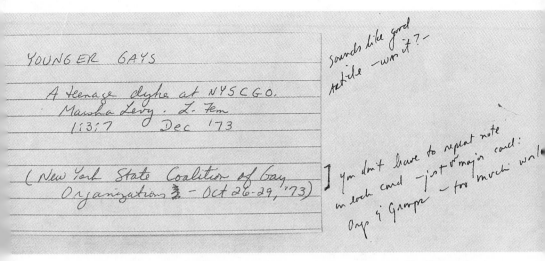

FIGURE 3.3 Index card written by Karen Brown, a member of the Circle of Lesbian Indexers, and annotated by the circle's coordinator, Clare Potter, early 1980s. The annotations read: "Sounds like good article—was it?" and "You don't have to repeat note on each card—just on major card: Orgs & Groups—too much work!" Circle of Lesbian Indexers Papers, folder 5. Image courtesy Lesbian Herstory Educational Foundation.

wide networks information activists called on for assistance—for example, a card that identifies a woman who owns a full set of the *Atlanta Lesbian Feminist Alliance (ALFA) Newsletter* and lists another woman who might have her contact information (figure 3.4). This card is part of the preparatory work necessary for making a community-based index. It indexes actual women—lesbian information activists—as data points, organized by last name, listing the resources they might offer the project. The connections between information activists and their shared media emerges through the card, which becomes a peculiar kind of archival document attuned to the networks of feminist cultural production behind the circle's project.

Cards record how a larger index counterpublic responded to the circle's requests for assistance. The circle recruited new members and located newsletter issues by publishing requests in lesbian periodicals, including *Matrices*, the subject of chapter 1. A *Matrices* listing from the circle's beginnings in 1979 states, "We need support from the lesbian community to make the index happen." The circle asks *Matrices* readers to send spare issues, provide missing titles or issue numbers, and provide information on publication history. Potential contributors also learn that "the records and materials gathered for the project will be deposited at the Lesbian Herstory

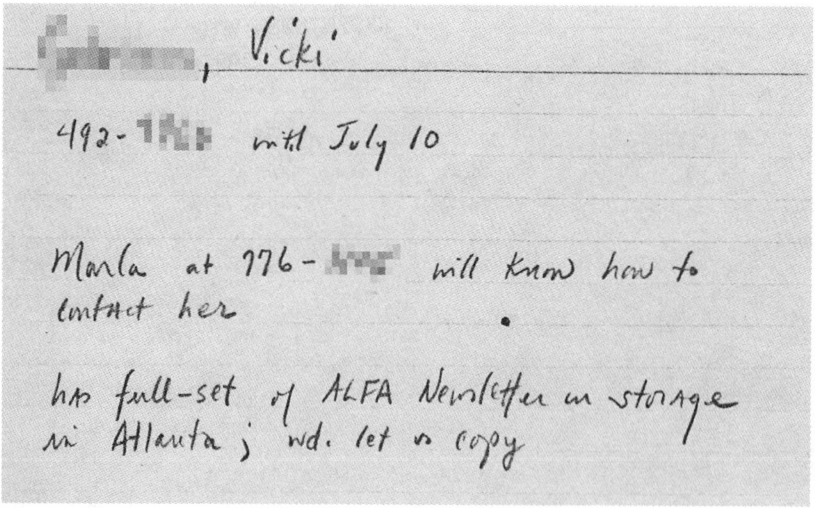

_____, Vicki*

492-1▓▓ mtl July 10

Marla at 776-▓▓ will know how to contact her

has full-set of ALFA Newsletter in storage in Atlanta; wd. let in copy

FIGURE 3.4 Index card written by Clare Potter describing a lead on a full collection of *ALFA Newsletters* (1978). Identifying information has been redacted. "Master List of Lesbian Serials Published in the United States since 1947," Lesbian Herstory Archives Collection, Brooklyn, NY. Image courtesy Lesbian Herstory Educational Foundation.

Archives in New York City."[137] The circle collaborated with the LHA to publish a list of titles they would index and asked readers for input and corrections.[138] Roberts also used *Matrices* and other periodicals to solicit support for *Black Lesbians*, including financial contributions to pay for printing: "Women with good jobs and surplus money are invited to contribute. Groups and organizations might help by doing fundraisers in their part of the country. This important publication will not be published without financial support from other lesbians and feminists."[139] Indexers supported lesbian feminism's print cultures by designing community-oriented pathways through this literature and relied on that very print culture's network to accomplish these goals.

The circle needed copies of newsletters that were hard to find to do their work. Potter remembers collecting most of the periodical issues herself, often with Roberts's help, by advertising in publications, following up on leads, and visiting collectors at their homes.[140] Once the indexing project was finished, Potter donated most of the periodicals to San Francisco's West Coast Lesbian Collections (now the Los Angeles June L. Mazer Archives), where she was an early coordinator.[141] She said, "At that time [the archive] was Cherie [Cox] and Lynn [Fonfa], and then it was me. It was in Cherie's house. We staffed it, we worked on building the collections. Eventually it ended up going to [Los Angeles], where it became the June Mazer [Archives]."[142] Drawing out the connections among indexers, subscribers, publications, and community archives illustrates the wide resource-sharing and support networks that build lesbian feminist historiographic tools. Lesbian information activists developed information infrastructures that brought these figures and sites into intimate exchange. The relatively small size and homophilic structure of lesbian studies was both a strength for this work and a formation that projects such as *Black Lesbians* needed to interrupt.

Committed to Revision, Ambivalent on Computing

Although it took the form of a book, *The Lesbian Periodicals Index* was also an information interface aimed at simplifying users' experience and caught up within the computational metaphors that characterized information-management projects during the 1980s. Like a desktop "window" or "file folder," "index" is a metaphor for understanding information as a series of objects (cards) that can be grasped and manipulated. Potter used the tools and strategies outlined in indexing manuals and designed the Circle of Lesbian Indexers' data-management techniques within the broader context of emergent database computing.

To make indexing easier and more efficient, Potter considered converting the circle's index to a computerized format. In letters to other members of the circle, she describes working with a new computer program called WYLBUR, which had a command-line interface. To enter data into WYLBUR or edit existing records, a user had to memorize and input a series of simple run commands that look like markup language. Potter tried WYLBUR right on the cusp of the graphic user interfaces (GUIs) that would revolutionize personal computing by making software much easier to manipulate. Working with code is less tactile than manipulating paper cards, even if it is potentially more efficient. The labor presented by converting an existing "database" of paper cards also deterred the circle. As Potter told me,

> Once I was knowledgeable about computers and what we could do, it was almost like I'm sitting on top of thousands of index cards, and converting that. . . . I had that thought at one time: if this could be converted. It was either charge ahead using the paper "technology" that existed at the time or turn around and input all the work that had already been done using a program. So in the end I just said, "Let's forge ahead and get this

done." . . . I had to make a decision to go back and convert to a different technology or move ahead and get it done. I was working full time. . . . The decision was just: it works.[143]

For Potter, computing held out promising applications for indexing but was too time-consuming and opaque for an activist indexer working evenings and weekends.

The application of computing to indexing was on Potter's mind while she was coordinating the circle; it was also in the background of the wider indexing culture. Like computers, indexes promote efficiency and usability. As tools they promise to help users stay on top of the information abundance characterized by late twentieth-century mass mediation. The index wants to work as a computer would, by mastering a quantity of information that a human being cannot in service of human knowledge pursuits.[144] Gitelman locates the index at the apex of an "unresolved tension" between "a machinic or an informatics sensibility" and "a more humanist" one.[145] Indexing manuals tend to include anecdotes that celebrate the fantasy of rapid information retrieval and clean management. Collison draws on the effusive rhetoric that often accompanies the introduction of new media technologies: "Indexing can be used to make life easier and more efficient." Although it is "not a panacea for all modern evils, . . . it can certainly be a palliative for some of the more common of them."[146] For Collison, the index is an elaborate system for managing a quantity of information that could not be managed otherwise. Indexes would provide a "modern substitute" for memory, which could not possibly "grapple with a thousand facets of a complex industrial civilization" on its own.[147] This investment in indexes as memory substitutes mirrors the ways digital storage technologies promise perpetual memory that they cannot actually provide.[148]

Collison writes as if he has computers in mind when he describes the revolution indexing could bring. The "mechanized indexing" chapter that concludes his book describes how advanced indexers could adapt computer punch cards, or "edge-notched" cards, to their indexing work. Similarly, Knight's *Indexing, The Art of* outlines the need for indexers to design alphabetizing systems that will anticipate the needs of computer languages, or what a future computer can read and sort.[149] During the late 1970s and early 1980s, when the circle did its work, computers were emerging widely into office environments and had begun to enter the public imagination as tools that might find value in personal use, and in social movement work. Relational database programs aimed at average users (think precursors to

Microsoft Access) entered the market in the 1980s.[150] As Kevin Driscoll argues, hobbyists' imaginative applications of relational databases led to the populist vision of personal computing that historians associate with the 1980s.[151] Lesbian information activists can be counted among these hobbyists, as both actual users of database programs and as *potential* users who gave up on these technologies for reasons that matter. Conscientious non-adoption by sexual and gender minorities is a rubric through which queer computing histories ought to be understood.

Lesbian indexers thought about computers and their potential for tasks they worked on, just as software designers created computing applications amenable to existing paperwork. In the early 1980s, the LHA, used by both the circle and Roberts to do their work, borrowed and later bought its first computer to manage a simple flat-file database of newsletter subscribers, a process detailed in the next chapter. In the circle's *How-to-Index* guide, Potter imagines the role computer databases might eventually play in her project: "That brings us to the subject of computers and their marvelous facility to sort and file. If anybody out there knows a lesbian programmer who could write a lesbian periodicals indexing program gratis, we need this woman! Beyond the need for an indexing program, using computers involves money—for computing time on the machine, for inputting, for storage—and who knows what else."[152] Potter was compelled by circulating ideas about what new computing technologies might offer to amateur indexers but unsure about the skills and costs involved in starting down this path.

In 1979, when Potter wrote these words, several relational database software packages were already available to skilled users with access to computing resources. This software primarily served institutions, but hobbyists also took it up.[153] The RAND Corporation developed a text-based abstract and index system in 1967 to manage internal bibliographic records, which was later sold to many institutions.[154] Four hundred miles up the California coastline, Stanford University developed WYLBUR, a much simpler text editing program Potter tried to learn at the university's computer center. Developed at Stanford in the late 1960s, WYLBUR is a line-oriented text editor, not a robust database system. It could be adapted to make simple "databases" that were more like lists. The program had wide applications for bibliographic management, text editing, and simple programming and was used at large institutions, including the National Institutes of Health, the City University of New York, and the University of California system.

Potter consulted with computer specialists about the circle's needs before she began her attempt to learn WYLBUR and input the circle's thesaurus. In one of her regular updates to circle members, she related this process:

> I have been devoting a lot of time to trying to learn how to use Stanford's text editing computer system. Like all of these machines it is somewhat more difficult to use than the manuals say it will be, or at least it takes a bit of time to become really efficient in using it. I met with . . . a consultant for WYLBUR, the system name, although I found it difficult to communicate with her through the maze of her jargon. I have one more contact: a gay man who uses both WYLBUR and a related system that is specifically an information retrieval system called SPIRES. I can only tell you that I will keep trying to get as much information as I can about how these systems might help us, what the potential cost would be both financially and in terms of time, and whether or not these systems can be effective for our purposes.[155]

Potter drew on queer connections to computing experts in the Palo Alto area, where she lived, to interpret the system's viability for a nonexpert, community-based project. When considering adoption or refusal of new computing technologies, lesbians weighed the time constraints they faced as activists with day jobs and the accessible presentation of technologies. Cost also mattered because they were funding projects out of their own pockets or through modest community donations.

Stanford engineers did aim at accessibility with WYLBUR, designing a command language that corresponded to commonsense English (natural language), so that it might be "usable by both novices and experts," including users who had no knowledge of programming.[156] Users of WYLBUR input text on teletype terminals, preferably the IBM Selectric.[157] The system used a shared mainframe computer to store and process data, while users interacted with the system using individual terminals that looked and felt like typewriters and used paper ribbon (rather than a monitor) to show users what they had typed. By the early 1980s, when Potter visited the Stanford lab, terminals were equipped with simple video displays.

The WYLBUR system stored a user's work in progress on a shared hard drive that could be output to a disk or printed, at cost to the user. The program represented a computational way of understanding information and documents: information could be stored and manipulated within a kind of "cloud" and then output as a traditional document, at which point that information became fixed in print. RAND's program offered the ability to store entries out of order and then order them differently for output according to particular needs—for example, by generating a list organized by author or subject. Stanford's WYLBUR program stored information *in* order, on numbered lines. To edit a WYLBUR text file, users had to call up and then revise or replace individual line numbers. Only a small range of lines could be viewed at once. More than any other task, WYLBUR promised to make simple revision easy, either line by line or by batch editing words throughout a file using a command equivalent to today's "find/replace" function in Microsoft Word. Manuals for WYLBUR play out scenario after scenario in which users make small changes to the larger project they are working on, even though they cannot "see" the whole file they have created because terminals could display only a limited range of lines at a time.

The promise of easy revision made WYLBUR appealing for managing the circle's thesaurus of vocabulary terms that indexers use to classify materials. A thesaurus of subject terms is a key document for any indexer. It acts as a framework, or system design. The thesaurus has to be good if the finished index has a hope of being any good. The circle used a thesaurus to maintain consistency across the work members were doing in different corners of the country. Potter managed the thesaurus by hand. She incorporated new headings into a central document based on suggestions she got from other circle indexers.

The thesaurus was an in-process document that required ongoing revision. Potter and other circle indexers uncovered new material that required more and more specialized terms of description. At other times, identity-based language politics changed in ways that required the circle to update its descriptions. In an essay published as part of the finished index, Potter describes the thesaurus's political implications: "We . . . see our attempts to build a thesaurus of subject terms applicable to lesbian realities as a way to help us pose the kinds of questions we need to ask about our experience. The thesaurus is truly a conceptualizing medium with an organic relationship to the culture—its people and ideas—from which it is derived."[158] The thesaurus's "organic" status begs for a dynamic technological solution in the form of an editable electronic file.

The circle revised or considered revising many terms over the course of the project. For example, the indexers discussed adding "Pro-" to "Abortion Movement" to improve clarity and lend it the same weight as "Anti-Abortion Movement" but settled on "Abortion Movement" in the final index (this occurred before the term "Pro-Choice" came into wide use).[159] The term "Lesbian Experience," used at the beginning of the project to "describe us trying to speak in relatively broad terms what it means to be a lesbian or to be gay in this world," was abandoned at some point during the project when it became too broad.[160] "Beauty (Personal)" was replaced with the toothier "Beauty (Standards)," and a "Women's Oppression" subdivision was added.[161] "Transpeople (men)" and "Transpeople (women)" became "Transpeople (male to female)" and "Transpeople (female to male)," which added precision and better reflected language used by trans community in the 1980s.[162] The circle's revisions made indexing more precise and granular as the project dug deeper into periodicals literature. Revision also offered indexers flexibility so they could listen closely and respond to grounded counterpublic taxonomies.

Each circle indexer who signed onto the project received a photocopy of the thesaurus in the mail. As subject headings evolved, Potter issued new copies or sent addenda to members via letter mail. This process was time-consuming and centralized—part of the burnout-inducing labor Potter shouldered as coordinator. Understandably, Potter imagined the thesaurus would benefit from automation and easier editability. As Geoffrey Bowker and Susan Leigh Star write, classification standards exist to ensure interoperability.[163] The thesaurus vocabulary acted as a standard all circle indexers shared, so that their work was compatible with the group's larger project. The thesaurus facilitated a necessary relationship among Circle members, their shared documents, and their indexing norms. But it was a standard the circle was willing to adjust as part of a lesbian-feminist commitment to accountability and consciousness-raising, despite the inconvenient extra work presented by such revisions.

As Potter explained to me, the circle "would be a collaborative project . . . like a hub and spoke with the thesaurus and communication. We would funnel it out. I felt like it would really work, and the work would get done more quickly if it was a group working on it."[164] Part of the circle's failure to collaborate effectively was about the thesaurus failing to produce this interoperability among members. As Potter explained, "The work would come in, and the cards weren't following the rules and procedures that were set up. In order to make this work as a cohesive publication, it had to be correct; it had to be accurate."[165] Potter used the thesaurus to train and condition circle members to produce uniform cards.

Considering WYLBUR's functionality in direct relation to the circle's thesaurus update procedure helps to illustrate the program's potential amenability to lesbian-feminist revision politics. "Addition 10" is a one-page list of thirty-one revisions to the thesaurus issue by Potter to circle indexers by mail.[166] Among this long list of revisions, Potter instructs each member to update the thesaurus terms for describing transgender materials to identify trans people, with respect, as women who have transitioned rather than as "men":

Clarify: TRANSPEOPLE (Men) = TRANSPEOPLE (Male to female)
and TRANSPEOPLE (Women) = TRANSPEOPLE (Female to male)

Consider this instruction alongside this excerpt from a WYLBUR manual that shows users how to change the name "James" to "Jim" throughout a text file:[167]

```
? LIST 'James'(CR)

5. James is now working at
9. a phone call from James
17. recommend James for the

? CHANGE 'James' TO 'Jim' IN ALL NOT LIST (CR)

? LIST 5,9,17(CR)
5. Jim is now working at
9. a phone call from Jim
17. recommend Jim for the

?
```

The first command (LIST 'James') shows the user a list of each instance that the word "James" appears in the file, along with corresponding line numbers (5, 9, 17). The second command (Change 'James' TO 'Jim'...) instructs WYLBUR to replace all instances of "James" with "Jim." The third command (LIST 5, 9, 17) instructs WYLBUR to show the user the lines that formerly contained "James" so that she can confirm that the desired revision has been made.

In this manual, changing "James" to "Jim" is just an arbitrary, jocular stand-in for any word a WYLBUR user might want to revise. But changing a term, renaming a person, or changing a gender marker with ease are fundamental to ensuring the dignity of trans representation in databases. The circle's addendum proposes changes that are significant, given the ways in which lesbian feminism is often remembered for its exclusion of trans people and its transmisogyny. If the circle had converted its thesaurus to a WYLBUR text file, Potter could have made her revisions with the simple command phrase: CHANGE 'Transpeople (male)' TO 'Transpeople (male to female)' IN ALL.

Attending to the minor adjustments information activists made in data-management contexts contributes to an etymology of language use for queer and trans communities. The circle's use of "transpeople" during the early 1980s shows that this term was in circulation beyond trans activist contexts prior to the wider adoption of "transpeople" in the 1990s, inspired by writers and activist such as Leslie Feinberg. As K. J. Rawson argues, community-based etymologies matter for understanding the changing cultural conditions in which trans communities make themselves intelligible or are recognized by others.[168]

Computer databases promised to enhance the work of second-wave feminist consciousness-raising, in which the ability to explain, listen to, understand, and revisit and revise a position were all key.[169] When Potter felt uncertain about a term, she noted her uncertainty on the card and returned to it once she discovered "*the* perfect term to describe a specific reality."[170] Potter explained, "I think we have to recognize that there will be a certain degree of re-indexing involved in creating *The Lesbian Periodicals Index*. . . . That's ok, but we have to have a good communication network."[171] Put simply, reindexing enacted the indexer's commitment to feminist methods, and computers promised to make this practice easier to carry out.

The circle's emphasis on revising its subject terms to achieve greater precision using the revision-oriented technologies of cards and computers is echoed in the Lesbian Herstory Archives' assignment (and reassignment) of metadata descriptors to its photography collection as it is scanned and put online. While Potter sought "the perfect term to describe a specific reality," the photograph coordinator Saskia Scheffer revises keywords whenever she realizes that she "can be more exact . . . more precise."[172] Potter found herself revising through a feminist commitment to lived experience and self-description developed out of the women's liberation movement. Scheffer grapples with the shifting signifiers and identifications for materials that resist classification under some of lesbian feminism's narrower terms. Despite different time periods, technologies, and publics, both Potter and Scheffer approach revision as a feminist practice that requires sensitive and open approaches to working with data.

Computing affordances such as revision and automated sorting remediate the paper index, but cards are also favored for their editability. Cards are singular, modular entries that can be reordered, edited, replaced, shuffled, sorted, and re-sorted. As Markus Krajewski explains, paper card indexes satisfy all the "basic operations" of Alan Turing's universal discrete machine (the theoretical prototype for the computer): paper indexes store, process, and transfer data, and "information is available on separate, uniform, and *mobile* carriers" that "can be further arranged and processed according to strict systems of order."[173] The computer index transcends some of the limits of a paper system because it allows instantaneous sorting and re-sorting, without any material file handling. But even "simple" programs such as WYLBUR required significant technical skill to operate, and they did not readily embrace capable amateurism—the feminist politics of trying things out using accessible materials, tools, and processes, practiced by the circle.

While most published manuals to WYLBUR imagine a user who already has some familiarity with computers, though not programming, the manual created specifically for use at Stanford took a unique focus on amateurs.[174] This manual was written by the Stanford engineer John Ehrman in 1975 to support basic users. Ehrman worked at Stanford's Linear Accelerator Lab and taught programming to computer science students. He made the manual to help others and worked hard to affect a lighthearted tone. The hand-drawn cover reads, "EVERYTHING You ALWAYS Wanted to Know About WYLBUR But Were Too: {Shy, Busy, Intelligent, Uninterested, Unavailable, Uptight, Scared} to Ask!" (figure 3.5).[175] Ehrman wrote the one hundred-page manual by hand on mismatched foolscap. This document about how to use a text editor is conspicuously *not* written with a text editor. The reason for this may be simple: most men in computer engineering in 1975 did not use word processors because typing was women's work. However, Ehrman's playful asides and informal scrawl seem intentional, in that they contribute to a look and feel for the manual he was trying to create. The manual looks accessible and tactile, unlike other WYLBUR tutorials that seem polished because they are typeset.

In another drawing from inside the manual (figure 3.6), Ehrman tries to explain to laypeople how a computer works—specifically, how the terminal on which they were typing connects to the larger apparatus. The drawing is user-focused, depicting a smiling figure with long, curly hair, seated at a computer center terminal. Although Ehrman probably wasn't imagining a bunch of lesbians taking up WYLBUR, he wanted amateurs to learn the program he loved. Accessible tools and warm invitations to learning these tools are key to activist movements and to bringing unconventional users into computing.

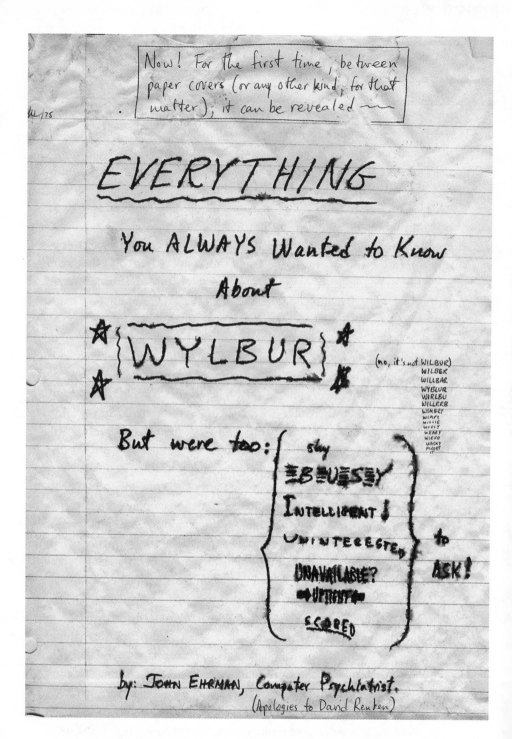

FIGURE 3.5 Hand-drawn cover for John Ehrman's "WYLBUR Tutorial," 1975: "EVERYTHING You ALWAYS Wanted to Know About WYLBUR But Were Too {Shy, Busy, Intelligent, Uninterested, Unavailable, Uptight, Scared} to Ask!" "WYLBUR Tutorial," 1998-014, John Ehrman Papers, SLAC National Accelerator Laboratory, Archives, History and Records Office, Stanford, CA. Image Courtesy SLAC Archives, History and Records Office.

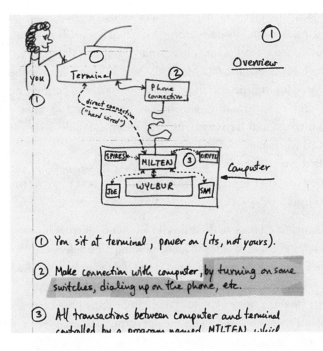

Potter's investment in learning computers, even though it often felt like a waste of precious "spare time" she could otherwise be spending on more pressing circle-related tasks, is its own kind of digital imperative, not unlike the pressures that guide community archives toward digitization. Potter imagined computers would allow the Circle of Lesbian Indexers to do the same things they were already doing with cards, but more easily and efficiently, a technical solution to the flood of cards with which she struggled to keep pace.[176]

The WYLBUR manual and Potter's interest in converting the circle's thesaurus into a text file illustrate how computers emulated the functions of "more material" indexes, which were also under constant revision. Editions of bibliographies such as Barbara Gittings's *Gay Bibliography* were edited each year and recompiled from a shifting stable of cards. Individual cards could be removed, modified, or reorganized and then output in a number of different ways.[177] Gittings performed this kind of modification when she crossed out outdated information about a periodical on an index card or when she used her existing collection of cards to re-sort a more specialized bibliography on a subtopic.

Although lesbian indexers used paper cards, pens, and pencils to build their indexes, their work was animated by the potential of computer databases in other information contexts they knew. These included the archives from which they drew their print sources and the more institutional information contexts—public and university archives—where some of these women had day jobs. During her final years working on *The Lesbian Periodicals Index*, Potter experienced a workplace transition to computer databases in her job as a librarian for the California Medical Association.[178] During the late 1970s and early 1980s, online search retrieval and database computing were the cutting edge of information studies, at the forefront of library school curricula, professional development, and technical skills acquisition for information workers.[179]

In correspondence with other circle members, Potter describes spending evenings at the computer center learning how to use WYLBUR. At the outset of her experiment with WYLBUR, Potter wrote to the circle:

> Given that the only time I have to do this is on weekends and on an occasional weekday evening, it will probably be some time before the updated thesaurus is out for everyone. Ergo, don't hold your breath. The only way I can see to expedite matters is if I can find some help with the "data entry" part (there's some jargon for you); I hope there might be an interested dyke out there just waiting for the opportunity to both learn WYLBUR and spend hours inputting *The Lesbian Periodicals Index!*[180]

The figure in Ehrman's drawing (see figure 3.6) is smiling at her computer center terminal, but Potter was not. Two months later, Potter describes frustration with WYLBUR in a letter to one of the other indexers: "I find I just can't spend my every night and weekend at the Stanford center learning and then inputting. I need to spread some of the parts of this to others!"[181] Potter's willingness to show up at the Stanford computer lab to learn demonstrates a familiarity with institutional information contexts and a facility with learning new technology acquired no doubt through her exposure to library school and professional library work.

Computing's potential for lesbian indexers' work was not always positive or generative. It also acted as a normative trajectory against which these women designed their resolutely manual indexing systems. Reflecting on her lack of experience with indexing despite completing library school, Potter writes in the circle's manual: "JR [Roberts] and I are both librarians, but must confess to having been rotten students. I remember my course in 'Indexing and Abstracting' as one long, hot (it was summer) dull panegyric to computers and information science."[182] In her letters to the circle, Potter seems to resent WYLBUR's opacity and expresses skepticism about whether the program's value for managing the thesaurus or index would ever pay off: "I haven't quite been able to understand the costing of all this. Computers have such a jargon."[183] In the same set of letters, alongside her perplexity at trying to learn computers, Potter describes paper cards with fondness for both the materials and her collaborators' acuity: "Judy works [on the index] on Sunday afternoons. She has proceeded so quickly . . . that I'm passing on to her the title of ace-indexer. My role is becoming filer of 3 × 5 cards! I'm serious. I have about 12 inches of Judy's indexing to incorporate, plus about that much of my own."[184]

Lesbian indexers were skeptical about computers because they were expensive: users of shared labs had to pay for computer time and to have their work output. Computers also took a long time to learn and were difficult to use, and university computer labs were not generally welcoming spaces for women.[185] Despite Potter's complaints about these systems, she also invested a great deal of time and hope in the possibilities computer databases presented for managing *The Lesbian Periodicals Index*. In the circle's guide to indexing, she writes, "The numbers of cards we can safely manage without the help of machines seems finite. We can keep on top of hundreds (no problem), or a few thousand cards, but even dykedom has its limits."[186] At the limits of dykedom, Potter wanted to find emergent computing, but in the end she stuck with her paper system.

The circle was based in a lesbian dream of collaboration. The organization's collective work processes failed because they were too labor-intensive, but using a computer in isolation was also at odds with the desire information activists had to work together. Potter lamented the nights spent alone at the computer center when she could be participating in more obviously productive circle activities and expressed hope that other women with facility for computers would join the circle so she could "ask every question [about computers] I've always wanted to ask but had no one to ask."[187] Potter didn't want to be working alone at her keyboard in a sterile computer lab; she wanted to collaborate. In the circle's how-to guide, she recalls workshopping subject headings with Roberts while sitting in rocking chairs in Potter's front room. In a letter to another circle member, Potter envisions a grand, collaborative end to the project one day: "I always hoped that several indexers would be based in N[ew] Y[ork] to use the archives, and of course to give each other support. Anyway, for the time being I guess we are pen pals. I certainly hope we can come together somehow for all the interfiling that will need doing. . . . I always thought of that happening around a big table with one person doing a–f, another g–m, etc., etc., plus breaks for food and drink."[188] An affective imaginary of shared space, shared tools, and dedicated social time with other activists guides this vision of finishing the index in collaboration with others.

In reality, women dropped out and disappeared, and Potter completed the indexing herself. She hired a woman with facility for word processing to turn the finished card index into a word-processed document. The lesbian-feminist press Naiad ultimately published the document as is, skipping the step of typesetting the manuscript. As a result, the finished book has the look and feel of a printout from an early word processor and daisy-wheel printer.

Potter's willingness to sit with and explore her shifting, frustrated feelings toward both computers and cards enacts a feminist practice of carrying on alongside and in acknowledgment of one's ambivalence, a position given language in feminist texts of this period, such as Adrienne Rich's *Of Woman Born* (1977).[189] Potter's reflections on computers offer a critical intervention with progress narratives about technology and information management during the early days of widespread database computing and text editing. Emergent database logics and informational sensibilities take on new valences in the context of lesbian-feminist research, publishing, and counterpublic formation. Here, nonadoption matters for understanding who was imagined and served by the pedagogical, spatial, temporal, and financial infrastructures of mainframe computing. The circle's story shows how it looked and felt when nonexpert queer users encountered barriers to entering computing, even when a program's bare-bones affordances perfectly suited their work.

Conclusion

The women who imagined, designed, and carried out bibliographic and indexing projects wrangled a mass of information into something useful through the reference tools they built. They managed a range of materials (cards, computers, thesauruses) and served a number of intersecting and competing publics (feminist, Black feminist, lesbian feminist). They worked in service of future users: those who were *not yet* any of these labels but might want to be. Lesbian-feminist indexing in the 1980s asks us to reckon with the politics of various information tools during a moment when computing was new but limited in its accessibility. Pathfinding with new digital tools continues to guide lesbian-feminist information work in the present, as I explore at the LHA in the next chapter. Digitization at these archives shares with 1980s indexes investments in compression, rationalization, and streamlined access to information for queer publics. The next chapter explores how contemporary investments in digitization reimagine past feminist engagements with information across paper and digital tools.

FOUR

Feminist Digitization Practices
at the Lesbian Herstory Archives

Colette Denali Montoya-Sloan is escorting me to the basement of the Lesbian Herstory Archives (LHA) for a tour of the "spoken word" collection. I am expecting to find a few boxes of cassette tapes, maybe even a shelf full. As it turns out, the basement of the LHA in Brooklyn is overrun with audiotapes, among many other collections. A full wall of bookshelves is lined top to bottom with acid-free boxes, each of which contains about twenty tapes, mostly consumer-grade compact cassettes manufactured in the 1980s. The very existence of the collection—the sheer number of tapes—speaks to the mediated conditions of possibility behind the feminist oral history movement: a combination of technological changes that made audio recording affordable and easy to do, and an ideological shift in feminist history toward the active recovery of women's lost stories, told in their own words.[1] Today these tapes—all three thousand of them—are being digitized and offered online as streaming audio, an endeavor that brings this history and the archives' operation into relation with a new set of technologies and publics.

During my three months volunteering while doing documentary research and interviews at the LHA, I spent an afternoon hanging out with Colette, the volunteer audio archivist and archives coordinator who works on digitizing these tapes every Friday. I asked her questions as she showed me how the tapes are digitized, and I was shocked by the scale of this task relative to what Colette can actually do in a day, a week, or a year. Nonplussed by my surprise, Colette explained, "All these boxes are tapes," pointing at the wall, "and they're in sort of an order. I'm on my third box and I've been doing this for almost two years."[2] Colette is in her early thirties, and she is Native American (Pueblo). She is of average height, which

I note because watching her pose confidently in front of a massive wall of three thousand tapes and pull down the third box out of hundreds is a striking image that reflects a larger politics of digitization at this archives.

Completing the digitization of this collection may not be possible, but the LHA is doing it anyway, following the same kind of philosophically utopian but technologically pragmatic feminist media politics that guided the oral history movement that created these tapes in the first place. Any digitization project, with its big promises of preservation and access, can only ever be a partial gesture or "attempt" in practice. Volunteer-driven digitization at these lesbian archives is a slow-and-steady response to the urgency of preservation through format migration and the desires for access archival publics have in an era increasingly mediated by online interfaces. This lesbian-feminist organization's investments in digitization lays bare the labor practices and horizons of possibility behind digitization.

This chapter examines how improvised lesbian-feminist digitization practices challenge and enrich understandings of technological values such as access, usability, engagement, and preservation. As a contemporary form of information activism, these digitization practices put historical materials about lesbian feminism out into the world and do so by adapting digitization technologies and standards, often on the fly, to a larger set of political ideals. The volunteers working on digitization at the archives move with great care, forethought, and caution in designing and implementing digitization projects that will support the organization's long-standing mandates to preserve and share lesbian histories while also making the tools of archiving widely accessible. These volunteers extend information activism into the future as they find ways to make lesbian histories come alive through digital interfaces. This chapter shows how lesbian politics and digital technologies are entangled through the imaginative technical labor volunteers perform at the LHA. Their work matters in how we understand digitization more broadly, because it offers alternative models in practice for improving technological accessibility, doing digitization ethically, and seeking justice in how data are created to represent marginalized communities.

Guided by a lesbian-feminist mandate, and drawing on a long history of do-it-yourself (DIY) feminist appropriations of consumer media technologies such as videotape and index cards, the LHA balances a desire to digitize to better serve its public with commitments to ideals such as self-funding of the archives from within the community and a willful embrace of capable amateurism that demands the accessibility of archival tools to volunteers of all ages and abilities. The archives are digitizing their spoken-word tapes and photography collection and upgrading their catalog to move online, using a variety of cobbled-together tools, blocks of irregular volunteer hours, and varied levels of expertise. Emerging out of this ongoing negotiation are thoughtful digital tactics through which the community archives reimagines ideals such as acquisition, access, and the lifespan of ephemeral documents.

Digitization at the LHA is an expansive set of practices not limited to the creation of digital files from "analog" sources; digitizing also encompasses online user-interface design and implementation, descriptive metadata assignment, and the selection of which materials to offer online. Digitizing the archives' holdings is a process that extends beyond the act of scanning an image. This extension is, of course, temporal: the process goes backward in time to decisions that were made before the scanner lid is lifted, such as discussing what it would mean to offer access to "private" snapshots online, deciding how to allocate volunteer hours to the project, or choosing which scanner to buy. After the act, there are choices to make about how to classify a digital object in the database, and more long-range considerations, such as how to decide when the project is "finished."

At every level, these choices matter to the archives' volunteers and the queer and lesbian publics they serve. The LHA's shift to using digital technologies in work processes and outreach takes up established methods for doing information activism toward building unique lesbian feminist information infrastructures. Volunteer digital archivists perform information-management techniques that are similar, in many ways, to those of the newsletter makers, hotline operators, and indexers who appeared in previous chapters. They think deeply about how to mediate information about lesbian history as they design online engagements.

This chapter explores digital archives as sites where lesbian feminist information activism moves online through a focused study of the LHA's digitization practices. I chose the Lesbian Herstory Archives because they are the largest lesbian-focused community archives in the United States and Canada, and a monolith in dyke culture. Although records span the twentieth and twenty-first centuries, the LHA has been most successful at documenting the late twentieth-century lesbian-feminist political movements out of which it emerged.[3] Records document the archives' own imbrication in the larger information infrastructures explored in previous chapters: the LHA facilitated information sharing through newsletter networks, provided material support for bibliographers and indexers, and was one among dozens of places to which a hotline caller might be referred in search of information.

My methods draw on archival research in the organization's records of its own work and interviews with the volunteers most closely engaged with designing and carrying out digitization. I conducted unstructured interviews with six volunteers leading these projects, five of whom were coordinators (collaborative administrators) of the archives.[4] They ranged in age from the early twenties to early seventies. Three were white, and three were women of color. I also interviewed figures adjacent to this work, including Beth Haskell, a former volunteer who led the archives' transition to computing in the 1980s, and Anthony Cocciolo, an information studies professor at Pratt Institute whose students help the archives with digitization work. Finally, I interviewed two summer interns engaged with shorter-term digitization projects.[5] I refer to volunteers by first name to signal the feeling of community space and horizontal power structure at place in the organization, as well as my own feelings of closeness to the archives that developed during the months I spent researching, interviewing, and volunteering there.

I began these interviews in 2013, when the LHA was several years into digitization work. Because these projects were at an intermediate stage, volunteers remembered rich details about their origins but could also offer perspective on how the projects had evolved through trial and error and where they might go next. Following up on these interviews as I completed this book five years later, I learned that the projects continued, with small changes: the archives had started an Instagram account to share digitized photographs and begun digitizing videotape in partnership with Pratt. Aside from these developments, digitization carries on through volunteers' everyday investments of their labor. More photos have been scanned and put online; more tapes from the basement have been preserved; and more data from the archives' catalog have been standardized, bit by bit.

This chapter begins by introducing how the archives' lesbian-feminist political orientations guide its approach to digital technologies. The next section examines how this broader orientation manifests in a practical, good-enough approach in which committed volunteer labor and a belief in collective organizing drives digitization projects. Turning to a history of technological decision making at the LHA, I show that contemporary digitization work builds on computing politics developed in practice since the early 1980s. Finally, I analyze how volunteers think about, write, and revise the data describing the archives' materials in online databases, specifically considering how this lesbian archives' evolving trans collections policies are worked out, in part, through practical work with databases.

In its most basic form, digitization converts analog data, including images, video, and text, to digital forms so they can be processed, stored, or viewed on computers.[6] Digitization has become an expectation publics have of archives, whose users may not be occupied with questions about preservation, but anticipate that online interfaces will be the means through which they encounter holdings. Digitization in queer archival contexts addresses this expectation through an affective and transmedial process Daniel Brouwer and Adela Licona call a "third space between print and digital."[7] Deciding to digitize an object imagines new queer networks in which it might circulate, along with a different kind of life for the object. An encounter with a digital object is perhaps less tactile than its "analog" counterpart but remains grounded in a sense of that analog object's former life. Digitization, for Brouwer and Licona, is a site of deep ambivalence and even mourning for the mediated, relational life-worlds afforded by the queer of color zine archives they study. A digitized issue of a zine or newsletter does not carry the same records of use and wear apparent on a print copy shared by generations of archives users.

Digitization changes the kinds of encounters we have with objects because, quite simply, different media *feel* different.[8] Queer digital archives built by community groups find ways to maintain traces of how objects were used by activists, such as the high-resolution photographs of actual tapes that accompany each streaming audio file produced by the Lesbian Herstory Archives (figure 4.1). These tapes have sticky paper labels, handwritten by their makers in different colors of ink, using unique scripts and terminology. Although users encounter these tapes as two-dimensional JPEGs, the close-up images lend tactility and a clear sense of format to streaming audio files.

Despite efforts to do this transmedial work at grassroots organizations such as the LHA, most digital "archives" of LGBTQ+ materials work at a pace informed by user demand and the business end of primary source databases. More and more undergraduate students manage to avoid ever setting foot in a library, thanks to the wide availability of full-text databases and ebooks. These include online collections of primary source materials created by scanning community archives collections. Large clearinghouses such as Gale's Primary Sources produce themed microfilm and digital collections of full-text LGBTQ materials.[9] Gale's LGBT Rights Movement & Activists series draws from many LGBTQ community archives, including

FIGURE 4.1 Photograph of digitized cassette tape from the Buffalo Women's Oral History Project, which accompanies streaming audio on the Lesbian Herstory Archives's digital collections site. Identifying information was redacted by the archives before this image was posted online (see top right). The image was created by the Projects in Digital Archives course at Pratt Institute's School of Information: Judy T., "Judy T., 1978 (Tape 2)," Herstories: Audio/Visual Collections of the LHA, accessed May 13, 2019, http://herstories.prattinfoschool.nyc/omeka/document /SPW451. Image courtesy Lesbian Herstory Educational Foundation.

the LHA's subject files and newsletter collection.[10] These digitization companies pay community archives large sums of money to scan their collections as part of mass digitization initiatives, which can involve bringing industrial document scanners and outside contract workers into these community spaces for weeks at a time.[11] Contracts generally provide copies of digitized files for the community archives' use, but at a lower resolution and without metadata, limiting their usability. These lump-sum payments and long-term royalty structures are enticing for community organizations that rely primarily on small donations and grants.

Gale and their competitors place these amalgamated collections behind paywalls that do not align with the community archiving values through which these materials were originally acquired. This matters because mass digitization has made more LGBTQ+ historical materials available online, but behind paywalls, for those with access to university libraries that can afford subscriptions. In comparison, the digitization work carried out by volunteers at community archives may be modest in scale but has a much wider reach.

Digitization takes on a hegemonic function in the strategic planning of libraries and archives through a combination of factors that include user expectation, the service-oriented shift in undergraduate education, the political economy of academic publishing, and technological change. I call this the "digital imperative": the idea that digitization is a necessary, inherently progressive process archives must carry out to stay relevant and preserve their holdings. Information professionals work under constant pressure from institutional employers, granting agencies, and users to invest time and financial resources in measures that will provide easy online access to materials.

Set apart from these large institutions, the LHA works through but also around the digital imperative, developing tools, procedures, and pacing through the archives' political and community ties. This volunteer-run community archives operates on a shoestring budget funded mostly by individual donations—the LHA will not accept state-supported grants and is skeptical of institutional partnerships.[12] The LHA is part of a larger community archives tradition that relies on volunteers, donations, and intergenerational knowledge sharing.[13] These community archives can be understood as activist organizations that redress the "symbolic annihilation" of marginalized sexual and gender expression from the historical record.[14] Many of these archives were founded by or grew significantly through the gay liberation and women's liberation movements and have collections that showcase the cultural heritage materials produced through this activism. LGBTQ community archives operate as vital technologies for survival and political organizing and evidence a long history of this work.[15]

The LHA responds to the intersection of LGBTQ activism and feminism with a statement of purpose that makes explicit the ways in which lesbian history, like all women's experience, is underrepresented: "The process of gathering this material will uncover and collect our herstory denied to us previously by patriarchal historians in the interests of the culture which they serve."[16] These lesbian-feminist goals emphasize the need to provide not only safekeeping for, but, moreover, *access to* lesbian materials. This access is disarticulated from instrumental research goals, emphasizing the emotional relations to objects ignored by conventional archives.[17] Writing in 1990, the LHA's cofounder Joan Nestle described wanting to satisfy a lesbian public's desires rather than any single research agenda: "We had to clarify that our archives, our family album, our library, was not primarily for academic scholars but for any lesbian woman who needed an image or a word to survive the day."[18] Here Nestle connects information access with the affective labor involved in building archives, which are technologies for everyday survival. Digitization can extend these goals by facilitating scrolling, browsing, and searching practices for lesbian and queer researchers, and community members, who still need these words and images today.

To satisfy these needs, an evolving, intergenerational committee of coordinators manages the archives, making decisions on a consensus basis.[19] The archives' founders, Nestle and Deborah (Deb) Edel, have remained on the coordinating committee into their seventies. The archives were originally housed in their apartment—they were lovers at the time. The archives are administered today very much as they were then. Most coordinators also work at the LHA, staffing open hours, leading tours, and processing collections alongside a loyal group of interns and volunteers, many of whom are information studies students in their twenties.

Materials are spread over the basement and first two stories of the archives' three-story brownstone in Park Slope, while the top floor is home to the archives' caretaker in residence, who also serves on the coordinating committee. The collection includes vertical subject files on dozens of topics related to lesbian culture (bathhouses, fat liberation, matriarchy, nuns, utopia, women of color), a book collection, three thousand spoken-word tapes, videos, "special collections" that consist of personal papers donated by individuals and organizations, periodicals, and all kinds of artifacts, including sex toys, buttons, posters, and T-shirts. The space feels unlike a conventional archive in that there are cozy reading nooks, macramé adornments, and a kitchen where coffee is often brewing, and visitors are allowed to access and handle any part of the collection without prior request (figures 4.2 and 4.3).

Tactility and in-the-flesh encounters with lesbian history are fundamental to this archives' design, and digital interfaces do not immediately map on to the LHA's established model for connecting with visitors. This warm, welcoming environment is deliberately constructed to reflect, in material terms, the archives' guiding commitments that "all Lesbian women must have access to the Archives," which "shall be housed in the community."[20] The "Statement of Principles," first written in 1979 and updated often since, includes several collection and admission policies that influence the LHA's decisions about technology, including an anti-institutional position (one coordinator I interviewed wouldn't say the word "Google" because of its

FIGURE 4.2 The desk at the Lesbian Herstory Archives' first office in the apartment of Joan Nestle and Deborah Edel, late 1970s. Image courtesy the Lesbian Herstory Educational Foundation.

FIGURE 4.3 Upstairs computer station at the Lesbian Herstory Archives, 2013. Photograph by the author.

corporate connotations), rejecting funding that isn't community based, making archival tools accessible to volunteers of all abilities, and training volunteer staff without archival experience.[21]

These feminist commitments at the Lesbian Herstory Archives complicate normative imperatives that can accompany digitization, such as purchasing expensive tools or pursuing project-based funding that can compromise long-term organizational goals. The archives' mandate, history, organizational structures, and intergenerational volunteer base act as the guiding, sometimes acrimonious, political frame within which the organization makes practical, ethical, and, above all, *everyday* choices about media technologies. In other words, digital media are not a neutral site exempt from the LHA's lesbian-feminist politics, past and present. Choices about interface design, hardware and software, the selection of materials to digitize, and classification schemes remediate the purposeful and always political design of information infrastructures by lesbian-feminist activists in the 1970s, '80s, and '90s.

Digitization foregrounds one way in which lesbian feminism, as a political orientation and a reason for working together, is ongoing. Digital information can become a site of tension between the history and identity-laden category "lesbian" and queerness, which is often figured as highly mobile in its digital manifestations.[22] Through digital technologies, lesbian information circulates among a network on a different scale: the small, print-based networks built among subscribers to a single print newsletter are tiny, enclaved counterpublics when compared with the wide-reaching, diverse, and dispersed publics who might access digital collections or peruse the archives' Instagram account.[23] Online, information activism finds a somewhat invisible audience of many different sexualities and genders, whose encounters with the history of lesbian feminism in the present engender collisions or attachment formations that cannot be fully anticipated or traced.[24]

The LHA views its lesbian-feminist stance as necessary for providing the kind of digital archival system that can accommodate the unusual, messy, emotional, queer cultural "material" that the archives house.[25] Yet the archives' identity politics also impose organizing logics, classifying materials and the lives they index through evolving subject headings that emerge out of larger political and philosophical conversations about the kinds of gendered subjects and bodies that come to matter as "lesbian." Like the Circle of Lesbian Indexers' always-in-process approach to its subject thesaurus, taxonomy at the LHA remains as open to revision as possible. A prominent example from my research is that the archives grapple on an ongoing basis with how to describe accurately and sensitively the collections of trans (most often trans-masculine) donors who have varied, complex relations to the category "lesbian," a matter on which members of the coordinating committee sometimes disagree. The archives' formal attention to how lesbian-adjacent trans narratives are told in the process of writing data is one instance of how archival politics shift through their entanglement with media and information technologies. The opening up of both "lesbian" and archival standards happens in and through this kind of work as it unfolds. Queer cultural politics and aesthetics shape how online media technologies are deployed in historical, archival, and commemorative lesbian-feminist contexts.

Distinctions between queer and lesbian feminism are deliberately cloudy in my analysis and experience of the LHA. Previous chapters approached lesbian feminism as an identity-based, coalitional position staked out against both patriarchy and the mainstreaming of women's liberation-era feminism and invested in information work as a way to extend these commitments and build counterpublic capacities. Turning to the twenty-first century in this chapter, lesbian feminism is also an ongoing position that generates attachments to the past that have both material and affective implications for the present.[26] Many of the archives' volunteers readily identify as lesbians, and the LHA sees itself as an institution whose primary, ongoing responsibility is to a lesbian public. Intergenerational encounters are made possible via the wide age range among coordinators. I assumed, wrongly, going into this research that "lesbian" as a specific term of identification had fallen out of favor with a younger generation of queer-identified activists. Young volunteers articulate deep attachments to lesbian history and to dyke culture partly through their own identities and aesthetics.[27] As I explore in the epilogue, expressing attachment to lesbian history by wearing a labrys necklace or identifying as "high femme" is part of a broader trend toward mediated but also embodied engagement with these histories.

At the same time, young volunteers are often fresh out of gender studies classrooms, and their work at the archives is steeped in theoretical understandings of queerness as a shifting signifier, often articulated in opposition to categorical identity. Queerness weaves its way through the LHA via the broader political milieu in which this service organization operates. Longtime volunteers understand the shifting needs and diverse identifications of the archives' public, even when "lesbian" might remain a comfortable position for them as individuals. Coordinators and volunteers want to serve a diverse group of researchers, and anyone is welcome in the space. I watched this open policy in practice many times during my research period.

Queerness and lesbian feminism operate in complex interrelation at the archives; they are perhaps inseparable in any real sense. Still, being aware of their potential to oppose each other in a crude analytic sense is useful for understanding the historical acrimonies and ongoing tensions through which volunteers approach digitization work. This chapter questions the temporal logics that bracket lesbian feminism to the past and place queerness ever in the future. Lesbian feminism was and is queer when queer is thought of as an intervention with archival norms. Building on previous scholarship on queer temporality, we might understand this as the *queer time of lesbian archives.*[28]

Here I am indebted to Ann Cvetkovich's research on the LHA. Cvetkovich holds lesbian feminism's identitarian commitments in productive tension with the space's queer archival impulses, documenting the "queer collections and strategies" at work in the grassroots lesbian archives.[29] The archives become a site where past, present, and future meet through the rubric of feeling; such is the encounter staged by what she calls "queer lesbian archives."[30] Similarly, Jack Gieseking dismisses the possibility that the "Lesbian Herstory Archives can be read as solely a lesbian, feminist, and/or lesbian feminist project." The LHA is both lesbian-feminist and "a predecessor and ancestor to queer ideas and concepts." Gieseking insists that "the experience of the social and spatial Lesbian Herstory Archives demonstrates what can be generated by holding a dialectic in tension while working firmly against the projects of heteronormativity and patriarchy."[31]

José Muñoz's work on futurity further shapes my approach to the archives as a space of encounter between lesbian feminist and queer. Muñoz theorizes queerness as a future orientation that is perhaps unrealizable in any concrete, here-and-now form. He writes, "Queerness is a structuring and educated mode of desiring that allows us to see and feel beyond the quagmire of the present."[32] Although Muñoz writes about futurity, his words provide a brilliant take on archives as sites of temporal rupture; queerness becomes an educated mode of desiring history *in order to desire a future.* Archives and their information infrastructures are "quagmire(s) of the present" in which this complex desire for history as futurity is managed.

Debates over the appropriateness and scale of the archives' digitization projects are conversations situated in larger, emotionally and politically informed relationships among volunteers who have commitments to differ-

Chapter Four

ent kinds of feminism. Young volunteers orient to the space of the archives following forms of socialization and affective interpellation to lesbian history via actually existing lesbians. In other words, they learn how to be community archivists from experienced women whom they look up to and admire. The erotics of activist mentorship at the LHA transcends the normative expectations of skill development and résumé building associated with internships. At a previous internship, Colette said, she "worked in a really toxic environment. . . . [P]eople were just not queer friendly . . . , [and] they don't typically hire anyone of color to work." When I asked Colette what she liked about working at the LHA, she said, "Everyone's just so nice, and you can be open about who you are. It's comfortable, and you can chat with everybody, and the material is really fascinating. . . . I like the social aspect, and I like working on stuff that matters to me as a person."

Working intergenerationally matters to Colette for many reasons, the most important of which is mentorship. "I've learned so much from Maxine [Wolfe] because she knows everything about everybody," Colette said. "At the same time, if I come here and Maxine's not here, I've learned a lot from a lot of the older women who are here, like Teddy and Deb." Colette likens this one-on-one mentorship to what it means to listen to the stories of older generations of queer women on the tapes she digitizes: "It's just interesting to hear their stories and feel like, wow, people lived such almost scary lives. They didn't know. . . . Of course, you know all that theoretically, but hearing these individual women tell their life stories, it's really powerful." These women lived queer lives that Colette could imagine only in theory before hearing their stories, with which she then identified deeply.

Working intimately alongside older women matters to Colette, who connects her reverence for intergenerational mentorship to her queer but also Indigenous identity: "I'm American Indian, and I was always taught that you respect, that there's always something to learn from people of other generations. I think Native American culture, at least mine, is very focused on intergenerational learning and talking and everything. Working with Maxine, it's cool." Ronika McClain, a person of color in her twenties, also described her experience of identity in relating what she likes about working on the photography collection with Saskia Scheffer, who is white and in her fifties:

I'm twenty-one [at time of interview]. . . . I came out as queer when I was in high school, but I was sort of in this place where I didn't really feel like I had any sort of tie to history or community. I grew up in the

[San Francisco] Bay area, and my parents are Mormon. I feel like every time Saskia will pull out a folder, it will be someone I don't know, and Saskia will teach me about who they are. . . . I feel like there's so much information that I feel really lucky to be able to learn from her, as well, and have her perspective on the history of the archives.

Just as the Circle of Lesbian Indexers' members saw their work as a gift from their hands to the hands of their "daughters," any archiving project imagines a future subject for whom what is archived has value and relevance. To some extent, these subjects will inadvertently and perhaps productively fail this project because they may not use what is archived toward the ends for which it was intended. As Robyn Wiegman argues, "Objects can resist what we try to make of them [because] objects of study are bound to multiple relationships, such that the conscious attempt to refuse an identification is in no way a guarantee that one can, let alone that one has done so."[33] Building on Wiegman's work, Kadji Amin argues that the idealization of queer history "binds us to the circular process [of] idealization, disappointment, and the search for a new object thought to be better able to fulfill the aspirations of the field."[34] The multivalent relationship among lesbian, queer, feminist, ascendency, and refusal negotiated at the archives is further complicated in the face of trans. What is perceived as "queer" can quickly stabilize as a recapitulation of gay/lesbian politics when trans identities, or bodies in transition, are introduced into archives, challenging their sensibilities of accumulation and capture.[35]

"Woman Power" and the Digital Imperative

As a hegemonic operation, what I call the "digital imperative" relies on the construction of norms of practice in archives. Perceptions of what institutional archives are doing with digitization becomes a standard against which other institutions measure themselves. This professional standard is set against community archives to articulate what it is that makes them "community" archives in the first place.[36] But there is a significant gap between the perceptions publics have about what deep-pocketed institutions are doing, or ought to be doing, to digitize their collections and the actual standards of practice in these archives. Paper and microfilm are thought to be more stable and cost-effective preservation formats than the creation of a digital file, so institutions have sometimes prioritized this kind of duplication.[37] Due to budget constraints and staffing issues, large institutions often take temporary, stop-gap measures with materials as they are acquired instead of digitizing them as part of an initial processing procedure.[38] This can include the "disk in a box" approach to managing born-digital acquisitions, which literally means placing a disk in an acid-free box among the stacks, a procedure that "can result in easy media degradation and format obsolescence when the media ages out of sight and out of mind."[39] The perception that digitization is *the way forward* for twenty-first-century archives, and the primary task institutional archivists work on is out of step with actual practices.

And yet the assumption that large-scale digitization is the rightful domain of deep-pocketed institutions persists and seems to discourage LGBTQ community archives from taking on these kinds of projects on a large scale.[40] When I began this research in 2013, other community-based LGBTQ archives appeared to be hesitant to undertake even partial digitization of their collections, partly because of a perception that these projects, any way one imagined them, were beyond the capacity of available labor hours, expertise, and financial resources.[41] While sharing my research at conferences or during visits to other LGBTQ archives, I often told volunteers and professional archivists about digitization at the Lesbian Herstory Archives and was consistently greeted with surprise at the kinds of projects they have dared to imagine and carry out with a relatively small volunteer base and limited outside institutional support. In the intervening years, digitization has become more widespread in LGBTQ community archives. This is due to the wider accessibility of digital collections tool, more literacy around "tagging" digital objects (creating metadata), and popularity of sharing archival documents via social media platforms, to be sure.[42] But the models provided by ambitious organizations such as the LHA are perhaps another, less formal lineage for this turn at community archives.

The LHA's ambitious pursuit of digitization initiatives is unexpected, given the organization's limited financial resources. In general, digitization's high cost, combined with limited staff hours and related lack of adequate database records, present common challenges to digitization for community archives.[43] Given the rarity of LGBTQ+ archival materials and the danger of deterioration, digitization and online access are more vital in these archives.[44] The ongoing accessibility of small collections depends on archives' having the means to provide materials with long-term custody, which can mean simply keeping track of where materials are located in storage and keeping good records that document where they came from and what they represent. Lacking these records can lead to the accidental neglect or destruction of the material in question.[45]

Digitization *can* be expensive—prohibitively so for community archives. These organizations must consider the staff resources and equipment required to initially digitize material, data storage needs, bandwidth and server space costs, ongoing staff costs, and "migration" costs, which means transferring digital files from one format to another as technology changes.[46] Outsourcing this work to a third-party vendor is beyond the means of almost all grassroots organizations. The LHA has some large-format, U-matic videocassettes in its collection, which were the archival standard among broadcasters from the mid-1970s through the early 1990s. During my time at the archives, an intern tasked with researching preservation of U-matic tapes explained that the archives had been quoted a rate of $1,000 per tape from a third-party digitization outlet. The intern, a library science student specializing in moving-image preservation, spoke with confidence and expertise, explaining the crux of the problem to me: once a broadcast standard, this particular format is no longer in use, and the machines that can play the tapes are not manufactured or serviced. So while audiocassettes, photographs, and even VHS tape can be digitized in-house, digitizing U-matic cassettes, Zip disks, and other obsolete or obscure formats without outside support can present insurmountable hardware challenges.

Preserving these tapes is one problem, providing access to them is another: researchers can't watch the tapes because the archives does not have a U-matic playback machine. Media-archaeology approaches in the digital humanities build working labs in which old hardware is restored and maintained so that obsolete formats such as U-matic tape can be played.[47] Video archives do the same, and offer access to digitization services for a fee. These labs are beyond the technical and financial resources of community archives.

While community archives often receive donations of old equipment, the machines tend to be commercial-grade VHS and DVD players rather than working or serviceable Beta or U-matic players. Volunteer-led digitization of videotape at community archives is possible—the ArQuives: Canada's LGBTQ2S+ Archives has begun to do this work with VHS tape—but requires well-maintained, reliable equipment and massive digital storage capacity (uncompressed video files are large). Simply having a working U-matic player in house at the LHA would offer access to these tapes via the original means of display but would not preserve degrading videotape.

If U-matic or VHS tapes in the collection were digitized, the archives would need to deal with uncompressed master files—that is, large quantities of data that must be stored securely and described well with metadata—to actually provide the "preservation" digitization promises. Large quantities of data present a problem for community archives.[48] As Maxine Wolfe (white, in her seventies), the longtime LHA coordinator told me, "Mostly what we're lacking is a server . . . because you really need someone who is a full-time technician, because servers go down."[49] Large institutions build and maintain robust Trustworthy Digital Repositories (TDRS) to store and monitor the stability of digital objects in their archives. For community archives, TDRS are an expensive, technically complex pipe dream. Partnering with universities and other public institutions willing to donate space on their stable servers is possible. Online access copies of photographs and audio/video files are stored on the servers of the Metropolitan New York Library Council and Pratt Institute, respectively. The Lesbian Herstory Archives maintains control of the master files, storing digitized photographs and audio files on a series of redundant external hard drives. For community archives, storing material on outside servers can come with strings attached or raise concerns about maintaining community ownership over data in the long term.

U-matic tapes are an example of a format that cannot really be digitized without specialized technology, expert input, and significant cost. Other formats support a DIY approach. Audiocassette tapes and still photographs can be digitized by volunteers using consumer-grade equipment and a fearless approach to working with media technology. Undertaking the work of digitization in-house can be just as daunting as figuring out what to do with tapes of an unfamiliar size: equipment such as hard drives, computers, high-quality scanners, audio digitizers, and software can be expensive to purchase, difficult to integrate into existing systems, and need to be maintained and replaced as they become obsolete.

Talking with the volunteers at the archives about their digitization projects and the archives more generally gives a clear picture of the LHA's rootedness in a long history of organizing in pursuit of what *seems like* too much to take on. The Lesbian Herstory Archives have always worked ambitiously to sort and create data about media in their collection, using a collaborative and consensus-based model. When the archives moved into their Park Slope home in the early 1990s, volunteers began the process of cataloging the unruly, ten-thousand-volume book collection. Working together, volunteers set up an accessible protocol for creating catalog records and met once a month as a working group to refine this process. Book by book, they cataloged the collection, completing the task over five years.

A working-group model structures most long-term projects at the archives. During my time there I became a part of the Special Collections Working Group. My assigned volunteer work involved working mostly alone, one day a week, processing special collections by organizing material into folders and creating a detailed finding aid and catalog record. This work can be interesting when it requires conceptual, high-level decisions about how to organize a collection. Decisions I made mediate access to these materials, shaping the collection's usability for future researchers. Most of the time, though, archival labor can be isolating and painstaking. To learn how collections are processed, I rolled up my sleeves and spent two days organizing a box filled with hundreds of party flyers from Shescape, a for-profit, New York-based lesbian party promoter popular in the 1990s. Most of the flyers were duplicates, which needed to be identified and removed from the collection, turning the task into an unending children's memory card game steeped in '90s "lesbian-chic" aesthetics. I did enjoy chatting with other volunteers around the main-floor work table. I learned how to perform basic materials-processing tasks such as deciding how to organize a collection into folders and describing materials by writing a finding aid to guide future researchers.

Rachel Corbman, the coordinator in charge of special collections, patiently taught me how to do this work. I continued to use these skills when I returned home to Toronto and the ArQuives, where, alongside other volunteers, I processed the papers of the trans artist, activist, and sex worker, Mirha-Soleil Ross.[50] My trajectory shows how the LHA contributes to a broader, grassroots community archiving movement by teaching interested volunteers the practical skills of archiving. The tasks involved in this work helped me develop a hands-on understanding of my research objects and gave me the skills to become an amateur archivist in my own community. Despite these outcomes, most of the job was repetitive and slow. I learned quickly that running archives generates work that is not always glamorous or fun.

The small tasks required to steward collections into the future make the archives' political project possible, just as this larger political project allows the everyday work to feel tenable. Feminism is critical of the present and oriented toward an alternative future, running on what Sara Ahmed calls "strange and perverse mixtures of hope and despair, optimism and pessimism."[51] As an affect modality, feminist activism turns on a complex temporality in which investments in a particular vision of the past from which "we" have come and the future to which "we" aspire motivate action in the present. This temporal formation is particularly salient in archives; establishing a complete lesbian history is an undoubtedly utopian endeavor: an imagined alternative future aspired to despite the possibility that this future may not be realizable. It is precisely failure, loss, and impossibility that motivate the ongoing regeneration of feminism in the present.[52] Wiegman describes this "pedagogy of failure," in which feminism is always chasing the materialization of the desires we invest in it, as "the constitutive condition of feminism's futurity."[53]

In this respect, feminism as an ideal operates in the realm of imagination and aspiration. Joan Scott argues that we owe some of feminism's political manifestations to "the operations of fantasies that can never fully satisfy the desire, or secure the representation, they seek to provide."[54] Grand ideals and fantastic visions manifest in more modest feminist collectives, events, and spaces that attempt to produce conditions denied elsewhere. Feminist archives develop supportive structures for the kind of historical research that is devalued by other institutions. Feminist archival activism is motivated by an end to the violence of historical erasure, so feminist archives act "as sites of promise and desire."[55] In micro-moments such as creating a finding aid or sorting out duplicate party fliers, the larger vision can be glimpsed; it is precisely the oscillation between this idealization and an everyday practice of living—what *I can do right now*—that motivates feminists to carry on with their work, however modest it may seem: sorting index cards, putting mailing labels on newsletters, answering the telephone every time it rings.

Victoria Hesford has described this oscillation in the context of the early 1970s women's liberation movement out of which the Lesbian Herstory Archives was formed. Hesford identifies a divide between the "world-making intentions of women's liberation" and the "micropolitics of vacuuming and sexual intercourse as sites for feminist resistance," charged political sites that can be written off as unimportant because of their everyday character.[56] These sites are where "the personal as political" meets everyday work with tools, including media technologies. Situated in this realm of the micropolitical, small, everyday dents in substantial projects take on a significance that makes the larger project seem feasible. This is less a pedagogy of failure than a pedagogy of perpetually catching up: hope mitigated by frustration produces a gap that can be measured by each small attempt to fill it. The everyday work of running the LHA, the cataloging of one book among thousands, is a modest, singular act driven by hope about what the archives, and lesbian history, could be.

Maxine, who is one of the archives' longest-serving coordinators and who leads the audio digitization project with Colette, suggests that part of the LHA's readiness to take on what seem like massive digitization projects comes from this history of balancing what she calls a "vision of the world" with the smaller tasks required to get there.[57] A history of direct action guides Maxine's approach. She has been an activist all her life. Maxine grew up working-class Jewish in Brooklyn in the 1940s and '50s. She got involved in civil rights organizing as a college student in the early 1960s and then in feminist activism in the late 1960s and '70s.[58] She started working at the LHA in the early 1980s and was an organizer with the AIDS Coalition to Unleash Power (ACT UP) from the group's inception in 1987.

As a lifelong direct-action practitioner, Maxine understands how a single action designed to achieve one small, attainable change can contribute to a much larger politic. Referencing her own biography as an activist, Maxine likened what motivated her work with ACT UP—"a vision of a world without AIDS"—to the archives' campaign to purchase a building in the late 1980s:

> I always say, about everything that I do, including when I was in ACT UP: you need to have a vision. Like in AIDS, I have a vision of a world without AIDS. If you don't have a vision of world without AIDS, you can't make it happen. Anything that you do you have to [have a vision]. We bought this house with no money. We had no money in the bank. We had no income. We bought a $300,000 house with no money in the bank, no guaranteed income, and figured out a way to get a bank to lend us a mortgage. You can only do that if you have a vision. You have to believe you can do it.[59]

Turning a vision of what the archives could be into a realistic, step-by-step plan, the LHA solicited donations and loans from community members to make a down payment and qualify for a mortgage on the Park Slope property, which opened to the public in 1993.

The grandiose is quickly translated into the mundane, everyday tasks needed to get there. Says Maxine, crediting one of the archives' founders Joan Nestle, "Joan was always that way. She always felt that you have to have a vision. You have to believe that you can do something. I think that's how we enter into everything. OK, so the books are going to take us six years [to catalog]. Where are we going? We're not going anywhere. We're just going to be here."[60] To facilitate working together efficiently on cataloging the books over many years, the archives developed a classification system and set of database standards that new volunteers could quickly learn and put into practice. Maxine explained the importance of thinking in a pedagogic and systematic way when designing collaborative approaches to organizing information: "If we develop a system where, as we do it, we know what we're doing, then it's not going to get screwed up. That's why it has dots [color coded, on the books' spines]. It was a whole system developed that made it possible to do it over time. Because you couldn't know what was in there and what wasn't in there [in advance]."[61]

These kinds of information management projects take work—work that is inevitably gendered, both because of the lesbian scope of the archives and, more generally, because of the ways in which volunteerism and behind-the-scenes, glamourless tasks are often carried out by women, trans people, and people of color. Describing the kind of volunteerism that makes years of laboring at a seemingly insurmountable task seem reasonable, Maxine uses the phrase "woman power," evoking the language and iconography of the women's liberation movement: "So we've been wanting to digitize everything, as much as we possibly can, and anything we haven't done already, it's a matter of woman power and not of not wanting to do it." The concept of "woman power" describes a feminist approach to laboring with information toward helping one's community, very much in line with information activism more generally. Says Maxine, "I would say that it is a feminist thing. It's a kind of belief in the women who come here. That they're coming here to help the archives, to help make this place be. And be available."[62]

Much of the actual, everyday work that gets done at the archives is carried out by interns and volunteers in their twenties. Some are enrolled in information studies programs to become librarians or archivists and receive practicum credit for their work. Library and information studies are gendered professions: the majority of students at information schools are women. This is also true of the profession historically.[63] The political economy of internships in the culture industries is similarly gendered.[64] Skills in digital archives management are sought after by the Lesbian Herstory Archives when they recruit interns from the information schools in the New York City area. As Maxine put it, "The last couple of years, Imogen [the coordinator responsible for modernizing the archives database] has been great at getting library interns who want to do digitization stuff but also have a specific amount of time to give that's larger. So I think that's how we do it."[65] The steady, intensive labor these interns perform is key to sustaining the ongoing pace of digitization at the archives. Coordinators with day jobs or other community-based commitments mentor these interns, most of whom have chosen to work at the LHA because of deep, abiding interests in lesbian history. The "woman hours" that keep the archives operational are part of a feminist practice of being both willing and available to do the hard, often thankless work required to effect change. This readiness likewise informs the archives' approach to digitization.

Digitization as Improvisation

There is something quite brave yet totally unassuming in the way Maxine and other archives volunteers describe what motivates their engagement with digitization projects at the archives. This technological bravery is exemplified by the audio digitization project's willingness to not only make do with available resources but also understand a DIY approach as part of the organization's commitment to technological accessibility. Although the LHA is traditionally wary of institutional partnerships, it answered an inquiry Pratt's Anthony Cocciolo posted on a listserv in 2008 looking for community-based oral history tapes that his students could digitize. Cocciolo's teaching and research support LGBTQ community groups as they establish digital archives in ways that center community members' values and skills.[66] Each semester, Cocciolo works with students in his Projects in Digital Archives course to digitize a selection of the LHA tapes, which are then offered online as streaming audio.[67] Students not only practice the technical skills involved in doing this work but also learn how lesbian feminist politics shape the practice of archiving. Students learn about the community's approach to categorizing materials and making ethical choices about what to put online.

Cocciolo's students started with the archives' audio collection and later expanded their work to include videotape. Maxine selects grouped, thematic collections of tapes for the students to work on, ensuring that the archives has explicit permission to offer access to these materials online.[68] The Pratt-led project has created highly visible digital collections for some of the archives' most popular audiovisual holdings, but thousands of other tapes in the collection also require digitization to preserve the stories they tell, as audio tape degrades, dries out, and can snap over time. Modeling an in-house system on the ongoing Pratt-led project, the LHA works diligently on its own, small-scale digitization of the bulk of the collection. Maxine, Colette, and other volunteers work on this project, listening to each tape to create a catalog record; interpreting donor agreement forms to confirm that audio may be circulated online; and creating uncompressed, preservation-quality masters and compressed, noise-reduced, streaming-ready MP3 versions of each tape.

The precious audio recorded on these tapes documents an exciting time in U.S.-based feminist organizing and constitutes the material remnants of an active feminist oral history movement that was politically conscious of its role in constructing documentary evidence of women's history. There are big names—speeches and readings by Adrienne Rich, Audre Lorde, Cherríe Moraga, Barbara Smith, and Sarah Schulman—and big events, recorded without knowledge of how they would be memorialized. The Barnard College conference "The Scholar and the Feminist" of 1982, for instance, is often touted in retrospect as the moment when the porn wars exploded.[69] These "events" share space with more modest recordings: scratchy, hard-to-decipher sounds of some lesbians' birthday party. These "regular" recordings evidence the democratic ideals behind recording lesbian audio. Maxine, for example, mentioned "these two women in Minneapolis who tape-recorded every lesbian event they ever went to. It's called Radical Rose Recordings and they got every single person to agree that we could use it and tape it and digitize and do whatever we want with it."

When Maxine began to research how much it would cost to send the tapes out for digitization—which was far beyond the means of the archives—she learned that the expense was due mostly to labor hours: audio digitization must be completed in real time, regardless of whether it is done "professionally" or in-house. If the LHA has anything in abundance, it is "woman hours." Colette showed me the digitization system she researched and designed, which included a physical digitizer that connects a basic tape player to a laptop via a USB cable; the free, open-source audio software Audacity; two hard drives for storing digital files; and an access laptop where the compressed versions of each tape are cataloged for visiting researchers who want to listen.

The archives use the same software as Pratt but cobbled together a less expensive hardware system, including portable hard drives instead of the stable online repository the archives wants but cannot afford. Colette researched, designed, purchased, and operates this system and talked with pride about her ability to come up a system within the budget that works just as well as professional equipment. The system is, above all, good enough—the audio quality is remarkable, actually. A commercial-grade Behringer analog-to-digital converter does not quite replicate the professional standard 96,000 kiloHertz sample rate, but the difference represented by 48,000 kiloHertz is unintelligible when dealing with the kinds of scratchy, noisy sounds these tapes record.

Choices such as compromised fidelity put into practice an aesthetics of access that expand what it means to preserve records from a community archives perspective. The media studies scholar Lucas Hilderbrand attributes an "aesthetics of access" to videotape and the queer bootlegging cultures of pornography, art, and the video chain letter.[70] The "compromised" aesthetics that result from prioritizing access forces a confrontation with what we mean when we talk about preservation, the kinds of "degradations" we avoid, and what is lost in this avoidance. Celebrating access means privileging reproducibility and circulation over perfect fidelity and adherence to standards established elsewhere, outside the lesbian community. In the LHA context, this can mean recognizing that being able to listen to a tape and easily understand the audio is the primary purpose of digitization.

As is standard in audiocassette digitization, the archives create an unaltered master file from each tape and then a compressed, noise-reduced version aimed at accessibility. Old tapes often contain loud background "hiss" that can make speech hard to decipher—noise reduction removes the sound-waves that create this hiss, but can also clip the full spectrum of a narrator's voice, making the recording less "true" to the original audio. The archives does not yet create written transcripts, a slow, labor-intensive process of listening and typing that would significantly improve access, particularly for researchers with hearing impairments. Maxine recommends that researchers listen to the noise-reduced versions of audio files, even though they are compressed, to improve legibility. Because of noise reduction, she said, "Somebody who came here to listen to Audre Lorde's speech could hear her, despite the fact that it was at the March on Washington, and there were 9,000 sounds in the background." Like calling a telephone hotline, this is about the affective experience of listening to another person's voice in your ear, but it's also about an information activist approach to sharing information within necessary constraints that can be worked around. Says Maxine, "It's so different when you hear somebody, and you hear people talking about their lives. Even people listening to Audre Lorde's speeches— it's so different from reading them." "Hearing" Lorde and "listening" to her words means not only experiencing the sound of her voice, but also taking her words in as information that has been rendered more accessible through practices of noise reduction and compression.

Improved access and preservation, the goals most often attributed to digitization, exist in complex relation to each other. At times they are amenable; at other times, one must be prioritized over the other. For example, archives justify restricting access to original artifacts of which they have a digital copy to reduce the handling these artifacts receive (audiotapes wear out eventually, and playing tape that has dried out risks breaking it).[71] However, circulating digitized material online helps to ensure the modernization and survival of the archives by making a select group of high-demand materials readily accessible to a larger network of researchers and casual listeners. Online finding aids and catalog records also create access-oriented interfaces between the public and archival holdings, telling potential visitors what is available for research.

Digitization aimed at democratizing community access reaches non-professional researchers and distributes select archival materials online to those without institutional credentials.[72] Digitization can also conceal an implicit mandate of finding long-term institutional cost savings by deskilling information workers and reducing the obligation to provide *in-person* access to community members. Despite these concerns, digitization is thought to have a democratizing function overall. In community archives, digitation can be thought in a longer continuum of archival media practices that imagine opening up the field of who gets to participate in history making. Online access has the potential to shift who finds representation in history by making relevant primary sources available to marginalized researchers.[73]

While all digital archives want to provide access in some way, access has different valences for digitization at a community-oriented lesbian-feminist organization. Information activists have unique concerns about digital access, from aesthetics to ethical concerns about privacy and political choices about a chosen technology's cost and ease of use. For Hilderbrand, an aesthetics of access describes how investments in accessibility get distilled in media's formal qualities. The "technical faults" of stretched taped, noise, distortion, and tracking problems become "indexical evidence of use and duration through time."[74] Digitization makes a powerful promise to preserve original artifacts by preventing this kind of degradation, but the process can also exchange tactility, fidelity, and aura for access. This is not a bad thing. Colette's "good enough" technological decisions enact and celebrate formal qualities such as affordability and compression. These values manifest in a lower dynamic-frequency range and cleaned-up, noise-reduced files that offer users an easier listening experience but become less "authentically noisy" in the process. Noise-reduced oral history interviews, for example, privilege making it possible to understand a narrators' words by eliminating background noises and hiss over the full-spectrum authenticity of the original recording.

Colette showed me how to set up the digitization station, how to watch for and eliminate clipping, and how to reduce noise in files using Audacity, all of which she learned through a process of trial and error made possible by a willingness at this organization to try something at which one is not an expert, to be wrong, even to fail. The system's pace is a striking example of deceleration due to limited resources and collective models of deliberation and processing that contrast with the ever-faster speeds often articulated to digital modalities. Technology here is neither fetishized nor caught up in idealizations of digital mediation; rather, the slow pace required to operate a cumbersome but entirely functional audio digitization station is amenable to the archives' larger digitization strategy and what is possible in the now. This pace is unlike the fast feminisms practiced in other areas of digitally mediated life, such as in online meme culture, the ultimate celebration of collective feminist response speed.[75]

At the same time, work to bring feminist archives into digitally mediated spaces is often tactile, scrappy, and unremunerated labor. Cassius Adair and Lisa Nakamura's study of women of color online archives and the "digital afterlives" of *This Bridge Called My Back* recovers the networked labor and clandestine, activist scanning and copying practiced by women of color to ensure ongoing digital access to PDFs of this significant 1981 collection.[76] Adair and Nakamura document how activists stitched together many different files and scans as a form of antiracist feminist pedagogy—that the pagination is off, or that some pages are better scanned than others, is beside the point. Online feminist archives can be purposefully quick and dirty or methodical and careful, like the slow pace of digitizing tapes in real time. Both practices seek a digital future for feminism.

The Lesbian Herstory Archives works with limited resources, with volunteers in some cases literally rigging affordable technological systems together like lesbian MacGyvers or making do with accessible data storage that isn't perfect for the job. Colette researched and designed the system with guidance from Cocciolo, Maxine, and a sales person at the large B&H audiovisual store in New York City, where Colette "realized we could do it on the cheap because this thing [pointing to the digitizer] cost, like, ten dollars, and we get the same quality."[77] When I asked Maxine about the equipment, she resisted my framing of it as system apart from values of "professionalism":

Yeah, but that *is* professional. . . . When Anthony [Cocciolo began digitizing the tapes], I said to him, "What can we do here? How are you doing this?" . . . I found out that it's all being done in real time, and it doesn't matter if you have the most sophisticated lab in the world. . . . The stuff that we're doing is archival quality. Audacity is an open-source program that anybody can get, and it's archival quality. It's not shoddy, unprofessional stuff. And then we're backing it up on a hard drive. There's no such thing as an "archival hard drive."[78]

Maxine's sarcastic dismissal of an "archival hard drive" matters precisely because such devices do exist (redundant arrays of hard drives, for example) but are fundamentally absurd for a community archives; here, data are data, just as labor hours are labor hours, two aspects of digitization demystified by the LHA's feminist critique of digital technology. This resolute approach to pace and scale at community archives mirrors the Minimal Processing Movement (More Product, Less Process) within the archives field, which works with strained resources to make collections accessible faster.[79] There are all kinds of resource-related reasons that the archives aren't ready to take on a large-scale digitization project such as this one. The task might be impossible, as Colette, handcuffed by the "realness" of time, gets through two or three tapes a week, and there are three thousand. But the LHA is doing it anyway. Maxine's assurance that this slow pace is not a problem because "We're not going anywhere. We're just going to be here" speaks to information activism's long horizon: the work will carry on because there is work to do, and there are people to do it. Digitization is daunting in the cost, strategic planning, labor, and technological expertise it seems to require, but something about a scrappy, lesbian feminist work ethic makes endeavoring to achieve the "impossible" seem reasonable.

The Lesbian Herstory Archives' investment in digitization as being primarily about improved access does not come at the cost of preservation. Instead, it points to the ways in which digitization *never* promises preservation. Archives do not just "digitize" a document one time; technological changes require ongoing format migration to avoid obsolescence, one of the reasons paper is actually one of the most stable formats for preservation. So while "digital networks have enabled the acceleration of access by reducing text to data," as Hilderbrand notes, "digitization is not preservation"—or at least, not the kind of singular act of preservation we might hope for it to be.[80] As Maxine described it, "My biggest concern . . . is that our tapes have lasted a very long time, but the truth is that the only things that people know [will] last are paper and microfilm. Nobody knows if any of the stuff they're digitizing is going to be accessible in ten years, five years, three years. Who knows? Even now they don't make laptops with a CD drive."[81] The archives burned access copies of digitized audio files to CDs at their project's outset in the early 2010s but had switched to storing files on a listening laptop by the end of the decade. With audiovisual materials such as the spoken word collection, analog formats outlast digital ones, which can become corrupted in the case of a scratched CD or failed hard drive, or they can grow obsolete and inoperable.

Community archives have limited capacity for dealing with born-digital documents, and the LHA has started to receive more and more of these materials—hard drives, disks, USB thumb drives—as the lives of donors move increasingly off paper. I experienced this born-digital problem firsthand in my volunteer work at the archives. The Shescape collection included a number of Zip disks. I had not seen a Zip disk since the computer lab at my high school, and it took me a moment, handling the small square of purple-blue plastic, to remember how this obsolete storage technology worked. I was unable to run the disks without access to a Zip drive—or, for that matter, a computer capable of operating a Zip drive. I never learned what was on those Zip disks, so the finding aid I created to accompany the collection is incomplete. For that matter, it is *incompletable*, given the technological constraints. My finding aid simply lists the Zip disks in their state as hardware destined to sit in a box.

Rachel Corbman wanted to improve online access to personal papers of individuals and organizations such as Shescape. Rachel is white, she was twenty-eight when I interviewed her, and she was the youngest active coordinator at the archives. She had just finished her certificate in archival management to begin a doctorate in gender and women's studies, which she has since finished.[82] On the born-digital problem, she said,

> We don't really know how to handle it at this point. . . . We got floppy disks from this one poet. They basically just sit in the box because what are we going to do with a floppy disk? I think there is going to be a time in the not too distant future where we're going to start getting people's computers or hard drives. Same thing: it's probably going to sit in a box. But that's not a problem that's unique to us.

Rachel touched on the lack of capacity for born-digital acquisitions that is widespread not only among community archives and small institutions but also at large university archives.[83]

Many, though not all, of the Lesbian Herstory Archives' volunteer staff have worked in these kinds of large institutions. They have library or archival training or attend an information school such as Pratt. These skilled librarians and archivists share what they know with others in the community. Like chapter 3's indexers, the LHA welcomes untrained volunteers who have no experience doing information work (like me) to help process collections. This embrace of what I call capable amateurism is rooted in the appropriation and adaptation of professional skills and new media technologies to do information activism.

Privacy, Ethics, and Institutional Knowledge Sharing

Queer and feminist archivists and librarians working on digital preservation in institutional settings often develop their critical media praxis by drawing on work at community archives.[84] Mutual exchange occurs among feminist practitioners at all kinds of archives, big, small, grassroots, or institutional. Wholesale calls to "queer" the archive rely on a binary in which institutions preserve some pure institutional status. But activism doesn't pay, so Riot Grrrl archivists need day jobs, too. These activist information workers can act as benevolent infiltrators at their institutional jobs, performing clandestine forms of resource extraction to benefit the community. Archivist and scholar Angela DiVeglia argues that they subvert the "uneven power dynamics inherent in the structure of archives" by drawing on the institution's substantial resources.[85] By engaging with community archives outside their professional lives, feminist information workers also bring subcultural and activist knowledge to their institutional contexts.[86]

The LHA benefits from its partnership with Pratt Institute and Cocciolo's digital projects course, but learning at Pratt is also enriched by experiencing how community archives approach digital media and think about access. In their encounters with the LHA, Pratt students learn the intricacies of working with marginalized archival materials and subjects, grappling with how the political urgencies and eccentricities of these materials manifest in mediating access to them online.[87] The Pratt project is aimed at preservation—Cocciolo explains that the fragility of magnetic tape is a significant issue in archival circles, and the ability to assess the condition of these tapes and preserve them by creating digital copies is an important technical competency for students to develop.[88] Students are also exposed to the desires marginalized archival publics have for materials whose online availability is all the more vital because of its scarcity and articulation to resiliency and survival.

Seeking permission to put queer materials online is about more than just copyright clearance or a take-down policy. Community-generated understandings of privacy, vulnerability, and the ethics of exposure matter more.[89] While for-profit digital clearinghouses will just put questionable material online and wait for affected parties to complain, the LHA is extremely risk-averse in making decisions about offering online access to digitized materials. The archives look for clearly articulated desire by participants to have their materials made widely available, including from everyone who is mentioned by name on a tape or depicted in a photograph. Maxine explained, "For us, that's never just a legal issue. That's also a big difference. We have a lot of ethical issues. There are things we can legally do but we wouldn't do them ethically."

The expectations of privacy that donors associate with analog versus digital formats factors in these decisions:

> When people give us stuff here, and especially years ago, nobody expected anybody to really be interested in it except lesbians, in the community, but if your uncle Al goes online and puts in the word lesbian and your name comes up, and you're not out to him, Hello . . . ! There are still radical feminists that want only lesbians to look at their stuff, and there are still people in the s/m community who don't want people to use [their material] for prurient interest.[90]

As T. L. Cowan and Jas Rault argue, despite the momentum and excitement generated by digitizing rare queer and feminist materials, community-engaged archivists must consider how these materials might reflect "a set of experiences that the people involved had not agreed to share with a search-engine-enabled, entitled, and emboldened public beyond the initial, intended, integral audience."[91]

Cocciolo's class is general education for aspiring archivists and librarians. It is not aimed at LGBTQ students. Working with the LHA leaves students with a sense of the unique concerns all archivists ought to have for materials and publics marginalized because of gender and sexuality. Says Cocciolo, "This was hugely radical what these women were doing, subversive and anti-establishment. These days it's not very radical at all. But people get it. They see that folks being interviewed on the oral histories were doing something very radical."[92] Students are eager to complete their professional degree and get any kind of institutional job they can scrounge up within an austerity economy. Students engaged critically with the exclusions practiced by cultural institutions such as archives through a lesson on the National Endowment for the Humanities' history of defunding gay and lesbian cultural projects.

Cocciolo's students are generally "shocked" when they learn that the LHA will not accept government funding to support any of its work, including the state-sponsored digitization grants that are becoming more readily available to small-scale cultural organizations. "But then you start getting into it with them and the history," Cocciolo said. "Eventually they start to get the fact of why the U.S. government is not a trusted source. . . . You could very well have a congressperson say, 'Please deaccession that.' It's basically not a safe space. You still need community archives."[93] The infrastructures that undergird information work are profound areas of concern for information activists, whose communities have long experienced marginalization from access to good information.

This small-scale institutional partnership shows how large archives, libraries, community archives, students, researchers, professionals, and information activists are always engaged in mutual exchanges of knowledge, which extend to the minutia of digitizing these materials. Cocciolo explained that his students began tagging each audio file with Library of Congress (LOC) subject headings but found them inadequate to the materials. When every tape gets tagged with the subject heading "lesbian," the sorting and search functions mediated by an online database become inoperably general.

Confronted with the ways in which marginalized materials quite literally do not fit within the epistemological frames of the institutional information contexts for which they are training, students began to use the Lesbian Herstory Archives' own, unique subject heading system, which has been generated and maintained by scores of volunteers since the 1970s. This database represents a community-generated subject thesaurus that replaces high-level, poorly descriptive LOC standards with language used by the community. Melissa Adler cites this subject classification scheme as an exemplary community-generated taxonomy that "rewrites certain archival and library practices by foregrounding and universalizing lesbians' desires and positionalities" and ought to be emulated.[94]

One student in Cocciolo's class at Pratt who was also interning at the Lesbian Herstory Archives took a leadership role in relating the importance of how these materials are described in the database. Her class was working on digitizing the original tapes used by Elizabeth Kennedy and Madeleine Davis for the Buffalo Women's Oral History Project. The intern/student explained to the class the complexities of historical terms such as "stone butch" when they are used in the present, potentially as metadata.[95] In the mid-twentieth century, this term meant a very butch woman who did not want to be touched genitally by a partner. Stone butch is often understood in retrospect as a trans-masculine identity. In the process of classifying materials, honoring historical terms alongside present-day relationships between lesbian and trans-masculine identities becomes a data justice issue.

By working through these problems, students learn that the profession they are training for is a site of struggle on which information activists have long worked. A sample tape from the *Boots of Leather* collection includes the subject tags "Lesbian Conduct of Life"; "Roles: Butch and Femme"; and "Gay Bars," among other vernacular classifications, all of which render the audio more searchable and accessible through the Omeka collections-management software that forms the website's infrastructure.

Like the Circle of Lesbian Indexers' thesaurus, the LHA's subject heading database represents an early, predigital effort to create a database system that meaningfully interprets LGBTQ information. Homosaurus is a contemporary example. This open-source, standard vocabulary for LGBTQ+ cultural heritage materials can be imported across platforms to create metadata for digital collections.[96] It has been used most notably by the Digital Transgender Archive, who turned the vocabulary into a linked data project so that others can more readily use it. Custom subject headings are not just about representing the LHA's tapes using the language subjects might choose to describe themselves. They also purposefully organize a digital interface that mediates access to archival materials. For these audio files to be "found" by interested researchers, they must be labeled using descriptive terms that make sense to those who search them out. Otherwise, the audio is just data, lost to poor classification strategies that do not represent the language these communities use. Lesbian feminist information activism turns metadata into a key access issue for digital objects, steeped in a much longer political history of database description.

Making Technological Decisions

The subject headings database the Lesbian Herstory Archives uses to describe materials with community-generated, standardized vocabulary was one of the organization's first applications of computing. How and why this database was built the way that it was and how it informed the LHA's investments in the political possibilities of computing during the early 1980s are important historical contexts for how the organization approaches digitization today.

Early in my documentary research at the archives, I pulled a small, seaweed-green, cloth-bound notebook out of a vertical file called "archive of the archives"—the cabinet that stores the LHA's administrative and operational records. The first page in the notebook reads, "Computer Log, Begins July 25, 1985"; the words are handwritten in black ink, and the first entry describes setting up training on the archives' new computer for "all interested women."[97] The log details arranging meetings to collaboratively design a bibliographic format and subject headings vocabulary. There are notes about an ongoing project of maintaining a database for the archive's mailing list to facilitate distribution of the newsletter and fundraising materials. Entries in the log are infrequent and span a two-year period (1985–86), eventually dropping off after about fifteen pages. The notebook is mostly empty, an incomplete record.

The log that is there documents an emerging computing politics at the archives. First, there is a willingness to experiment, record what is learned for others, and share knowledge. Second, accessible systems design and training are prioritized. And third, concern for how existing text records do not translate to a standard set of database fields is expressed, as is hesitation about the politics of shaping these fields *to* the database. All of these concerns continue to press on the archives' technological approach in the present.

The engagement with digital technologies began long before the LHA developed its first website in 1997. What follows is a brief history of computing, database creation, and the use of digital technologies at the archives from its founding, emphasizing decision-making practices. Decisions situate new media technologies in larger cultural formations, among a specific public whose shifting desires and expectations of what the archives mean and how they would like to encounter them are entangled with technologies in practice.[98] The adoption of new media technologies within organizations does not necessarily offer either momentary rupture or long-term transformation, just as the introduction of new media into larger societal contexts reflects their amenability to earlier media practices.[99]

Focusing on decisions, decision making, and non-decisions or decisions that never get made is one method of attending to the ongoing negotiation of meaning that occurs around technological transitions. Decisions about new media matter, even when they are arbitrary. They are culturally and historical specific choices that have material effects at both technological and social levels. The choice of one database program over another is the beginning of a system that functions as a "protocol," a set of techniques, routines, and control mechanisms that exert ongoing, operational pressure.[100] We have this database program; it's installed on all of the machines; everyone knows how to use it; and it would be too hard to change. So subsequent decisions about technology are made, in part, to achieve compatibility with earlier ones.

These decisions are rarely monolithic; rather, they take place in unremarkable ways that require methodological attention to the potential significance of everyday actions, such as sending in a donation check, which the lesbian feminist writer Dorothy Allison, author of *Bastard out of Carolina* (1992), did in 1983 (figure 4.4). Allison was responding to the LHA's fundraising drive to buy its first computer. The white, working-class southern writer did information technology–related work by day and thought the archives should choose a machine called the Eagle Spirit, because it would be great for converting their paper card catalog into a computer database. She described the computer with affection, bordering on lust, using some pretty colorful language.

Despite her affection for the Eagle Spirit—"a motherfucking incredible honey"—Allison also writes that "computers are boring."[101] She would much rather talk about "something interesting," such as "gardening or sex, or even costume fantasy, or the wonders of lesbian perseverance." When Allison calls computers boring, she makes a flippant remark that actually says a great deal about technological accessibility, community norms around decision making and advice giving, and the everyday labor that sustains community archives and queer lives. Understanding the textures through which technology matters to information activists, and within social movements, means approaching shopping for a computer as much more than just a task on a to-do list.

A mixed method of interviews, ethnographic observation—actually hanging out with archive volunteers while they digitize—and documentary research in the "archive of the archive" (letters, meeting minutes, internal and external print communications such as emails and newsletters) helped me find my way through these quotidian practices. I consider documents, interviews, and observation pathways to tracing not only how social movement discourse is formed, what it says, and how and why it has meaning, but also *what it does*.[102] Decisions about media and technology in these organizations are neither, as Carrie Rentschler puts it, "mysterious nor magical" but everyday facets of larger discursive formations that have

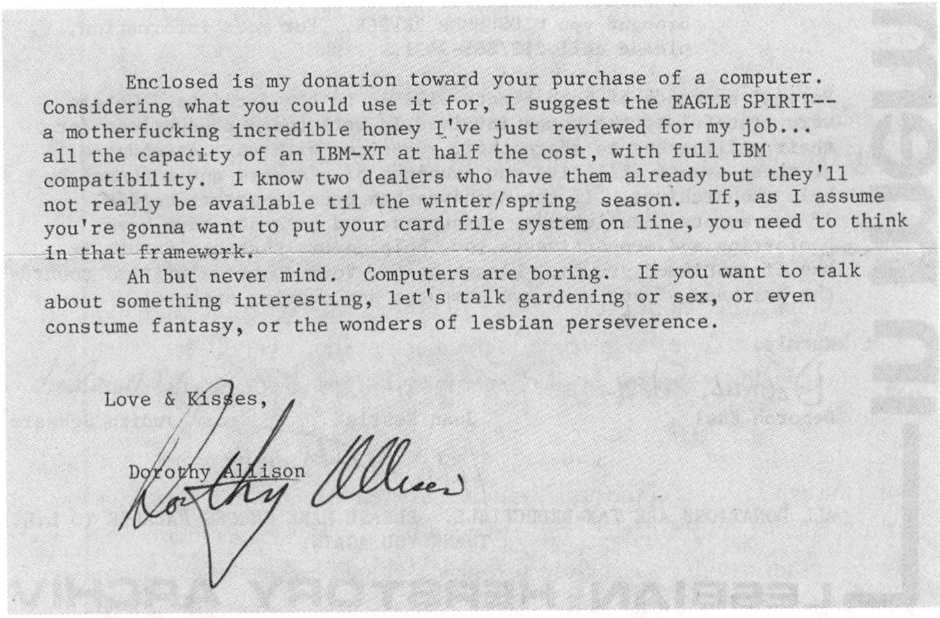

Enclosed is my donation toward your purchase of a computer.
Considering what you could use it for, I suggest the EAGLE SPIRIT--
a motherfucking incredible honey I've just reviewed for my job...
all the capacity of an IBM-XT at half the cost, with full IBM
compatibility. I know two dealers who have them already but they'll
not really be available til the winter/spring season. If, as I assume
you're gonna want to put your card file system on line, you need to think
in that framework.

Ah but never mind. Computers are boring. If you want to talk
about something interesting, let's talk gardening or sex, or even
constume fantasy, or the wonders of lesbian perseverance.

Love & Kisses,

Dorothy Allison

FIGURE 4.4 Letter from Dorothy Allison to the Lesbian Herstory Archives recommending a computer purchase (donation check enclosed), 1983. Image courtesy Lesbian Herstory Educational Foundation.

effects through the way they orient organizations and their publics—in this case, the archives itself.[103]

As both a social movement organization and an archives, the LHA tries to keep good records of its own operation, but the everyday practice of documenting administrative tasks can be abandoned as attention is devoted to more immediate concerns. Because decisions about technology often feel mundane to the activists making them, it can be hard for historians to recover these histories—they are underdocumented or decades pass and people understandably forget details such as what machine they bought or what software they used. The incomplete computer log, with its smattering of entries, is one such example. My documentary research in the LHA works with what is available, reading across the documents that do remain, looking for modest articulations of bigger ideals in complex relation to one another across time. These methods approach social movements through their "complex eventfulness," which understands feminist histories as unsettled, unfinished, and surprising in the twists and turns, steps forward and backward, that they take.[104] This methodological practice is attuned to diverse proliferations, micro-moments, conflicts, antagonisms, contradictions, and attachments to and detachments from technologies.

As chapter 2's attention to telephone hotline call logs argues, the paper remainders information activists leave behind are complex and utterly partial. The "archived minutiae" of feminist organizing challenges normative temporal orientations to digital histories suggested by terms such as "the consumer computer revolution" or "planned obsolescence."[105] At the Lesbian Herstory Archives, I cobbled together nuggets of information about technological decisions gathered here and there, whether from a log book on database creation, an instruction manual that shows volunteers how to create a catalog record, or a story remembered in casual conversation with a longtime volunteer.

The history of digital technology at the archives begins by understanding the explicit aims of the organization, gathered from documents such as the "Statement of Principles" and early newsletters. These documents were written in the mid-1970s, before anyone imagined how database software, networked communication, the World Wide Web, and other digital technologies would shape the community archives movement. Regardless of their original political and technological moment, the principles related in these documents echo the archives' digitization projects. "Funding shall be sought from within the communities the Archives serves, rather than from outside sources" informs the LHA's skepticism about state-related digitization grants and makes necessary the design of affordable, DIY digitization systems such as the audio digitizer featured earlier in this chapter.[106] "Archival skills shall be taught, one generation of Lesbians to another, breaking the elitism of traditional archives" fosters an emphasis on ease-of-use and accessibility for this system and is a value Cocciolo used when he explained the selection of the Omeka platform: "Wordpress for collections; it's super simple."[107] To accompany the system, Colette has produced what she calls a "protocol," a step-by-step text- and image-based guide to using an audio digitizer that is accessible to volunteers who "know how to use a mouse and how to use a computer" but otherwise could have "zero" knowledge of the system.[108] Colette's protocol is part of a longer legacy of accessible how-to guides that accompany archiving work at the LHA: a set of manuals from the 1980s show new volunteers how to catalog a book, process a special collection, or add an image to the photo collection.

Policy and protocol documents such as these archives manuals, or the Circle of Lesbian Indexer's *How to Index in the Circle of Lesbian Indexers*, relate the high-level contexts guiding information activists' decisions.

When they are available, activists' own memories add richness and depth to reading these documents, along with stories of the affective attachments volunteers form with new technologies. So I can make better sense of the archives' mysterious green computer log, Rachel puts me in touch with Beth Haskell, the former volunteer who led the archives' transition to computing. Beth, a white woman, volunteered at the archives in the 1980s and '90s, from her late twenties to her early forties. She is now a technologist in the nonprofit sector.

Beth started using a Kaypro computer while she was in graduate school at New York University (NYU) in the late 1970s. She has learning disabilities and was hooked by the word-processing features, which made it easier for her to write. "So I got very fascinated by the power of what a computer could do," she said, "and took a little programming class at NYU and was like, "Oh, is that what this is about? This isn't very hard.' I'm kind of one of these people who's a natural with it. . . . I was very, very interested in what a computer could do for an organization."[109] Beth's interest would transform the archives' mailing system.

Technological transitions at grassroots organizations are often ignited by a trustworthy new person who brings a different set of skills and ideas about how established processes might be improved using those skills. As I outline in chapter 1, the Lesbian Herstory Archives first used a computer to create an electronic database for its mailing list. Volunteers had been transcribing 2,500 addresses onto mailing labels by hand every time a newsletter or fundraising letter needed to go out. Beth saw this cumbersome process and had an idea: "When I got to the archives at the [volunteer] orientation, I found out that they had their mailing list on 3×5 cards, written out by Joan [Nestle], who had atrocious handwriting. I just said. 'Well, how about we computerize these?' And they kinda looked at me, like, 'What?'"[110] The archives didn't have a computer when this work started in 1982, so Beth borrowed a friend's Kaypro and set it up at the apartment of Morgan Gwenwald (an LHA coordinator). Beth spent her spare time that summer inputting each index card into a flat file—a basic text database. She told me, laughing, "I became an expert at reading Joan's handwriting."

The work was repetitive and took months, but Beth liked working on computers, she said, and hanging out with Morgan's "[pet] snake! And her photographs, and her knife collection, and her cowboy boots, and Morgan herself, who, of course, everyone was smitten with."[111] Networks of interdependence support information activists as they undertake technological transitions: Beth's decision to join the archives; the friend who lent the computer; Morgan, who invited Beth to work in her apartment; the other coordinators who were open to trying something new and unfamiliar. A push to finish the project that September brought more volunteers into the fold. Reporting on the project, the *Lesbian Herstory Archives Newsletter* announced, "In 1983, on one of the hottest September weekends on record, about 20 Archives volunteers and 2 borrowed Kaypro computers got together in an un-air-conditioned apartment in Brooklyn and put the Archives' 2,500 name mailing list on a database. This was the first step in the long-term goal of having a fully computerized Archives catalog system."[112]

The archives' volunteers were hooked by this successful first experiment with computing and raised the money to purchase their own machine, an IBM-XT, in 1984.[113] As I argue in chapter 1, digitizing the mailing list expanded the archives' network, allowed mailings to be sent more easily and frequently, and improved fundraising capacities. Computing and database capabilities promised not just to organize information well, but also to improve communication and outreach and even recruit new volunteers. The newsletter explained this plan to readers: "Our computer project coordinators Beth Haskell and Judith Schwarz are also available to work out long distance projects for those of you who have access to an IBM-compatible PC and would like to assist the archives from your own home."[114] Although this "telecommuting" plan for new volunteers was never realized, others gradually got involved in computing at the archives, trained by Beth, or through exposure in other areas of their work lives.[115] The archives kept up with progress in desktop computing, moving next to a Gateway machine, and volunteers began using the computer to create more sophisticated listings of actual holdings.[116]

Beth's memories of early computing at the archives help to fill in important details that documents don't capture, including some of the affective dimensions of working with other activists using new and intimidating technologies. Records of everyday communication are also invaluable for filling in the more mundane practices that may not register as significant enough to hold on to as memories for thirty years. Documents such as the computer log, multiple drafts of the subject heading database, meeting minutes, and the newsletter are vital because conversations about technology go on for so long—sometimes years, as in the case of the planning, design, and implementation of the archives' first website. I follow these processes the best I can through the minutes, often alerted to when a decision has actually been made and implemented by a public announcement in the newsletter.

In 1995, the coordinating committee began to discuss whether the archives should "be on the World Wide Web," because it would provide for greater outreach to lesbians who could not visit the archives in person or did not receive the newsletter.[117] From its first encounters, the LHA's investments in online spaces were animated by the possibility of extending access to lesbian history. Meeting minutes document discussions of every aspect of the archives' developing website, including the formation of a committee in 1996, the year the archives also installed a modem so internet access would be available inside the building. Between 1996 and 1998, as the website was being developed, the committee mapped how existing archival politics could take shape online: they discussed managing costs, preserving donors' privacy, and how server space with a politically sympathetic hosting company should be arranged.[118] The Lesbian Herstory Archives' website went live at the end of 1997, after a printed draft had been circulated, modified, and approved by the committee. The draft process demonstrates how a consensus model extended to the web project and to interface design. Printing out the website ensured that the archives coordinators who were not internet users could participate in the decision-making process by evaluating the site on paper, a more familiar medium.[119]

Social movement mandates are discursive. Even when they stay the same formally, what they mean changes over time, as technologies evolve along with understandings of sexuality and gender. Decisions about technology are one way that the archives' principles come up for discussion. The ongoing discussion about the place of transgender materials and volunteers is another, pushing on the category of lesbian itself. Digitization invites reckoning with financing models and outside partnerships. Many LGBTQ community archives, including the Lesbian Herstory Archives, accept remuneration and indirect technical assistance from large primary-source clearinghouses such as Gale. The LHA is also deciding how its established understandings of privacy and consent from donors will apply as catalog records and finding aids for collections move online. Rather than from concerns for copyright, these issues emerge from lesbian feminist and queer ethics entangled with social understandings of technology.

These negotiations show that the archives is always already in flux, as is the organization's relation to lesbian feminism and queerness. The LHA is often described using the short-hand term "lesbian-feminist archives," but the reality is far more complex, where what "lesbian feminism" means and how it is practiced as an approach to archiving varies from volunteer to volunteer. Moreover, the long-term volunteers I interviewed described how their politics had changed along with technology and their evolving understandings of online communications. Rachel, who worked with special collections, had to ask what it means to list the contents of a donor's collection on a public-facing website. This can involve interpreting a form completed in the 1970s by a donor who gave over copyright for her materials to the archives but penciled "for lesbian eyes only" into the margins.[120]

During my volunteer hours at the archives I was assigned the task of sorting through these donor forms to make exactly this kind of assessment and create a spreadsheet that would help guide planning about putting special collections material online. I sorted through hundreds of forms and was confronted with temporally complex questions about media at the archives. Did these donors imagine every encounter with their materials taking place in the domestic space of the archives? What does the condition "for lesbian eyes only" mean now that the archives welcome visitors and researchers of any sexual or gender identification? Donor forms were often missing altogether. Tara Robertson and Elizabeth Groeneveld have explored how attempts to mediate access to lesbian history through digital interfaces raise significant ethical issues. Digital archives must ask media-archaeology questions about how makers might have understood the choices they made about mediated exposure in the past in relation to how they might feel about their representation on digital platforms.[121]

The LHA has checked in with donors over the years to find out how technological changes map onto their original bequests. In 1999, the newsletter distributed a website agreement form after a lengthy discussion by coordinators about the ethics of offering descriptions of special collections online. The form gave donors the opportunity to be explicit about whether they wanted to have their special collections listed online; it explained that the LHA was checking in with donors because the transition to digital environments represents a fundamentally different form of exposure, beyond earlier outreach strategies aimed at a contained community of lesbians: "The Web is part of the Internet and is accessible to an audience more vast than those who visit the archives or receive our newsletter."[122] To be clear, the LHA has never tried to put scans of actual materials from personal papers online; rather, it provides titles and short descriptions of these collections. Rachel added the descriptions to the LHA's website in 2012. By 2013, ongoing and ultimately inconclusive discussions had begun about adding digital versions of finding aids and select documents to highlight collections.[123]

Interpreting these donor agreement and website agreement forms has a complex temporality bound up with the archives as a constantly changing site of mediation. It is also inseparable from the coordinators' interpretive archival work and stewardship. These decision-making processes are often acrimonious and complex. Rachel told me, "I can get frustrated by the resistance [of other coordinators] even though I understand it. It feels like I have to strategize things, and it can make me uncomfortable, even though I know that is part of working in any ostensibly structureless group. I don't understand the point of creating such detailed finding aids and having this information if we're not going to have it on the internet."[124] Mediated by shifting feminist politics and intergenerational conversations, digitization is above all improvisational. In her own words, Rachel must "strategize," and this is part of the work.[125]

There is no master plan; rather, these kinds of projects are taken on, as the photography collection coordinator Saskia told me, by "whoever does it. Whoever knows about it. Whoever is available to work with it. Whoever has some expertise or some resources. It's whatever you know most about and where you're most helpful."[126] This improvisational approach honors collaboration and trusts in the unique technological skills each volunteer brings to information work. Ultimately, this way of working together has been practiced at the archives since the beginning. Beth described a similar approach to delegating technological responsibility in the archives' transition to computing in the 1980s: "I don't think there was resistance. I think there was a 'That would be nice if we could do it [mentality], but we don't know how to do it. If you know how to do it, that would be great.' . . . [The archives coordinators at the time] just realized or felt that it was a lot of work, and it really took somebody to take it on and do it."

Decisions are made through a consensus-building process that often involves careful navigation of interpersonal relationships, and varied levels of comfort with technology. Imogen Peach, a professional metadata expert and coordinator of the archives' catalog, related a similar experience:

> One of the benefits of being here is that you have women who are actively engaged and want to know. There's two people who don't really care about technology, and that's OK. . . . But for the people who do want to know, they're willing to stretch themselves to meet me where I can explain. In that respect, we've been able to overcome the differences. I'm pretty good at being able to figure out what is meaningful for you and then explaining whatever it is in a way that's meaningful for you. There's still times when people's lack of patience or personalities make it difficult, and then I just work around. That's something that [information technology]

people do all the time. So you do a lot of that, too, because I can't expect that everybody at the archives will be as excited about URL linking as I am.[127]

While these encounters across difference are exciting, there are also moments of frustration. Rachel's use of "strategize" and Imogen's explanation that she "work[s] around . . . people's lack of patience or personalities" point to decisions about media and technology as loaded sites where established protocols for working at this archives are quietly usurped. Rachel told me that decisions at the archives were made through "consensus, but because it's consensus and it's horizontally run, it actually has very complex internal workings of who has informal power."[128]

Feeling encounters with technology and with others tend to manifest through the consensus-building process. I asked all of the coordinators I interviewed to describe how the archives made decisions about technology. It can be difficult for the coordinators to remember practicalities but they often described what it felt like to make a decision or how they subtly pried open established practices, recalling the work of building consensus, the tone in the room, the feelings of others to which they worked to be sensitive. These information activists try to meet their collaborators where they are at and understand that decisions about new technology sometimes need to be slow and purposeful. As I argue in the next section, this caring practice extends to everyday decisions the archives make about database description as volunteers assign metadata to digital objects.

Writing, Revising, and "Cleaning Up" Databases

Digitization requires volunteers to create metadata that describes objects and makes them findable in the archives' databases. Ostensibly simple choices about how to describe the people in a photograph or the topics discussed on an oral history tape become complicated because they remediate how lesbian and queer identity politics change over time. New descriptive interfaces such as the archives' online photo collection and in-progress online catalog are substantial digital access provisions that reflect these conflicts. The LHA's online public access catalog (OPAC) project seeks to make materials held at the archives easy to find by standardizing the existing database; "OPAC" is a library term for the front-end, public-facing part of a catalog database. An OPAC allows libraries and archives to make their materials findable through their own websites or through larger bibliographic databases such as WorldCat.

The OPAC is one of the most strategically significant digitization projects at the archives, representing digital transition at an infrastructural level. While the archives' catalog has taken the form of a computer database since the 1980s, it is stored on local machines, to be used on-site by volunteers assisting researchers. Imogen, the coordinator responsible for the project, expects that putting the catalog online will reduce the volume of questions the archives field from researchers, raise the profile of the archives, perform outreach to potential visitors who cannot come to New York, and create connections to other LGBTQ+ archival holdings by making the LHA collection searchable across popular platforms such as Google and WorldCat.[129] The OPAC is an infrastructure for making public the archives collections, so the minutia of its design matters. The rollout of the OPAC is a long-term project, years in the making, that demands massive investments of volunteer hours. Coordinators must make a series of decisions about technology and the database that will shape the archives ontologically by structuring the public's future encounters with the collection.

The main obstacle in the way of moving the archives' existing catalog online is the messiness of the database, which needs to be "cleaned up" to migrate the records to the OPAC.[130] Imogen describes this cleanup as "going through each record and confirming that everything's spelled correctly and everything's in the right field."[131] She went on to explain how this data-hygiene process aims at efficient search and allowing databases to "read" and index the archives' catalog in relation to materials stored at other libraries and archives. A common form of information work, this data processing standardizes records so they become "pristine." Once these clean records "join" larger indexes, the prior cleaning of data becomes invisible.[132]

Resisting these sanitizing aspects of the digital imperative, the LHA's data processing highlights how data infrastructures are built and maintained by volunteers with particular values. Their process preserves the archives' idiosyncratic record of how materials have been cataloged differently at the archives *over time*.[133] This means implementing new, standardized subject headings for future database compatibility while maintaining a field for existing headings. The DIY classifications are preserved as archival documents, in and of themselves.[134] Imogen explained:

> We are a volunteer organization, and over the last forty years many
> lesbian hands have touched the catalog. Well-meaning, well-intentioned
> hands. Whatever lesbian created that record and how she cataloged it, it's
> there for posterity. Each one of those records is an archival document in

itself. Some lesbian who knew nothing about library science or nothing about cataloging came in—completely useless for the actual catalog, but so wonderful in terms of looking at what some lesbian just sat down and did for, like, three years. She just wrote stuff about each video she watched. The numbers are all wrong, but it doesn't matter. . . . That little document she created is wonderful.[135]

What might be viewed as "bad data" in a standard sense is considered added value by this archives—indeed, a source of "wonder." Amateur classifications are part of the materials' queer historical status. These old classifications are useless for search retrieval, in practical terms, but they do other kinds of work by framing information activism as a key facet of lesbian history.

Maintaining these records preserves how lesbians have described their communities and identities differently over time rather than casting outdated terms aside when the burden of their untimeliness becomes too heavy. By preserving identity-related terms that might be considered old-fashioned or even offensive today, the catalog contributes to community-based etymologies.[136] Maintaining the old catalog records echoes the scratched-out handwriting and records of revision that are key to the Circle of Lesbian Indexers' reindexing process. All this behind-the-scenes work to conscientiously build information infrastructures for lesbian history matters enough to archive.

Descriptive practices can have significant effects on how users perceive and navigate materials when materials are encountered through a digital interface. Digital interfaces rely on metadata description to organize materials and provide access according to the logics behind these descriptions. They do so through set vocabularies that reflect how information workers who write metadata deploy their knowledge of the communities they work in and for. Descriptive practices can shape what an archive becomes in its digital form while potentially effacing the evidence of that shaping. "Good" digital interfaces resolve tensions by providing search retrieval and navigability that work so well the interface virtually disappears.[137] In contrast, lesbian-feminist history is complex, acrimonious, and multivalent, rooted in affective histories where sex, gender, race, class, and ability meet. The Lesbian Herstory Archives' digital interface must struggle to find ways to represent the acrimony, ambivalence, and tension critical to lesbian-feminist histories.

Transgender subjects and materials present an ongoing challenge to a lesbian archives, given the ways lesbian feminism is often remembered for excluding transgender people (especially trans women) from participation.

While the LHA has no official policy on how it understands the relationship between "lesbian" and "transgender," it is working to make its practices amenable to the trans donors, visitors, and records that search out a place there. Creating an explicit, gender-inclusive "Statement of Principles" has been discussed by the coordinators, resulting in the formation of a sub-committee.[138] In the meantime, less explicit evidence of this work appears through the maintenance of database records.

While exploring the archive's photography files to gain a sense of the physical collection's scope in relation to the smaller "Online Photo Sampler," I found a simple index card that read "Del LaGrace Volcano (2010)" inserted into a folder long ago labeled "Della Grace." Index cards often assert their materiality where the labor of revision has been necessary. The folder contained work by Volcano, a well-known nonbinary, intersex photographer who focuses on portraiture of queer, trans, and intersex people and communities.[139] The collection at the archives documents lesbian punk and S/M scenes in London and San Francisco in the 1980s. At first blush, the handwritten card suggests a straightforward categorical rupture that could be traced to a singular moment in Volcano's gender chronology. Volcano's self-described "gender terrorism" and "intentional mutation" began long before 2010 and resist teleological notions of transition.[140] The date on the card describes not Volcano but, rather, the moment in which the archives altered the data about herm.[141]

Trans, nonbinary, and intersex identities can pose unique problems for the sense-making impetus that accompanies digitization. Writing on trans subjects in the archives and the challenge of metadata, K. R. Roberto theorizes trans as resistance to a categorizing epistemology inherent in archiving. This resistance is temporal in its openness to various levels of between-ness in relation to transition. Classification schemes, which are hierarchical by nature, don't do well with the unfixedness of gender. Roberto writes, "If [LOC] subject headings should represent people's identities, it also should acknowledge that identities can be complex and temporal."[142] As Roberto, Anna Lauren Hoffmann, and Rena Bivens have argued, databases are both challenges to open-ended epistemologies and opportunities to design new schemes and systems that can think differently about subjects and their ontologies.[143] Database and software design and revisions are opportunities for "severing and opening up possibilities for gendered life," according to Bivens.[144]

At play here is a larger question about *archives in transition*; in the case of the Lesbian Herstory Archives, this manifests in an unmooring of archiving's structures, where trans* becomes a force unsettling the lesbian-feminist status quo.[145] The trans studies scholars Susan Stryker, Paisley Currah, and Lisa Jean Moore discuss the relation of trans to feminism as one of productive motion: "The lines implied by the very concept of 'trans-' are moving targets, simultaneously composed of multiple determinants. 'Transing,' in short, is a practice that takes place within, as well as across or between, gendered spaces. It is a practice that assembles gender into contingent structures of association with other attributes of bodily being, and that allows for their reassembly."[146] Trans puts the Lesbian Body con-stituted through the archives in motion in ways that "queer" archival prac-tices do not.[147] Where efforts to queer the archives affectionately maintain "lesbian," but with an asterisk—as in, "We're 'queerer' than lesbian femi-nism but love it anyway"—trans might shake up the signifier of lesbian by emphasizing its need for ongoing movement and actual groundlessness in practice. Perhaps trans even shares with the digital an emphasis on move-ment, motion, revision, and process and an ontological willingness to sit with "incompleteness."[148]

I asked Saskia whether Volcano's photos would be digitized. Saskia works in digital projects at the New York Public Library and is an accom-plished photographer herself. She had been volunteering at the archives since 1987. She told me quite practically that she would "love to put up those images" but needed to ask Volcano about permissions and how to catalog the material, something she hadn't gotten around to yet.[149] Some of the photos included images of "totally recognizable people," which compli-cates the archives' policy of obtaining enthusiastic consent from subjects of photographs before putting them online.[150] Saskia then told me about several examples of materials in the collection in which the photographers or subjects are trans men who once identified as butch lesbians.

We had a long conversation about trans* inclusion at the Lesbian Her-story Archives, and Saskia explained some of the archives' ongoing engage-ments with these questions as they extend to digitization. When Saskia chose photos to digitize, she scanned them but also carefully interpreted the images as she wrote the metadata. The archives' Online Photo Sampler is hosted by Digital Culture of Metropolitan New York, a historical image sharing service for members of the Metropolitan New York Library Coun-cil. The LHA has its own collection of nearly seven hundred photographs on the site. Each image is richly described by Saskia and her collaborators using Dublin Core, a standard set of metadata that includes, among other fields, "Title," "Subject," "Creator," "Date," and "Description."

A thoughtful, slow approach to writing metadata also guides Saskia's direction for the archives' Instagram account, @lesbianherstoryarchives, which began in December 2016. The account shares digitized photographs from the collection with more than twenty-four thousand followers. For each post, Saskia writes detailed captions that contain dates, full names of everyone pictured, and full histories that contextualize events. Followers are asked to "include complete caption when reposting" the images. This practice sets the archives apart within Instagram's quick and dirty LGBTQ history world, where attribution and context are often in short supply.

I had hoped to find Volcano's images from the file cabinet online, not just as a researcher, but as a fan. If nothing else, they represent a significant body of work by a well-known, critically successful photographer. Saskia seemed to feel the same way. "They're really cool," she said. "I would love to put up those images." As mentioned earlier, Saskia said that contacting the photographer to ask, "What shall we do? Can we publish? . . . Do you want to see each one?" was on her to-do list. "I have no idea what to expect," she said, "but my guess is that there will be openness about discussing that."[151]

My questions about these materials were rooted in a larger desire to understand how a contemporary lesbian-feminist organization practices trans* inclusivity—questions that were not just about digitizing photographs, but also about my own growing attachment to the archives. What was my relationship to "lesbian" and "trans" as a masculine, nonbinary person who is kind of a "lesbian," doesn't feel like a "woman" but does not register as "trans" within many circles, either? While I might once have found a home within the archives' proud celebration of "butch," I wondered whether the edges of masculine identification move too close to trans-masculinity to maintain a relationship with lesbian in the present.[152] I was also aware of myself appearing like the sort of awful academic-type who descends on a community organization with a list of complaints and questions, communicated in overly theoretical terms, to volunteers who are already pressed for time. All these feelings were perhaps caused by my own ambivalence working in a lesbian space while feeling attached to but not quite as if I fit within that concept.

Perhaps anticipating these thoughts or working to show how her own questions aligned with my own, Saskia began:

> The [questions] "What is a lesbian?" and "How do we include every lesbian?" and how do you have the discussion about who is a lesbian, or who was, and what do you do with that is incredibly relevant, cer-

tainly for an organization like ours. It's a very emotional issue. It's a very political issue. It's a very complicated issue. Not just for the photo collection. . . . The whole trans discussion, I think we really need to have it. I really want to have it. . . . I think that should be totally part of the archives, but I think that it also, it's complicated. It's really complicated.

Five years later, the LHA's 2018 revised "Statement of Principles" gestured to this complexity in a more formalized context: "The Archives collects material by and about all Lesbians, acknowledging changing concepts of Lesbian identities. All expressions of Lesbian identities, desires and practices are important, welcomed and included."[153] In 2013, Saskia rehearsed some of these complicated debates for me, pointing out how circular they can become: "I think at the moment the question is really who calls themselves a lesbian and who calls themselves a woman and do you include people in your organization who reject the concept of them being female and why would they even want to be here? This is about women. What is a woman? It's complicated as hell."[154] Saskia's collaborator and intern Ronika told me about finding work by or about transgender subjects in the photo files and feeling excited that these materials might present "a real challenge for the LHA to sink its teeth into," as the organization works to become more trans-inclusive by exploring practices and policies for selecting, describing, and contextualizing trans* materials.[155] Ronika's newer relationship to the archives is inevitably less steeped in an acrimonious history of trans exclusion in lesbian-feminist movements and spaces.

In her work digitizing the photo collection, Saskia is committed to working through these kind of questions in very practical ways, asking donors whether and how they want their photographs represented online. A month after my interview with Saskia, she emailed to say that she had gotten in touch with Volcano, who was excited to start putting the photographs online. The digitized collection of Volcano's work offers an unusual, artful pictorial record of lesbian kink. The black-and-white photographs were taken in the late 1980s and early 1990s in San Francisco and London and donated to the Lesbian Herstory Archives in the early 1990s. The images show groups of dykes clad in leather and hanging out in bars, in public space, and at marches. They are pro-S/M photographs of lesbians who took big risks to live their sexualities in public, with others. Volcano has written about the work: "I think it gave us all a sense of satisfaction to see the looks on some faces when confronted with two dozen dykes in leathers and looking fierce and fabulous."[156]

Title	Jane, Jane, Queen of Pain
Identifier	dellagrace_08.jp2
Creator	Volcano, Del Lagrace
Subject-Topic	dykes
	leather
	SM
Location	London, England
Date Created	1988
Description	dyke in leather with sunglasses
Description	Del LaGrace Volcano, previously known as Della Grace and Della Disgrace
Note	Digitized by the Lesbian Herstory Educational Foundation.
Type	still image
Genre	Black & white photographs
Extent	8 x 10
Digital Format	image/jp2
Digital Origin	reformatted digital
Rights (Use and Reproduction)	Del LaGrace Volcano
Collection	Lesbian Herstory Archives Photo files, Del LaGrace Volcano folders

FIGURE 4.5 Metadata for *Jane, Jane, Queen of Pain*, by Del LaGrace Volcano, 1988. Lesbian Herstory Archives digital photography collection.

Looking underneath the confident grins of these '80s leather dykes, users find metadata description that references the photographer's shifting identifications over time: the "creator" and "rights" holder for the image is listed as Del LaGrace Volcano, the filename is "dellagrace_08.jp2," with the further addition of a "Description" that reads, "Del LaGrace Volcano, previously known as Della Grace and Della Disgrace" (figure 4.5). On the surface, this seems like an archives deadnaming one of its donors, but this description was conceived by Saskia after consultation with Volcano.[157] It reflects the complexity of trans, intersex, and non-binary artists' archives, Volcano's career-long commitment to "gender terrorism," and the artist's own use of language when writing about these photographs on herm's website.[158] This is careful metadata description that attempts to open space for a historical subject in transition—in this case, the non-binary, intersex subject often effaced from how lesbian archives are understood.[159]

Saskia's metadata description, like much work with digital technology at the Lesbian Herstory Archives, remains open to revision and critique. The LHA responds dynamically to lesbian feminist politics, past and present, as it works to improve description. Saskia explained:

> If changes need to be made, that will happen. I think that discussion will come; clearly, we're having one now. And maybe you will make me aware of something, or I will make you aware of something, and something changes in the metadata. I have no problem going in the system and adding or taking something away in terms of description. The more I work with it, the more that actually happens, because I realize that I can be more exact, I can be more precise. It will be better, it will be easier to use, more informative.

Writing metadata is an ongoing process that begins when the archives uploads a photograph, and continues as information activists like Saskia care for and maintain these digital objects over time.

Materials that intersect with trans* or that trans the collection often do so in relation to digitization and to media practices in transition. As a process that requires the archives to make ongoing technological decisions about historical materials, digitization can turn frustrations, controversies, and affective attachments that seem like ancient history into present-day matters of concern. My search for Volcano's photos in the online database set just such a process in motion; in failing to find what I was looking for, I became ever more aware of the interface *as an interface* built by activists who care. Lesbian-feminist history is a productively unstable collection of events that the archives constructs through volunteer-driven practices with media technologies.[160]

Conclusion

Even as it offers preservation, digitization at the Lesbian Herstory Archives exchanges the aura of a perfectly reproduced digital version for wider access. This exchange manifests in all kinds of interface and database qualities that reflect the organization's politics, such as the paradoxical messiness of the catalog data, which must be "cleaned up" or repaired to function but also maintained in its beautiful messiness for posterity's sake. Similarly, by reducing the noise in access copies of spoken-word audio files, the archives carry out a compression process that prioritizes usability. For the LHA, this choice is obvious. Maxine expressed surprise that anyone would oppose noise reduction aimed at making audio easier to understand, because understanding is precisely the point of doing oral histories.[161] She explained, "A lot of preservation and conservation is sort of like the people who are into the wilderness as a place that nobody can go to. It's like, 'You're preserving this for whom?' If nobody can listen to it, then what's the point?"[162]

Maxine sets the digital imperative's emphasis on preservation apart from the Lesbian Herstory Archives' goal to serve a public with precarious access to its own histories:

> The point for us is that we have a right to our history. And people have a right to hear this. The point isn't just to conserve it, preserve it. The point is to make it accessible. So you try to do both those things at once. You don't just say, "OK, we're going to conserve this, and no one's going to touch it." What's the point? For us, there's no point because the whole reason for the Lesbian Herstory Archives is a belief that people have a right to their own history. And it's not just about putting it into a drawer and a hundred years from now somebody will know it was put into a drawer.[163]

Maxine and Colette create digital files that are stored on hard drives for now but may ultimately be destined for streaming via the LHA's website.

The archives' administration is guided by a simple question Maxine lays out for me: "Can people find it, and can they get here? People always say, 'Oh, you're not open that many hours,' but if you come from out of town, you can come here all the time. We've had people sleep here, and [at] Joan's apartment, too, when it was at her apartment. I guess . . . the major thing is just making sure that people can get it and that it's kept in decent condition and that we know what we have."[164] For Maxine, these are "the basics."[165] Access guides the Lesbian Herstory Archives' fearlessness about taking on large digitization projects in the first place. An improvisational approach to digitization means being willing to take risks or roll out projects imperfectly in pursuit of improved access. Giving the archives' public opportunities to engage with the collection justifies project design aimed at "getting it done." This is digitization guided by an abiding belief in how profound it can be to encounter information.

The archives' improvisational approach to digitization guides decisions about technology and, ultimately, the future of this archives. Choosing what to digitize and figuring out how to describe those objects in online databases is a significant responsibility because these decisions shape the ontology of the twenty-first-century archives as it becomes a space of primarily digital encounter. Processes of selection and description made on an improvisational or ad hoc basis might seem insignificant in their singularity but add up to chains of decisions with profound effects on the archives' direction. At the Lesbian Herstory Archives, everyday choices about digital technologies matter because they build the information infrastructure through which lesbian history might continue to be enlivened, guiding how histories of sexuality are accessed and imagined.

Epilogue

Doing Lesbian Feminism
in an Age of Information Abundance

"THE PATRIARCHY IS A PYRAMID SCHEME" reads the hand-painted sign held aloft by the artist and activist Ginger Brooks Takahashi, who stands in front of a densely postered wall at the 2006 New York Art Book Fair (figure E.1). The sign's red letters look finger painted and a bit as if they are written in menstrual blood, in the style of Judy Chicago's deep-lez Central Core Imagery.[1] They follow a crude typography that stretches and compresses to accommodate the upside-down black triangle in the placard's center. Although it's hard to make out in the photo, Takahashi wears a baseball cap emblazoned with a fist inside a Venus symbol, the woman-power emblem familiar from second-wave lesbian-feminist typography. This is mid-2000s queer lesbian-feminist revival. Handmade aesthetics, second-wave protest techniques, and a critique of patriarchy appear alongside clear markers that locate the image in a later time: the upside-down triangle symbol made famous by ACT UP and Queer Nation and Takahashi's role as a founding member of LTTR, the feminist genderqueer artists' collective and journal (2001–2006) whose first issue was titled "Lesbians to the Rescue."[2]

The artist A. L. Steiner took the photo as part of the larger multimedia project *The Patriarchy Is a Pyramid Scheme* (2008), but that is not how most people encounter it today. Instead, the image lives on via Instagram, the retailer Otherwild, and the hashtag #thepatriarchyisapyramidscheme. Otherwild is a store and graphic design studio based in Los Angeles and New York that makes contemporary clothing and housewares, some of which are based on archival images from lesbian-feminist activist histories drawn from Instagram. Promoting its work through social media, the retailer has partnered with the popular Instagram account @h_e_r_s_t_o_r_y to produce wearable encounters with lesbian-feminist print ephemera.

FIGURE E.1 A. L. Steiner with Ginger Brooks Takahashi, "Untitled (The Patriarchy Is a Pyramid Scheme)," digital photograph, 2006. Courtesy of the artists.

On Otherwild's ecommerce site, users can buy a "The Patriarchy Is a Pyramid Scheme" T-shirt for $40. The white, long-sleeved shirt is screen-printed with Takahashi's sign, which emblazons the wearer's chest: same blood-red color, same hand-drawn font, same black triangle. Users shopping the site confront an image of a model wearing the shirt standing in front of a woven, Pride-rainbow wall-hanging. The model is posing in a way that replicates Takahashi's sign-holding posture. When the user rolls over the image of the model, the graphic flips to Steiner's original photo of Takahashi.[3]

Otherwild's Instagram account, which boasts eighty thousand followers, also shares the archival photos that form the basis of the company's clothing. Those who buy and wear the shirt are encouraged to share selfies under hashtags such as #thepatriarchyisapyramidscheme. Users who take the time to read Otherwild's Instagram captions encounter a brief history of the original photo and are reminded that the patriarchy taken on by their queer and lesbian predecessors is alive and well, theirs to inherit and dismantle: "Systemic patriarchal oppression and racism are multilayered and multi-functional, often hiding themselves so successfully that they're ineffable, invisible, and unquestioned. With this phrase, the name of the game is exposed and its players laid bare."[4] Users also learn that Otherwild donates 25 percent of sales from this particular shirt to ENLACE, an antiracist prison abolition organization focused on women of color.[5] The rest is split by Takahashi, Dean Daderko, Steiner, and Otherwild, who came to this arrangement after some acrimony over whose work is represented on the shirt—Steiner's photo or the concept for the sign, developed collectively out of "a series of social interactions" among Steiner, Daderko, Takahashi and other friends in the early 2000s.[6]

Nostalgia for lesbian feminism is certainly at play here, but this is not a depoliticized longing for the past.[7] Otherwild's interface insists on maintaining connections to each item's historical referent through the site's rollover function—a user cannot "look" at details on a particular item without also browsing its history—the reproduction and its referent are mechanically stitched together. This interface design insists on pedagogical encounters with historical information. At the same time, Otherwild is a business that trades in the abundance of iconography from lesbian history, which is no longer rarefied, marginalized, or subject to erasure in the same ways it once was.

Otherwild's work responds to a desire for encounters with lesbian-feminist activist archives through networked digital interfaces. The sometimes tenuous connection to history is what gives this clothing interest. A navy blue tote bag screen-printed with yellow text that reads "We Are Everywhere" reproduces two images of this popular gay liberation slogan in action: one depicts a pin button from the Lesbian Herstory Archives collection, the other is a photograph of balloons printed with the slogan from a 1978 issue of Lesbian Tide.[8] The balloon photograph was taken by Bourge Hathaway at a lesbian rally that took place at the 1977 National Women's Conference in Houston, though the Otherwild caption reads simply, "'We Are Everywhere' Lesbian Tide, 1978."[9] Without the reference to the button, or the grainy black-and-white photo of the balloons, scanned from a newsletter, the tote bag is still cute, but it's just a tote bag. With the original photos for context, the bag becomes a point of pride, identification, and membership. The "We" invoked on the bag transcends generations and distinctions between digital and analog media, and it brings the archives out into the streets. This connection to the past is drawn out of digital networks and can be yours, for a price.

Otherwild is merely one player in a larger aestheticized revival of lesbian-feminist history. This aesthetic emerges from an affective and commercial economy in which a wide range of primary source materials are reblogged, scanned, copied, and circulated through social media. Lesbian information is no longer scarce; rather, it is readily available online via digital collections produced by institutional and community archives, artists, and public history projects.[10] These abundant conditions inspire looser ideas about what digitized objects from the past are for, who ought to control them, and how the integrity of the histories they represent should be presented online.

Instagram's photo-sharing cultures are not known for the didactic strength of their captions, but queer and feminist historical Instagram accounts do try to provide context and to name the people pictured in digitized materials.[11] Conflicts often erupt in the comments sections when accounts do not bother to include this information or get it wrong.[12] Some users are reading these posts carefully and critically, suggesting a temporal orientation to Instagram that is at odds with the image-sharing platform's reputation for distracted, perpetual scrolling.[13] Kelly Rakowski's @h_e_r_s_t_o_r_y is the most popular of these accounts, with more than 160,000 followers and a tagline on its profile that qualifies its historical responsibilities as merely social media: this is "A DYKE IG Acct, Not An Archive" responds to the intense representational expectations queer feminist communities express on social media.[14] The tagline also disarticulates @h_e_r_s_t_o_r_y from a specific, *actual* archives with a similar name: the Lesbian Herstory Archives (LHA). Where @h_e_r_s_t_o_r_y and Otherwild are community-oriented "brands" with business interests related to lesbian history, the LHA is a nonprofit community organization committed to the preservation of records related to lesbian politics and life. The archives' own popular Instagram account also uses social media to do outreach with materials the LHA houses, in keeping with its long-standing practice of using media to make materials accessible for those who are unable to visit New York. Though these organizations have different goals, they all operate within a larger economy of attention in which LGBT visibility on social media platforms is leveraged toward neoliberal equity, diversity, and inclusion regimes (think for example, of specially animated #Pride hashtags released by platforms each June). Public libraries, community archives and cultural heritage organizations play a role in this process.[15]

Instagram posts that share lesbian ephemera don't always provide context for the histories they reference, particularly when images and iconography circulate beyond the queer networks that initially gather and digitize this information. For example, Otherwild's first and best-known reproduction is a T-shirt with the slogan "The Future Is Female," based on a photograph of the lesbian folk singer Alix Dobkin wearing the shirt while standing in front of New York City's first women's bookstore, Labyris Books, in 1975. The photo was taken by Dobkin's girlfriend at the time, the photographer Liza Cowan. Forty years later, on May 26, 2015, @h_e_r_s_t_o_r_y posted the image. Labyris Books had created the shirt in 1975 to promote the store and the women's publishing movement. From the present, the garment is difficult to separate rhetorically from histories of trans-exclusionary feminist organizing, particularly given Dobkin's history as a political columnist who often published transphobic views about lesbian feminism.[16] In 2015, the "The Future Is Female" shirt became a uniform for a certain kind of liberal, often white feminist, as it was taken up by Hillary Clinton's supporters during and after her 2016 presidential campaign.[17] What once articulated a commitment to publishing as a form of world building outside patriarchal structures becomes enmeshed in celebrity culture and "lean-in" styles of popular, white feminism aimed at equality for some. The shirt has been knocked off by countless retailers and circulates as mainstream feminist fast fashion. Otherwild's follow-up T-shirt, "The Future Is Female Ejaculation," is willfully less portable.

"The Future Is Female" is an easy slogan to coopt and separate from its lesbian-feminist roots: it is a hopeful, palatable mainstream feminist sentiment grounded in reproductive futurity and a celebration of the category "woman." The very different temporality of "The Patriarchy Is a Pyramid Scheme" locates the need for radical queer feminist practices in both the future and the past: pyramid schemes grow exponentially, but lesbian history is full of tools for dismantling them, including the digital networks that revive all this print ephemera. Photographs, scans from newsletters and other print documents, deeply researched captions, and hashtags all organize lesbian feminist history as information that can be circulated through digital networks.

Images that accounts such as @h_e_r_s_t_o_r_y, @lesbianherstoryarchives, and @lgbt_history choose to share on their feeds frame how Instagram users visualize lesbian history. Most of these users are far too young to have "been there." Like the information activists before them, these accounts use the interface to redress transphobia and white supremacy in movement histories through photo selection and captioning practices that highlight activism by queer and trans people of color. These efforts at inclusion do not necessarily shift the white gaze through which many queer history Instagram accounts look.[18] As China Medel argues, archivally engaged accounts made and maintained by and for people of color foreground unique aesthetic practices that approach knowing about the past in ways that depart from an emphasis on capture and accumulation.[19]

Instagram and Tumblr—the other image-sharing platform formerly popular with queer users, especially youth—are also subject to platform constraints via profit-oriented practices, including content moderation aimed at upholding "community values."[20] Sisterhood, protest, and aesthetic aspects of dyke culture abound, but there is little overt sexuality. Seminude images, images that are too sexually suggestive, and even Zoe Leonard's 1992 poem *I Want a Dyke for President* are regularly flagged and removed by Instagram. Users fight back, editing images slightly so they conform technically with policies (for example, by placing "stickers" over nipples and genitals), avoiding risky hashtags, altering metadata, or simply reposting an image in the hope that a few hundred more users will catch a glimpse before the offending nipples are taken down once again.

This information work takes places under conditions in which the rapid and abundant online circulation of ephemera from late twentieth-century lesbian-feminist activism has the potential to isolate all of these images from the real, laboring bodies who first made them. Within the flows of online image sharing cultures, T-shirt slogans, and the monetization and mainstreaming of queer and trans history, it is easy to scroll distractedly through these faces, marches, and even memorials. That casual, rapid flick of the thumb characterizing my habitual scroll through Instagram is far removed from the methodical pace at which hundreds of print newsletters might be folded and stamped for mailing by dedicated volunteers. Earlier generations of information activists labored to share whatever good lesbian information they could scrounge up. Historical Instagrams operate within abundant conditions produced precisely by these earlier generations of information activists, who preserved their work in archives. While differences of pace, scale, and rhythm are plain, something else ties this contemporary work with digital technologies to information activism of the past: a media praxis deeply committed to the ongoing, everyday work of managing information. Through tagging, reblogging, and holding other users accountable to the histories they engage, information activists continue working on lesbian-feminist infrastructures within queer digital networks.

Binding original archival references to the contemporary projects that enliven them is a way to slow down the speed at which digital networks operate: take a breath; think about where this comes from; hold space for those who did this work; read the caption or citation. This practice is a way of marking the economic and temporal discontinuities between lesbian historical legibility in the 1970s and today, and a response to information abundance. Finding strategies to cope with feeling overwhelmed by information is a practice shared by earlier information activism with paper tools. A single image comes up over and over again when information activists write about their work: being overwhelmed by too much paper and attempting to stay on top of the influx. Clare Potter describes this feeling in her handbook to indexing in the Circle of Lesbian Indexers:

> I suddenly realized that I had accumulated overnight—or so it seemed—hundreds of 3×5 cards. Although they sat quietly in the file drawers in front of me, I began to get this very distinct feeling that they were surreptitiously plotting to disrupt my best laid plans and would in a pique come raining down on me in gleeful anarchy. What I'm intimating here is that the numbers of cards we can safely manage without the help of machines seems finite.[21]

Potter gives life to her paper database of lesbian periodicals. The cards become a rogue army, stalking her from the drawers as they grow their ranks in anticipation of just the right moment to sabotage the system she put in place to order them.

The "very distinct feeling" Potter tries to describe through this image is one of precarity: an existence of "radical contingency," without predictability, security, or guarantees.[22] I have argued that information activists do their work because access to good lesbian information is so *precarious*: unavailable, inconsistent, temporary, or even impossible. Information activism attempts to build stable infrastructures that ameliorate this problem. It also produces more paper on the verge of disorganization or even erasure, through misfiling or neglect. Precarity has a certain temporality experienced when singular agents do not seem to have control over events that have been set in motion.[23] Try as Potter might to keep her collection of cards within the limits of what "we can safely manage" by hand, the collection continued to grow; such is the paradoxical sequence that seems to come along with committing to any information-management project, particularly ones carried out by activists, on the margins of institutional structures and their supports. What seems like so much possibility at the project's outset—a usable subject guide to all lesbian periodical literature—quickly becomes precisely the project's undoing as information accumulates in unmanageable ways.

Lauren Berlant describes "cruel optimism" as "the condition of maintaining an attachment to a significantly problematic object."[24] Lesbian-feminist information is one such problematic object. Digital technology's promise of newer and ever-greater methods of management, preservation, and access are optimistic sites of attachment. Optimism informs the belief that digital archives can remember, commemorate, and preserve. But as Wendy Hui Kyong Chun has shown, digital media rhetoric often conflates storage with memory. For Chun, "Memory is an active process, not static. A memory must be held in order to keep it from moving or fading."[25] Lesbian-feminist work with digital media is an active process of holding, where efforts such as selection and description ensure more than mere storage. But this work is ongoing and incompletable, perpetually chasing after a lasting, usable archive and always trying to catch up.

Berlant understands living with precarity through affective attachments to "good life" fantasies as they motivate ways of being in the present.[26] Good-life fantasies can be individual (love, happiness, a comfortable middle-class life) or they can be collective (about family, a political scene, or dreams of a reciprocal world). The projects I have examined straddle the singular/private and collective/public, imagining information to serve both kinds of good-life fantasies: the figure of the well-informed "lesbian" is used to imagine a political collective with organized demands, but also to shore up livable lives for individual women. This collective-singular tension is expressed in the LHA's founder Joan Nestle's assertion that the archives existed "for any lesbian woman who needed an image or a word to survive the day" and in JR Roberts's hope that her Black lesbian bibliography would "lead to a better understanding of Black lesbian life and that this knowledge [would] help us all as we attempt to revolutionize our relationships with one another."[27] Nestle and Roberts both propose an active stance for those brought into lesbian-feminist information infrastructures, evoking struggle met by revolution. These optimistic scenes stand in contrast to Potter's sense of trying not to get too overwhelmed by her drawers full of index cards.

Potter's words are closer to the register of "styles, active habits, and modes of responsivity" that add up to a politics of getting by.[28] In more recent work, Berlant has described these "getting by" modalities as the "poetics of infrastructure," where regular people find ways to adjust to and work on and in systems not of their own making.[29] These forms of adjustment and improvisation guide what I have argued is a lesbian-feminist approach to information work: carrying on with the routine and repetitive tasks required to achieve a greater "good-life" vision of what information might do for movements. I have argued that lesbian feminism hinges on visions of the future, sometimes modest ones grounded in making lesbian lives more inhabitable, with information.

Potter describes having too much of the thing she sought in the first place: cards. The tyranny of abundance is a common complaint among information activists who face growing pressure exerted by too much stuff and too little time. These conditions shape information activists' everyday approaches to their work processes. Saskia Scheffer at the LHA described her willingness to assign less-than-perfect metadata to a digital image this way: "At some point I just need to get stuff up [online], and I can't spend more time waiting for inspiration."[30] As I have argued, this approach accepts provisionality and welcomes revision, critiquing categorical description's inherent inadequacies to complex forms of life. Here the limitations of time and space have productive effects for the project: at some point, Scheffer just makes a decision because she trusts her judgment and built a system in which she can change that decision later on.

Scheffer, Potter, and other information activists navigate a careful balance between abundance and scarcity, always catching up to the information they work to wrangle. *Matrices'* paper newsletter network made countless connections possible, but these connections outgrew the pages of the newsletter and became impossible to document. The network's success became an obstacle for its very status as a publication. As Berlant explains, optimism is cruel when the "very vitalizing or animating potency of an object/scene of desire contributes to the attrition of the very thriving that is supposed to be made possible in the work of attachment in the first place."[31] Here the object/scene of desire—the newsletter, the cards, the ringing telephone, or the archives—continues to produce information in need of management, and activists burn out as they try to keep up.

Community archives bring their own scenes of carrying on in the face of tasks that seem endless. Writers who set the scene of encountering the Lesbian Herstory Archives often try to get across a sense of being overwhelmed by stuff through descriptions of "piles" and "overflow" that are nearly genre writing about the space. The LHA's vertical subject files are "bulging"; the collections are "overwhelming" and "confusing"; the building's walls are "filled"; the special collections are "piled to the ceiling" and "crammed into every available corner"; the basement is filled with "hundreds of paper documents"; and "the rooms, bathrooms, and closets burst," while "piles of unsorted publications formed a two-foot-high mound in a corner of what was once a bedroom overlooking a tree-lined street."[32] I made this turn myself in the introduction to this book, describing a basement "overcrowded" with "stuff." The feeling of being overwhelmed comes up over and over again, but attempts to address this problem through media practices can end up creating more paper, as with Potter's cards.

The LHA's mandate to preserve and provide access to any records of lesbian lives that otherwise would be lost presents the irony that these lives, once collected, might get lost in the archives' piles. A pivotal scene in Leslie Feinberg's semiautobiographical novel *Stone Butch Blues* (1993) imagines the protagonist Jess leaving a letter for a long-lost lover, Theresa, at an archives that is probably the Lesbian Herstory Archives. Jess writes, "Since I can't mail you this letter, I'll send it to a place where they keep women's memories safe. Maybe someday, passing through this big city, you will stop and read it. Maybe you won't."[33] Ann Cvetkovich reads this scene as emblematic of the LHA's role in making trauma and "erotic feelings the subject of archival history."[34] While rereading *Stone Butch Blues* around the time of Feinberg's death in 2014, as I was working on the research that would become this book, I came to this passage and felt stressed out. Would Jess/Feinberg's letter get accessioned properly? Might it get lost in the piles of materials waiting to be processed—the "unsorted, two-foot high mounds" Jack Gieseking describes? Would Jess remember not only to sign but to mail in the donor agreement form that will allow researchers future online access to the letter? Will the letter get scanned? How will a finding aid describe the complexity of Jess/Feinberg's trans identity in relation to "lesbian?"

These overly technical worries about a piece of paper in *Stone Butch Blues* (a work of fiction) are irrational thoughts furnished by the isolation of academic research and writing. But there is also something here about the impossible temporalities of attachment. An imagined future subject who might shore up or challenge the status quo guides information activists. Archiving the past is work motivated by attachment to this subject in the future. The ongoing management of information about the past generates more and more material for this future subject who is always in the process of arriving, and is only anticipated in certain forms. Put simply, the archives, by its very nature, can never catch up to what, and who, it wants to serve.

Describing the LHA's overwhelming abundance of stuff takes up Cvet-kovich's argument that "the history of any archive is a history of space, which becomes the material measure and foundation of the archive's power and visibility as a form of public culture."[35] Remarking on this history of space, Gieseking reads many of the Lesbian Herstory Archives' spatial id-iosyncrasies as material evidence of a productive, queer instability. The or-ganized chaos is evidence of how "activist archives are notoriously under-funded and always in process," but it also marks how the "Lesbian Herstory Archives enacts a specific way of destabilizing what *archive* means."[36] These descriptions also set a scene in which lesbian history is always being made, and we are always catching up to its making. As Barbara Godard has ar-gued, the challenge of archives in the twenty-first century is that their once black-boxed processes are being put on display.[37] In placing the archives' digital media practices on display, I situate these practices in an ongoing, perpetual state of information abundance that digital media cannot ex-actly solve, despite promises that it will do so. All kinds of "digital" media promise mastery over information: the newsletter through its network; the telephone hotline through its "neutral" search-query method; the index cards through their nearly computational ability to store and sort; the digi-tal archives with its promise of access and preservation. Lesbian feminists probe the limits of the digital through resourceful practices that contribute to a gendered history of emergent media technologies: digitization as strat-egizing and working around constraints.

I have argued that a "digital imperative" shapes the direction of archives in the present, becoming a normative trajectory or standard with the po-tential to solve the too-much-stuff crisis. This is the same digital imperative that led Potter to consider abandoning her cards for a computer program. Compression is a potent fantasy of digital formats, guiding the develop-ment of media infrastructures and technical standards as they encounter users.[38] Compression's potential is a factor when an organization such as the LHA thinks about digitizing the special collections that are "piled to the ceiling" and "crammed into every available corner."[39] Digital collections "compress" the space that materials take up in a number of ways: digitized materials are easier to relocate to offsite storage; fewer visitors need to take up space in the physical archives if they can get what they want online; and, finally, the "fidelity" of original formats is compressed, as in the case of the noise-reduced, streaming-ready MP3s that archives offer in place of cassette tapes. But compression does little to address the ongoing precari-ous conditions information activists must navigate. Digitization creates an abundance of data that must be managed, kept track of, stored, and sorted, all processes with which information activists must catch up and stay afloat. Digitization also opens records of lesbian-feminist information activism to contemporary social media, through which their historical specificities may, or may not, be preserved.[40] Somehow these Instagram feeds feel endless—scroll, scroll, scroll, scroll, scroll—although the images they offer merely scratch the surface of what's available.

Rather than a rupture or solution to the archives' problem of stuff, digital media in practice can often seem quite banal: the LHA continues to digitize tape after tape just as it continued to catalog book after book thirty years ago. The differences among media formats matter, but situating digitization at the twenty-first-century archives in a longer genealogy of activism aimed at building lesbian information infrastructures emphasizes continuities and discontinuities among styles of media practice over technologically determined changes.

By connecting lesbian-feminist information from the early 1970s to the present, I have argued that activists have long thought carefully and intentionally about their work with media, whether with paper or an online interface. To be more modest about the digital is not to dismiss or diminish the work information activists do. Quite the opposite. Through media practices, lesbian feminist activists take on a familiar killjoy role, supplanting fantasies of the digital with attention to everyday operations and uses that matter. In refusing to share the same orientation to "good" digital objects, they make room for other possible encounters with digital media.[41] Through the systems they design and the everyday decisions they make, their work brings into relief such vital questions as what access really means, given its often-forgotten gendered dimensions, or how subject classification and metadata perpetuate categorizations that wound.

This work, organized around ongoing negotiations about "lesbian's" relevance and leverage in the past and present, is critical, to be sure. It also puts forward visions of joy motivated by collectivity, the erotics of taking part in a sexual public and the idea that more livable lives in the present might be built out of loving attention paid to the past. Lesbian-feminist information activism intervenes with fantasies of digital mastery and abundance but does so to make room for its own modest practices of keeping up under the precarious weight of information. That there will continue to be more and more paper to do something with ensures a past that matters, a present animated by vital technologies, and a future with value in it.

Notes

INTRODUCTION

1. "The National Women's Mailing List," *Matrices*, vol. 4, no. 1, 1980, 21.
2. "The National Women's Mailing List," 21.
3. Other scholars have used the term "information activism" to describe digital activism oriented toward affecting political and policy outcomes by consuming, aggregating and distributing information (Max Halupka, "The Rise of Information Activism: How to Bridge Dualisms and Reconceptualise Political Participation," *Information, Communication & Society* 19, no. 10 [2016]: 1487–1503), or performing data-driven forms of activism (Kelly Hannah-Moffat, "Algorithmic Risk Governance: Big Data Analytics, Race and Information Activism in Criminal Justice Debates," *Theoretical Criminology* 23, no. 4 [2018]: 453–70). My use of the term departs in its emphasis on media history and on information as constitutive of queer and feminist social movements.
4. Information activism approaches feminism at a similar register to Carrie Rentschler and Samantha Thrift's "Doing Feminism" methodology. Carrie A. Rentschler and Samantha C. Thrift, "Doing Feminism in the Network: Networked Laughter and the 'Binders Full of Women' Meme," *Feminist Theory* 16, no. 3 (2015): 329–59, https://doi.org/10.1177/1464700115604136; Carrie A. Rentschler, "Making Culture and Doing Feminism," in *The Routledge Handbook of Contemporary Feminism,* ed. Tasha Oren and Andrea L. Press, 127–47 (New York: Routledge University Press, 2019). "Doing Feminism" is a framework for understanding how dispersed groups of women collectively perform media activism in ways that exceed many of the established scholarly methods for studying this activism via the products it leaves behind (zines, buttons, posters, and so on). This method attends to the affects and assemblages that exceed the creation of traditional tools or artifacts, and are less likely to find their way into archives or object-oriented understandings of feminist media production.
5. A "queer" history of information describes both a methodological imperative to bend what and who is understood as significant in histories of information management. It also references the process of looking queerly from the present at lesbian-feminist history, a temporality I unpack later in this introduction.

6. Lucas Hilderbrand, *Inherent Vice: Bootleg Histories of Videotape and Copyright* (Durham NC: Duke University Press, 2009); Tara Macpherson, "DH by Design: Alternative Origin Stories for the Digital Humanities," Center for Digital Scholarship and Curation, Washington State University, Pullman, March 3, 2016, accessed April 6, 2019, https://www.youtube.com/watch?v=S4VRAQLLjRg; Michelle Meagher, "Difficult, Messy, Nasty, and Sensational," *Feminist Media Studies* 14, no. 4 (2013): 578–92; Trysh Travis, "The Women in Print Movement: History and Implications," *Book History* 11 (2008): 275–300.

7. Susan Leigh Star, "Misplaced Concretism and Concrete Situations," in *Boundary Objects and Beyond: Working with Leigh Star*, ed. Geoffrey C. Bowker et al. (Cambridge, MA: MIT Press, [1994] 2016), 152.

8. Geoffrey B. Pingree and Lisa Gitelman, "What's New about New Media?" in *New Media, 1740–1915*, ed. Geoffrey B. Pingree and Lisa Gitelman (Cambridge MA: MIT Press, 2003), xii. See also Carolyn Marvin, *When Old Technologies Were New: Thinking about Electrical Communication in the Nineteenth Century* (New York: Oxford University Press, 1988); Jonathan Sterne and Dylan Mulvin, "The Low Acuity for Blue: Perceptual Technics and American Color Television," *Journal of Visual Culture* 13, no. 2 (2014): 122.

9. Barbara Sjoholm, "She Who Owns the Press," in *Make Your Own History: Documenting Feminist and Queer Activism in the 21st Century*, ed. Lyz Bly and Kelly Wooten (Sacramento, CA: Litwin, 2012). On the history of this print culture, see Agatha Beins, *Liberation in Print: Feminist Periodicals and Social Movement Identity* (Athens: University of Georgia Press, 2017); Kristen Hogan, *The Feminist Bookstore Movement: Lesbian Antiracism and Feminist Accountability* (Durham, NC: Duke University Press, 2016); Tessa Jordan, "*Branching Out*: Second-Wave Feminist Periodicals and the Archive of Canadian Women's Writing," *English Studies in California* 36, nos. 2–3 (2010): 63–90; Meagher, "Difficult, Messy, Nasty, and Sensational"; Martin Meeker, *Contacts Desired: Gay and Lesbian Communications and Community, 1940s–1970s* (Chicago: University of Chicago Press, 2006); SaraEllen Strongman, "The Sisterhood: Black Women, Black Feminism, and the Women's Liberation Movement" (PhD diss., University of Pennsylvania, Philadelphia, 2018).

10. On the digital afterlives of these print materials, particularly within women of color online spaces, see Cassius Adair and Lisa Nakamura, "The Digital Afterlives of *This Bridge Called My Back*: Women of Color Feminism, Digital Labor, and Networked Pedagogy," *American Literature* 89, no. 2 (2017): 255–78.

11. Lisa Gitelman, *Paper Knowledge: Toward a Media History of Documents* (Durham NC: Duke University Press, 2014), 7–9.

12. My methodological emphasis on the materiality of media and nonlinear histories places this work in dialogue with media archaeology; however, my primary commitment is to the laboring activists who imagine and carry out this work. The video game historian Laine Nooney writes, "Media archaeology so often ignores: human specificity, the way enactments of power fall upon certain types of bodies more than others": Laine Nooney, "A Pedestal, a Table, a Love Letter: Archaeologies of Gender in Videogame History," *Game Studies* 13, no. 2 (2013), http://gamestudies

.org/1302/articles/nooney. I hope this book contributes to the corrective Nooney and others have launched.

13. See Rachel Corbman, "A Genealogy of the Lesbian Herstory Archives, 1974–2014," *Journal of Contemporary Archival Studies* 1, no. 1 (2014): 1–16; Ann Cvetkovich, *An Archive of Feelings: Trauma, Sexuality and Lesbian Public Cultures* (Durham, NC: Duke University Press, 2003).

14. "Statement of Purpose and Principles" ([1978] 2017), Lesbian Herstory Archives, http://www.lesbianherstoryarchives.org/history.html. Rachel Corbman has traced the origin of these principles back to Joan Nestle, "Voice 2: Radical Archiving: A Lesbian Feminist Perspective," OutHistory.org, 1978, http://outhistory .org/exhibits/show/an-early-conversation-about-ga/voice-2-joan-nestle.

15. My approach to the entanglement of politics, technology, and practice is influenced by feminist science and technology studies. See esp. Karen Barad, *Meeting the Universe Halfway: Quantum Physics and the Entanglement of Matter and Meaning* (Durham, NC: Duke University Press, 2007); Lucas Introna, "Ethics and the Speaking of Things," *Theory, Culture and Society* 26, no. 4 (2009): 25–46, https://doi.org/10.1177/0263276409104967; Wanda J. Orlikowski, "The Sociomateriality of Organizational Life: Considering Technology in Management Research," *Cambridge Journal of Economics* 34 (2010): 125–41; Lucy Suchman, *Human-Machine Reconfigurations: Plans and Situated Actions* (Cambridge: Cambridge University Press, [1987] 2006), https://doi.org/10.1017/CBO9780511808418.008.

16. Geoffrey C. Bowker, Karen Baker, Florence Miller, and David Ribes, "Toward Information Infrastructure Studies: Ways of Knowing in a Networked Environment," in *International Handbook of Internet Research*, ed. Jeremy Hunsinger, Lisbeth Klastrup, and Matthew M. Allen (Dordrecht: Hunsinger, 2009), 98.

17. Susan Leigh Star and Karen Ruhleder, "Steps Toward an Ecology of Infrastructure: Design and Access for Large Information Spaces," *Information Systems Research* 7, no. 1 (1996): 111–34.

18. See Melissa Adler, *Cruising the Library: Perversities in the Organization of Knowledge* (New York: Fordham University Press, 2017).

19. For recent work that exemplifies the methodological approaches required to make this turn see Rachel Corbman, "Conferencing on the Edge: A Queer History of Feminist Field Formation, 1969–89" (PhD diss., Stony Brook University, Stony Brook, 2019); Hogan, *The Feminist Bookstore Movement*; SaraEllen Strongman, "'Creating Justice between Us': Audre Lorde's Theory of the Erotic as Coalitional Politics in the Women's Movement," *Feminist Theory* 19, no. 1 (2018): 41–59. Jack Gieseking's "Size Matters to Lesbians, Too: Queer Feminist Interventions into the Scale of Big Data," *Professional Geographer* 70, no. 1 (2018): 150–56, https://doi.org /10.1080/00330124.2017.1326084, uses data visualization techniques to surface connections among activists by coding organizational records at the Lesbian Herstory Archives. It is an especially illustrative example of what methodological experimentation can offer here, as is Michelle Moravec's Scalar project "Unghosting Apparitional (Lesbian) Histories," *Ada* 5 (2014), http://doi.org/10.7264/N3GF0RS6. This scholarship departs in radical ways from monolithic histories of the women's liberation movement.

20. Anna Feigenbaum, "Written in the Mud: (Proto)zine-Making and Autonomous Media at the Greenham Common Women's Peace Camp," *Feminist Media Studies* 13, no. 1 (2012): 1–13; Victoria Hesford, *Feeling Women's Liberation* (Durham, NC: Duke University, 2013); Carrie A. Rentschler and Samantha C. Thrift, "Doing Feminism: Event, Archive, Techné," *Feminist Theory* 16, no. 3 (2015): 239–49, https://doi.org/10.1177/1464700115604138; Rianka Singh, "Platform Feminism: Protest and the Politics of Spatial Organization," *Ada* 14 (2018), https://doi.org/10.5399/uo/ada.2018.14.6; Rianka Singh and Sarah Sharma, "Platform Uncommons," *Feminist Media Studies* 19, no. 2 (2019), https://doi.org/10.1080/14680777.2019.1573547.

21. Carrie A. Rentschler and Samantha C. Thrift, "Doing Feminism in the Network: Networked Laughter and the 'Binders Full of Women' Meme," *Feminist Theory* 16, no. 3 (2015): 329–59, https://doi.org/10.1177/1464700115604136.

22. Star and Ruhleder, "Steps Toward an Ecology of Infrastructure," 113.

23. Star and Ruhleder, "Steps Toward an Ecology of Infrastructure," 112.

24. Carrie A. Rentschler, *Second Wounds: Victims' Rights and the Media in the U.S.* (Durham, NC: Duke University Press, 2011), 17.

25. Rentschler, *Second Wounds*, 19.

26. Cf. Corbman, "A Genealogy of the Lesbian Herstory Archives"; Cvetkovich, *An Archive of Feelings*; Jack Gieseking, "Useful Instability: The Dialectical Production of the Social and Spatial Lesbian Herstory Archives," *Radical History Review* 122 (2015): 25–37.

27. Martin Frické, "The Knowledge Pyramid: A Critique of the DIKW Hierarchy," *Journal of Information Science* 35, no. 2 (2008): 131–42; Lisa Gitelman and Virginia Jackson, "Introduction," in *Raw Data Is an Oxymoron*, ed. Lisa Gitelman and Virginia Jackson (Cambridge MA: MIT Press, 2013), 1–14.

28. *Oxford English Dictionary*, "Information, n."

29. Angela L. DiVeglia, "Accessibility, Accountability, and Activism," in Bly and Wooten, *Make Your Own History*, 72–73.

30. On database flexibility and standards, see Tineke Egyedi, "Infrastructure Flexibility Created by Standardized Gateways: The Cases of XML and the ISO Container," *Knowledge, Technology, and Policy* 14, no. 3 (2001): 41–54.

31. Jennifer S. Light, "When Computers Were Women," *Technology and Culture* 40, no. 3 (1999): 455–83; Lisa Nakamura, "Indigenous Circuits: Navajo Women and the Racialization of Early Electronic Manufacture," *American Quarterly* 66, no. 4 (2014): 919–41; Patrick Keilty, "Tedious: Feminized Labor in Machine-Readable Cataloging," *Feminist Media Studies* 18, no. 2 (2018): 191–204, https://doi.org/10.1080/14680777.2017.1308410.

32. On cultural infrastructure, see Fred Turner, "Burning Man at Google: A Cultural Infrastructure for New Media Production," *New Media & Society* 11, nos. 1–2 (2009): 73–94.

33. Dylan Mulvin, *Proxies: The Cultural Work of Standing In* (Cambridge, MA: MIT Press, forthcoming).

34. Quinn DuPont and Alana Cattapan, "Alice and Bob: A History of the World's Most Famous Cryptographic Couple," n.d., http://cryptocouple.com.

35. Mulvin, *Proxies*.

36. Warren Weaver, "Recent Contributions to the Mathematical Theory of Communication," 1949, http://www.ffzg.unizg.hr/fonet/kolegij/tinfo/weaver.pdf, 15.

37. Brenton J. Malin argues that the nineteenth-century telegraph was thought to incite emotional response that might harm recipients, where telegraph operators (Malin mentions the "telegraph boy" who delivers telegrams on the run) provide emotional mediation among senders, receivers, and technology: Brenton J. Malin, *Feeling Mediated: A History of Media Technology and Emotion in America* (New York: New York University Press, 2014), 35–36. Malin also discusses the effects of Taylorism on communications workers; the prevailing idea during the time of the telegraph was that "emotionally controlled workers could create more efficient industries": Malin, *Feeling Mediated*, 78.

38. Yola de Lusenet and Pieter J. D. Drenth, "Preservation and Access: Two Concepts, One Goal—The Work of the European Commission on Preservation and Access (ECPA)," *Journal of the Society of Archivists* 20, no. 2 (1999): 162; Peter J. Astle and Adrienne Muir, "Digitization and Preservation in Public Libraries and Archives," *Journal of Librarianship and Information Science* 34, no. 2 (2002): 67.

39. Astle and Muir, "Digitization and Preservation"; Michèle Valerie Cloonan, "W(H)ITHER Preservation?" *Library Quarterly* 71, no. 2 (2001): 231–42; de Lusenet and Drenth, "Preservation and Access"; Lilly Kolton, "The Promise and Threat of Digital Options in an Archival Age," *Archivaria* 47 (1999): 114–35.

40. Hilderbrand, *Inherent Vice*.

41. C. M. Bolick, "Digital Archives: Democratizing the Doing of History," *International Journal of Social Education* 21, no. 1 (2006): 122.

42. See, e.g., Wendy Hui Kyong Chun, "The Enduring Ephemeral, or The Future Is a Memory," in *Media Archaeology: Approaches, Application, and Implications*, ed. Erkki Huhtamo and Jussi Parikka (Berkeley: University of California Press, 2011), 184–203; Abigail De Kosnik, *Rogue Archives: Digital Cultural Memory and Media Fandom* (Cambridge, MA: MIT Press, 2016); Kate Eichhorn, *The Archival Turn in Feminism: Outrage in Order* (Philadelphia: Temple University Press, 2013); Gabriella Giannachi, *Archive Everything: Mapping the Everyday* (Cambridge, MA: MIT Press, 2016); Shannon Mattern, *Code and Clay, Data and Dirt: Five Thousand Years of Urban Media* (Minneapolis: University of Minnesota Press, 2017).

43. Michel Foucault, *The Archaeology of Knowledge* (New York: Vintage, [1972] 2002).

44. Ann Laura Stoler, *Along the Archival Grain: Epistemic Anxieties and Colonial Common Sense* (Princeton, NJ: Princeton University Press, 2010).

45. Jarrett M. Drake, "RadTech Meets RadArch: Towards A New Principle for Archives and Archival Description," *On Archivy*, April 6, 2016, https://medium.com/on-archivy/radtech-meets-radarch-towards-a-new-principle-for-archives-and-archival-description-568f133e4325.

46. Eichhorn, *The Archival Turn in Feminism*.

47. Michelle Caswell, "Seeing Yourself in History: Community Archives and the Fight against Symbolic Annihilation," *Public Historian* 36, no. 2 (2014): 36.

48. Caswell, "Seeing Yourself in History." See also Michelle Caswell, Alda Allina Migoni, Noah Geraci and Marika Cifor, "'To Be Able to Imagine Otherwise':

Community Archives and the Importance of Representation, *Archives and Records* 38, no. 1 (2017): 5–26.

49. Caswell et al., "To Be Able to Imagine Otherwise."

50. Jamie A. Lee, "Mediated Storytelling Practices and Productions: Archival Bodies of Affective Evidences," *Networking Knowledge* 9, no. 6 (2016): 74–87.

51. Tonia Sutherland, "Archival Amnesty: In Search of Black American Transitional and Restorative Justice," *Journal of Critical Library and Information Studies* 1, no. 2 (2017); Drake, "RadTech Meets RadArch."

52. Syrus Marcus Ware, "All Power to All People? Black LGBTTI2QQ Activism, Remembrance, and Archiving in Toronto," *Transgender Studies Quarterly* 4, no. 2 (2017): 170–80; Rio Rodriguez, "Mapping QTBIPOC Toronto" (master's thesis, York University, Toronto, 2016).

53. For an exceptional example of queer librarian-scholar work on these questions, see Emily Drabinski, "Gendered S(h)elves: Body and Identity in the Library," *Women and Environments International Magazine* 78–79 (2009–10): 16–18.

54. Sanford Berman, "Introduction: Cataloging Reform, LC, and Me," in *Radical Cataloging: Essays at the Front*, ed. K. R. Roberto (Jefferson, NC: MacFarland, 2008), 5–11; Dee Garrison, "The Tender Technicians: The Feminization of Public Librarianship, 1876–1905," *Journal of Social History* 6, no. 2 (1972–73): 131–59; Matt Johnson, "A Hidden History of Queer Subject Access," in Roberto, *Radical Cataloging*, 18–27.

55. Garrison, "The Tender Technicians," 143.

56. See Maria T. Accardi, *Feminist Pedagogy for Library Instruction* (Sacramento, CA: Litwin, 2013); Bly and Wooten, *Make Your Own History*; Patrick Keilty and Rebecca Dean, eds., *Feminist and Queer Information Studies Reader* (Sacramento, CA: Litwin, 2013); Alana Kumbier, *Ephemeral Materiality: Queering the Archive* (Sacramento, CA: Litwin, 2014); Tracy Nectoux, ed., *Out Behind the Desk: Workplace Issues for LGBTQ Librarians* (Sacramento, CA: Litwin, 2011).

57. Michelle Caswell, "'The Archive' Is Not an Archives: Acknowledging the Intellectual Contributions of Archival Studies," *Reconstruction* 16, no. 1 (2016); Maryanne Dever, "Editorial: Archives and New Forms of Feminist Research," *Australian Feminist Studies* 32, nos. 91–92 (2017): 1–4; Drabinski, "Gendered S(h)elves"; K. J. Rawson, "Accessing Transgender//Desiring Queer(er?) Archival Logics," *Archivaria* 68 (2009): 123–40; K. R. Roberto, "Inflexible Bodies: Metadata for Transgender Identities," *Journal of Information Ethics* 20, no. 2 (2011): 56–64.

58. DiVeglia, "Accessibility, Accountability, and Activism"; Elizabeth Ellcessor, *Restricted Access: Media, Disability, and the Politics of Participation* (New York: New York University Press, 2016); Margaret Hedstrom, "Archives, Memory, and Interfaces with the Past," *Archival Science* 2 (2002): 21–43; Marlene Manoff, "Archive and Database as Metaphor: Theorizing the Historical Record," *Portal* 10, no. 4 (2010): 385–98; Tara Robertson, "Not All Information Wants to Be Free: The Case Study of *On Our Backs*," in *Applying Library Values to Emerging Technology: Decision-Making in the Age of Open Access, Maker Spaces, and the Ever-Changing Library*, ed. Peter D. Fernandez and Killy Tilton, Publications in Librarianship 72 (Chicago: American Library Association, 2018), 225–39; Jen Wolfe, "Playing Fast and Loose

with the Rules: Metadata Cataloging for Digital Library Projects" in Roberto, *Radical Cataloging*, 69–74.

59. Michael Warner, "Publics and Counterpublics," *Public Culture* 14, no. 1 (2002): 49–90. Warner's work on counterpublics emphasizes these tactile discursive modes.

60. Nancy Fraser, "Rethinking the Public Sphere: A Contribution to the Critique of Actually Existing Democracy," *Social Text* 25/26 (1990): 68.

61. On feminist organizing against this private-public distinction in the context of counterpublic theory, see Rita Felski, *Beyond Feminist Aesthetics: Feminist Literature and Social Change* (Cambridge, MA: Harvard University Press, 1989), 72.

62. Jane Gerhard, *Desiring Revolution: Second-Wave Feminism and the Rewriting of American Sexual Thought: 1920–1982* (New York: Columbia University Press, 2001), 111.

63. Radicalesbians, "The Woman Identified Woman: Atlanta Lesbian Feminist Alliance Archives," 1970, http://library.duke.edu/digitalcollections/wlmpc _wlmms01011, 1.

64. Hesford, *Feeling Women's Liberation*, 94. Hesford performs her own feminist historiography carefully, warning against an "overly schematic presentation" of feminist history in which branches of feminism are thought as discrete splinters: Hesford, *Feeling Women's Liberation*, 8–9.

65. Becki Ross, *The House That Jill Built: A Lesbian Nation in Formation* (Toronto: University of Toronto Press, 1995), 61.

66. Dana Heller, "Purposes: An Introduction," in *Cross Purposes: Lesbians, Feminists, and the Limits of Alliance*, ed. Dana Heller (Bloomington: Indiana University Press, 1997), 7–9; Meeker, *Contacts Desired*, 225–50; Julie Podmore and Manon Tremblay, "Lesbians, Second-Wave Feminism and Gay Liberation," in *The Ashgate Companion to Lesbian and Gay Activism*, ed. David Paternotte and Manon Tremblay (Farnham, UK: Ashgate, 2015); Robert O. Self, *All in the Family: The Realignment of American Democracy since the 1960s* (New York: Hill and Wang, 2012), 225–28.

67. The Combahee River Collective Statement (1977) reads: "Our situation as Black people necessitates that we have solidarity around the fact of race, which white women of course do not need to have with white men, unless it is their negative solidarity as racial oppressors. We struggle together with Black men against racism, while we also struggle with Black men about sexism." Roderick Ferguson also argues that Black lesbians worked in dialogue with men against the nationalism present in Black radicalism through an anti-essential understanding of race, gender, and sexuality that constitutes queer critique prior to the institutionalization of (white) queer theory: Roderick Ferguson, *Aberrations in Black: Toward a Queer of Color Critique* (Minneapolis: University of Minnesota Press, 2003).

68. Felski, who is cited by Nancy Fraser, discusses divisions within feminism through the concept of public formation: Felski, *Beyond Feminist Aesthetics*, 170.

69. Strongman, "Creating Justice between Us," 49–50. In this article, Strongman is specifically interested in Audre Lorde's use of the erotic to build interracial coalitions. Strongman's dissertation and book manuscript in process, "The Sisterhood:

Black Women, Black Feminism, and the Women's Liberation Movement," asks these questions in a broader frame, with attention to how Black feminists assembled reading lists as an activist practice.

70. Catherine Squires, "Rethinking the Black Publish Sphere: An Alternative Vocabulary for Multiple Public Spheres," *Communication Theory* 12, no. 4 (2002): 458, 460.

71. While censorship of information about sexuality in the United States had waned by the late twentieth century as feminist and gay liberation organizations successfully challenged the Comstock laws, censorship of LGBT materials, including print, film, and video, remained prevalent in Canada into the 1990s: see Brenda Cossman, "Censor, Resist, Repeat: The History of Censorship of Gay and Lesbian Sexual Representations in Canada," *Duke Journal of Gender, Law and Policy* 45 (2014).

72. Beins, *Liberation in Print*; Travis, "The Women in Print Movement."

73. Travis, "The Women in Print Movement," 276.

74. Finn Enke, *Finding the Movement: Sexuality, Contested Space, and Feminist Activism* (Durham NC: Duke University Press, 2007), 2.

75. Meeker, *Contacts Desired*, 15.

76. Avery Dame-Griff, "Talk amongst Yourselves: 'Community' in Transgender Counterpublic Discourse Online, 1990–2014" (PhD diss., University of Maryland, College Park, MD, 2017); Regina Kunzel, "Lessons in Being Gay: Queer Encounters in Gay and Lesbian Prison Activism," *Radical History Review* 10 (2008): 14; Cait McKinney, "Printing the Network: AIDS Activists and Online Access in the 1980s," *Continuum: Journal of Media and Cultural Studies* 32, no. 1 (2018): 7–17.

77. Cvetkovich, *An Archive of Feelings*, 7. Building on Cvetkovich, Jack Halberstam researches through a queer "archival method" that brings unlikely objects and fragments into nonhierarchical relationships guided by meanings and emotions that are both singular and shared: Jack Halberstam, *In a Queer Time and Place: Transgender Bodies: Subcultural Lives* (New York: New York University Press, 2005), 24. See also Jack Haberstam, *The Queer Art of Failure* (Durham, NC: Duke University Press, 2011); Jack Halberstam, "Unfound," in *Cruising the Archive: Queer Art and Culture in Los Angeles, 1945–1980*, ed. David Evans Frantz and Mia Locks (Los Angeles: ONE Archives, 2011), 158–61.

78. Marika Cifor, "Affecting Relations: Introducing Affect Theory to Archival Discourse, "*Arch Science,* 16 (2016), 12–18. See also Marika Cifor, "Stains and Remains: Liveliness, Materiality, and the Archival Lives of Queer Bodies," *Australian Feminist Studies* 32, nos. 91–92 (2017): 5–21.

79. Audre Lorde, "Uses of the Erotic: The Erotic as Power" (1978), in *Sister Outsider: Essays and Speeches* (Trumansburg, NY: Crossing, [1984] 2007), 53–59.

80. Grace Kyungwon Hong, *Death beyond Disavowal: The Impossible Politics of Difference* (Minneapolis: University of Minnesota Press, 2015), 78–79.

81. Lorde, "Uses of the Erotic," 56–57.

82. Lorde, "Uses of the Erotic," 55, emphasis added.

83. Strongman, "Creating Justice between Us"; Hong, *Death beyond Disavowal*.

84. Amber Jamilla Musser, *Sensational Flesh: Race, Power, and Masochism* (New York: New York University Press, 2014), 147. "Affect" and "emotion" are slippery theo-

retical terms, and while I am interested in holding open some of the ways that they can overlap, I use "emotion" to describe feelings when they are articulated as cultural and ascribed to subjects. Affect, following Sara Ahmed (*The Cultural Politics of Emotion* [New York: Routledge, 2004]) or Teresa Brennan (*The Transmission of Affect* [Ithaca, NY: Cornell University Press, 2004]), describes the force of emotions as they circulate and move either among individuals and groups. In my work, this affective movement happens through media practices, alongside or "as" information.

85. Malin, *Feeling Mediated*, 6–7. Although it is not historical in focus, Sherry Turkle's work exemplifies this emphasis on the shifting intimacies that accompany technological change. See Sherry Turkle, *Alone Together: Why We Expect More from Technology and Less from Each Other* (New York: Basic, 2011).

86. Malin, *Feeling Mediated*, 6, emphasis added.

87. Michael Hardt, "Affective Labor," *boundary 2* 26, no. 2 (1999): 89.

88. Arlie Hochschild, *The Managed Heart: Commercialization of Human Feeling* (Berkeley: University of California Press, [1983] 2003). See also Arlie Hochschild and Anne Machung, *The Second Shift: Working Parents and the Revolution at Home* (New York: Viking, 1989); Melissa Gregg, *Work's Intimacy* (Cambridge: Polity, 2011), 54.

89. Melissa Gregg and Michael Hardt both emphasize immateriality in their work: Gregg, *Work's Intimacy*; Hardt, "Affective Labor."

90. Sara Ahmed's work on queer pathways and books guides my thinking here: see Sara Ahmed, *Queer Phenomenology: Orientations, Objects, Others* (Durham, NC: Duke University Press, 2006).

91. For a selection of work on these topics, see Sara Ahmed, *The Promise of Happiness* (Durham, NC: Duke University Press, 2010); Sara Ahmed, *Willful Subjects* (Durham, NC: Duke University Press, 2014); Sara Ahmed, *Living a Feminist Life* (Durham, NC: Duke University Press, 2017); Kate Davy, "Outing Whiteness: A Feminist/Lesbian Project, *Theatre Journal* 47, no. 2 (1995): 189–205; Hogan, *The Feminist Bookstore Movement*; bell hooks, *Feminist Theory: From Margin to Center* (London: Pluto, [1984] 2000); Aileen M. Moreton-Robinson, "Troubling Business: Difference and Whiteness within Feminism," *Australian Feminist Studies* 15, no. 33 (2000): 343–52; Viviane K. Namaste, *Invisible Lives: The Erasure of Transsexual and Transgendered People* (Chicago: University of Chicago Press, 2000); Viviane K. Namaste, *Oversight: Critical Reflections on Feminist Research and Politics* (Toronto: Women's Press, 2015); Bobby Noble, *Songs of the Movement: FtMs Risking Incoherence on a Post-Queer Cultural Landscape* (Toronto: Women's Press, [1978] 2006); Susan Stryker, "My Words to Victor Frankenstein above the Village of Chamounix: Performing Transgender Rage," *GLQ* 1, no. 3 (1994): 237–54; Susan Stryker, *Transgender History* (Berkeley, CA: Publishers Group West, 2008).

92. See Jessie Daniels, "The Trouble with White Feminism: Whiteness, Digital Feminism and the Intersectional Internet," in *The Intersectional Internet: Race, Sex, Class and Culture Online*, ed. Safiya Umoja Noble and Brendesha M. Tynes (New York: Peter Lang, 2016), 41–60; Susana Loza, "Hashtag Feminism, #SolidarityIsForWhiteWomen, and the Other #FemFuture," *Ada* 5 (2014), https://adanewmedia.org/2014/07/issue5-loza; Namaste, *Invisible Lives*; Namaste, *Oversight*; Carrie A. Rentschler, "Bystander Intervention, Feminist Hashtag Activism, and the Anti-carceral

Politics of Care," *Feminist Media Studies* 17, no. 4 (2017): 565–84, https://doi.org/10
.1080/14680777.2017.1326556; Rodriguez. "Mapping QTBIPOC Toronto."

93. Barbara Smith, "Foreword," in *Black Lesbians: An Annotated Bibliography*,
ed. JR Roberts (Tallahassee, FL: Naiad, 1981), ix.

94. Smith, "Foreword," ix–x.

95. Smith, "Foreword," x.

96. Ahmed, *Living a Feminist Life*, 230.

97. Stryker, *Transgender History*, 109.

98. Finn Enke, "Collective Memory and the Transfeminist 1970s: Toward a
Less Plausible History," *Transgender Studies Quarterly* 5, no. 1 (2018): 9–29; Emma
Heaney, "Women-Identified Women: Trans Women in 1970s Lesbian Feminist
Organizing," *Transgender Studies Quarterly* 3, nos. 1–2 (2016): 137–45; Cristan
Williams, "Radical Inclusion: Recounting the Trans Inclusive History of Radical
Feminism," *Transgender Studies Quarterly* 3, nos. 1–2 (2016): 254–58.

99. Enke, "Collective Memory and the Transfeminist 1970s," 10, 12.

100. Namaste, *Invisible Lives*, 65.

101. Ahmed, *Living a Feminist Life*, 227.

102. "Deep-Lez" comes from Allyson Mitchell's "Deep Lez I Statement:" see
Allyson Mitchell and Ann Cvetkovich, "A Girl's Journey into the Well of Forbid-
den Knowledge," GLQ 17, no. 4 (2011): 603–18. A labrys is a double-edged ax that
symbolizes matriarchy and in the 1970s was a popular icon of lesbian feminism
often worn as jewelry.

103. This approach to thinking across lesbian-feminist and queer is adapted
from: Cvetkovich, *An Archive of Feelings;* Enke, *Finding the Movement;* Jack
Gieseking, *A Queer New York* (New York: New York University Press, 2020);
Elizabeth Freeman, *Time Binds: Queer Temporalities, Queer Histories* (Durham,
NC: Duke University Press, 2010); Hesford, *Feeling Women's Liberation;* Hogan,
The Feminist Bookstore Movement.

104. Freeman, *Time Binds*, 62.

105. Adair and Nakamura, "The Digital Afterlives of *This Bridge Called My
Back*"; Clare Hemmings, *Why Stories Matter: The Political Grammar of Feminist
Theory* (Durham, NC: Duke University Press, 2011); Hesford, *Feeling Women's
Liberation;* Hong, *Death beyond Disavowal;* Alex Pauline Gumbs, *M Archive: After
the End of the World* (Durham, NC: Duke University Press, 2018); Freeman, *Time
Binds;* Joan Wallach Scott, *The Fantasy of Feminist History* (Durham, NC: Duke
University Press, 2011); Robyn Wiegman, "The Intimacy of Critique: Ruminations
on Feminism as a Living Thing," *Feminist Theory* 11, no. 1 (2010): 79–84; Robyn
Wiegman, *Object Lessons* (Durham, NC: Duke University Press, 2012).

106. Freeman, *Time Binds*, 62–64.

107. Hesford, *Feeling Women's Liberation*, 32–33.

108. Kadji Amin, *Disturbing Attachments: Genet, Modern Pederasty, and Queer
History* (Durham, NC: Duke University Press, 2017); David L. Eng, *The Feeling of
Kinship: Queer Liberalism and the Racialization of Intimacy* (Durham, NC: Duke
University Press, 2010); Jasbir K. Puar, *Terrorist Assemblages: Homonationalism in
Queer Times* (Durham, NC: Duke University Press, 2007).

109. On "archive stories" as an autoethnographic method, see Antoinette Burton, ed., *Archive Stories: Facts, Fictions, and the Writing of History* (Durham, NC: Duke University Press, 2006).

110. Agatha Beins estimates that upward of 500 individual feminist periodicals were created in the 1970s: Beins, *Liberation in Print*, 8. Some lasted only a few issues and reached small numbers of readers, while others lasted many years and reached thousands. By my count, based on archival collections and *The Lesbian Periodicals Index*, at least seventy-five publications founded during this decade specifically targeted lesbians: see Clare Potter, ed., *The Lesbian Periodicals Index* (Tallahassee, FL: Naiad, 1986). The precarity and ephemerality of these publications makes it impossible to know precisely how many individual periodicals existed. The practice of sharing issues, combined with the lack of organizational records, makes circulation estimates impossible. Despite a lack of numbers here, it is undeniable the newsletters made feminist organizing on a large scale possible, and Beins's work provides an excellent theorization of this history.

111. Capable amateurism builds on feminist media studies work about "amateur" approaches to technology in activist and maker contexts: see esp. Christina Dunbar-Hester, *Low Power to the People: Pirates, Protest, and Politics in FM Radio Activism* (Cambridge, MA: MIT Press, 2014); Daniela K. Rosner, *Critical Fabulations: Reworking the Methods and Margins of Design* (Cambridge, MA: MIT Press, 2018).

112. Lauren Berlant, *Cruel Optimism* (Durham, NC: Duke University Press, 2011).

113. Jacques Derrida, "Archive Fever: A Freudian Impress," *Diacritics* 25, no. 2 (1995): 9–63.

114. As Ahmed writes, "When a world does not give us standing, we have to create other ways of being in the world. You acquire the potential to make things, create things. Lesbian feminism: the actualization of a potential we have to make things": Ahmed, *Living a Feminist Life*, 223.

CHAPTER ONE: THE INTERNET THAT LESBIANS BUILT

1. Victoria Brownworth, "In Remembrance: Julia Penelope, Lesbian Theorist," *Lambda Literary*, February 1, 2013, accessed January 30, 2014, http://www .lambdaliterary.org/features/rem/02/01/in-remembrance-julia-penelope-lesbian -theorist.

2. Brownworth, "In Remembrance."

3. Julia Penelope Stanley, personal communication, April 27, 1977, Circle of Lesbian Indexers Papers, Lesbian Herstory Archives, Brooklyn, NY (hereafter, LHA).

4. *Matrices*, vol. 4, no. 1, 1980, 1.

5. There is no definitive list of lesbian periodicals, so I have drawn this estimate from Clare Potter, ed., *Lesbian Periodicals Index* (Tallahassee, FL: Naiad, 1986), combined with additional titles housed at the Canadian Lesbian and Gay Archives and the LHA. "At least 100" is a conservative estimate based on what I have been able to count and reflects publications that were significant enough to have been archived. It likely leaves out many local and regional titles.

6. Jack Gieseking describes lesbian constellations as material but also ephemeral imaginaries that sustain the idea of collectivity and belonging over time: Jack Gieseking, *A Queer New York* (New York: New York University Press, 2020). Here I build on Gieseking to think about the role of information, rather than space, in these imaginaries.

7. Sarah Hoagland, JR Roberts, Susan Leigh Star, and Julia Penelope Stanley, "Editorial," *Matrices*, vol. 1, nos. 1–2, 1977–78, 3.

8. While the early 1970s saw a veritable explosion of grassroots periodicals publishing by feminists, this movement modeled technics already developed in the midcentury through such publications as *The Ladder*, an early lesbian periodical published by the Daughters of Bilitis between 1956 and 1972. Although *The Ladder* also included reader-generated material, its project was assimilationist; rooted in the homophile movement, the publication disarticulated itself from any radical feminist project of social transformation: Marianne Cutler, "Educating the 'Variant,' Educating the Public: Gender and the Rhetoric of Legitimation in *The Ladder* Magazine for Lesbians," *Qualitative Sociology* 26, no. 2 (2003): 233–55.

9. For a detailed history of this periodicals movement, see Agatha Beins, *Liberation in Print: Feminist Periodicals and Social Movement Identity* (Athens: University of Georgia Press, 2017); on xerography and queer counterpublics, see Kate Eichhorn, *Adjusted Margin: Xerography, Art and Activism in the Late Twentieth Century* (Cambridge, MA: MIT Press, 2016).

10. On the distinctions and entwinements between the women's and LGBT history movements, see Margot Canaday, "LGBT History," *Frontiers* 35, no. 1 (2014): 11–19.

11. Steven Maynard, "The Burning, Willful Evidence: Lesbian/Gay History and Archival Research," *Archivaria* 33 (1991): 195–201.

12. At the Lesbian Herstory Archives, the creation of a mailing list database to circulate the annual newsletter was the task through which women at the archives learned how to use a personal computer, a precursor to the development of a computerized catalog of the archives' holdings (see chapter 4 in this volume).

13. Maynard, "The Burning, Willful Evidence," 200.

14. This oral history project became Madeline Davis and Elizabeth Kennedy, *Boots of Leather, Slippers of Gold* (New York: Routledge, 1993).

15. On the emergences of humanities and social science listservs, see Avi Hyman, "Twenty Years of ListServ as an Academic Tool," *Internet and Higher Education* 6 (2003): 17–24. On feminist listservs, see Elisabeth Jay Friedman, *Interpreting the Internet: Feminist and Queer Counterpublics in Latin America* (Oakland: University of California Press, 2017).

16. K. J. Rawson, "Archival Justice: An Interview with Ben Power Alwin," *Radical History Review* 122 (2015): 178.

17. On following citation as a feminist method, see Clare Hemmings, *Why Stories Matter: The Political Grammar of Feminist Theory* (Durham, NC: Duke University Press, 2011).

18. Kate Eichhorn, *The Archival Turn in Feminism: Outrage in Order* (Philadelphia: Temple University Press, 2013).

19. Lisa Sloniowski, "In the Stacks of Barbara Godard, or Do Not Confuse the Complexity of this Moment with Chaos," in *Trans/acting Culture, Writing, and Memory: Essays in Honour of Barbara Godard*, ed. Eva C. Karpinski et al. (Waterloo, ON: Wilfred Laurier University Press, 2013), 478–95.

20. Shannon Mattern's *Deep Mapping the Media City* (Minneapolis: University of Minnesota Press, 2017) provides a useful media-archaeology model for understanding the entanglement of conceptual and technical infrastructures.

21. Janet Abbate, *Inventing the Internet* (Cambridge, MA: MIT Press, 1999), 8–21. The heavy citation of Baran's diagram is also about ARPANET's outsize place in internet historiography.

22. Abbate, *Inventing the Internet*, 8–21.

23. Alexander Galloway, *Protocol: How Control Exists after Decentralization* (Cambridge, MA: MIT Press, 2004), 201.

24. Galloway, *Protocol*, 201.

25. Galloway, *Protocol*, 200; Roy Rosenzweig, "Wizards, Bureaucrats, Warriors, and Hackers: Writing the History of the Internet," *American Historical Review* 103, no. 5 (1998): 1532–33.

26. Galloway, *Protocol*, 234.

27. *The Grapevine*, February–March 1983, 1.

28. *Telewoman*, "masthead," 1983, 1.

29. See Victoria Hesford, *Feeling Women's Liberation* (Durham, NC: Duke University Press, 2013).

30. Friedman, *Interpreting the Internet*.

31. Cassius Adair and Lisa Nakamura, "The Digital Afterlives of *This Bridge Called My Back*: Women of Color Feminism, Digital Labor, and Networked Pedagogy," *American Literature* 89, no. 2 (2017): 268.

32. Julia Penelope was expelled from two universities as a graduate student and fired from one academic job because she was a lesbian: Brownworth, "In Remembrance." The pages of *Matrices* often featured stories and questions about workplace discrimination experienced by lesbian researchers working in institutions. Doing lesbian research in universities during this period was risky business, particularly for those without tenure, and *Matrices* served as survival literature in this context.

33. Beins, *Liberation in Print*; Martin Meeker, *Contacts Desired: Gay and Lesbian Communications and Community, 1940s–1970s* (Chicago: University of Chicago Press, 2006).

34. Meeker, *Contacts Desired*, 13.

35. Meeker, *Contacts Desired*, 243.

36. Hesford, *Feeling Women's Liberation*, 178–79. Feminist research on housework, such as Ruth Cowan's *More Work for Mother: The Ironies of Household Technology from the Open Hearth to the Microwave* (New York: Basic, 1983), and activist campaigns such as Wages for Housework (founded 1973) contributed to growing understanding of domestic and "behind-the-scenes" labor as a site of struggle.

37. On the relationship between hope and feminist labor, see Sara Ahmed, *The Promise of Happiness* (Durham, NC: Duke University Press, 2010); Robyn Wiegman,

"The Intimacy of Critique: Ruminations on Feminism as a Living Thing," *Feminist Theory* 11, no. 1 (2010): 79–84.

38. Anna Feigenbaum, "Written in the Mud: (Proto)zine-Making and Autonomous Media at the Greenham Common Women's Peace Camp," *Feminist Media Studies* 13, no. 1 (2012): 2.

39. Bobby Lacy, "Editorial," *Matrices*, vol. 4, no. 1, 1980, 1.

40. Gayle Rubin, "Letter to *Matrices* subscribers," *Matrices* vol. 3, no. 3, May 1980, 1–2.

41. See "Miss Major's Monthly Giving Circle," https://www.gofundme.com /MsMajorRetirement; "Barbara Smith Caring Circle," https://fundly.com/barbara-2.

42. *Matrices*, vol. 8, no. 3, 1985–86.

43. *Matrices* vol. 1 no. 3, 1978, 7. The State University of New York, Buffalo, was the site of one of the first women's studies departments in the United States, founded in 1969: Elizabeth Kennedy, "Dreams of Social Justice: Building Women's Studies at the State University of New York, Buffalo," in *The Politics of Women's Studies: Testimony from 30 Founding Mothers*, ed. Florence Howe (New York: Feminist Press, 2000), 244–63.

44. *Matrices*, vol. 1, no. 3, 1978, 7.

45. Newsletter networks bring a public into existence because of how they support doing feminist history collaboratively. The social media scholar danah boyd describes networked publics that emerge through online social media as distinct from other kinds of mediated publics. Networks fundamentally extend the reach of publics beyond a singular website. They facilitate participation by "invisible audiences" that *"could* consist of all people across space and time" because they are not "constrained by geography and temporal collocation": danah boyd, "Why Youth (Heart) Social Network Sites: The Role of Networked Publics in Teenage Social Life," in *MacArthur Foundation Series on Digital Learning: Youth, Identity, and Digital Media Volume*, ed. David Buckingham (Cambridge, MA: MIT Press, 2007), 9. The *Matrices* network attempts to transcend these spatiotemporal limitations in search of a networked public for lesbian historiography but does so using print media.

46. Editorial, *Matrices*, vol. 1, no. 3, 1978, 1.

47. Friedman, *Interpreting the Internet*.

48. Rosenzweig, "Wizards, Bureaucrats, Warriors, and Hackers," 1552. See also Kevin Driscoll and Camille Paloques-Berges, "Searching for Missing 'Net Histories,'" *Internet Histories* 1, no. 1 (2017): 1–13, https://doi.org/10.1080/24701475.2017 .1307541; Friedman, *Interpreting the Internet*.

49. Kevin Driscoll, "Hobbyist Inter-networking and the Popular Internet Imaginary: Forgotten Histories of Networked Personal Computing, 1978–1998" (PhD diss., University of Southern California, Los Angeles, 2014); Friedman, *Interpreting the Internet* (Oakland: University of California Press, 2017); Eden Medina, *Cybernetic Revolutionaries: Technology and Politics in Allende's Chile* (Cambridge, MA: MIT Press, 2011); Benjamin Peters, *How Not to Network a Nation: The Uneasy History of the Soviet Internet* (Cambridge, MA: MIT Press, 2016); Fred Turner, *From Counterculture to Cyberculture: Stewart Brand, the Whole Earth Network, and the Rise of Digital Utopianism* (Chicago: University of Chicago Press, 2006). For

example, Turner locates the idea of networks—a computational metaphor—in antibureaucratic, libertarian back-to-the land movements organized around personal tool use as a key frame through which "the American public understood the social possibilities of computers and computer networking": Turner, *From Counterculture to Cyberculture*, 237.

50. Wanda J. Orlikowski, "The Sociomateriality of Organizational Life: Considering Technology in Management Research," *Cambridge Journal of Economics* 34 (2010): 125–41.

51. Marisa Elena Duarte, *Network Sovereignty: Building the Internet across Indian Country* (Seattle: University of Washington Press, 2017).

52. Beins, *Liberation in Print*; Feigenbaum, "Written in the Mud"; Gieseking, *A Queer New York*; Lucas Hilderbrand, *Inherent Vice: Bootleg Histories of Videotape and Copyright* (Durham, NC: Duke University Press, 2009); Hande Eslen-Ziya, "Social Media and Turkish Feminism: New Resources for Social Activism," *Feminist Media Studies* 13, no. 5 (2013): 860–70.

53. Hilderbrand, *Inherent Vice*, 197.

54. Lacy, "Editorial," 1.

55. Leila Pourtavaf, ed., *Féminismes électriques* (Montreal: Centrale Galerie Powerhouse, 2012), 9.

56. Lisa Sloniowski, "This Is Not a Love Story: Libraries and Feminist Porn," *Access* 18, no. 2 (2012): 14–17.

57. *Matrices*, vol. 7, no. 2, 1984, 13.

58. *Matrices*, vol. 5, no. 1, 1982, 13–14.

59. Eichhorn, *The Archival Turn in Feminism*.

60. Hemmings, *Why Stories Matter*.

61. Cindy Ingold, "Preserving the Literature of Women's and Gender Organizations: The Availability of Newsletters in Libraries, Commercial Online Databases, and Organizational Web Sites," *Feminist Formations* 23, no. 1 (2011): 182–211.

62. Meagher, "Difficult, Messy, Nasty, and Sensational," 579.

63. Julia Penelope and Bobby Lacy, "Editorial," *Matrices*, vol. 3, no. 1, 1979, 1.

64. This challenge parallels the work of many feminist print culture scholars, perhaps most closely Kristen Hogan's work with *Feminist Bookstore News*, which involved mapping the precarious institutions of "Book Women" through the equally precarious pages of a community newsletter: Kristen Hogan, *The Feminist Bookstore Movement: Lesbian Antiracism and Feminist Accountability* (Durham, NC: Duke University Press, 2016).

65. *Lesbian Herstory Archives Newsletter*, vol. 5, 1979, 5. The archives also incorporated as a "research center" rather than as an archives to avoid oversight by New York State's Board of Regents, which supervises all archives: Corbman, email to the author, July 15, 2018.

66. *Lesbian Herstory Archives Newsletter*, vol. 5, 1979, 5.

67. Today, the Lesbian Herstory Archives communicates primarily via its website, Facebook, Instagram, and email blasts sent every few months to promote events.

68. *Lesbian Herstory Archives Newsletter*, vol. 5, 1979; *Lesbian Herstory Archives Newsletter*, vol. 1, 1975; *Lesbian Herstory Archives Newsletter*, vol. 2, 1976.

69. *Lesbian Herstory Archives Newsletter*, vol. 1, 1975, 5.

70. Gieseking describes these imagined connections between urban and rural lesbians through the metaphor of constellations in *A Queer New York*.

71. *Lesbian Herstory Archives Newsletter*, vol. 4, 1978. The LHA still maintains subject files of clippings mailed in to the archives, as do many LGBTQ community archives.

72. The motorcycle tour occurred in 1996: see Alexis Danzig, "Tales from the Road: Diaries of a Biker Chick," *Lesbian Herstory Archives Newsletter*, vol. 16, 1996, 4–5.

73. *Lesbian Herstory Archives Newsletter*, vol. 5, 1979, 15, emphasis added.

74. Gieseking, *A Queer New York*.

75. *Lesbian Herstory Archives Newsletter*, vol. 4, 1978, 2.

76. *Lesbian Herstory Archives Newsletter*, vol. 7, 1981, 17.

77. Lisa Gitelman, *Paper Knowledge: Toward a Media History of Documents* (Durham, NC: Duke University Press, 2014), 9. Jonathan Sterne's turn to "format" in *MP3: The Meaning of a Format* (Durham, NC: Duke University Press, 2013) makes a similar gesture for media-history methods.

78. "Chicago Resource Center Funds LHA Computer," *Lesbian Herstory Archives Newsletter*, vol. 9, 1986, 6.

79. "Chicago Resource Center Funds LHA Computer."

80. "Chicago Resource Center Funds LHA Computer."

81. *Lesbian Herstory Archives Newsletter*, vol. 9, 1986.

82. *Lesbian Herstory Archives Newsletter*, vol. 9, 1986.

83. *Lesbian Herstory Archives Newsletter*, vol. 7, 1981, 53.

84. The faith required to sustain a newsletter's public through an erratic print schedule can be contrasted with the constant engagement many contemporary organizations, including community archives, perform through social media outreach.

85. Lacy, "Editorial," 1.

86. Jack Halberstam, *The Queer Art of Failure* (Durham, NC: Duke University Press, 2011).

87. Wendy Hui Kyong Chun, *Control and Freedom: Power and Paranoia in the Age of Fiber Optics* (Cambridge, MA: MIT Press, 2006); Galloway, *Protocol*.

88. JR Roberts, "Letter of Resignation," *Matrices*, vol. 2, no. 3, 1979, 2.

89. Karla Jay, *The Gay Report* (New York: Summit, 1979).

90. Amethyst, "Letter to the Editor," *Matrices*, vol. 2, no. 3, 1979, 3.

91. Amethyst, "Letter to the Editor," 3.

92. A 2018 roundtable by feminist digital studies scholars outlines some key aspects of network "safety," exposure, and power dynamics across a range of platforms: Dorothy Kim, et al., "Race, Gender, and the Technological Turn: A Roundtable on Digitizing Revolution," *Frontiers* 39, no. 1 (2018): 149–77, https://www.muse.jhu.edu/article/690813.

93. Che Gossett, "We Will Not Rest in Peace: AIDS Activism, Black Radicalism, Queer and/or Trans Resistance," in *Queer Necropolitics*, ed. Adi Kuntsman, Jin Haritaworn, and Silvia Posocoo (New Brunswick, NJ: Routledge, 2014), 31–50; José Esteban Muñoz, *Disidentifications* (Minneapolis: University of Minnesota Press, 1999); Syrus Marcus Ware, "All Power to All People? Black LGBTTI2QQ Activism,

Remembrance, and Archiving in Toronto," *Transgender Studies Quarterly* 4, no. 2 (2017): 170–80.

94. Barbara Smith, "Foreword," in *Black Lesbians: An Annotated Bibliography*, ed. JR Roberts (Tallahassee, FL: Naiad, 1981), ix.

95. *Matrices*, vol. 3, no. 1, 1979, 11.

96. Examples include Mabel Hampton, a black lesbian activist whose photograph graced the cover of *Lesbian Herstory Archives Newsletter*, vol. 5, 1979. Hampton's coming-out story from her oral history was transcribed in volume 7 (1981), and volume 8 (1984) featured a collage of Asian lesbians of the East Coast, with a cover image designed by a socialist lesbian organization from Mexico.

97. "The International Collection," *Lesbian Herstory Archives Newsletter*, vol. 8, 1984, 25.

98. *Matrices*, vol. 11, no. 2, 1996, 8.

99. Barbara Sjoholm, "She Who Owns the Press," in *Make Your Own History: Documenting Feminist and Queer Activism in the 21st Century*, ed. Lyz Bly and Kelly Wooten (Sacramento, CA: Litwin, 2012), 166.

100. On feminist zine cultures, see Alison Piepmeier, *Girl Zines: Making Media, Doing Feminism* (New York: New York University Press, 2009).

101. Adair and Nakamura, "The Digital Afterlives of *This Bridge Called My Back*."

102. See Herstories: Audio/Visual Collections at http://herstories.prattsils.org /omeka.

CHAPTER TWO: CALLING TO TALK AND LISTENING WELL

1. Call log, August 1, 1973, Lesbian Switchboard of New York City, Inc., Records, LBGT Community Center National History Archive, Lesbian, Gay, Bisexual and Transgender Community Center, New York (hereafter, Lesbian Switchboard Records), box 3, folder 25.

2. Names recorded in the call logs have been changed throughout the chapter to protect anonymity.

3. Ann Cvetkovich, *An Archive of Feelings: Trauma, Sexuality, and Lesbian Public Cultures* (Durham, NC: Duke University Press, 2003).

4. Eliza Stewart, untitled article about Lesbian Switchboard, January 17, 1995, Lesbian Switchboard Records, box 2, folder 15.

5. Jessica Slote, "Lesbian Switchboard: 'Raps and Referrals,'" unpublished ms., n.d. Lesbian Switchboard Records, box 2, folder 15, 9.

6. ASTRAEA Foundation Grant Application, 1990, Lesbian Switchboard Records, box 1, folder 3.

7. Susan Stryker, *Transgender History* (Berkeley, CA: Publishers Group West, 2008). The activist, scholar, and artist Tourmaline (formerly known as Reina Gossett) has devoted years to assembling an online archive that documents STAR's work: see the website at http://www.reinagossett.com/tag/street-transvestite-action -revolutionaries.

8. Kate Eichhorn, *The Archival Turn in Feminism: Outrage in Order* (Philadelphia: Temple University Press, 2013).

9. Meeting minutes, March 14, 1977, Lesbian Switchboard Records, box 1, folder 5.

10. Oral history methods have also been key to the field: see Elspeth H. Brown, "Trans/Feminist Oral History: Current Projects," *Transgender Studies Quarterly* 2, no. 4 (2015): 666–72, https://doi.org/10.1215/23289252-3151583; Elise Chenier, "Hidden from Historians: Preserving Lesbian Oral History in Canada," *Archivaria* 68 (2009): 247–69. Recent work on excavating the second-wave feminist film and video archive has been undertaken by Rox Samer, "Revising 'Re-vision': Documenting 1970s Feminisms and the Queer Potentiality of Digital Feminist Archives," *Ada* 5 (2014), https://doi.org/10.7264/N3FF3QMC.

11. Craig Robertson, "Learning to File: Reconfiguring Information and Information Work in the Early Twentieth Century," *Technology and Culture* 58, no. 4 (2017): 955–81, https://doi.org/10.1353/tech.2017.0110.

12. Lisa Gitelman, *Paper Knowledge: Toward a Media History of Documents* (Durham, NC: Duke University Press, 2014).

13. Theodore Schellenberg, *Modern Archives: Principles and Techniques* (Chicago: University of Chicago Press, 1956).

14. Luciana Duranti, "The Concept of Appraisal and Archival Theory," *American Archivist* 57 (1994): 339.

15. Michelle Caswell, "Community-centered Collecting: Finding Out What Communities Want from Community Archives," *Proceedings of the American Society for Information Science Technology* 51, no. 1 (2014): 1–9, https://doi.org/10.1002/meet.2014.14505101027.

16. On affect in social-justice archives, see Marika Cifor, "Affecting Relations: Introducing Affect Theory to Archival Discourse," *Archival Science,* 16 (2016): 7–31.

17. Community archives sometimes follow a practice called "original order," which maintains a donor's existing filing system as a record of how this donor organized their work. Often community organizations do not have consistently organized filing systems to begin with, in which case maintaining paper records' original order is mostly meaningless, except to preserve disorganization. Sometimes original order is preserved simply because a community archive lacks the resources to reorganize a collection and thus practices the "More Product, Less Process" approach to organizing records: Mark A. Greene and Dennis Meissner, "More Product, Less Process: Revamping Traditional Archival Processing," *American Archivist* 68 (2005): 208–63.

18. Gitelman, *Paper Knowledge*, 4.

19. John Guillory, "The Memo and Modernity," *Critical Inquiry* 31(1), (2004): 113.

20. Craig Robertson, "A Documentary Regime of Verification," *Cultural Studies* 23, no. 3 (2009): 329–54, https://doi.org/10.1080/09502380802016253. Robertson is primarily interested in identification documents, such as passports.

21. Guillory, "The Memo and Modernity," 113.

22. Samantha Thrift, "Feminist Eventfulness: Boredom and the 1984 Canadian Leadership Debate on Women's Issues," *Feminist Media Studies* 13, no. 3 (2011): 416.

23. Thrift, "Feminist Eventfulness," 416.

24. Name withheld, interview with the author, August 14, 2017.

25. Jennifer Brier, *Infectious Ideas: U.S. Political Responses to the* AIDS *Crisis* (Chapel Hill : University of North Carolina Press, 2009); Marty Fink, *Forget Burial:* HIV/AIDS *and Queer/Trans Narratives of Care* (New Brunswick, NJ: Rutgers University Press, 2020); Cindy Patton, *Last Served? Gendering the* HIV *Pandemic* (London: Taylor and Francis, 1994); Deborah B. Gould, *Moving Politics: Emotion and* ACT UP*'s Fight against* AIDS (Chicago: University of Chicago Press, 2009).

26. Feminist social movement studies has also critiqued the transition to service provision as a product of the neoliberalization of social-justice organization: See esp. Shana L. Maier, "Are Rape Crisis Centers Feminist Organizations?" *Feminist Criminology* 3, no. 2 (2008); Debra C. Minkoff, "The Emergence of Hybrid Organizational Forms: Combining Identity-based Service Provision and Political Action," *Nonprofit and Voluntary Sector Quarterly* 31, no. 3 (2002), 377–401.

27. Call log, January 22, 1973, Lesbian Switchboard Records, box 3, folder 24.

28. The switchboard was also housed in the firehouse at the time of this call; it remained there until the building's renovation in 1987, at which point the switchboard moved to the Gay and Lesbian Center: see "Women's Liberation Center," New York City LBGT Historic Sites Project website, https://www.nyclgbtsites.org /site/womens-liberation-center.

29. Call log, October 3, 1980, box 3 folder 35; call log, November 4, 1972, box 3, folder 23; call log, February 19, 1973, box 3, folder 24, all in Lesbian Switchboard Records.

30. Call log, July 11, 1984, Lesbian Switchboard Records, box 3, folder 40.

31. Lisa Duggan, *The Twilight of Equality? Neoliberalism, Cultural Politics, and the Attack on Democracy* (Boston: Beacon, 2003); Katherine Sender, *Business, Not Politics: The Making of the Gay Market* (New York: Columbia University Press, 2004).

32. Call log, January 11, 1990, Lesbian Switchboard Records, box 3, folder 34.

33. On orienting away or toward shared objects of happiness see Sara Ahmed, *The Promise of Happiness* (Durham, NC: Duke University Press, 2010).

34. Mary Bryson et al., "Virtually Queer? Homing Devices, Mobility, and Un/ Belongings," *Canadian Journal of Communication* 31, no. 4 (2006): 791–814, https:// doi.org/10.22230/cjc.2006v31n4a1795; Alexander Cho, "Default Publicness: Queer Youth of Color, Social Media, and Being Outed by the Machine," *New Media & Society* 20, no. 9 (2018): 3183–3200, http://doi:10.1177/1461444817744784; Susan Driver, *Queer Girls and Popular Culture: Reading, Resisting, and Creating Media* (New York: Peter Lang, 2007); Mary L. Gray, *Out in the Country* (New York: New York University Press, 2009); Daniel Marshall, "Popular Culture, the 'Victim' Trope and Queer Youth Analytics," *International Journal of Qualitative Studies in Education* 23, no. 1 (2010): 65–85.

35. Call log, June 8, 1979, Lesbian Switchboard Records, box 3, folder 33.

36. On burnout, see Gould, *Moving Politics*.

37. Ann Cvetkovich, *Depression: A Public Feeling* (Durham, NC: Duke University Press, 2012).

38. Sara Ahmed, *Living a Feminist Life* (Durham, NC: Duke University Press, 2017); Ahmed, *The Promise of Happiness*; bell hooks, *Feminist Theory: From Margin to Center* (London: Pluto, [1984] 2000); Audre Lorde, *Sister Outsider: Essays and Speeches* (Trumansburg, NY: Crossing, [1984] 2007).

39. "Some Common Dos and Don'ts," insert handout in *Switchboard Handbook*, Lesbian Switchboard Records, box 1, folder 1.

40. Teresa Brennan, *The Transmission of Affect* (Ithaca, NY: Cornell University Press, 2004).

41. Call log, June 21, 1973, Lesbian Switchboard Records, box 3, folder 25.

42. Call log, June 5, 1984, Lesbian Switchboard Records, box 3, folder 40.

43. This process of evaluation was not always simple or straightforward. For example, an ongoing discussion at the switchboard in 1976 concerned designing a questionnaire that could be used to ensure therapists given as referrals were feminist enough: see meeting minutes, 1976, Lesbian Switchboard Records, box 1, folder 5.

44. Hannah Zeavin, "The Communication Cure: Tele-therapy, 1890–2015" (PhD diss., New York University, 2018).

45. Michael C. Dixon and J. L. Burns "Crisis Theory, Active Learning and the Training of Telephone Crisis Volunteers," *Journal of Community Psychology* 2, no. 2 (1974): 120–25.

46. On the relationship between 1970s hotlines and social movements, see Lennis Echterling and Mary Lou Wylie, "Crisis Centers: A Social Movement Perspective," *Journal of Community Psychology* 9 (1981): 342–46.

47. U.S. census figures track this increase and show a notable difference in access between the northern and southern states: "Historical Census of Housing Tables: Telephones," U.S. Census Bureau, October 31, 2011, https://www.census.gov/hhes/www/housing/census/historic/phone.html.

48. Echterling and Wylie, "Crisis Centers," 343.

49. Christina Hanhardt documents the relationship among gay and lesbian hotlines, AIDS response, and antiviolence initiatives in the early 1980s: Christina B. Hanhardt, *Safe Space: Gay Neighborhood History and the Politics of Violence* (Durham, NC: Duke University Press, 2013), 159–61. AIDS response and antiviolence were intertwined because of a violent AIDS-phobic backlash. Handhardt argues that hotlines were "among the first large-scale lesbian and gay activist projects to receive governmental and foundation funding on both coasts": Hanhardt, *Safe Space*, 159.

50. Jennifer Ryan, "A Report on the 4th Annual National Gay and Lesbian Switchboard Conference held on June 27, 1997," Lesbian Switchboard Records, box 1, folder 9.

51. Lisa Power, "Voice in My Ear," in *Radical Records: Thirty Years of Lesbian and Gay History, 1957–1987*, ed. Bob Cant and Susan Hemmings (London: Routledge, 1988), 143.

52. Power, "Voice in My Ear."

53. Bobby Noble, *Songs of the Movement: FtMs Risking Incoherence on a Post-Queer Cultural Landscape* (Toronto: Women's Press, 2006), 19. Noble is signifying this concept's monolithic status with this spelling.

54. Stephen Tropiano, "'A Safe and Supportive Environment': LBGTQ Youth and Social Media," in *Queer Youth and Media Cultures*, ed. Christopher Pullen (New York: Palgrave, 2014), 46–62.

55. On critique of this politics of visibility vis-à-vis media, see Gray, *Out in the Country*. On dominant narratives about millennials and online identity formation, see Mary Bryson and Lori McIntosh, "Can We Play Fun Gay?: Disjuncture and Difference, and the Precarious Mobilities of Millennial Queer Youth Narratives," *International Journal of Qualitative Studies in Education* 23.1 (2010): 101–24.

56. Kenneth Lipartitto, "When Women Were Switches: Technology, Work and Gender in the Telephone Industry, 1890–1920," *American Historical Review*, 99, no. 4 (1994): 1075–1111.

57. Danielle Van Jaarsveld and Winifred R. Poster, "Call Centers: Emotional Labour over the Phone," in *Emotional Labor in the 21st Century: Diverse Perspectives on the Psychology of Emotion Regulation at Work,* ed. Alicia Grandey, James Diefendorff, and Deborah E. Rupp (New York: Routledge Academic, 2013), 153–73; Kalindi Vora, "The Transmission of Care: Affective Economies and Indian Call Centers," in *Intimate Labors: Cultures, Technologies, and the Politics of Care*, ed. Eileen Boris and Rhacel Salazar Parreñas (Stanford, CA: Stanford Social Sciences, 2010), 33–48.

58. Lana F. Rakow, *Gender on the Line: Women, the Telephone, and Community Life* (Urbana: University of Illinois Press, 1992), 5.

59. Rakow, *Gender on the Line*, 5.

60. Cristan Williams, "Radical Inclusion: Recounting the Trans Inclusive History of Radical Feminism," *Transgender Studies Quarterly* 3, nos. 1–2 (2016): 254–58.

61. Meeting minutes, October 5, 1977, Lesbian Switchboard Records, box 1, folder 5.

62. Call log, May 31, 1973, Lesbian Switchboard Records, box 3, folder 25.

63. On trans etymologies see K. J. Rawson and Cristan Williams, "*Transgender**: The Rhetorical Landscape of a Term," *Present Tense* 3, no. 2 (2015), http://www .presenttensejournal.org/volume-3/transgender-the-rhetorical-landscape-of-a -term; Stryker, *Transgender History*.

64. Call log, August 22, 1977, Lesbian Switchboard Records, box 3, folder 29.

65. Call log, August 14, 1984, Lesbian Switchboard Records, box 3, folder 40.

66. Avery Dame-Griff, "Talk amongst Yourselves: 'Community' in Transgender Counterpublic Discourse Online" (PhD diss., University of Maryland, Baltimore, 2017).

67. Williams, "Radical Inclusion," 206; Heaney, "Women-Identified Women"; Stryker, *Transgender History*; Enke, "Collective Memory and the Transfeminist 1970s."

68. Stryker, *Transgender History*.

69. Kristen Hogan, *The Feminist Bookstore Movement: Lesbian Antiracism and Feminist Accountability* (Durham, NC: Duke University Press, 2016); Emily K. Hobson, *Lavender and Red: Liberation and Solidarity in the Gay and Lesbian Left* (Oakland: University of California Press, 2016), 33–35, 40.

70. ASTRAEA Foundation Grant Application, 1990, Lesbian Switchboard Records, box 1, folder 3.

71. ASTRAEA Foundation Grant Application (1990).

72. Training evaluation form, Lesbian Switchboard Records, box 2, folder 12.

73. Many volunteer operators would note a caller's race when it was provided and worked to explain how this shaped the referrals they gave.

74. Name withheld, interview with the author, August 14, 2017.

75. Call log, July 20, 1977, Lesbian Switchboard Records, box 3, folder 28.

76. Ann Allen Shockley, "The Salsa Soul Sisters," *Off Our Backs* 9, no. 10 (1979): 13.

77. Switchboard training logs, name of volunteer withheld, October 31, 1989, Lesbian Switchboard Records, box 2, folder 12.

78. Rachel Corbman, "Remediating Disability Activism in the Lesbian Feminist Archive," *Continuum* 32, no. 1 (2018): 18–28.

79. See Eileen Reynolds, "Beyond Braille: A History of Reading by Ear," *NYU News Story*, January 29, 2015, https://www.nyu.edu/about/news-publications/news /2015/january/mara-mills-blind-reading.html.

80. Harry G. Lang, *A Phone of Our Own: The Deaf Insurrection against Ma Bell* (Washington, DC: Gallaudet University Press, 2000).

81. Call log, February 15, 1974, box 3, folder 27; call log, December 4, 1979, box 3, folder 33, both in Lesbian Switchboard Records.

82. Writer's and recipient's name redacted, letter, February 12, 1981, Lesbian Switchboard Records, box 1, folder 9.

83. Robert McRuer and Anna Mollow have argued that the intersection of marginalized sexualities with disability is generative for new modes of theorizing and political imagination: Robert McRuer and Anna Mollow, "Introduction," in *Sex and Disability*, ed. Robert McRuer and Anna Mollow (Durham, NC: Duke University Press, 2012), 1–35.

84. *Switchboard Handbook.*

85. "Lesbian Phone Line Flyer," Lesbian Organization of Toronto (LOOT) files, the ArQuives, Toronto.

86. Nancy K. Baym, *Personal Connections in the Digital Age* (Cambridge: Polity, 2010), 8.

87. See, e.g., Audre Lorde, "Uses of the Erotic: The Erotic as Power" (1978), in *Sister Outsider: Essays and Speeches* (Trumansburg, NY: Crossing, [1984] 2007), 53–59; Audre Lorde, *Zami: A New Spelling of My Name* (Berkeley, CA: Crossing, 1982). Ahmed provides a wonderful overview of this work in *Living a Feminist Life*.

88. "Interviews with Lesbian Phone Line Members Sue Cook and Darlene McDougall," sound recording, 2003-007/01T, the ArQuives.

89. Amy Flowers, *The Fantasy Factory: An Insider's View of the Phone Sex Industry* (Philadelphia: University of Pennsylvania Press, 1998), 3.

90. Flowers, *The Fantasy Factory*, 4.

91. Baym, *Personal Connections in the Digital Age*, 140. See also Nancy K. Baym, Yan Bing Zhang, and Mei-Chen Lin, "Social Interactions across Media: Interpersonal Communication on the Internet, Telephone, and Face-to-Face," *New Media and Society* 6, no. 3 (2004): 299–318, and Sherry Turkle, *Reclaiming Conversation: The Power of Talk in a Digital Age* (New York: Penguin, 2015).

92. David Suisman, *Selling Sounds: The Commercial Revolution in American Music* (Cambridge MA: Harvard University Press, 2009), 149.

93. Call log, November 9, 1972, 9:45 PM, Lesbian Switchboard Records, box 3, folder 23.

94. Christin Scarlett Milloy, "Trans Customers Locked out of TD Bank Accounts." *Xtra*, December 22, 2014, https://www.dailyxtra.com/trans-customers -locked-out-of-td-bank-accounts-65644.

95. Sherry Turkle's *Reclaiming Conversation* exemplifies this argument about young people and "phone-phobia."

96. See, e.g., Toronto's LBGT Youthline, which received 55 percent of its contacts via the telephone in 2015–16, versus 23 percent by text message and 21 percent by online chat: *LBGT Youthline Annual Report*, 2015–16, http://cdn.youthline.ca/wp -content/uploads/2016/11/YLAnnualReportFinaltoLoad.pdf.

97. Sara Ahmed's ideas about how we make feminist life livable are the strongest influence on my thinking here, but I wish to bring these ideas into conversation with media and information studies. In other words, what role does access to mediated information play in making a feminist life livable?

98. Hogan, *The Feminist Bookstore Movement*.

99. Susan Leigh Star and Karen Ruhleder, "Steps toward an Ecology of Infrastructure: Design and Access for Large Information Spaces," *Information Systems Research 7*, no. 1 (1996): 111–34.

100. Geoffrey C. Bowker and Susan Leigh Star, *Sorting Things Out: Classification and Its Consequences* (Cambridge, MA: MIT Press, 1999).

101. Jane Sandberg, "Organizing the Transgender Internet: Web Directories and Envisioning Inclusive Digital Spaces," in *Queers Online: LGBT Digital Practices in Libraries, Archives, and Museums*, ed. Rachel Wexelbaum (Sacramento, CA: Litwin, 2015), 43–60.

102. *Switchboard Handbook*, emphasis added.

103. Name withheld, interview with the author, August 14, 2017.

104. Name withheld, interview with the author, August 14, 2017.

105. See, e.g., lesbian theorists such as Gloria Anzaldúa, Audre Lorde, Robin Morgan, and Adrienne Rich. They frame "lesbian" differently but always as a contentious, political category.

106. "Some Common Dos and Don'ts."

107. Jack Halberstam, "Straight Eye for the Queer Theorist: A Review of 'Queer Theory without Antinormativity,'" *Bully Bloggers*, September 12, 2015, https:// bullybloggers.wordpress.com/2015/09/12/straight-eye-for-the-queer-theorist-a -review-of-queer-theory-without-antinormativity-by-jack-halberstam; Heather Love, "Review: A Gentle Angry People," *Transition 84* (2000): 98–113.

108. *Switchboard Handbook*.

109. Naomi E. Goodhart, "Lesbian Switchboard Evaluation Checklist," Lesbian Switchboard Records, box 2, folder 12.

110. Naomi E. Goodhart, "Lesbian Switchboard Trainee Evaluation," Lesbian Switchboard Records, box 2, folder 12.

111. Call log, June 14, 1973, Lesbian Switchboard Records, box 3, folder 25.

112. Call log, February 9, 1977, Lesbian Switchboard Records, box 3, folder 28.

113. Jack Halberstam, *Female Masculinity* (Durham, NC: Duke University Press, 1998); Joan Nestle, *A Restricted Country* (San Francisco: Cleis, 2003); Minnie Bruce Pratt, *s/HE* (Ithaca, NY: Firebrand, 1995).

114. Fred Turner, "Burning Man at Google: A Cultural Infrastructure for New Media Production," *New Media and Society* 11, nos. 1–2 (2009): 83.

115. Slote, "Lesbian Switchboard," 3.

CHAPTER THREE: THE INDEXERS

1. Clare Potter, "The Lesbian Periodicals Index," in *Lesbian Studies Present and Future*, ed. Margaret Cruikshank (Old Westbury, NY: Feminist Press, 1982), 152–61; Clare Potter, ed., *The Lesbian Periodicals Index* (Tallahassee, FL: Naiad, 1986).

2. Clare Potter, "How to Index in the Circle of Lesbian Indexers, Part 1," 1979, Circle of Lesbian Indexers Papers, Lesbian Herstory Archives, Brooklyn, NY (hereafter, LHA), 1.

3. Geoffrey C. Bowker and Susan Leigh Star, *Sorting Things Out: Classification and Its Consequences* (Cambridge, MA: MIT Press, 1999).

4. On interfaces and digital imaginaries, see Ann Friedberg, *The Virtual Window: From Alberti to Microsoft* (Cambridge, MA: MIT Press, 2009).

5. Potter, "How to Index in the Circle of Lesbian Indexers, Part 1," 4, emphasis added.

6. Jonathan Sterne, *MP3: The Meaning of a Format* (Durham, NC: Duke University Press, 2012).

7. On experience in feminist theory and politics, see Joan Wallach Scott, "The Evidence of Experience," *Critical Inquiry* 17, no. 4 (1993): 773–97.

8. JR Roberts, "Introduction," in *Black Lesbians: An Annotated Bibliography*, ed. JR Roberts (Tallahassee, FL: Naiad, 1981), xi–xv.

9. Marcel Danesi, *Encyclopedia Dictionary of Semiotics, Media, and Communications* (Toronto: University of Toronto Press, 2000), 119.

10. Jessie Daniels, "Race and Racism in Internet Studies: A Review and Critique," *New Media and Society* 15, no. 5 (2013): 695–719; Michele White, *The Body and the Screen: Theories of Internet Spectatorship* (Cambridge, MA: MIT Press, 2006).

11. Raymond Williams, *Marxism and Literature* (Oxford: Oxford University Press, 1977), 132.

12. Ronald Day traces the twentieth-century transition of indexes from paper documents to infrastructural devices operating in the background of digital technologies. He argues that fundamental ideas such as the user-document distinction developed out of paper indexes and eventually led to the modern "subsumption of both documents and users as data": Ronald Day, *Indexing It All: The Subject in the Age of Documentation* (Cambridge, MA: MIT Press, 2014), 2.

13. Safiya Umoja Noble, *Algorithms of Oppression* (New York: New York University Press, 2018).

14. Michel Foucault, *The Archaeology of Knowledge* (New York: Vintage, 1972).

15. Scott, "The Evidence of Experience," 776.

16. Clare Potter, interview with the author, telephone, November 16, 2014.

17. Potter interview.

18. Clare Potter, "How to Index in the Circle of Lesbian Indexers, Vol. 2," 1979, LHA, 1–2.

19. Potter interview.

20. Potter interview.

21. Potter interview.

22. Margaret Cruikshank, "Lesbian Studies: Present and Future" (New York: Feminist Press, 1982).

23. Potter, "The Lesbian Periodicals Index," 153.

24. Potter, "The Lesbian Periodicals Index," 153.

25. Potter, "The Lesbian Periodicals Index," 153.

26. Sara Ahmed, *Queer Phenomenology: Orientations, Objects, Others* (Durham, NC: Duke University Press, 2006), 19–20. "Desire Lines" does not appear in *Queer Phenomenology*'s index.

27. Ahmed, *Queer Phenomenology*, 20.

28. Sara Ahmed, *Willful Subjects* (Durham, NC: Duke University Press, 2014), 14.

29. Ahmed, *Willful Subjects*, 21.

30. Barbara Smith, "Foreword," in *Black Lesbians: An Annotated Bibliography*, ed. JR Roberts (Tallahassee, FL: Naiad, 1981), x, emphasis added.

31. Potter interview.

32. Roberts, "Introduction," xiii.

33. JR Roberts, "Master List of Lesbian Serials Published in the United States since 1947," 1978, LHA.

34. Roberts, "Introduction," xi.

35. Kristen Hogan, *The Feminist Bookstore Movement: Lesbian Antiracism and Feminist Accountability* (Durham, NC: Duke University, 2016), 72.

36. Hogan, *The Feminist Bookstore Movement*, 72n15.

37. Hazel V. Carby, "White Woman Listen! Black Feminism and the Boundaries of Sisterhood" (1982), in *Theories of Race and Racism: A Reader*, ed. Les Back and John Solomos (London: Routledge, 2000), 110–28; bell hooks, *Ain't I a Woman? Black Women and Feminism* (Boston: South End, 1981); Audre Lorde, "An Open Letter to Mary Daly" (1979), in *Sister Outsider: Essays and Speeches* (Trumansburg, NY: Crossing, [1984] 2007), 66–71; Bernice Johnson Reagon, "Coalition Politics: Turning the Century," in *Home Girls: A Black Feminist Anthology*, ed. Barbara Smith (New York: Kitchen Table: Women of Color, [1981] 1983). Reagon's essay was originally delivered as an address at the West Coast Women's Music Festival in 1981. On the relationship between Reagon's address and lesbian antiracism more generally, see Hogan, *The Feminist Bookstore Movement*, 69–71. The earlier Combahee River Collective Statement set the stage and terms for this debate. The collective wrote, "Black, other Third World, and working women have been involved in the feminist movement from its start, but both outside reactionary forces and racism and elitism within the movement itself have served to obscure our participation": Combahee River Collective, "The Combahee River Collective Statement," 1977, https://americanstudies.yale.edu /sites/default/files/files/Keyword%20Coalition_Readings.pdf.

38. SaraEllen Strongman, "The Sisterhood: Black Women, Black Feminism, and the Women's Liberation Movement" (PhD diss., University of Pennsylvania, Philadelphia, 2018).

39. Liza Taylor, "Coalition from the Inside Out: Women of Color Feminism and Politico-Ethical Coalition Politics," *New Political Science* 40, no. 1 (2018): 119–36. https://doi.org/10.1080/07393148.2017.1416447.

40. Carby, "White Woman Listen!" 120.

41. Hogan develops this concept of antiracism as accountability in *The Feminist Bookstore Movement*.

42. Roberts, "Introduction," xi.

43. Emily Hobson documents how radical gay and lesbian activists who were white worked to learn from intersectional feminism created by lesbians of color: Emily Hobson, *Lavender and Red: Liberation and Solidarity in the Gay and Lesbian Left* (Oakland: University of California Press, 2016), 33–35, 40.

44. Aimee Carrillo Rowe, *Power Lines: On the Subject of Feminist Alliances* (Durham, NC: Duke University Press, 2008), 4.

45. Roberts, "Introduction," xi.

46. Smith, "Foreword," ix.

47. Smith, "Foreword," ix.

48. Combahee River Collective, "Combahee River Collective Statement"; Lorde, "An Open Letter to Mary Daly"; SaraEllen Strongman, "'Creating Justice between Us': Audre Lorde's Theory of the Erotic as Coalitional Politics in the Women's Movement," *Feminist Theory* 19, no. 1 (2018): 41–59.

49. Amber Jamilla Musser, *Sensational Flesh: Race, Power, and Masochism* (New York: New York University Press, 2014), 157.

50. Audre Lorde, "I Am Your Sister: Black Women Organizing across Sexualities" (New York: Kitchen Table: Women of Color, 1985).

51. Roderick Ferguson, *Aberrations in Black: Toward a Queer of Color Critique* (Minneapolis: University of Minnesota Press, 2004), 126–27. See, e.g., the much-quoted passage from the "Combahee River Collective Statement": "We believe that sexual politics under patriarchy is as pervasive in Black women's lives as are the politics of class and race. We also often find it difficult to separate race from class from sex oppression because in our lives they are most often experienced simultaneously."

52. Smith and Audre Lorde founded Kitchen Table: Women of Color Press in 1980 while Roberts was working on her bibliography. Kitchen Table published significant women of color anthologies featuring work by lesbian feminists of color, including Cherríe Moraga and Gloria Anzaldúa's *This Bridge Called My Back : Writings by Radical Women of Color*, 2d ed. (New York: Kitchen Table: Women of Color Press, [1981] 1983), and Barbara Smith, *Home Girls: A Black Feminist Anthology* (New York: Kitchen Table: Women of Color Press,1983).

53. Catherine Squires, "Rethinking the Black Public Sphere: An Alternative Vocabulary for Multiple Public Spheres," *Communication Theory* 12, no. 4 (2002): 446–68.

54. See Alexis Pauline Gumbs, "Eternal Summer of the Black Feminist Mind," in *Make Your Own History: Documenting Feminist and Queer Activism in the 21st Century*, ed. Lyz Bly and Kelly Wooten (Sacramento, CA: Litwin, 2012), 59–68.

55. Roberts, "Introduction," xi.

56. Roberts, "Introduction," xv.

57. Potter, "How to Index in the Circle of Lesbian Indexers, Part 1," 10.

58. Roberts, "Introduction," xiv.

59. See the Cite Black Women Collective's website at https://www .citeblackwomencollective.org.

60. JR Roberts, "Suggested Activities," in *Black Lesbians: An Annotated Bibliography*, ed. JR Roberts (Tallahassee, FL: Naiad, 1981), xiii.

61. Potter, "How to Index in the Circle of Lesbian Indexers, Part 1," 4.

62. These indexing societies are the two leading professional associations for indexers, publishing most of the books in circulation on the topic.

63. Potter, "How to Index in the Circle of Lesbian Indexers, Part 1," 4.

64. Lisa Gitelman and Virginia Jackson, "Introduction," in *Raw Data Is an Oxymoron*, ed. Lisa Gitelman and Virginia Jackson (Cambridge, MA: MIT Press, 2013), 9.

65. G. Norman Knight, *Indexing, the Art of* (London: George Allen and Unwin, 1979).

66. Fred Turner analyzes accessibility and the tool cultures of information management in *From Counterculture to Cyberculture: Stewart Brand, the Whole Earth Network and the Rise of Digital Utopianism* (Chicago: University of Chicago Press, 2006).

67. Data are distinguished as "confusing mass," in opposition to information, in Gitelman and Jackson, *Raw Data Is an Oxymoron*, 8.

68. On indexing in the gay and lesbian archives movement, see Robert B. M. Ridinger, "Playing in the Attic: Indexing and Preserving the Gay Press," in *Liberating Minds: The Stories and Professional Lives of Gay, Lesbian, and Bisexual Librarians and Their Advocates*, ed. Norman G. Kester (Jefferson, NC: McFarland, 1997), 92–97. Ridinger, who created a complete index to *The Advocate* during his tenure at Northern Illinois University Library, describes sending out a survey to all sixty-seven member collections of the International Association of Lesbian and Gay Archives and Libraries in 1986. In response, he learned that ten distinct indexes of gay and lesbian periodicals were being produced at various archives and libraries. Ridinger worked with others to merge the listings into a common indexing thesaurus, which was then redistributed to each contributing institution: see Ridinger, "Playing in the Attic," 95.

69. Robert L. Collison, *Indexes and Indexing* (London: Ernest Benn, 1959), 19.

70. Collison, *Indexes and Indexing*, front matter (n.p.).

71. Markus Krajewski, *Paper Machines: About Cards and Catalogs, 1548–1929* (Cambridge, MA: MIT Press, 2011).

72. Knight, *Indexing, The Art of*, xx.

73. *Paperwork Explosion* (1967) is a short film by Jim Henson commissioned by IBM to advertise its MT/ST word processor. It also uses a crisis tone to describe this proliferation of documents, which could be ameliorated through bureaucratic management strategies, especially computing.

74. Lisa Gitelman, *Paper Knowledge: Toward a Media History of Documents* (Durham, NC: Duke University Press, 2014), 54.

75. Gitelman, *Paper Knowledge*, 58.

76. Day, *Indexing It All*; Gitelman, *Paper Knowledge*; Krajewski, *Paper Machines*.

77. Gitelman, *Paper Knowledge*, 59.

78. Sasha Archibald, "Indexes, In Praise of," *Cabinet* 52 (2013–14), 58.

79. Archibald, "Indexes, In Praise of," 59.

80. Archibald, "Indexes, In Praise of," 59.

81. Gitelman, *Paper Knowledge*, 58.

82. Day, *Indexing It All*; Shannon Mattern, "Small, Moving, Intelligent Parts," *Words in Space* (blog), June 28, 2016, http://wordsinspace.net/shannon/2016/06/28/small-moving-intelligent-parts/.

83. Collison, *Indexes and Indexing*, 19–20.

84. Roberts, "Introduction," xi.

85. On marginalization from institutional contexts, see Gumbs, "Eternal Sunshine of a Black Feminist Mind"; Matt Johnson, "A Hidden History of Queer Subject Access," in *Radical Cataloging: Essays at the Front,* ed. K. R. Roberto (Jefferson, NC: McFarland, 2008), 18–27; Trysh Travis, "The Women in Print Movement: History and Implications," *Book History* 11 (2008): 275–300.

86. Jonathan Guillory, "Genesis of the Media Concept," *Critical Inquiry* 36 (2010): 357.

87. Guillory, "Genesis of the Media Concept," 357.

88. Finn Enke, *Finding the Movement: Sexuality, Contested Space, and Feminist Activism* (Durham, NC: Duke University Press, 2007); Jack Gieseking, *A Queer New York* (New York: New York University Press, 2020).

89. Barbara Gittings, "Feeding the Hungry Gay Bookworm," box 116, folder 6, 1983, 1. Barbara Gittings and Kay Tobin Lahusen gay history papers and photographs 1855–2009. Manuscripts and Archives Division, New York Public Library. See also Cait McKinney, "Finding the Lines to My People: Media History and Queer Bibliographic Encounter," GLQ 24, no. 1 (2018): 55–83.

90. On "raw" or preprocessed information, see Jonathan Sterne and Tara Rodgers, "The Poetics of Signal Processing," *Differences* 22, nos. 2–3 (2011): 36.

91. Potter, "Introduction," x, emphasis added.

92. Melissa Adler, *Cruising the Library: Perversities in the Organization of Knowledge* (New York: Fordham University Press, 2017); Matt Johnson, "GLBT Controlled Vocabularies and Classification Schemes," Gay, Lesbian, Bisexual, and Transgender Round Table, American Library Association, 2007, http://www.ala.org/glbtrt/popularresources/vocab.

93. Potter, "How to Index in the Circle of Lesbian Indexers, Part 1."

94. Lisa Nakamura, *Digitizing Race: Visual Cultures of the Internet* (Minneapolis: University of Minnesota Press, 2008), 28.

95. Nakamura, *Digitizing Race*, 28.

96. Margaret Hedstrom, "Archives, Memory, and Interfaces with the Past," *Archival Science* 2 (2002): 21.

97. Hedstrom, "Archives, Memory, and Interfaces with the Past," 21.

98. Potter, "How to Index in the Circle of Lesbian Indexers, Part 1," 4–5.

99. Michael Warner, "Publics and Counterpublics," *Public Culture* 14, no. 1 (2002): 89.

100. Warner, "Publics and Counterpublics," 88.

101. Warner, "Publics and Counterpublics," 85.

102. Warner, "Publics and Counterpublics," 88.

103. Potter, "How to Index in the Circle of Lesbian Indexers, Part 1," 1–2.

104. Julia Creet, "Daughters of the Movement: The Psychodynamics of Lesbian s/m Fantasy," *Differences* 3, no. 2 (1991): 135–59; Bobby Noble, *Sons of the Movement: FtMs Risking Incoherence on a Post-Queer Cultural Landscape* (Toronto: Women's Press, [1978] 2006), 19.

105. Joan Scott, *The Fantasy of Feminist History,* (Durham, NC: Duke University Press, 2011), 51.

106. Archibald, "Indexes, In Praise of," 57.

107. Potter, "How to Index in the Circle of Lesbian Indexers, Part 1," 8.

108. On the DIY sensibility of feminist activism, see Alison Piepmeier, *Girl Zines: Making Media, Doing Feminism* (New York: New York University Press, 2009); Amy Spencer, *DIY: The Rise of Lo-Fi Culture* (London: Marion Boyars, 2008).

109. I am grateful to Kate Eichhorn for this insight on index cards via a discussion we had about her research on the recipe box as a paper database.

110. Margot Canaday, "Queer Career: Precarious Labor, Law, and Sexuality in Postwar America" (forthcoming).

111. Potter interview.

112. Potter interview.

113. Potter interview, 12.

114. The construction of library work as easy because women can do it is a frequent discursive tactic in the history of the political economy of libraries, explored in Dee Garrison, "The Tender Technicians: The Feminization of Public Librarianship, 1876–1905," *Journal of Social History* 6, no. 2 (1972–73): 131–59. She argues that the feminization of library work had the effect of diminishing the status of public libraries. "Above all, women's dominance of librarianship did much to shape the inferior and precarious status of the public library as an important cultural resource and to cause it to evolve into a marginal kind of public amusement service": Garrison, "The Tender Technicians," 132.

115. See Potter, "How to Index in the Circle of Lesbian Indexers, Part 1."

116. Potter, "How to Index in the Circle of Lesbian Indexers, Part 1," 1.

117. Potter interview.

118. Travis, "The Women in Print Movement."

119. Travis, "The Women in Print Movement," 280.

120. Potter, "How to Index in the Circle of Lesbian Indexers, Part 1," 3.

121. On these characteristics of women's liberation, see Victoria Hesford, *Feeling Women's Liberation* (Durham, NC: Duke University Press, 2013), 117–32.

122. Potter, "How to Index in the Circle of Lesbian Indexers, Part 2," 1–2.

123. Scott, *The Fantasy of Feminist History,* 73.

124. See Bowker and Star, *Sorting Things Out*; Emily Drabinski, "Queering the Catalog: Queer Theory and the Politics of Correction," *The Library Quarterly* 83, no. 2 (2013): 94–111.

125. Potter, "How to Index in the Circle of Lesbian Indexers, Part 2," 2.

126. See Potter, "How to Index in the Circle of Lesbian Indexers, Part 1," 7.

127. Potter, "How to Index in the Circle of Lesbian Indexers, Part 1," 2.

128. Dale Spender, *Women of Ideas and What Men Have Done to Them: From Aphra Behn to Adrienne Rich* (London: Routledge, 1982). See also Archibald, "Indexes, In Praise of," 57n7. Other projects were similar to Spender's. Matt Johnson identifies Mary Ellen Capek's *A Women's Thesaurus* (New York, NY Harper and Row, 1987) as a "unique project which resulted in a list of descriptors novel in both form and content" that was "tested in many libraries and other information retrieval settings": Johnson, "A Hidden History of Queer Subject Access," 22–23.

129. "Resolution on Gay Subject Headings passed at Annual Conference," July 11, 1974, Social Responsibilities Round Table Task Force on Gay Liberation Business Meeting, Barbara Gittings and Kay Tobin Lahusen Gay History Papers and Photographs, 1855–2009, MssCol 6397, Manuscripts and Archives Division, New York Public Library, box 51, folder 2. See also Sanford Berman, "Introduction: Cataloguing Reform, LC, and Me," in *Radical Cataloging: Essays at the Front*, ed. K. R. Roberto (Jefferson, NC: MacFarland, 2008), 5–11; Adler, *Cruising the Library*.

130. Potter, "How to Index in the Circle of Lesbian Indexers, Part 1," 7.

131. Potter, "How to Index in the Circle of Lesbian Indexers, Part 1," 7–8.

132. Garrison, "The Tender Technicians," 131–32. See also Patrick Keilty, "Tedious: Feminized Labor in Machine-Readable Cataloging," *Feminist Media Studies* 18, no. 2 (2017): 191–204, https://doi.org/10.1080/14680777.2017.1308410.

133. Garrison, "The Tender Technicians," 137.

134. Francis L. Miksa, "The Columbia School of Library Economy, 1887–1888," *Libraries and Culture* 23, no. 3 (1988): 250.

135. On Dewey and the feminization of librarianship, see Garrison, "The Tender Technicians," 148–51.

136. Clare Potter and Karen Brown, copies of cards (revised and corrected), Circle of Lesbian Indexers Papers, LHA, folder 5.

137. "Circle of Lesbian Indexers," *Matrices*, vol. 2 no. 2, 1979, 2.

138. Debora Edel, Clare Potter, and JR Roberts, "Guide to Current Lesbian Periodicals," *Matrices*, vol. 4, no. 1, 1980, 17.

139. "Black Lesbian Bibliography Needs Financial Sponsors," *Matrices*, vol. 2, no. 1, 1978, 12. The same announcement was published in *Out and About*, no. 22, 1979.

140. Potter interview.

141. Potter interview.

142. Potter interview. The June L. Mazer Archives, in West Hollywood, California, are similar to the LHA but focused on West Coast materials.

143. Potter interview.

144. Mark Goble, *Beautiful Circuits: Modernism and the Mediated Life* (New York: Columbia University Press, 2010), 289.

145. Gitelman, *Paper Knowledge*, 64.

146. Gitelman, *Paper Knowledge*, 15.

147. Collison, *Indexes and Indexing*, 13–14.

148. Wendy Hui Kyong Chun, *Updating to Remain the Same: Habitual New Media* (Cambridge, MA: MIT Press, 2016).

149. Knight, *Indexing, The Art of*, 116.

150. Kevin Driscoll, "From Punched Cards to 'Big Data': A Social History of Database Populism," *Communication +1* 1, (2012), https://scholarworks.umass.edu/cpo/vol1/iss1/4.

151. Driscoll, "From Punched Cards to 'Big Data.'"

152. Potter, "How to Index in the Circle of Lesbian Indexers, Part 1," 9.

153. Driscoll, "From Punched Cards to 'Big Data.'"

154. RAND Corporation, *Specifications for the RAND Abstract and Index System* (Santa Monica, CA: RAND Computation Center, 1975), iii.

155. Clare Potter to the Circle of Lesbian Indexers, letter, May 16, 1981, Circle of Lesbian Indexers Papers, LHA.

156. Roger Rajman and John Borgelt, "WYLBUR: An Interactive Text Editing and Remote Job Entry System," *Communications of the ACM* 16 no. 5 (1973): 315.

157. Rajman and Borgelt, "WYLBUR," 315.

158. Potter, "The Lesbian Periodicals Index," 153.

159. This rationale is outlined in Clare Potter to Karen Brown, another Circle indexer, letter, December 23, 1980, Circle of Lesbian Indexers Papers, LHA.

160. Potter to Karen Brown, letter (December 23, 1980).

161. Clare Potter, "Revisions, Edition 10," n.d. [1981], Circle of Lesbian Indexers Papers, LHA, folder 2 (*The Basic Thesaurus*, edited).

162. Potter, "Revisions, Edition 10."

163. On standards see Bowker and Star, *Sorting Things Out*.

164. Potter interview.

165. Potter interview.

166. Karen Brown and Clare Potter, "Addition 10," copies of cards (revised and corrected), Circle of Lesbian Indexers Papers, LHA, folder 5.

167. National Institutes of Health, *WYLBUR Fundamentals* (Bethesda, MD: Division of Computer Research and Technology, 1980), 75.

168. K. J. Rawson, "The 'Trans + Gender' Project," http://kjrawson.net/trans-gender-timeline.

169. See Jo Freeman, "The Tyranny of Structurelessness," *Women's Studies Quarterly* 41, nos. 3–4 (2013): 231–46.

170. Potter, "How to Index in the Circle of Lesbian Indexers, Part 1," 7.

171. Potter, "How to Index in the Circle of Lesbian Indexers, Part 1," 7.

172. Saskia Scheffer, interview with the author, Brooklyn, NY, May 10, 2013.

173. Krajewski, *Paper Machines*, 4.

174. For example, RAND's WYLBUR manual "presumes knowledge of basic microcomputer procedures": Gail Covitt Roberts, *CUE R3.0 Tutorial for WYLBUR*, RAND Corporation, February 1989, https://www.rand.org/content/dam/rand/pubs/notes/2009/N2673.pdf, iii.

175. My reading of Ehrman's manual drew on the original version available to users at Stanford: John Ehrman, "WYLBUR Tutorial," 1998-014, John Ehrman Papers, SLAC National Accelerator Laboratory, Archives, History and Records Office,

Stanford, CA. An adapted version of the manual is also available online via CERN's archives at http://cds.cern.ch/record/2273001.

176. See Clare Potter to Karen Brown, letter, July 17, 1981, Circle of Lesbian Indexers Papers, LHA.

177. McKinney, "Finding the Lines to My People."

178. Potter interview.

179. The late 1970s and early 1980s saw the publication of many instructional manuals for information workers who wanted to learn how to use databases: see John Convey, *Online Information Retrieval: An Introductory Manual to Principles and Practice*, 3d ed. (London: Library Association, [1977] 1989); Peter Judge and Brenda Gerrie, eds. *Small Scale Bibliographic Databases* (Orlando, FL: Academic, 1986); Brian Wilks, *What Every Librarian Should Know about On-line Searching* (Ottawa: Canadian Library Association, 1982). See also Charles Bourne and Trudi Bellardo Hahn, *A History of Online Information Services, 1963–1976* (Cambridge, MA: MIT Press, 2003), 1.

180. Potter to the Circle members (May 16, 1981).

181. Potter to Karen Brown (July 17, 1981).

182. Potter, "How to Index in the Circle of Lesbian Indexers, Part 1," 2.

183. Clare Potter to Karen Brown, letter, May 2, 1981, Circle of Lesbian Indexers Papers, LHA.

184. Potter to Karen Brown (July 17, 1981).

185. Nathan Ensmenger, "Beards, Sandals, and Other Signs of Rugged Individualism': Masculine Culture within the Computing Professions," *Osiris* 30 (2015): 38–65.

186. Potter, "How to Index in the Circle of Lesbian Indexers, Part 1," 9.

187. Clare Potter to Karen Brown, letter, April 19, 1981, Circle of Lesbian Indexers Papers, LHA. See also Potter to Karen Brown (July 17, 1981).

188. Clare Potter to Karen Brown, letter, February 21, 1981, Circle of Lesbian Indexers Papers, LHA.

189. Adrienne Rich, *Of Woman Born: Motherhood as Experience and Institution* (New York: W. W. Norton, 1977).

CHAPTER FOUR: FEMINIST DIGITIZATION PRACTICES AT THE LESBIAN HERSTORY ARCHIVES

1. Nan Alamilla Boyd, "Who Is the Subject? Queer Theory Meets Oral History," *Journal of the History of Sexuality* 12, no. 2 (2008): 177–89; Elise Chenier, "Hidden from Historians: Preserving Lesbian Oral History in Canada," *Archivaria* 68 (Fall 2009): 247–69; Madeline Davis and Elizabeth Kennedy, "Oral History and the Study of Sexuality in the Lesbian Community: Buffalo, New York, 1940–1960," *Feminist Studies* 12, no. 1 (1986): 7–26, https://doi.org/10.2307/3177981.

2. Colette Denali Montoya-Sloan, interview with the author, Brooklyn, NY, April 26, 2013. Working away at a potentially incompletable task is not without precedent in the history of libraries and archives, where historical book collections have tended to expand faster than they could be cataloged on paper. This is notable in the legend of the Great Library at Alexandria, which could never catch

up, though its custodians continued to try. It also was a common work pace during the introduction of card catalogs in the United States in the early nineteenth century, as documented in Markus Krajewski, *Paper Machines: About Cards and Catalogs, 1548–1929* (Cambridge, MA: MIT Press, 2011). New card catalog systems struggled to input existing collections and catch up to the influx of new books libraries acquired. Backlogs in "processing" new acquisitions so that they are ready for researchers to use are universal across community and institutional archives. In other words, catching up, to some extent, is the norm in information work, but the Lesbian Herstory Archives brings a particular lesbian feminist sensibility to carrying on with this (impossible) work.

3. Angela Willey, *Undoing Monogamy: The Politics of Science and the Possibilities of Biology* (Durham, NC: Duke University Press, 2016), 142.

4. The volunteers were Rachel Corbman, Ronika McClain, Colette Denali Montoya-Sloan, Imogen Peach, Saskia Scheffer, and Maxine Wolfe. Imogen Peach is a pseudonym that this coordinator chose to participate in the interview anonymously. Demographic information about Imogen has also been withheld for this reason.

5. I have withheld the names of these interns because they are no longer involved in the organization and I was unable to follow up with them to confirm their ongoing consent to be named in the research. I checked in with participants about using their names prior to publication because the nature of online indexing of scholarly books and trolling/harassment of feminist and queer people has changed significantly since 2013, when participants initially consented to participate. Though this was not part of my original ethics protocol, it highlights crucial ethical concerns for feminist digital research methods.

6. This simple understanding of digitization is exemplified by the Oxford English Dictionary, sv. "digitize." Digitization at community archives, or perhaps in any institutional context, is a much broader process that involves questions about labor, technology, accessibility, and the long-term stewardship of materials.

7. Daniel C. Brouwer and Adela C. Licona, "Trans(affective)mediation: Feeling Our Way from Paper to Digitized Zines and Back Again," *Critical Studies in Media Communication* 33, no. 1 (2016): 78–79.

8. Brouwer and Licona, "Trans(affective)mediation," 81.

9. On the cultural politics of microfilm, see Nicholson Baker, *Double Fold: Libraries and the Assault on Paper* (New York: Random House, 2001).

10. The ArQuives: Canada's LGBTQ2S+ Archives was also a major contributor to this project: see LGBT Rights Movement & Activists, https://www.gale.com/primary-sources/archives-of-sexuality-and-gender/collections/gay-rights-movement.

11. On mass digitization and cultural memory, see Nanna Bonde Thylstrup, *The Politics of Mass Digitization* (Cambridge, MA: MIT Press, 2019).

12. The Lesbian Herstory Archives' annual budget varies from year to year but is generally about $60,000, most of which is spent on basic upkeep such as utility bills, folders, and acid-free boxes: 2013 Annual Income, Rachel Corbman, email to the author, December 11, 2014. The archives runs many modest fundraising events throughout the year, including a speed-dating event at which I volunteered

to sell raffle tickets during my research period. There are also book sales, services auctions, and a commemorative tote bag drive. A semiannual art auction features donated works by notable lesbian artists including Carrie Moyer and Allyson Mitchell.

13. Rebecka Sheffield, "Community Archives," *Currents of Archival Thinking, 2nd Ed.* (Denver, CO: Libraries Unlimited, 2017): 351–76. Grassroots, community-based archives documenting marginal social groups emerged in the late 1960s following the British New Left idea that historical research could be used against class oppression as the "forgotten" histories of socially marginalized groups are recovered and made to matter: see Chenier, "Hidden from Historians"; Bill Luckenbill, "Modern Gay and Lesbian Libraries and Archives in North America: A Study in Community Identity and Affirmation," *Library Management* 23, nos. 1–2 (2002): 93–100.

14. Michelle Caswell, Alda Allina Migoni, Noah Geraci, and Marika Cifor, "'To Be Able to Imagine Otherwise': Community Archives and the Importance of Representation," *Archives and Records* 38, no. 1 (2017): 5–26. See also Andrew Flinn, Mary Stevens, and Elizabeth Shepherd, "Whose Memories, Whose Archives? Independent Community Archives, Autonomy and the Mainstream," *Archival Science* 9 (2009): 74.

15. Stephen Maynard, "The Burning, Willful Evidence: Lesbian/Gay History and Archival Research," *Archivaria* 33 (1991): 200.

16. "Statement of Principles," 1979, Lesbian Herstory Archives, http://www .lesbianherstoryarchives.org/history.html.

17. Ann Cvetkovich, *An Archive of Feelings: Trauma, Sexuality and Lesbian Public Cultures* (Durham, NC: Duke University Press, 2003).

18. Joan Nestle, "The Will to Remember: The Lesbian Herstory Archives of New York," *Feminist Review* 34 (1990): 88.

19. During my research there were fifteen Lesbian Herstory Archives coordinators, ten of whom were active and attending meetings.

20. "Statement of Principles." The most recent version of the principles is dated Fall 2018. It is similar in spirit to the original version but includes explicit language about welcoming users of all gender identities and acknowledges "changing concepts of lesbian identities."

21. "Statement of Principles." See also Polly Thistlethwaite, "Building 'A Home of Our Own': The Construction of the Lesbian Herstory Archives," in *Daring to Find Our Names: The Search for Lesbigay Library History*, ed. James V. Carmichael Jr. (Westport, CT: Greenwood, 1998), 153–74.

22. Kara Keeling, "Queer OS," *Cinema Journal* 53, no. 2 (2014): 152–57; Kate O'Riordan, "Queer Theories and Cybersubjects: Intersecting Figures," in *Queer Online: Media Technology and Sexuality*, ed. Kate O'Riordan and David J. Phillips (New York: Peter Lang, 2007), 13–30.

23. See the formulation of enclaves and counterpublics in Catherine Squires, "Rethinking the Black Public Sphere: An Alternative Vocabulary for Multiple Public Spheres," *Communication Theory* 12, no. 4 (2002): 446–68. On counterpublics and enclaves in social media contexts, see Sarah J. Jackson, Moya Bailey, and Brooke Foucault Welles, "#GirlsLikeUs: Trans Advocacy and Community Building Online," *New Media and Society* 20, no. 5 (2018): 1868–88.

24. On invisible publics, see dana boyd, "Why Youth (Heart) Social Network Sites: The Role of Networked Publics in Teenage Social Life," in *MacArthur Foundation Series on Digital Learning: Youth, Identity, and Digital Media Volume*, ed. David Buckingham (Cambridge, MA: MIT Press, 2007), 119–142.

25. Here I draw on Ann Cvetkovich's study of the Lesbian Herstory Archives' emotional role in collecting, representing, and providing engagements with histories of public culture and trauma: see Cvetkovich, *An Archive of Feelings*.

26. On lesbian feminism's pull, or drag, on "queer," see Elizabeth Freeman, *Time Binds: Queer Temporalities, Queer Histories* (Durham, NC: Duke University Press, 2010).

27. Rachel Corbman, email to the author, January 15, 2018.

28. Freeman, *Time Binds*; Jack Halberstam, *In a Queer Time and Place: Transgender Bodies: Subcultural Lives* (New York: New York University Press, 2005); José Esteban Muñoz, *Cruising Utopia: The Then and There of Queer Futurity* (New York: New York University Press, 2009).

29. Cvetkovich, *An Archive of Feelings*, 11, 245.

30. Cvetkovich, *An Archive of Feelings*, 14.

31. Jack Gieseking, "Useful In/stability: The Dialectical Production of the Social and Spatial Lesbian Herstory Archives," *Radical History Review* 122 (2015): 28.

32. Muñoz, *Cruising Utopia*, 1.

33. Robyn Wiegman, *Object Lessons* (Durham, NC: Duke University Press, 2012), 30.

34. Kadji Amin, *Disturbing Attachments: Genet, Modern Pederasty, and Queer History* (Durham, NC: Duke University Press, 2017), 8.

35. Cassius Adair writes about a "trans anti-archival orientation" that reflects "a long history of trans world-making as anti-archival, surreptitious, multiplicitous, unfixed." Cassius Adair, "Delete Yr Account: Speculations on Trans Digital Lives and the Anti-Archival, Part II: Turning Away," Digital Research Ethics Collaboratory, accessed October 31, 2019, http://www.drecollab.org/delete-yr-account-part-iI/.

36. On community archives, see Anne Gilliland and Andrew Flinn, "Community Archives: What Are We Really Talking About?" keynote speech delivered at the CIRN Prato Community Informatics Conference, Prato, Italy, October 28–30, 2013, https://www.monash.edu/__data/assets/pdf_file/0007/920626/gilliland_flinn_keynote.pdf; Michelle Caswell, "Seeing Yourself in History: Community Archives and the Fight against Symbolic Annihilation," *Public Historian* 36, no. 2 (2014): 26–37; Sheffield, "Community Archives."

37. Mary Lynn Ritzenhaler, *Preserving Archives and Manuscripts*, 2d ed. (Chicago: Society of American Archivists, 2010).

38. Erin O'Meara, "Perfecting the New Wave of Collecting," in *Make Your Own History: Documenting Feminist and Queer Activism in the 21st Century*, ed. Lyz Bly and Kelly Wooten (Sacramento, CA: Litwin, 2012), 107–22.

39. O'Meara, "Perfecting the New Wave of Collecting," 118.

40. There are parallels here with Gieseking's argument about "small" data gathered by lesbian archives in relation to Big Data rhetorics: Jack Gieseking, "Size Matters to Lesbians, Too: Queer Feminist Interventions into the Scale of Big Data,"

Professional Geographer 70, no. 1 (2017): 150–56, https://doi.org/10.1080/00330124
.2017.1326084 He argues that lesbians and queers confront their invisibilization in
part by failing to measure up to having large, normatively actionable datasets.

41. Don McLeod at the ArQuives (formerly the Canadian Lesbian and Gay
Archives) explained that these were the main reasons the organization had not
undertaken any kind of digitization program: Don McLeod, conversation with the
author, Toronto, August 27, 2013. Since my initial conversation with McLeod in
2013, the ArQuives has partnered with a project funded by the Social Sciences and
Humanities Research Council of Canada and directed by Dr. Elspeth Brown at the
University of Toronto that has digitized a selection of the archives' audiotapes and
supported their development of a digitization infrastructure. I was a postdoctoral
fellow on this project in 2016–17 and developed the organization's audio digitization system based on what I learned from Colette at the Lesbian Herstory Archives.

42. On the challenges of establishing digital LGBTQ community archives, see
Anthony Cocciolo, "Community Archives in the Digital Era: A Case from the LGBT
Community," *Preservation, Digital Technology and Culture* 45, no. 4 (2017): 157–65,
https://doi.org/10.1515/pdtc-2016-00182017.

43. Luckenbill, "Modern Gay and Lesbian Libraries and Archives in North
America," 99.

44. Chenier, "Hidden from Historians."

45. Jacqueline Spense, "Small Organizations and Cultural Institutions—A Digital Future?" *Program* 39, no. 4 (2005): 367.

46. Peter J. Astle and Adrienne Muir, "Digitization and Preservation in Public
Libraries and Archives," *Journal of Librarianship and Information Science* 34, no. 2
(2002): 70. The library science literature on digital archives always makes a point
of reminding readers that digitization does not present a permanent solution for
the preservation of material. In addition to the ongoing issue of migration, digital
records "are easier to destroy than their paper equivalents or they are considered
ephemeral anyway": Spense, "Small Organizations and Cultural Institutions," 368.

47. On media archaeology labs, see Lori Emerson, *Reading Writing Interfaces:
From the Digital to the Bookbound* (Minneapolis: University of Minnesota Press,
2014); Wolfgang Ernst, *Digital Memory and the Archive*, ed. Jussi Parikka (Minneapolis: University of Minnesota Press, 2013). The systematic production of
digital files from obsolete formats runs counter to media archaeology's emphasis
on encounters with original hardware—"the utterly unique material specificity" of
particular interfaces and platforms: Emerson, *Reading Writing Interfaces*, x.

48. Gieseking, "Size Matters to Lesbians, Too: Queer Feminist Interventions
into the Scale of Big Data."

49. Maxine Wolfe, interview with the author, Brooklyn, NY, October 1, 2013.

50. I have been both a volunteer at the ArQuives, and a paid postdoctoral
fellow at the LGBTQ+ Oral History Digital Collaboratory, a partnership with the
ArQuives. The latter supported the processing of Ms. Ross's archives, and the volunteers I collaborated with most closely were Sid Cunningham and Aaron Cain.

51. Sara Ahmed, *The Promise of Happiness* (Durham, NC: Duke University
Press, 2010), 163.

52. Wiegman, *Object Lessons*, 82.

53. Wiegman, *Object Lessons*, 82.

54. Joan Wallach Scott, *The Fantasy of Feminist History* (Durham, NC: Duke University Press, 2011), 19.

55. Maryanne Dever, "Editorial: Archives and New Forms of Feminist Research," *Australian Feminist Studies* 32, nos. 91–92 (2017): 1.

56. Victoria Hesford, *Feeling Women's Liberation* (Durham, NC: Duke University Press, 2013), 178–79.

57. Wolfe interview.

58. Jim Hubbard, "Interview of Maxine Wolfe," ACT UP Oral History Project, interview no. 43, February 19, 2004, http://www.actuporalhistory.org/interviews /images/wolfe.pdf.

59. Wolfe interview.

60. Wolfe interview.

61. Wolfe interview.

62. Wolfe interview.

63. Melodie J. Fox and Hope A. Olsen, "Essentialism and Care in a Female-Intensive Profession," in *Feminist and Queer Information Studies Reader*, ed. Patrick Keilty and Rebecca Dean (Sacramento, CA: Litwin, 2013), 48–61.

64. Elaine Swan, "The Internship Class: Subjectivity and Inequalities—Gender, Race and Class" in *Handbook of Gendered Careers in Management: Getting In, Getting On, Getting Out*, ed. Adelina M. Broadbridge and Sandra L. Fielden (Cheltenham, UK: Edward Elgar, 2015), 30–43.

65. Wolfe interview.

66. Cocciolo, "Community Archives in the Digital Era."

67. Anthony Cocciolo, interview with the author, New York, April 24, 2013.

68. So far, students at Pratt have digitized a selection of Audre Lorde's speeches (audio); the original oral history interviews from Madeline Davis and Elizabeth Kennedy's *Boots of Leather, Slippers of Gold* (audio); oral history interviews with members of the Daughters of Bilitis, the first lesbian homophile group in the United States (video); Dyke TV, the cable access television program created by the Lesbian Avengers (video); oral history of Mabel Hampton, an African American lesbian who lived in New York City from 1909 until her death in 1989 (audio); and audio recordings related to ACT UP New York's Women's Committee.

69. Jane Gerhard, *Desiring Revolution: Second-Wave Feminism and the Rewriting of American Sexual Thought, 1920–1982* (New York: Columbia University Press, 2001), 183–95. Rachel Corbman's work on the history of the Barnard conference makes great use of these tapes: see Rachel Corbman, "The Scholars and the Feminists: The Barnard Sex Conference and the History of the Institutionalization of Feminism," *Feminist Formations* 27, no. 3 (2016): 49–80.

70. Lucas Hilderbrand, *Inherent Vice: Bootleg Histories of Videotape and Copyright* (Durham, NC: Duke University Press, 2009).

71. Astle and Muir, "Digitization and Preservation in Public Libraries and Archives," 69.

72. C. M. Bolick, "Digital Archives: Democratizing the Doing of History," *International Journal of Social Education* 21, no. 1 (2006): 122.

73. Bolick, "Digital Archives," 130.

74. Hilderbrand, *Inherent Vice*, 15.

75. Samantha Thrift and Carrie Rentschler, "Binders Full of Women: A Feminist Meme to Bind Them All," *Flow* 21, no. 2 (2014), http://flowtv.org/2014/11/binders -full-of-women.

76. Cassius Adair and Lisa Nakamura, "The Digital Afterlives of *This Bridge Called My Back*: Women of Color Feminism, Digital Labor, and Networked Pedagogy," *American Literature* 89, no. 2 (2017): 255–78.

77. Montoya-Sloan interview. The converter actually costs between $30 and $40.

78. Wolfe interview.

79. Mark A. Greene and Dennis Meissner, "More Product, Less Process: Revamping Traditional Archival Processing," *American Archivist* 68 (2005): 208–63.

80. Hilderbrand, *Inherent Vice*, 21.

81. Wolfe interview.

82. Rachel Corbman, "Conferencing on the Edge: A Queer History of Feminist Field Formation, 1969–89," PhD diss., Stony Brook University, Stony Brook, NY, 2019.

83. Rachel Corbman, interview with the author, Brooklyn, NY, May 14, 2013. On community archiving and born-digital materials, see O'Meara, "Perfecting the New Wave of Collecting," 112.

84. O'Meara, "Perfecting the New Wave of Collecting."

85. Angela L. DiVeglia, "Accessibility, Accountability, and Activism," in Bly and Wooten, *Make Your Own History*, 72–73.

86. DiVeglia, "Accessibility, Accountability, and Activism," 72–73.

87. Cocciolo interview.

88. Cocciolo interview.

89. T. L. Cowan and Jasmine Rault, "Onlining Queer Acts: Digital Research Ethics and Caring for Risky Archives" *Women and Performance* 28, no. 2 (2018): 121–42, https://doi.org/10.1080/0740770X.2018.1473985; Tara Robertson, "Not All Information Wants to Be Free: The Case Study of *On Our Backs*," in *Applying Library Values to Emerging Technology: Decision-Making in the Age of Open Access, Maker Spaces, and the Ever-Changing Library*, ed. Peter D. Fernandez and Kelly Tilton, Publications in Librarianship no. 72 (Chicago: American Library Association, 2018), 225–39.

90. Wolfe interview.

91. Cowan and Rault, "Onlining Queer Acts," 4.

92. Cocciolo interview.

93. Cocciolo interview. The interview took place in 2013, before Donald Trump's systematic dismantling of government websites about climate change, HIV, and transgender rights.

94. Melissa Adler, *Cruising the Library: Perversities in the Organization of Knowledge* (New York: Fordham University Press, 2017), 159.

95. Cocciolo interview.

96. "The Homosaurus: An International LGBTQ Linked Data Vocabulary," at http://homosaurus.org, was compiled by Jack van der Wel, with support from Ellen Greenblatt, in 2013 and has been converted into a linked data project by K. J. Rawson and the Digital Transgender Archive.

97. Computer log, "Archive of the Archives" collection, Lesbian Herstory Archives, Brooklyn, NY (hereafter, LHA), vertical file cabinets, second floor.

98. Lucas Introna, "Ethics and the Speaking of Things" *Theory, Culture and Society* 26, no. 4 (2009): 25–46, https://doi.org/10.1177/0263276409104967; Wanda J. Orlikowski, "The Sociomateriality of Organizational Life: Considering Technology in Management Research," *Cambridge Journal of Economics* 34 (2010):125–41; Lucy Suchman, *Human-Machine Reconfigurations: Plans and Situated Actions* (Cambridge: Cambridge University Press, [1987] 2006), https://doi.org/10.1017/CBO9780511808418.008.

99. Lisa Gitelman writes, "The introduction of new media is never entirely revolutionary: new media are less points of epistemic rupture than they are socially embedded sites for the ongoing negotiation of meaning as such": Lisa Gitelman, *Always Already New; Media, History, and the Data of Culture* (Cambridge, MA: MIT Press, 2006), 6.

100. Alexander Galloway, *Protocol: How Control Exists after Decentralization* (Cambridge, MA: MIT Press, 2004).

101. Dorothy Allison to "Friends at Lesbian Herstory Archives," undated letter, 1983, LHA.

102. Rentschler's approach to studying social movements at the "midlevel scale of their communication," described in detail in this book's introduction, has been helpful for finding my way: Carrie A. Rentschler, *Second Wounds: Victims' Rights and the Media in the U.S.* (Durham, NC: Duke University Press, 2011), 17.

103. Rentschler, *Second Wounds*, 18.

104. Hesford, *Feeling Women's Liberation*, 14.

105. On the archival minutia of feminist social movements records, see Samantha Thrift, "Feminist Eventfulness: Boredom and the 1984 Canadian Leadership Debate on Women's Issues," *Feminist Media Studies* 13, no. 3 (2011): 416.

106. "Statement of Principles."

107. Cocciolo interview.

108. Montoya-Sloan interview.

109. Beth Haskell, interview with the author, telephone, June 28, 2018.

110. Haskell interview.

111. Haskell interview. According to Beth, the snake was a six-foot constrictor.

112. "Chicago Resource Centre Funds LHA Computer," *Lesbian Herstory Archives Newsletter* vol. 9, 6.

113. "Chicago Resource Centre Funds LHA Computer," 6.

114. "Chicago Resource Centre Funds LHA Computer," 6.

115. Haskell interview.

116. Haskell interview.

117. Coordinating Committee meeting minutes, March 15, 1995, "Archive of the Archives" collection, LHA, vertical file cabinets, second floor.

118. Coordinating Committee meeting minutes, July 26, 1995; Coordinating Committee meeting minutes, September 10, 1997, both in "Archive of the Archives" collection, LHA, vertical file cabinets, second floor.

119. Coordinating Committee meeting minutes, September 10, 1997, "Archive of the Archives" collection, LHA, vertical file cabinets, second floor.

120. This example is one of several specific forms that include marginalia like this.

121. Elizabeth Groeneveld, "Remediating Pornography: The *On Our Backs* Digitization Debate," *Continuum* 32, no. 1 (2018): 73–83, https://doi.org/10.1080 /10304312.2018.1404677; Robertson, "Not All Information Wants to Be Free."

122. "LHA Enters Cyberspace," *Lesbian Herstory Archives Newsletter* vol. 17, 1999, 5.

123. Corbman email.

124. Corbman interview.

125. Corbman interview.

126. Saskia Scheffer, interview with the author, Brooklyn, NY, May 10, 2013.

127. Imogen Peach, interview with the author, Brooklyn, NY, April 23, 2013.

128. Corbman interview.

129. Peach interview.

130. On data as a maintenance practice, see Dylan Mulvin, *Proxies: The Cultural Work of Standing In* (Cambridge, MA: MIT Press, forthcoming).

131. Peach interview.

132. Jean-Christophe Plantin, "Data Cleaners for Pristine Datasets: Visibility and invisibility of data processors in social science," *Science, Technology and Human Values* 44, no. 1 (2019): https://doi.org/10.1177/0162243918781268.

133. Peach interview.

134. DiVeglia describes the "political act" of DIY categorization as emerging from a "desire for self-determination": DiVeglia, "Accessibility, Accountability, and Activism," 78.

135. Peach interview.

136. K. J. Rawson's digital humanities work does precisely this kind of etymological history through antecedents to the term "transgender": see "The Trans + Gender Project," http://kjrawson.net/trans-gender-timeline.

137. Emerson, *Reading Writing Interfaces*; Friedberg, The *Virtual Window*.

138. Rachel Corbman, email with the author, July 15, 2018.

139. "Gender variant" is Volcano's term. On the relationship between Volcano's photography and gender expression, see Del LaGrace Volcano, Jay Prosser, and Eliza Steinbock, "INTER*me: An Inter-Locution on the Body in Photography," in *Transgender and Intersex: Theoretical, Practical, and Artistic Perspectives*, ed. Stefan Horlacher (New York: Palgrave Macmillan, 2016), 189–224; Eliza Steinbock, "Generative Negatives: Del LaGrace Volcano's *Herm Body* Photographs," *Transgender Studies Quarterly* 1, no. 4 (2014): 539–51.

140. Volcano, Prosser, and Steibock, "INTER*me," 189.

141. Volcano uses the pronoun "herm" to reclaim "from medical and mythical discourse an ambiguity that interrupts gender binaries": Volcano et al., "INTER*me," 223.

142. K. R. Roberto, "Inflexible Bodies: Metadata for Transgender Identities," *Journal of Information Ethics* 20, no. 2 (2011): 60.

143. Anna Lauren Hoffmann, "Data, Technology, and Gender: Thinking About (and From) Trans Lives," in *Spaces for the Future: A Companion to Philosophy of Technology*, ed. Joseph C. Pitt and Ashley Shew (New York: Routledge, 2017), 3–13.

144. Rena Bivens, "The Gender Binary Will Not Be Deprogrammed: Ten Years of Coding Gender on Facebook," *New Media and Society* 19, no. 6 (2017): 880–98, https://doi.org/10.1177/1461444815621527.

145. I use "trans*" to make a broader point here about transgender, nonbinary, intersex, and gender-nonconforming archival records while marking the term as inadequate to the complexities, distinctions, and intersections among these identifications.

146. Susan Stryker, Paisley Currah, and Lisa Jean Moore, "Introduction: Trans-, Trans, or Transgender?" *Women's Studies Quarterly* 36, nos. 3–4 (2018): 11–22.

147. I set "lesbian body" against "Lesbian Body" to distinguish between the singular bodies of individual lesbians, and the monolithic idea of what constitutes a Lesbian Body within movement discourse.

148. See Adair, "Delete Yr Account."

149. Scheffer interview.

150. Scheffer interview.

151. Scheffer interview.

152. Joan Nestle's edited collection *The Persistent Desire: A Femme-Butch Reader* (New York: Alyson, 1992) explores lesbian masculinity. It was recently paid homage by the collection *Persistence: All Ways Butch and Femme*, which works to locate the persistent figure of the butch in the present, and in a trans-masculine milieu: Ivan E. Cayote and Zena Sharman, eds., *Persistence: All Ways Butch and Femme* (Vancouver, BC: Arsenal Pulp, 2011).

153. "Principles," Fall 2018, LHA, provided to me by Maxine Wolfe via email, November 21, 2018.

154. Scheffer interview.

155. Ronika McClain, email to the author, November 26, 2018.

156. Del LaGrace Volcano, "Reflections on Love Bites," accessed May 18, 2020, https://www.dellagracevolcano.se/gallery/love-bites-23196221.

157. "Deadnaming" describes harmfully referring to trans people who have undergone name changes by their old names rather than their affirmed names. On the importance of self-determination and donor collaboration for community archives doing transgender description see Jarrett M. Drake, "RadTech Meets RadArch: Towards A New Principle for Archives and Archival Description," *On Archivy*, April 6, 2016, https://medium.com/on-archivy /radtech-meets-radarch-towards-a-new-principle-for-archives-and-archival -description-568f133e4325; Jamie A. Lee, "Mediated Storytelling Practices and Productions: Archival Bodies of Affective Evidences," *Networking Knowledge* 9, no. 6 (2016): 74–87.

158. Volcano, "Reflections on Love Bites."

159. On the role of care in trans citational practices see Katja Thieme and Mary Ann S. Saunders, "How Do You Wish to Be Cited? Citation Practices and a Scholarly

Community of Care in Trans Studies Research Articles," *Journal of English for Academic Purposes* 32 (2018): 80–90, https://doi.org/10.1016/j.jeap.2018.03.010.

160. Lori Emerson has discussed how digital interfaces become most visible when they fail. She writes of productive attempts to "bring the interface back into view again via failure, discomfort, and dissonance": Emerson, *Reading Writing Interfaces*, 3. Writing specifically on the interface and marginalized users, Lisa Nakamura documents how critiques of the racialization of interfaces might render the interface visible as such: Lisa Nakamura, *Digitizing Race: Visual Cultures of the Internet* (Minneapolis: University of Minnesota Press, 2008), 27.

161. Wolfe interview.

162. Wolfe interview.

163. Wolfe interview.

164. Wolfe interview.

165. Wolfe interview.

EPILOGUE: DOING LESBIAN FEMINISM IN AN AGE OF INFORMATION ABUNDANCE

1. On "deep-lez," see Allyson Mitchell and Ann Cvetkovich, "A Girl's Journey into the Well of Forbidden Knowledge," *GLQ* 17, no. 4 (2011): 603–18

2. The T-shirt, situated within Steiner's and Takahashi's larger bodies of work, articulates radical second-wave feminist organizing to transfeminist practices in the 2000s and the present.

3. Otherwild, "The Patriarchy Is a Pyramid Scheme Long Sleeve Tee," ecommerce page, accessed April 11, 2019, https://otherwild.com/collections/collaborations/products/patriarchy-is-a-pyramid-scheme-long-sleeve-tee?variant=30751261069.

4. Otherwild, "The Patriarchy Is a Pyramid Scheme," Instagram post, accessed April 11, 2019, https://instagram.com/p/BLHKQ_uhoVw.

5. Otherwild selects various feminist charities as beneficiaries for the sales of some products, and these choices seem to pursue a connection between the message on a shirt and the goals of these organizations. Sales of "The Future Is Female," for example, benefits Planned Parenthood, qualifying any simple reading of the slogan as an endorsement of reproductive futurity.

6. Ginger Brooks Takahashi, correspondence with the author, April 5, 2019.

7. Marika Cifor, "'What Is Remembered Lives': The Disruptive Animacy of Archiving AIDS on Instagram," *Theory, Culture, and Society* (forthcoming); Susan Stewart, *On Longing: Narratives of the Miniature, the Gigantic, the Souvenir, the Collection* (Durham, NC: Duke University Press, 1993).

8. "We Are Everywhere Tote Bag," ecommerce page, https://otherwild.com/collections/collaborations/products/we-are-everywhere-tote-bag, accessed October 30, 2019.

9. Jeanne Córdova "Those Lesbians Are Everywhere!" *Lesbian Tide* 7, no. 4 (1978): 10.

10. For example, it took about ten minutes to locate the source for the "We Are Everywhere" balloon image by consulting J. D. Doyle's Houston LGBT History site,

which includes open-access, high-resolution scans of many *Lesbian Tide* issues: http://www.houstonlgbthistory.org/lesbian-tide.html.

11. See also @lgbt_history, @lesbianherstoryarchives, @thearquives, and @onearchives.

12. For example, a commenter criticized a photograph of the African American science-fiction writer Octavia Butler on the beach with her poodle, posted by @h_e_r_s_t_o_r_y on September 14, 2017, because Butler did not identify as a lesbian. Also, a @h_e_r_s_t_o_r_y caption misidentifying a woman standing with the writer Ingrid Sischy as her partner, Sandy Brant, posted on November 30, 2018, received a reply from k.d. lang: "Awww. I miss my buddy. But that's not Sandy." These corrective engagements speak to the intense expectations around research and accuracy that Instagram's queer counterpublics have of historical accounts.

13. On queer Instagram cultures and temporality, see Cifor, "What Is Remembered Lives."

14. This is current as of January 31, 2019.

15. Marika Cifor and Jamie A. Lee survey the literature on information studies and neoliberalism in "Towards an Archival Critique: Opening Possibilities for Addressing Neoliberalism in the Archival Field," *Journal of Critical Library and Information Studies* 1, no. 1 (2017): 1–22.

16. Alix Dobkin, "(In)famous Last Words (For Now)," *Windy City Times*, June 21, 2000; Alix Dobkin, "The Emperor's New Gender," *Off Our Backs* 30, no. 4 (2000): 14; Alix Dobkin, "Passover Revisited," *Windy City Times*, September 16, 1998.

17. Clinton's first public address after Donald Trump's inauguration in 2017 addressed the Women's March on Washington with the slogan "The Future Is Female."

18. Cifor, "What Is Remembered Lives."

19. China Medel, "Brown Time: Veteranas_and_Rucas and Latinx Image Archiving in the Face of Gentrification," paper presented at the annual conference of the Society for Cinema and Media Studies, Seattle, March 13, 2019.

20. Alexander Cho, "Default Publicness: Queer Youth of Color, Social Media, and Being Outed by the Machine," *New Media and Society* 20, no. 9 (2018): 3183–200.

21. Clare Potter, "How to Index in the Circle of Lesbian Indexers, Part 1," 1979, Circle of Lesbian Indexers Papers, Lesbian Herstory Archives, Brooklyn, NY, 9.

22. Michael Hardt and Antonio Negri, *Empire* (Cambridge, MA: Harvard University Press, 2000), 60–61.

23. Hardt and Negri, *Empire*, 61.

24. Lauren Berlant, *Cruel Optimism* (Durham, NC: Duke University Press, 2011), 24.

25. Wendy Hui Kyong Chun, "The Enduring Ephemeral, or The Future Is a Memory," in *Media Archaeology: Approaches, Application, and Implications*, edited by Erkki Huhtamo and Jussi Parikka (Berkeley: University of California Press, 2011), 195.

26. Berlant, *Cruel Optimism*, 27.

27. Joan Nestle, "The Will to Remember: The Lesbian Herstory Archives of New York," *Feminist Review* 34 (1990): 88; JR Roberts, "Introduction," in *Black Lesbians: An Annotated Bibliography*, edited by JR Roberts (Tallahassee, FL: Naiad, 1981): xii.

28. Berlant, *Cruel Optimism*, 20

29. Lauren Berlant, "The Commons: Infrastructures for Troubling Times," *Society and Space* 34, no. 3 (June 2016): 393–419, https://doi.org/10.1177 /0263775816645989.

30. Saskia Scheffer, interview with the author, Brooklyn, NY, May 10, 2013.

31. Berlant, *Cruel Optimism*, 24–25.

32. Judith Schwarz, "Living Herstory," *Off Our Backs* 8, no. 5, (May 1978): 20; Rachel Corbman, "A Genealogy of the Lesbian Herstory Archives, 1974–2014," *Journal of Contemporary Archival Studies* 1, no. 1 (2014): 13–14; Shawn(ta) Smith, "Tape-by-Tape: Digital Practices and Cataloguing Rituals at the Lesbian Herstory Archives," in *Queer Online: LGBT Digital Practices in Libraries, Archives, and Museums*, edited by Rachel Wexelbaum (Sacramento, CA: Litwin, 2015), 87; Kate Eichhorn, *The Archival Turn in Feminism: Outrage in Order* (Philadelphia: Temple University Press, 2013), 47; Jack Gieseking, "Useful In/stability: The Dialectical Production of the Social and Spatial Lesbian Herstory Archives," *Radical History Review* 122 (2015): 30.

33. Leslie Feinberg, *Stone Butch Blues* (Los Angeles: Alyson, 1993), 12.

34. Ann Cvetkovich, *An Archive of Feelings: Trauma, Sexuality and Lesbian Public Cultures* (Durham, NC: Duke University Press, 2003), 78.

35. Cvetkovich, *An Archive of Feelings*, 245.

36. Gieseking, "Useful Instability," 31.

37. Barbara Godard, "Contested Memories: Canadian Women Writers in and out of the Archive," in *Trans/Acting Culture, Writing, and Memory: Essays in Honour of Barbara Godard*, ed. Eva C. Karpinski et al. (Waterloo, ON: Wilfrid Laurier University Press, 2013).

38. Jonathan Sterne, *MP3: The Meaning of a Format* (Durham, NC: Duke University Press, 2012).

39. Corbman, "A Genealogy of the Lesbian Herstory Archives," 13–14.

40. Thinking through the cruel optimism of digitization takes up part of a larger turn in media studies toward theorizing the digital more modestly. Steven Jackson's approach to media through repair and "broken world thinking" has especially influenced my approach: see Steven J. Jackson, "Rethinking Repair," in *Media Technologies: Essays on Communication, Materiality and Society*, ed. Tarleton Gillespie, Pablo Boczkowski, and Kirsten Foot (Cambridge, MA: MIT Press, 2014), 221.

41. As Sara Ahmed writes, "To kill joy . . . is to open a life, to make room for life, to make room for possibility, for chance": Sara Ahmed, *The Promise of Happiness* (Durham, NC: Duke University Press, 2010), 20.

Bibliography

INTERVIEWS

Anthony Cocciolo. New York, NY, April 24, 2013.
Rachel Corbman. Brooklyn, NY, May 14, 2013.
Beth Haskell. Telephone, June 28, 2018.
Ronika McClain. Brooklyn, NY, May 3, 2013.
Colette Denali Montoya-Sloan. Brooklyn, NY, April 26, 2013.
Imogen Peach (pseudonym). Brooklyn, NY, April 23, 2013.
Clare Potter. Telephone, November 16, 2014.
Saskia Scheffer. Brooklyn, NY, May 10, 2013.
Maxine Wolfe. Brooklyn, NY, October 1, 2013.

PUBLICATIONS

Abbate, Janet. *Inventing the Internet*. Cambridge, MA: MIT Press, 1999.
Accardi, Maria T. *Feminist Pedagogy for Library Instruction*. Sacramento, CA: Litwin, 2013.
Adair, Cassius. "Delete Yr Account: Speculations on Trans Digital Lives and the Anti-Archival Part II: Turning Away." Digital Research Ethics Collaboratory, accessed October 31, 2019, http://www.drecollab.org/delete-yr-account-part-iI/.
Adair, Cassius, and Lisa Nakamura. "The Digital Afterlives of *This Bridge Called My Back*: Women of Color Feminism, Digital Labor, and Networked Pedagogy." *American Literature* 89, no. 2 (2017): 255–78.
Adler, Melissa. *Cruising the Library: Perversities in the Organization of Knowledge*. New York: Fordham University Press, 2017.
Ahmed, Sara. *The Cultural Politics of Emotion*. New York: Routledge, 2004.
Ahmed, Sara. *Living a Feminist Life*. Durham, NC: Duke University Press, 2017.
Ahmed, Sara. *The Promise of Happiness*. Durham, NC: Duke University Press, 2010.
Ahmed, Sara. *Queer Phenomenology: Orientations, Objects, Others*. Durham, NC: Duke University Press, 2006.
Ahmed, Sara. *Willful Subjects*. Durham, NC: Duke University Press, 2014.

Amin, Kadji. *Disturbing Attachments: Genet, Modern Pederasty, and Queer History.* Durham, NC: Duke University Press, 2017.

Archibald, Sasha. "Indexes, In Praise of." *Cabinet* 52 (2013–14): 57–63.

Astle, Peter J., and Adrienne Muir. "Digitization and Preservation in Public Libraries and Archives." *Journal of Librarianship and Information Science* 34, no. 2 (2002): 67–79.

Baker, Nicholson. *Double Fold: Libraries and the Assault on Paper.* New York: Random House, 2001.

Barad, Karen. *Meeting the Universe Halfway: Quantum Physics and the Entanglement of Matter and Meaning.* Durham NC: Duke University Press, 2007.

Baran, Paul. "On Distributed Communications: I. Introduction to Distributed Communications Networks." Memorandum RM-3420-PR prepared for the U.S. Air Force Project Rand. RAND Corporation, Santa Monica, CA, August 1964.

Baym, Nancy K. *Personal Connections in the Digital Age.* Cambridge, MA: Polity, 2010.

Baym, Nancy K., Yan Bing Zhang, and Mei-Chen Lin. "Social Interactions across Media: Interpersonal Communication on the Internet, Telephone, and Face-to-Face." *New Media and Society* 6, no. 3 (2004): 299–318.

Beins, Agatha. *Liberation in Print: Feminist Periodicals and Social Movement Identity.* Athens: University of Georgia Press, 2017.

Berlant, Lauren. "The Commons: Infrastructures for Troubling Times." *Society and Space* 34, no. 3 (2016): 393–419. https://doi.org/10.1177/0263775816645989.

Berlant, Lauren. *Cruel Optimism.* Durham, NC: Duke University Press, 2011.

Berman, Sanford. "Introduction: Cataloging Reform, LC, and Me." In *Radical Cataloging: Essays at the Front,* edited by K. R. Roberto, 5–11. Jefferson, NC: McFarland, 2008.

Bivens, Rena. "The Gender Binary Will Not Be Deprogrammed: Ten Years of Coding Gender on Facebook." *New Media and Society* 19, no. 6 (2017): 880–98. https://doi.org/10.1177/1461444815621527.

Bly, Lyz, and Kelly Wooten, eds. *Make Your Own History: Documenting Feminist and Queer Activism in the 21st Century.* Sacramento: CA: Litwin, 2012.

Bolick, C. M. "Digital Archives: Democratizing the Doing of History." *International Journal of Social Education* 21, no. 1 (2006): 122–34.

Bourne, Charles P., and Trudi Bellardo Hahn. *A History of Online Information Services, 1963–1976.* Cambridge, MA: MIT Press, 2003.

Bowker, Geoffrey C., Karen Baker, Florence Miller, and David Ribes. "Toward Information Infrastructure Studies: Ways of Knowing in a Networked Environment." In *International Handbook of Internet Research,* edited by Jeremy Hunsinger, Lisbeth Klastrup, and Matthew M. Allen, 97–117. Dordrecht: Springer, 2009.

Bowker, Geoffrey C., and Susan Leigh Star. *Sorting Things Out: Classification and Its Consequences.* Cambridge, MA: MIT Press, 1999.

boyd, danah. "Why Youth (Heart) Social Network Sites: The Role of Networked Publics in Teenage Social Life." In *MacArthur Foundation Series on Digital Learning: Youth, Identity, and Digital Media Volume,* edited by David Buckingham, 119–142. Cambridge, MA: MIT Press, 2007.

Boyd, Nan Alamilla. "Who Is the Subject? Queer Theory Meets Oral History." *Journal of the History of Sexuality* 12, no. 2 (2008): 177–89.

Brennan, Teresa. *The Transmission of Affect*. Ithaca, NY: Cornell University Press, 2004.

Brier, Jennifer. *Infectious Ideas: U.S. Political Responses to the AIDS Crisis*. Chapel Hill, NC: University of North Carolina Press, 2009.

Brouwer, Daniel C., and Adela C. Licona. "Trans(affective)mediation: Feeling Our Way from Paper to Digitized Zines and Back Again." *Critical Studies in Media Communication* 33, no. 1 (2016): 70–83.

Brown, Elspeth H. "Trans/Feminist Oral History: Current Projects." *Transgender Studies Quarterly* 2, no. 4 (2015): 666–72. https://doi.org/10.1215/23289252 -3151583.

Brownworth, Victoria. "In Remembrance: Julia Penelope, Lesbian Theorist." *Lambda Literary*, February 1, 2013. Accessed January 30, 2014. http://www.lambdaliterary .org/features/rem/02/01/in-remembrance-julia-penelope-lesbian-theorist.

Bryson, Mary and Lori McIntosh, "Can We Play Fun Gay?: Disjuncture and Difference, and the Precarious Mobilities of Millennial Queer Youth Narratives." *International Journal of Qualitative Studies in Education* 23.1 (2010): 101–24.

Bryson, Mary, Lori MacIntosh, Sharalyn Jordan, and Hui-Ling Lin. "Virtually Queer? Homing Devices, Mobility, and Un/Belongings." *Canadian Journal of Communication* 31, no. 4 (2006): 791–814. https://doi.org/10.22230/cjc .2006v31n4a1795.

Burton, Antoinette, ed. *Archive Stories: Facts, Fictions, and the Writing of History*. Durham, NC: Duke University Press, 2006.

Canaday, Margot. "LGBT History." *Frontiers* 35, no. 1 (2014): 11–19.

Canaday, Margot. "Pink Precariat: LGBT Workers in the Shadow of Civil Rights" (forthcoming).

Capek, Mary Ellen. *A Women's Thesaurus*. New York: Harper and Row, 1987.

Carby, Hazel V. "White Woman Listen! Black Feminism and the Boundaries of Sisterhood" (1982). In *Theories of Race and Racism: A Reader*, edited by Les Back and John Solomos, 110–28. London: Routledge, 2000.

Caswell, Michelle. "'The Archive' Is Not an Archives: Acknowledging the Intellectual Contributions of Archival Studies." *Reconstruction* 16, no. 1 (2016). https:// escholarship.org/uc/item/7bn4v1fk.

Caswell, Michelle. "Community-centered Collecting: Finding Out What Communities Want from Community Archives." *Proceedings of the American Society for Information Science Technology* 51, no. 1 (2014): 1–9. https://doi.org/10.1002 /meet.2014.14505101027.

Caswell, Michelle. "Seeing Yourself in History: Community Archives and the Fight against Symbolic Annihilation." *Public Historian* 36, no. 2 (2014): 26–37.

Caswell, Michelle, Alda Allina Migoni, Noah Geraci, and Marika Cifor. "'To Be Able to Imagine Otherwise': Community Archives and the Importance of Representation." *Archives and Records* 38, no. 1 (2017): 5–26.

Cayote, Ivan E., and Zena Sharman, eds. *Persistence: All Ways Butch and Femme*. Vancouver, BC: Arsenal Pulp, 2011.

Chenier, Elise. "Hidden from Historians: Preserving Lesbian Oral History in Canada." *Archivaria* 68 (2009): 247–69.

Cho, Alexander. "Default Publicness: Queer Youth of Color, Social Media, and Being Outed by the Machine." *New Media and Society* 20, no. 9 (2018): 3183–200. https://doi.org/10.1177/1461444817744784.

Chun, Wendy Hui Kyong. *Control and Freedom: Power and Paranoia in the Age of Fiber Optics.* Cambridge, MA: MIT Press, 2006.

Chun, Wendy Hui Kyong. "The Enduring Ephemeral, or The Future Is a Memory." In *Media Archaeology: Approaches, Application, and Implications,* edited by Erkki Huhtamo and Jussi Parikka, 184–206. Berkeley: University of California Press, 2011.

Chun, Wendy Hui Kyong. *Updating to Remain the Same: Habitual New Media.* Cambridge, MA: MIT Press, 2016.

Cifor, Marika. "Affecting Relations: Introducing Affect Theory to Archival Discourse." *Archival Science,* 16 (2016): 7–31.

Cifor, Marika. "Stains and Remains: Liveliness, Materiality, and the Archival Lives of Queer Bodies." *Australian Feminist Studies* 32, no. 91–92 (2017): 5–21.

Cifor, Marika. "'What Is Remembered Lives': The Disruptive Animacy of Archiving AIDS on Instagram." *Theory, Culture, and Society* (forthcoming).

Cifor, Marika and Jamie A. Lee. "Towards an Archival Critique: Opening Possibilities for Addressing Neoliberalism in the Archival Field." *Journal of Critical Library and Information Studies* 1, no. 1 (2017): 1–22.

Cloonan, Michèle Valerie. "W(H)ITHER Preservation?" *Library Quarterly* 71, no. 2 (2001): 231–42.

Cocciolo, Anthony. "Community Archives in the Digital Era: A Case from the LGBT Community." *Preservation, Digital Technology and Culture* 45, no. 4 (2017): 157–65. https://doi.org/10.1515/pdtc-2016-0018.

Collison, Robert L. *Indexes and Indexing.* London: Ernest Benn, 1959.

Combahee River Collective. "The Combahee River Collective Statement," 1977. https://americanstudies.yale.edu/sites/default/files/files/Keyword%20Coalition_Readings.pdf

Convey, John. *Online Information Retrieval: An Introductory Manual to Principles and Practice,* 3d ed. London: Library Association, (1977) 1989.

Corbman, Rachel. "Conferencing on the Edge: A Queer History of Feminist Field Formation, 1969–89." PhD diss., Stony Brook University, Stony Brook, 2019.

Corbman, Rachel. "A Genealogy of the Lesbian Herstory Archives, 1974–2014." *Journal of Contemporary Archival Studies* 1, no. 1 (2014): 1–16.

Corbman, Rachel. "Remediating Disability Activism in the Lesbian Feminist Archive." *Continuum* 32, no. 1 (2018): 18–28.

Corbman, Rachel. "The Scholars and the Feminists: The Barnard Sex Conference and the History of the Institutionalization of Feminism." *Feminist Formations* 27, no. 3 (2016): 49–80.

Córdova, Jeanne. "Those Lesbians Are Everywhere!" *Lesbian Tide* 7, no. 4 (1978): 10.

Cossman, Brenda. "Censor, Resist, Repeat: The History of Censorship of Gay and Lesbian Sexual Representations in Canada." *Duke Journal of Gender, Law and Policy* 45 (2014): 45–66.

Cowan, Ruth Schwartz. *More Work for Mother: The Ironies of Household Technology from the Open Hearth to the Microwave.* New York: Basic, 1983.

Cowan, T. L., and Jasmine Rault. "Onlining Queer Acts: Digital Research Ethics and Caring for Risky Archives." *Women and Performance* 28, no. 2 (2018): 121–42. https://doi.org/10.1080/0740770X.2018.1473985.

Creet, Julia. "Daughters of the Movement: The Psychodynamics of Lesbian S/M Fantasy." *Differences* 3, no. 2 (1991): 135–59.

Cutler, Marianne. "Educating the 'Variant,' Educating the Public: Gender and the Rhetoric of Legitimation in *The Ladder* Magazine for Lesbians." *Qualitative Sociology* 26, no. 2 (2003): 233–55.

Cvetkovich, Ann. *An Archive of Feelings: Trauma, Sexuality and Lesbian Public Cultures.* Durham, NC: Duke University Press, 2003.

Cvetkovich, Ann. *Depression: A Public Feeling.* Durham, NC: Duke University Press, 2012.

Dame-Griff, Avery. "Talk amongst Yourselves: 'Community' in Transgender Counterpublic Discourse Online, 1990–2014." PhD diss., University of Maryland, College Park, 2017.

Danesi, Marcel. *Encyclopedic Dictionary of Semiotics, Media, and Communications.* Toronto: University of Toronto Press, 2000.

Daniels, Jessie. "Race and Racism in Internet Studies: A Review and Critique." *New Media and Society* 15, no. 5 (2013): 695–719.

Daniels, Jessie. "The Trouble with White Feminism: Whiteness, Digital Feminism and the Intersectional Internet." In *The Intersectional Internet: Race, Sex, Class, and Culture Online,* edited by Safiya Umoja Noble and Brendesha M. Tynes, 41–60. New York: Peter Lang, 2016.

Davis, Madeline, and Elizabeth Kennedy. *Boots of Leather, Slippers of Gold.* New York: Routledge, 1993.

Davis, Madeline, and Elizabeth Kennedy. "Oral History and the Study of Sexuality in the Lesbian Community: Buffalo, New York, 1940–1960." *Feminist Studies* 12, no. 1 (1986): 7–26. https://doi.org/10.2307/3177981.

Davy, Kate. "Outing Whiteness: A Feminist/Lesbian Project." *Theatre Journal* 47, no. 2 (1995): 189–205.

Day, Ronald. *Indexing It All: The Subject in the Age of Documentation.* Cambridge, MA: MIT Press, 2014.

De Kosnik, Abigail. *Rogue Archives: Digital Cultural Memory and Media Fandom.* Cambridge, MA: MIT Press, 2016.

de Lusenet, Yola, and Pieter J. D. Drenth. "Preservation and Access: Two Concepts, One Goal—The Work of the European Commission on Preservation and Access (ECPA)." *Journal of the Society of Archivists* 20, no. 2 (1999): 161–68.

Derrida, Jacques. "Archive Fever: A Freudian Impression." *Diacritics* 25, no. 2 (1995): 9–63.

Dever, Maryanne. "Editorial: Archives and New Forms of Feminist Research." *Australian Feminist Studies* 32, nos. 91–92 (2017): 1–4.

DiVeglia, Angela L. "Accessibility, Accountability, and Activism." In *Make Your Own History: Documenting Feminist and Queer Activism in the 21st Century*, edited by Lyz Bly and Kelly Wooten, 69–88. Sacramento, CA: Litwin, 2012.

Dixon, Michael C., and J. L. Burns. "Crisis Theory, Active Learning and the Training of Telephone Crisis Volunteers." *Journal of Community Psychology* 2, no. 2 (1974): 120–25.

Dobkin, Alix. "The Emperor's New Gender." *Off Our Backs* 30, no. 4 (2000): 13.

Drabinski, Emily. "Gendered S(h)elves: Body and Identity in the Library." *Women and Environments International Magazine* 78–79 (2009–10): 16–18.

Drabinski, Emily. "Queering the Catalog: Queer Theory and the Politics of Correction." *The Library Quarterly: Information, Community, Policy* 83, no. 2 (2013): 94–111. https://doi.org/10.1086/669547.

Drake, Jarrett M. "RadTech Meets RadArch: Towards A New Principle for Archives and Archival Description." *On Archivy, Medium.com* (April 6, 2016). https://medium.com/on-archivy/radtech-meets-radarch-towards-a-new-principle-for-archives-and-archival-description-568f133e4325.

Driscoll, Kevin. "From Punched Cards to 'Big Data': A Social History of Database Populism." *Communication +1* 1 (2012). https://scholarworks.umass.edu/cpo/vol1/iss1/4

Driscoll, Kevin. "Hobbyist Inter-networking and the Popular Internet Imaginary: Forgotten Histories of Networked Personal Computing, 1978–1998." PhD diss., University of Southern California, Los Angeles, 2014.

Driscoll, Kevin, and Camille Paloques-Berges. "Searching for Missing 'Net Histories.'" *Internet Histories* 1, no. 1 (2017): 1–13. https://doi.org/10.1080/24701475.2017.1307541.

Driver, Susan. *Queer Girls and Popular Culture: Reading, Resisting, and Creating Media*. New York: Peter Lang, 2007.

Duarte, Marisa Elena. *Network Sovereignty: Building the Internet across Indian Country*. Seattle: University of Washington Press, 2017.

Duggan, Lisa. *The Twilight of Equality? Neoliberalism, Cultural Politics, and the Attack on Democracy*. Boston: Beacon, 2003.

Dunbar-Hester, Christina. *Low Power to the People: Pirates, Protest, and Politics in FM Radio Activism*. Cambridge, MA: MIT Press, 2014.

Duranti, Luciana. "The Concept of Appraisal and Archival Theory." *American Archivist* 57 (1994): 328–44.

Echterling, Lennis, and Mary Lou Wylie. "Crisis Centers: A Social Movement Perspective." *Journal of Community Psychology* 9 (1981): 342–46.

Egyedi, Tineke. "Infrastructure Flexibility Created by Standardized Gateways: The Cases of XML and the ISO Container." *Knowledge, Technology, and Policy* 14, no. 3 (2001): 41–54.

Eichhorn, Kate. *Adjusted Margin: Xerography, Art and Activism in the Late Twentieth Century*. Cambridge, MA: MIT Press, 2016.

Eichhorn, Kate. *The Archival Turn in Feminism: Outrage in Order.* Philadelphia: Temple University Press, 2013.

Ellcessor, Elizabeth. *Restricted Access: Media, Disability, and the Politics of Participation.* New York: New York University Press, 2016.

Emerson, Lori. *Reading Writing Interfaces: From the Digital to the Bookbound.* Minneapolis: University of Minnesota Press, 2014.

Eng, David L. *The Feeling of Kinship: Queer Liberalism and the Racialization of Intimacy.* Durham, NC: Duke University Press, 2010.

Enke, Finn. "Collective Memory and the Transfeminist 1970s: Toward a Less Plausible History." *Transgender Studies Quarterly* 5, no. 1 (2018): 9–29.

Enke, Finn. *Finding the Movement: Sexuality, Contested Space, and Feminist Activism.* Durham, NC: Duke University Press, 2007.

Ensmenger, Nathan. "'Beards, Sandals, and Other Signs of Rugged Individualism': Masculine Culture within the Computing Professions." *Osiris* 30 (2015): 38–65.

Ernst, Wolfgang. *Digital Memory and the Archive,* edited by Jussi Parikka. Minneapolis: University of Minnesota Press, 2013.

Eslen-Ziya, Hande. "Social Media and Turkish Feminism: New Resources for Social Activism." *Feminist Media Studies* 13, no. 5 (2013): 860–70.

Felski, Rita. *Beyond Feminist Aesthetics: Feminist Literature and Social Change.* Cambridge, MA: Harvard University Press, 1989.

Feigenbaum, Anna. "Written in the Mud: (Proto)zine-Making and Autonomous Media at the Greenham Common Women's Peace Camp." *Feminist Media Studies* 13, no. 1 (2012): 1–13.

Feinberg, Leslie. *Stone Butch Blues.* Los Angeles: Alyson, 1993.

Ferguson, Roderick. *Aberrations in Black: Toward a Queer of Color Critique.* Minneapolis: University of Minnesota Press, 2004.

Fink, Marty. *Forget Burial: HIV/AIDS and Queer/Trans Narratives of Care.* New Brunswick, NJ: Rutgers University Press, 2020.

Flinn, Andrew, Mary Stevens, and Elizabeth Shepherd. "Whose Memories, Whose Archives? Independent Community Archives, Autonomy and the Mainstream." *Archival Science* 9 (2009): 71–86.

Flowers, Amy. *The Fantasy Factory: An Insider's View of the Phone Sex Industry.* Philadelphia: University of Pennsylvania Press, 1998.

Foucault, Michel. *The Archaeology of Knowledge.* New York: Vintage, (1972) 2002.

Fox, Melodie J., and Hope A. Olsen. "Essentialism and Care in a Female-Intensive Profession." In *Feminist and Queer Information Studies Reader,* edited by Patrick Keilty and Rebecca Dean, 48–61. Sacramento, CA: Litwin, 2012.

Fraser, Nancy. "Rethinking the Public Sphere: A Contribution to the Critique of Actually Existing Democracy," *Social Text* 25/26 (1990): 56–80.

Freeman, Elizabeth. *Time Binds: Queer Temporalities, Queer Histories.* Durham, NC: Duke University Press, 2010.

Freeman, Jo. "The Tyranny of Structurelessness." *Women's Studies Quarterly* 41, nos. 3–4 (2013): 231–46.

Frické, Martin. "The Knowledge Pyramid: A Critique of the DIKW Hierarchy." *Journal of Information Science* 35, no. 2 (2008): 131–42.

Friedberg, Anne. *The Virtual Window: From Alberti to Microsoft*. Cambridge, MA: MIT Press, 2009.

Friedman, Elisabeth Jay. *Interpreting the Internet: Feminist and Queer Counterpublics in Latin America*. Oakland: University of California Press, 2017.

Galloway, Alexander. *Protocol: How Control Exists after Decentralization*. Cambridge, MA: MIT Press, 2004.

Garrison, Dee. "The Tender Technicians: The Feminization of Public Librarianship, 1876–1905." *Journal of Social History* 6, no. 2 (1972–73): 131–59.

Gerhard, Jane. *Desiring Revolution: Second-Wave Feminism and the Rewriting of American Sexual Thought: 1920–1982*. New York: Columbia University Press, 2001.

Giannachi, Gabriella. *Archive Everything: Mapping the Everyday*. Cambridge, MA: MIT Press, 2016.

Gieseking, Jack. *A Queer New York*. New York: New York University Press, 2020.

Gieseking, Jack. "Size Matters to Lesbians, Too: Queer Feminist Interventions into the Scale of Big Data." *Professional Geographer* 70, no. 1 (2017): 150–56. https://doi.org/10.1080/00330124.2017.1326084.

Gieseking, Jack. "Useful In/stability: The Dialectical Production of the Social and Spatial Lesbian Herstory Archives." *Radical History Review* 122 (2015): 25–37.

Gilliland, Anne, and Andrew Flinn. "Community Archives: What Are We Really Talking About?" Keynote speech delivered at the CIRN Prato Community Informatics Conference, Prato, Italy, October 28–30, 2013. https://www.monash.edu/__data/assets/pdf_file/0007/920626/gilliland_flinn_keynote.pdf.

Gitelman, Lisa. *Always Already New; Media, History, and the Data of Culture*. Cambridge, MA: MIT Press, 2006.

Gitelman, Lisa. *Paper Knowledge: Toward a Media History of Documents*. Durham, NC: Duke University Press, 2014.

Gitelman, Lisa, and Virginia Jackson. "Introduction." In *Raw Data Is an Oxymoron*, edited by Lisa Gitelman and Virginia Jackson, 1–14. Cambridge, MA: MIT Press, 2013.

Gitelman, Lisa, and Virginia Jackson, eds. *Raw Data Is an Oxymoron*. Cambridge, MA: MIT Press, 2013.

Goble, Mark. *Beautiful Circuits: Modernism and the Mediated Life*. New York: Columbia University Press, 2010.

Godard, Barbara. "Contested Memories: Canadian Women Writers in and out of the Archive." In *Trans/Acting Culture, Writing, and Memory: Essays in Honour of Barbara Godard*, edited by Eva C. Karpinski, Jennifer Henderson, Ian Sowton, and Ray Ellenwood. Waterloo, ON: Wilfrid Laurier University Press, 2013.

Gossett, Che. "We Will Not Rest in Peace: AIDS Activism, Black Radicalism, Queer and/or Trans Resistance." In *Queer Necropolitics*, edited by Jin Haritaworn, Adi Kuntsman, and Silvia Posocoo, 31–50. New Brunswick, NJ: Routledge, 2014

Gould, Deborah B. *Moving Politics: Emotion and ACT UP's Fight against AIDS*. Chicago: University of Chicago Press, 2009.

Gray, Mary L. *Out in the Country*. New York: New York University Press, 2009.

Greene, Mark A., and Dennis Meissner. "More Product, Less Process: Revamping Traditional Archival Processing." *American Archivist* 68 (2005): 208–63.

Gregg, Melissa. *Work's Intimacy*. Cambridge: Polity, 2011.

Groeneveld, Elizabeth. "Remediating Pornography: The *On Our Backs* Digitization Debate." *Continuum* 32, no. 1 (2018): 73–83. https://doi.org/10.1080/10304312.2018.1404677.

Guillory, John. "Genesis of the Media Concept." *Critical Inquiry* 36 (2010): 321–62.

Guillory, John. "The Memo and Modernity." *Critical Inquiry* 31, no. 1 (2004): 113.

Gumbs, Alexis Pauline. "Eternal Summer of the Black Feminist Mind." In *Make Your Own History: Documenting Feminist and Queer Activism in the 21st Century*, edited by Lyz Bly and Kelly Wooten, 59–68. Sacramento, CA: Litwin, 2012.

Gumbs, Alexis Pauline. *M Archive: After the End of the World*. Durham, NC: Duke University Press, 2018.

Halberstam, Jack. *Female Masculinity*. Durham, NC: Duke University Press, 1998.

Halberstam, Jack. *In a Queer Time and Place: Transgender Bodies: Subcultural Lives*. New York: New York University Press, 2005.

Halberstam, Jack. *The Queer Art of Failure*. Durham, NC: Duke University Press, 2011.

Halberstam, Jack. "Straight Eye For the Queer Theorist: A Review of 'Queer Theory without Antinormativity.'" *Bully Bloggers*, September 12, 2015. https://bullybloggers.wordpress.com/2015/09/12/straight-eye-for-the-queer-theorist-a-review-of-queer-theory-without-antinormativity-by-jack-halberstam.

Halberstam, Jack. "Unfound." In *Cruising the Archive: Queer Art and Culture in Los Angeles, 1945–1980*, edited by David Evans Frantz and Mia Locks, 158–61. Los Angeles: ONE Archives, 2011.

Halupka, Max. "The Rise of Information Activism: How to Bridge Dualisms and Re-conceptualise Political Participation." *Information, Communication and Society* 19, no. 10 (October 2, 2016): 1487–503. https://doi.org/10.1080/1369118X.2015.1119872.

Hanhardt, Christina B. *Safe Space: Gay Neighborhood History and the Politics of Violence*. Durham, NC: Duke University Press, 2013.

Hannah-Moffat, Kelly. "Algorithmic Risk Governance: Big Data Analytics, Race and Information Activism in Criminal Justice Debates." *Theoretical Criminology* 23, no. 4 (March 22, 2018): 453–70. https://doi.org/10.1177/1362480618763582.

Hardt, Michael. "Affective Labour." *boundary 2* 26, no. 2 (1999): 89–100.

Hardt, Michael, and Antonio Negri. *Empire*. Cambridge, MA: Harvard University Press, 2000.

Heaney, Emma. "Women-Identified Women: Trans Women in 1970s Lesbian Feminist Organizing." *Transgender Studies Quarterly* 3, nos. 1–2 (2016): 137–45.

Hedstrom, Margaret. "Archives, Memory, and Interfaces with the Past." *Archival Science* 2 (2002): 21–43.

Heller, Dana. "Purposes: An Introduction." In *Cross Purposes: Lesbians, Feminists, and the Limits of Alliance*, edited by Dana Heller, 1–18. Bloomington: Indiana University Press, 1997.

Hemmings, Clare. *Why Stories Matter: The Political Grammar of Feminist Theory*. Durham, NC: Duke University Press, 2011.

Hesford, Victoria. *Feeling Women's Liberation*. Durham, NC: Duke University Press, 2013.

Hilderbrand, Lucas. *Inherent Vice: Bootleg Histories of Videotape and Copyright*. Durham, NC: Duke University Press, 2009.

Hobson, Emily K. *Lavender and Red: Liberation and Solidarity in the Gay and Lesbian Left.* Oakland: University of California Press, 2016.

Hochschild, Arlie Russell. *The Managed Heart: Commercialization of Human Feeling.* Berkeley: University of California Press, (1983) 2003.

Hochschild, Arlie Russell, and Anne Machung. *The Second Shift: Working Parents and the Revolution at Home.* New York: Viking, 1989.

Hoffmann, Anna Lauren. "Data, Technology, and Gender: Thinking about (and from) Trans Lives." In *Spaces for the Future: A Companion to Philosophy of Technology,* edited by Joseph C. Pitt and Ashley Shew, 3–13. New York: Routledge, 2017.

Hogan, Kristen. *The Feminist Bookstore Movement: Lesbian Antiracism and Feminist Accountability.* Durham, NC: Duke University Press, 2016.

hooks, bell. *Ain't I a Woman? Black Women and Feminism.* Boston: South End, 1981.

hooks, bell. *Feminist Theory: From Margin to Center.* London: Pluto, (1984) 2000.

Hong, Grace Kyungwon. *Death beyond Disavowal: The Impossible Politics of Difference.* Minneapolis: University of Minnesota Press, 2015.

Hyman, Avi. "Twenty Years of ListServ as an Academic Tool." *Internet and Higher Education* 6 (2003): 17–24.

Ingold, Cindy. "Preserving the Literature of Women's and Gender Organizations: The Availability of Newsletters in Libraries, Commercial Online Databases, and Organizational Web Sites." *Feminist Formations* 23, no. 1 (2011): 182–211.

Introna, Lucas. "Ethics and the Speaking of Things." *Theory, Culture and Society* 26, no. 4 (2009): 25–46. https://doi.org/10.1177/0263276409104967.

Jackson, Sarah J., Moya Bailey, and Brooke Foucault Welles. "#GirlsLikeUs: Trans Advocacy and Community Building Online." *New Media and Society* 20, no. 5 (2018): 1868–88.

Jackson, Steven J. "Rethinking Repair." In *Media Technologies: Essays on Communication, Materiality and Society,* edited by Tarleton Gillespie, Pablo Boczkowski, and Kirsten Foot, 221–39. Cambridge, MA: MIT Press, 2014.

Jay, Karla. *The Gay Report.* New York: Summit, 1979.

Johnson, Matt. "GLBT Controlled Vocabularies and Classification Schemes." Gay, Lesbian, Bisexual, and Transgender Roundtable, American Library Association, 2007. http://www.ala.org/glbtrt/popularresources/vocab.

Johnson, Matt. "A Hidden History of Queer Subject Access." In *Radical Cataloging: Essays at the Front,* edited by K. R. Roberto, 18–27. Jefferson, NC: McFarland, 2008.

Jordan, Tessa. "*Branching Out:* Second-Wave Feminist Periodicals and the Archive of Canadian Women's Writing." *English Studies in Canada* 36, nos. 2–3 (2010): 63–90.

Judge, Peter, and Brenda Gerrie, eds. *Small Scale Bibliographic Databases.* Orlando, FL: Academic, 1986.

Keeling, Kara. "Queer OS." *Cinema Journal* 53, no. 2 (2014): 152–57.

Keilty, Patrick. "Tedious: Feminized Labor in Machine-Readable Cataloging." *Feminist Media Studies* 18, no. 2 (2018): 191–204. https://doi.org/10.1080/14680777.2017.1308410.

Keilty, Patrick, and Rebecca Dean, eds. *Feminist and Queer Information Studies Reader.* Sacramento, CA: Litwin, 2013.

Kennedy, Elizabeth. "Dreams of Social Justice: Building Women's Studies at the
State University of New York, Buffalo." In *The Politics of Women's Studies: Testimony from 30 Founding Mothers*, edited by Florence Howe, 244–63. New York:
Feminist Press, 2000.

Kim, Dorothy, TreaAndrea M. Russworm, Corrigan Vaughan, Cassius Adair,
Veronica Paredes, T. L. Cowan, Anna Everett, Guisela Latorre. "Race, Gender,
and the Technological Turn: A Roundtable on Digitizing Revolution." *Frontiers:
A Journal of Women Studies* 39, no. 1 (2018): 149–77. https://www.muse.jhu.edu
/article/690813.

Knight, G. Norman. *Indexing, the Art of.* London: George Allen and Unwin, 1979.

Kolton, Lilly. "The Promise and Threat of Digital Options in an Archival Age."
Archivaria 47 (1999): 114–35.

Krajewski, Markus. *Paper Machines: About Cards and Catalogs, 1548–1929.* Cambridge, MA: MIT Press, 2011.

Kumbier, Alana. *Ephemeral Materiality: Queering the Archive.* Sacramento, CA:
Litwin, 2014.

Kunzel, Regina. "Lessons in Being Gay: Queer Encounters in Gay and Lesbian
Prison Activism." *Radical History Review* 100 (2008): 11–37.

Lang, Harry G. *A Phone of Our Own: The Deaf Insurrection against Ma Bell.* Washington, DC: Gallaudet University Press, 2000.

Lee, Jamie A. "Mediated Storytelling Practices and Productions: Archival Bodies
of Affective Evidences." *Networking Knowledge*, 9, no. 6 (2016). http://www.ojs
.meccsa.org.uk/index.php/netknow/article/view/484/togetherWHILEapartLEE.

Light, Jennifer S. "When Computers Were Women." *Technology and Culture* 40,
no. 3 (1999): 455–83.

Lipartitto, Kenneth. "When Women Were Switches: Technology, Work and Gender
in the Telephone Industry, 1890–1920." *American Historical Review* 99, no. 4
(1994): 1075–1111.

Lorde, Audre. "I Am Your Sister: Black Women Organizing across Sexualities."
New York: Kitchen Table: Women of Color, 1985.

Lorde, Audre. "An Open Letter to Mary Daly" (1979). In *Sister Outsider: Essays and
Speeches*, 66–71. Trumansburg, NY: Crossing, (1984) 2007.

Lorde, Audre. *Sister Outsider: Essays and Speeches.* Trumansburg, NY: Crossing,
(1984) 2007.

Lorde, Audre. "Uses of the Erotic: The Erotic as Power" (1978). In *Sister Outsider:
Essays and Speeches*, 53–59. Trumansburg, NY: Crossing, (1984) 2007.

Lorde, Audre. *Zami: A New Spelling of My Name.* Berkeley, CA: Crossing, 1982.

Love, Heather. "Review: A Gentle Angry People." *Transition* 84 (2000): 98–113.

Loza, Susana. "Hashtag Feminism, #SolidarityIsForWhiteWomen, and the Other
#FemFuture." *Ada* 5 (2014). https://adanewmedia.org/2014/07/issue5-loza.

Luckenbill, Bill. "Modern Gay and Lesbian Libraries and Archives in North America: A Study in Community Identity and Affirmation." *Library Management* 23,
nos. 1–2 (2002): 93–100.

Macpherson, Tara. "DH by Design: Alternative Origin Stories for the Digital
Humanities." Center for Digital Scholarship and Curation, Washington State

University, Pullman, WA, March 3, 2016. Accessed April 6, 2019. https://www
.youtube.com/watch?v=S4VRAQLLjRg.

Maier, Shana L. "Are Rape Crisis Centers Feminist Organizations?" *Feminist Crimi-nology* 3, no. 2 (2008): 82–100.

Malin, Brenton J. *Feeling Mediated: A History of Media Technology and Emotion in America*. New York: New York University Press, 2014.

Manoff, Marlene. "Archive and Database as Metaphor: Theorizing the Historical Record." *Portal* 10, no. 4 (2010): 385–98.

Marshall, Daniel. "Popular Culture, the 'Victim' Trope and Queer Youth Analytics." *International Journal of Qualitative Studies in Education* 23, no. 1 (2010): 65–85.

Marvin, Carolyn. *When Old Technologies Were New: Thinking about Electrical Com-munication in the Nineteenth Century*. New York: Oxford University Press, 1988.

Mattern, Shannon. 2017. *Code and Clay, Data and Dirt: Five Thousand Years of Urban Media*. Minneapolis: University of Minnesota Press, 2017.

Mattern, Shannon. *Deep Mapping the Media City*. Minneapolis: University of Min-nesota Press, 2015.

Mattern, Shannon. "Small, Moving, Intelligent Parts" Words in Space, June 28, 2016. http://wordsinspace.net/shannon/2016/06/28/small-moving-intelligent -parts/.

Maynard, Steven. "The Burning, Willful Evidence: Lesbian/Gay History and Archi-val Research." *Archivaria* 33 (1991): 195–201.

McKinney, Cait. "Printing the Network: AIDS Activism and Online Access in the 1980s." *Continuum: Journal of Media and Cultural Studies* 32, no. 1 (2018): 7–17.

McRuer, Robert, and Anna Mollow. "Introduction." In *Sex and Disability*, edited by Robert McRuer and Anna Mollow, 1–35. Durham, NC: Duke University Press, 2012.

Meagher, Michelle. "Difficult, Messy, Nasty, and Sensational." *Feminist Media Stud-ies* 14, no. 4 (2013): 578–92.

Medel, China. "Brown Time: Veteranas_and_Rucas and Latinx Image Archiving in the Face of Gentrification." Paper presented at the annual conference of the Society for Cinema and Media Studies, Seattle, March 13, 2019.

Medina, Eden. *Cybernetic Revolutionaries: Technology and Politics in Allende's Chile*. Cambridge, MA: MIT Press, 2011.

Meeker, Martin. *Contacts Desired: Gay and Lesbian Communications and Commu-nity, 1940s–1970s*. Chicago: University of Chicago Press, 2006.

Miksa, Francis L. "The Columbia School of Library Economy, 1887–1888." *Libraries and Culture* 23, no. 3 (1988): 249–80.

Milloy, Christin Scarlett. "Trans Customers Locked out of TD Bank Accounts." *Xtra*, December 22, 2014. https://www.dailyxtra.com/trans-customers-locked -out-of-td-bank-accounts-65644.

Minkoff, Debra C. "The Emergence of Hybrid Organizational Forms: Combining Identity-based Service Provision and Political Action." *Nonprofit and Voluntary Sector Quarterly* 31, no. 3 (2002): 377–401.

Mitchell, Allyson, and Ann Cvetkovich. "A Girl's Journey into the Well of Forbid-den Knowledge." *GLQ* 17, no. 4: 603–18.

Moraga, Cherríe, and Gloria Anzaldúa, eds. *This Bridge Called My Back: Writings by Radical Women of Color*, 2d ed. New York: Kitchen Table: Women of Color Press, (1981) 1983.

Moravec, Michelle. "Unghosting Apparitional (Lesbian) Histories." *Ada* 5 (2014). https://doi.org/10.7264/N3GF0RS6.

Moreton-Robinson, Aileen M. "Troubling Business: Difference and Whiteness within Feminism." *Australian Feminist Studies* 15, no. 33 (2000): 343–52.

Mulvin, Dylan. *Proxies: The Cultural Work of Standing In*. Cambridge, MA: MIT Press, forthcoming.

Muñoz, José Esteban. *Cruising Utopia: The Then and There of Queer Futurity*. New York: New York University Press, 2009.

Muñoz, José Esteban. *Disidentifications*. Minneapolis: University of Minnesota Press, 1999.

Musser, Amber Jamilla. *Sensational Flesh: Race, Power, and Masochism*. New York: New York University Press, 2014.

Nakamura, Lisa. *Digitizing Race: Visual Cultures of the Internet*. Minneapolis: University of Minnesota Press, 2008.

Nakamura, Lisa. "Indigenous Circuits: Navajo Women and the Racialization of Early Electronic Manufacture." *American Quarterly* 66, no. 4 (2014): 919–41.

Namaste, Viviane K. *Invisible Lives: The Erasure of Transsexual and Transgendered People*. Chicago: University of Chicago Press, 2000.

Namaste, Viviane K. *Oversight: Critical Reflections on Feminist Research and Politics*. Toronto: Women's Press, 2015.

National Institutes of Health. WYLBUR *Fundamentals*. Betheseda, MD: Division of Computer Research and Technology, 1980.

Nectoux, Tracy, ed. *Out behind the Desk: Workplace Issues for LGBTQ Librarians*. Sacramento, CA: Litwin, 2011.

Nestle, Joan, ed. *The Persistent Desire: A Femme-Butch Reader*. New York: Alyson, 1992.

Nestle, Joan. *A Restricted Country*. San Francisco: Cleis, 2003.

Nestle, Joan. "Voice 2: Radical Archiving: A Lesbian Feminist Perspective." OutHistory.org, 1978. http://outhistory.org/exhibits/show/an-early-conversation-about-ga/voice-2-joan-nestle.

Nestle, Joan. "The Will to Remember: The Lesbian Herstory Archives of New York." *Feminist Review* 34 (1990): 86–94.

Noble, Bobby. *Songs of the Movement: FtMs Risking Incoherence on a Post-Queer Cultural Landscape*. Toronto: Women's Press, 2006.

Noble, Safiya U. *Algorithms of Oppression: How Search Engines Reinforce Racism*. New York: NYU Press, 2018.

Nooney, Laine. "A Pedestal, a Table, a Love Letter: Archaeologies of Gender in Videogame History." *Game Studies* 13, no. 2 (2013). http://gamestudies.org/1302/articles/nooney.

O'Meara, Erin. "Perfecting the New Wave of Collecting." In *Make Your Own History: Documenting Feminist and Queer Activism in the 21st Century*, edited by Lyz Bly and Kelly Wooten, 107–22. Sacramento, CA: Litwin, 2012.

O'Riordan, Kate. "Queer Theories and Cybersubjects: Intersecting Figures." In *Queer Online: Media Technology and Sexuality*, edited by Kate O'Riordan and David J. Phillips, 13–30. New York: Peter Lang, 2007.

Orlikowski, Wanda J. "The Sociomateriality of Organizational Life: Considering Technology in Management Research. *Cambridge Journal of Economics* 34 (2010): 125–41.

Patton, Cindy. *Last Served? Gendering the HIV Pandemic*. London: Taylor and Francis, 1994.

Peters, Benjamin. *How Not to Network a Nation: The Uneasy History of the Soviet Internet*. Cambridge, MA: MIT Press, 2016.

Piepmeier, Alison. *Girl Zines: Making Media, Doing Feminism*. New York: New York University Press, 2009.

Pingree, Geoffrey B., and Lisa Gitelman. "What's New about New Media?" In *New Media, 1740–1915*, edited by Geoffrey B. Pingree and Lisa Gitelman, xi–xxii. Cambridge, MA: MIT Press, 2003.

Plantin, Jean-Christophe. "Data Cleaners for Pristine Datasets: Visibility and Invisibility of Data Processors in Social Science." *Science, Technology, and Human Values* 44, no. 1 (2019): 52–73. https://doi.org/10.1177/0162243918781268.

Podmore, Julie, and Manon Tremblay. "Lesbians, Second-Wave Feminism and Gay Liberation." In *The Ashgate Companion to Lesbian and Gay Activism*, edited by David Paternotte and Manon Tremblay, 121–34. Farnham, UK: Ashgate, 2015.

Potter, Clare. "Introduction." In *The Lesbian Periodicals Index*, edited by Clare Potter, x–xii. Tallahassee, FL: Naiad, 1986.

Potter, Clare. "The Lesbian Periodicals Index." In *Lesbian Studies Present and Future*, edited by Margaret Cruikshank, 152–61. Old Westbury, NY: Feminist Press, 1982.

Potter, Clare, ed. *The Lesbian Periodicals Index*. Tallahassee, FL: Naiad, 1986.

Pourtavaf, Leila. "Introduction." In *Féminismes électriques*, edited by Leila Pourtavaf, 9. Montreal: Centrale Galerie Powerhouse, 2012.

Power, Lisa. "Voice in My Ear." In *Radical Records: Thirty Years of Lesbian and Gay History, 1957–1987*, edited by Bob Cant and Susan Hemmings, 142–54. London: Routledge, 1988.

Pratt, Minnie Bruce. *S/HE*. Ithaca, NY: Firebrand, 1995.

Puar, Jasbir K. *Terrorist Assemblages: Homonationalism in Queer Times*. Durham, NC: Duke University Press, 2007.

Rajman, Roger, and John Borgelt, "WYLBUR: An Interactive Text Editing and Remote Job Entry System." *Communications of the ACM* 16, no. 5 (1973): 314–22.

Rakow, Lana F. *Gender on the Line: Women, the Telephone, and Community Life*. Urbana: University of Illinois Press, 1992.

RAND Corporation. *Specifications for the RAND Abstract and Index System*. Santa Monica, CA: RAND Computation Center, 1975.

Rawson, K. J. "Accessing Transgender//Desiring Queer(er?) Archival Logics." *Archivaria* 68 (2009): 123–40.

Rawson, K. J. "Archival Justice: An Interview with Ben Power Alwin." *Radical History Review* 122 (2015): 177–87.

Rawson, K. J., and Cristan Williams. "Transgender*: The Rhetorical Landscape of a Term." *Present Tense* 3, no. 2 (2014). http://www.presenttensejournal.org /volume-3/transgender-the-rhetorical-landscape-of-a-term/.

Reagon, Bernice Johnson. "Coalition Politics: Turning the Century." In *Home Girls: A Black Feminist Anthology*, edited by Barbara Smith, 356–68. New York: Kitchen Table: Women of Color Press, (1981) 1983.

Rentschler, Carrie A. "Bystander Intervention, Feminist Hashtag Activism, and the Anti-carceral Politics of Care." *Feminist Media Studies* 17, no. 4 (2017): 565–84. https://doi.org/10.1080/14680777.2017.1326556.

Rentschler, Carrie A. "Making Culture and Doing Feminism." In *The Routledge Handbook of Contemporary Feminism,* edited by Tasha Oren and Andrea L. Press, 127–47. New York: Routledge, 2019.

Rentschler, Carrie A. *Second Wounds: Victims' Rights and the Media in the U.S.* Durham, NC: Duke University Press, 2011.

Rentschler, Carrie A., and Samantha C. Thrift. "Doing Feminism: Event, Archive, Techné." *Feminist Theory* 16, no. 3 (2015): 239–49. https://doi.org/10.1177 /1464700115604138.

Rentschler, Carrie A., and Samantha C. Thrift. "Doing Feminism in the Network: Networked Laughter and the 'Binders Full of Women' Meme." *Feminist Theory* 16, no. 3 (2015): 329–59. https://doi.org/10.1177/1464700115604136.

Reynolds, Eileen. "Beyond Braille: A History of Reading by Ear." *NYU News Story*, January 29, 2015. https://www.nyu.edu/about/news-publications/news/2015 /january/mara-mills-blind-reading.html.

Rich, Adrienne. *Of Woman Born: Motherhood as Experience and Institution.* New York: W. W. Norton, 1977.

Ridinger, Robert B. M. "Playing in the Attic: Indexing and Preserving the Gay Press." In *Liberating Minds: The Stories and Professional Lives of Gay, Lesbian, and Bisexual Librarians and their Advocates*, edited by Norman G. Kester, 92–97. Jefferson, NC: McFarland, 1997.

Ritzenhaler, Mary Lynn. *Preserving Archives and Manuscripts*, 2d ed. Chicago: Society of American Archivists, 2010.

Roberto, K. R. "Inflexible Bodies: Metadata for Transgender Identities." *Journal of Information Ethics* 20, no. 2 (2011): 56–64.

Roberts, Gail Covitt. *CUE R3.0 Tutorial for WYLBUR.* RAND Corporation, February 1989. https://www.rand.org/content/dam/rand/pubs/notes/2009/N2673 .pdf.

Roberts, JR. "Introduction." In *Black Lesbians: An Annotated Bibliography*, edited by JR Roberts, xi–xv. Tallahassee, FL: Naiad, 1981.

Robertson, Craig. "A Documentary Regime of Verification." *Cultural Studies* 23, no. 3 (2009): 329–54. https://doi.org/10.1080/09502380802016253.

Robertson, Craig. "Learning to File: Reconfiguring Information and Information Work in the Early Twentieth Century." *Technology and Culture* 58, no. 4 (2017): 955–81. https://doi.org/10.1353/tech.2017.0110.

Robertson, Tara. "Not All Information Wants to Be Free: The Case Study of *On Our Backs.*" In *Applying Library Values to Emerging Technology: Decision-Making in the Age of Open Access, Maker Spaces, and the Ever-Changing Library*, edited by Peter D. Fernandez and Kelly Tilton, 225–39. Publications in Librarianship no. 72. Chicago: American Library Association, 2018.

Rodriguez, Rio. "Mapping QTBIPOC Toronto." Master's thesis, York University, Toronto, 2016.

Rosenzweig, Roy. "Wizards, Bureaucrats, Warriors, and Hackers: Writing the History of the Internet." *American Historical Review* 103, no. 5 (1998): 1530–52.

Rosner, Daniela K. *Critical Fabulations: Reworking the Methods and Margins of Design*. Cambridge, MA: MIT Press, 2018.

Ross, Becki. *The House That Jill Built: A Lesbian Nation in Formation*. Toronto: University of Toronto Press, 1995.

Rowe, Aimee Carrillo. *Power Lines: On the Subject of Feminist Alliances*. Durham, NC: Duke University Press, 2008.

Samer, Rox. "Revising 'Re-vision': Documenting 1970s Feminisms and the Queer Potentiality of Digital Feminist Archives." *Ada* 5 (2014). https://doi.org/10.7264/N3FF3QMC.

Sandberg, Jane. "Organizing the Transgender Internet: Web Directories and Envisioning Inclusive Digital Spaces." In *Queers Online: LGBT Digital Practices in Libraries, Archives, and Museums*, edited by Rachel Wexelbaum, 43–60. Sacramento, CA: Litwin, 2015.

Schellenberg, Theodore. *Modern Archives: Principles and Techniques*. Chicago: University of Chicago Press, 1956.

Schwarz, Judith. "Living Herstory." *Off Our Backs*, 8, no. 5 (May 1978): 20.

Scott, Joan Wallach. "The Evidence of Experience." *Critical Inquiry* 17, no. 4 (1993): 773–97.

Scott, Joan Wallach. *The Fantasy of Feminist History*. Durham, NC: Duke University Press, 2011.

Self, Robert O. *All in the Family: The Realignment of American Democracy since the 1960s*. New York: Hill and Wang, 2012.

Sender, Katherine. *Business, Not Politics: The Making of the Gay Market*. New York: Columbia University Press, 2004.

Sheffield, Rebecka. "Community Archives." In *Currents of Archival Thinking*, 2d ed., edited by Terry Eastwood and Heather MacNeil, 351–76. Santa Barbara, CA: Libraries Unlimited, 2017.

Shockley, Ann Allen. "The Salsa Soul Sisters." *Off Our Backs* 9, no. 10 (1979): 13.

Singh, Rianka. "Platform Feminism: Protest and the Politics of Spatial Organization." *Ada* 14 (2018). https://doi.org/10.5399/uo/ada.2018.14.6.

Singh, Rianka, and Sarah Sharma. "Platform Uncommons." *Feminist Media Studies* 19, no. 2 (2019). https://doi.org/10.1080/14680777.2019.1573547.

Sjoholm, Barbara. "She Who Owns the Press." In *Make Your Own History: Documenting Feminist and Queer Activism in the 21st Century*, edited by Lyz Bly and Kelly Wooten, 159–70. Sacramento, CA: Litwin, 2012.

Sloniowski, Lisa. "In the Stacks of Barbara Godard, or Do Not Confuse the Complexity of this Moment with Chaos." In *Trans/acting Culture, Writing, and Memory: Essays in Honour of Barbara Godard*, edited by Eva C. Karpinski,

Jennifer Henderson, Ian Sowton, and Ray Ellenwood, 478–95. Waterloo, ON: Wilfred Laurier University Press, 2013.

Sloniowski, Lisa. "This Is Not a Love Story: Libraries and Feminist Porn." *Access* 18, no. 2 (2012): 14–17.

Smith, Barbara. "Foreword." In *Black Lesbians: An Annotated Bibliography*, edited by JR Roberts, ix–x. Tallahassee, FL: Naiad, 1981.

Smith Barbara, ed. *Home Girls: A Black Feminist Anthology*. New York: Kitchen Table: Women of Color, (1981) 1983.

Smith, Shawn(ta). "Tape-by-Tape: Digital Projects at the Lesbian Herstory Archives." In *Queers Online: LGBT Digital Practices in Libraries, Archives, and Museums*, edited by Rachel Wexelbaum, 85–110. Sacramento, CA: Litwin. 2015.

Spencer, Amy. *DIY: The Rise of Lo-Fi Culture*. London: Marion Boyars, 2008.

Spender, Dale. *Women of Ideas and What Men Have Done to Them: From Aphra Behn to Adrienne Rich*. London: Thorsons, 1983.

Spense, Jaqueline. "Small Organizations and Cultural Institutions—A Digital Future?" *Program* 39, no. 4 (2005): 366–80.

Squires, Catherine. "Rethinking the Black Publish Sphere: An Alternative Vocabulary for Multiple Public Spheres." *Communication Theory* 12, no. 4 (2002): 446–68.

Star, Susan Leigh. "Misplaced Concretism and Concrete Situations." In *Boundary Objects and Beyond: Working with Leigh Star*, edited by Geoffrey C. Bowker, Stefan Timmermans, Adele E. Clarke, and Ellen Balka Star, 143–70. Cambridge, MA: MIT Press, (1994) 2016.

Star, Susan Leigh, and Karen Ruhleder. "Steps toward an Ecology of Infrastructure: Design and Access for Large Information Spaces." *Information Systems Research* 7, no. 1 (1996): 111–34.

Steinbock, Eliza. "Generative Negatives: Del LaGrace Volcano's *Herm Body* Photographs." *Transgender Studies Quarterly* 1, no. 4 (2014): 539–51.

Sterne, Jonathan. *MP3: The Meaning of a Format*. Durham, NC: Duke University Press, 2012.

Sterne, Jonathan, and Dylan Mulvin. "The Low Acuity for Blue: Perceptual Technics and American Color Television." *Journal of Visual Culture* 13, no. 2 (2014): 118–38.

Sterne, Jonathan, and Tara Rodgers. "The Poetics of Signal Processing." *Differences* 22, nos. 2–3 (2011): 31–53.

Stewart, Susan. *On Longing: Narratives of the Miniature, the Gigantic, the Souvenir, the Collection*. Durham, NC: Duke University Press, 1993.

Stoler, Ann Laura. *Along the Archival Grain: Epistemic Anxieties and Colonial Common Sense*. Princeton, NJ: Princeton University Press, 2010.

Strongman, SaraEllen. "'Creating Justice between Us': Audre Lorde's Theory of the Erotic as Coalitional Politics in the Women's Movement." *Feminist Theory* 19, no. 1 (2018): 41–59.

Strongman, SaraEllen. "The Sisterhood: Black Women, Black Feminism, and the Women's Liberation Movement." PhD diss., University of Pennsylvania, Philadelphia, 2018.

Stryker, Susan. "My Words to Victor Frankenstein above the Village of Chamounix: Performing Transgender Rage." *GLQ* 1, no. 3 (1994): 237–54.

Stryker, Susan. *Transgender History*. Berkeley, CA: Publishers Group West, 2008.

Stryker, Susan, Paisley Currah, and Lisa Jean Moore. "Introduction: Trans-, Trans, or Transgender?" *Women's Studies Quarterly* 36, nos. 3–4 (2008): 11–22.

Suchman, Lucy. *Human-Machine Reconfigurations: Plans and Situated Actions*. Cambridge: Cambridge University Press, (1987) 2006. https://doi.org/10.1017 /CBO9780511808418.008.

Suisman, David. *Selling Sounds: The Commercial Revolution in American Music*. Cambridge, MA: Harvard University Press, 2009.

Sutherland, Tonia. "Archival Amnesty: In Search of Black American Transitional and Restorative Justice." *Critical Archival Studies* 1, no. 2 (2017). https://doi.org /10.24242/jclis.v1i2.42.

Swan, Elaine. "The Internship Class: Subjectivity and Inequalities—Gender, Race and Class." In *Handbook of Gendered Careers in Management: Getting In, Getting On, Getting Out*, edited by Adelina M. Broadbridge and Sandra L. Fielden, 30–43. Cheltenham, UK: Edward Elgar, 2015.

Taylor, Liza. "Coalition from the Inside Out: Women of Color Feminism and Politico-Ethical Coalition Politics." *New Political Science* 40, no. 1 (2018): 119–36. https://doi.org/10.1080/07393148.2017.1416447.

Thieme, Katja, and Mary Ann S. Saunders. "How Do You Wish to Be Cited? Citation Practices and a Scholarly Community of Care in Trans Studies Research Articles." *Journal of English for Academic Purposes* 32 (2018): 80–90. https://doi .org/10.1016/j.jeap.2018.03.010.

Thistlethwaite, Polly J. "Building 'A Home of Our Own': The Construction of the Lesbian Herstory Archives." In *Daring to Find Our Names: The Search for Lesbigay Library History*, edited by James V. Carmichael Jr., 153–74. Westport, CT: Greenwood, 1998.

Thrift, Samantha. "Feminist Eventfulness: Boredom and the 1984 Canadian Leadership Debate on Women's Issues." *Feminist Media Studies* 13, no. 3 (2011): 406–21.

Thrift, Samantha, and Carrie Rentschler. "Binders Full of Women: A Feminist Meme to Bind Them All." *Flow* 21, no. 2 (2014): 329–59. http://flowtv.org/2014/11 /binders-full-of-women.

Thylstrup, Nanna Bonde. *The Politics of Mass Digitization*. Cambridge, MA: MIT Press, 2019.

Travis, Trysh. "The Women in Print Movement: History and Implications." *Book History* 11 (2008): 275–300.

Tropiano, Stephen. "'A Safe and Supportive Environment': LBGTQ Youth and Social Media." In *Queer Youth and Media Cultures*, edited by Christopher Pullen, 46–62. New York: Palgrave, 2014.

Turkle, Sherry. *Alone Together: Why We Expect More from Technology and Less from Each Other*. New York: Basic, 2011.

Turkle, Sherry. *Reclaiming Conversation: The Power of Talk in a Digital Age*. New York: Penguin, 2015.

Turner, Fred. "Burning Man at Google: A Cultural Infrastructure for New Media Production." *New Media and Society* 11, nos. 1–2 (2009): 73–94.

Turner, Fred. *From Counterculture to Cyberculture: Stewart Brand, the Whole Earth Network, and the Rise of Digital Utopianism*. Chicago: University of Chicago Press, 2006.

Van Jaarsveld, Danielle, and Winifred R. Poster. "Call Centers: Emotional Labour over the Phone." In *Emotional Labor in the 21st Century: Diverse Perspectives on the Psychology of Emotion Regulation at Work*, edited by Alicia Grandey, James Diefendorff, and Deborah E. Rupp, 153–73. New York: Routledge Academic, 2013.

Volcano, Del LaGrace, "Reflections on Love Bites." Accessed May 11, 2019. https://web.archive.org/web/20190502202548/https://www.dellagracevolcano.com/gallery/love-bites-23196221.

Volcano, Del LaGrace, Jay Prosser, and Eliza Steinbock. "INTER*me: An Inter-Locution on the Body in Photography." In *Transgender and Intersex: Theoretical, Practical, and Artistic Perspectives*, edited by Stefan Horlacher, 189–224. New York: Palgrave Macmillan, 2016.

Vora, Khalindi. "The Transmission of Care: Affective Economies and Indian Call Centers." In *Intimate Labors: Cultures, Technologies, and the Politics of Care*, edited by Eileen Boris and Rhacel Salazar Parreñas, 33–48. Stanford, CA: Stanford Social Sciences, 2010.

Ware, Syrus Marcus. "All Power to All People? Black LGBTTI2QQ Activism, Remembrance, and Archiving in Toronto." *Transgender Studies Quarterly* 4, no. 2 (2017): 170–80.

Warner, Michael. "Publics and Counterpublics." *Public Culture* 14, no. 1 (2002): 49–90.

White, Michele. *The Body and the Screen: Theories of Internet Spectatorship*. Cambridge MA: MIT Press, 2006.

Wiegman, Robyn. "The Intimacy of Critique: Ruminations on Feminism as a Living Thing." *Feminist Theory* 11, no. 1 (2010): 79–84.

Wiegman, Robyn. *Object Lessons*. Durham, NC: Duke University Press, 2012.

Wilks, Brian B. *What Every Librarian Should Know about On-line Searching*. Ottawa: Canadian Library Association, 1982.

Willey, Angela. *Undoing Monogamy: The Politics of Science and the Possibilities of Biology*. Durham NC: Duke University Press, 2016.

Williams, Cristan. "Radical Inclusion: Recounting the Trans Inclusive History of Radical Feminism." *Transgender Studies Quarterly* 3, nos. 1–2 (2016): 254–58.

Williams, Raymond. *Marxism and Literature*. Oxford: Oxford University Press, 1977.

Wolfe, Jen. "Playing Fast and Loose with the Rules: Metadata Cataloging for Digital Library Projects." In *Radical Cataloging: Essays at the Front*, edited by K. R. Roberto, 69–74. Jefferson, NC: McFarland, 2008.

Zeavin, Hannah. "The Communication Cure: Tele-therapy, 1890–2015." PhD diss., New York University, 2018.

Index

Page numbers in italics refer to figures.

bisexual women, 87, 91

Bivens, Rena, 197

Black lesbians, 23, 78, 79, 123, 212; feminist struggles and, 120; history and source materials, 65, 118, 120, 121, 122; information referrals to, 90; solidarity around race, 18, 223n67; women's movements and, 118–19

Black Lesbians: An Annotated Bibliography (1981), 38–39, 130, 138; antiracist strategy, 108, 118–21; cover, *117*; emergence of, 116, 118, 127; foreword, 23, 65, 114, 120; primary aim, 122–23

Boots of Leather, Slippers of Gold (Davis and Kennedy), 66, 184, 228n14, 253n68

born-digital problem, 180

Bowker, Geoffrey C., 97, 144

boyd, danah, 230n45

Brennan, Teresa, 225n84

Brouwer, Daniel, 157

Buffalo Women's Oral History Project, 38, 50, *158*, 183

butch-femme dynamics, 25, 67–68, 100–101, 184

Butler, Octavia, 259n12

Canadian Lesbian and Gay Archives (CLGA), 53–54, 227n5. *See also* ArQuives

capable amateurism, 31, 132, 147, 154, 181; definition, 30, 227n111

care work, 22, 78–79. *See also* economies of care

Caswell, Michelle, 15

catalog databases, 31, 194–95, 202

censorship, 17, 19, 210, 224n71

centralized/decentralized networks, 41, *42*, 49–50, 53, 61–65

Chun, Wendy Hui Kyong, 62, 212

Cifor, Marika, 20

Circle of Lesbian Indexers, 11, 29, 38, 116; capable amateur ethos, 132–33; classification strategies, 106, 108, 131, 133–34, 135; collaborative work process, 111, 133, 137–38, 144, 151; database computing, 109, 139–42, 149–50; index cards, 136–37, *137*, *138*; overview of, 105–6; recruitment of indexers, 49, 111, 132; thesaurus of terms, 143–46. See also *Lesbian Periodicals Index, The* (1986)

citation practices, 40, 54

Cite Black Women, 122

classification: amateur, 196; choices and, 16, 108, 130; flexibilities around, 11, 111, 143–44; historical terms and, 183–84, 196, 256n136; Library of Congress (LOC), 7, 129, 135; standards, 144; of subject headings, 4, 110, 121–22, 130, 133–34, 162, 183, 216; of trans identities, 143–44, 146, 184, 197; women workers and, 135–36

Clinton, Hillary, 209, 259n17

Cocciolo, Anthony, 156, 174, 178–79, 181, 182–83, 188

collaboration, 230n45; of Circle of Lesbian Indexers, 111, 133, 136–38, 151; cross-racial, 119; of LHA, 172, 193–94; of *Matrices*, 51, 53–54

collective-singular tension, 212

Collison, Robert L., 123, 124–26, 127, 132, 140

colonial archives, 14

Combahee River Collective Statement (1977), 223n67, 241n37, 242n51

coming out, 79–81, 93

communication networks, 4, 8, 19–20; community care circles and, 48; conflicts, 62–63; emotional dimension of, 44; feminist organizing and, 1, 43–45; grassroots, 59, 122; histories, 51–53; LHA's, 58–59, 61, 190; *Matrices*, 27–28, 35–36, 40, 41–42, 48–51, 62–65, 213; newsletters as, 34–35, 41–46, 55, 60, 230n45; technologies, 34; telephones as, 86, 98

communications media, 18–19, 27–28, 34, 36, 95

communication studies, 12

communicative labor, 8, 86

community archives, 13–15, 106, 176, 213; as activist organizations, 159, 250n13; digitization and, 157–58, 167–68, 177, 252n41; equipment donations, 168; government funding, 183; importance of newsletters, 37–38, 54, 55–56; LGBTQ, 4, 15, 76, 157, 159, 167, 191; pace and scale, 179; paper records, 75–76, 234n17; servers, 169. *See also* archives; Lesbian Herstory Archives (LHA)

community care circles, 48

community formation, 21

computer databases: catalog standardization, 194–96; indexing and, 30, 109, 124, 139–41, 144–46; instructional manuals, 150, 248n179; LHA's use of, 37, 61, 141, 184–85, 189–90; neutrality of, 110; trans representation in,

emotions (*continued*)
212, 213–14; frustration, 85, 127, 150, 194; information activism and, 22, 216; loneliness and anxiety, 43, 68, 79, 82; optimism and hope, 45, 80; vulnerability, 67–68, 71, 80, 92–93, 95, 182

Enke, Finn, 24

erotic, the, 93, 165, 214, 216; Lorde's theory of, 21; racial difference and, 18, 223n69

ethics, 182, 191, 192, 249n5

eventfulness, 78, 187

exclusions, 87, 121, 123, 134, 182; trans, 23, 24, 88, 145–46, 200, 209

fantasies, 71, 131, 171, 215, 216; good-life, 212

Feigenbaum, Anna, 46

Feinberg, Leslie, 214

feminism: antiracism and, 118–19; archival activism and, 171, 178; critique of the present, 170–71; critiques of language, 134–35; information activism and, 2, 217n4; network thinking and, 27–28, 43–44; role of newsletters, 44–46; theory and politics, 3, 19, 23, 27, 45, 82, 133; women of color and, 21, 23, 43, 93, 120–21. *See also* lesbian feminism; second-wave feminism

Feminist Bookstore News (periodical), 96, 231n64

feminist historiographies, 8, 16, 36, 52, 55, 131, 223n64; second-wave, 14, 69

feminist social movements, 15, 24, 74, 102, 241n37; eventfulness of, 78; methodological approach to, 8, 187; networks and, 38, 46, 52, 60; racial aspects, 118, 241n37; service-provision work and, 78, 235n26; use of telephones, 86. *See also* social movements; women's liberation movement

Ferguson, Roderick, 223n67

Flowers, Amy, 94

Foster, Jeanette, 48–49, 113

Foucault, Michel, 14

Fraser, Nancy, 17

Freeman, Elizabeth, 24

Friedman, Elisabeth Jay, 43, 51

fundraising, 37–38, 186, 249n12

"Future Is Female" slogan, 209, 259n17

futurity, 62, 131, 164, 170–71, 209, 258n5

Gale, 61, 157–58, 191

Galloway, Alexander, 41, 62

Garrison, Dee, 16, 245n114

Gay Bibliography, A (1971–80), 128, 149

gay liberation movement, 17, 18, 37, 84, 159, 207, 224n71

Gay Report, The (Jay), 63–64

gendered labor, 11, 132–33, 136, 147, 173, 245n114

genres, 60

Gieseking, Jack, 59, 164, 214–15, 228n6, 251n40

Gitelman, Lisa, 5, 10, 77, 124, 255n99; on genres, 60; on indexes and bibliographies, 126, 140

Gittings, Barbara, 128, 149

Godard, Barbara, 215

Google, 110, 160, 195

Grapevine (newsletter), 42–43, 45

Great Library at Alexandria, 248n2

Groeneveld, Elizabeth, 192

Guillory, John, 77, 128

Gwenwald, Morgan, 189–90

Halberstam, Jack, 98, 224n77

Hampton, Mabel, 233n96, 253n68

handwriting, 82, 136, 189

Hanhardt, Christina, 236n49

harassment, 71, 74, 249n5

hard drives, 175, 179, 180

hardware, 168, 252n47

Haskell, Beth, 156, 189–90, 193

Hesford, Victoria, 25, 171, 223n64

heteronormativity, 12, 100, 164

Hilderbrand, Lucas, 13, 52, 176, 177, 179

history and archives movement, 27, 36, 56, 77–78; incompletable tasks, 248n2; research and pedagogical goals, 37, 38, 171

HIV/AIDS, 84, 172, 236n49

hobbyists, 141

Hobson, Emily, 242n43

Hogan, Kristen, 96, 118, 231n64

homophobia, 33, 84, 95, 105, 121

Homosaurus, 184, 255n96

hotlines. *See* Lesbian Switchboard of New York; telephone hotlines

iconography, 173, 205, 207, 209; labrys, 25, 226n102

identity: affect and, 21; archival work and, 40, 165; butch, 100, 184; coming out and, 80; lesbian, 9, 19, 87, 97–98, 118, 119, 122, 162–63,

language politics, 134–35, 143, 246n128

Lee, Jamie A., 15

lesbian, category of, 98, 118, 122, 191, 239n105; ambivalent identifications with, 26, 199; LHA's views, 40, 162–63, 200; New York Lesbian Switchboard's views, 87, 88, 91

Lesbian Body, 198, 257n147

lesbian feminism: attachments to, 26, 163; circulation of ephemera, 205–7, 209–10; computer databases and, 1–2, 30; cultural infrastructure for, 102; digitization and, 154, 162; indexes and, 111, 126, 130–31; information infrastructure and, 3, 7, 44, 96, 98; networks and, 37, 41, 44–45, 62; queerness and, 162, 163–64, 191; race and, 118–21, 127; social movements and counterpublics, 17–19; trans exclusion/inclusion, 23, 87–88, 145, 196, 198, 199, 200

Lesbian/Gay History Researchers Network Newsletter, 37

Lesbian Herstory Archives (LHA), 40, 65, 111, 112; approach to digitization, 6, 13, 30, 154–55, 174, 203–4; born-digital materials, 180; budget and fundraising, 159, 183, 186, 249n12; catalog records and database, 169–70, 172–73, 194–96; collaboration and decision-making, 138, 193–94; computing and technological transition, 37, 61, 185–90, 193–94; coordinators and staff, 25, 38, 160, 172, 180, 189, 191, 193–94, 250n19; founders, 26, 39, 58, 172; how-to guides, 188; incorporation, 56, 231n65; interns, 173; lesbian-feminist stance, 162–64, 191, 202; online access, 66, 181–82, 191–93, 231n67; open access policy, 13, 116; photography collection, 146, 169, 197–202, 201; physical space, 5, 9, 160, 161, 213–14; record keeping, 136, 185, 187, 190, 195–96, 214; Special Collections Working Group, 170; "Statement of Principles," 6, 159, 160, 188, 197, 200, 250n20; U-matic tape collection, 168, 169; volunteers, 10–11, 45, 46, 154–56, 164–66, 191–92, 249n4; website and donor agreements, 191–92. *See also* audiocassette digitization

Lesbian Herstory Archives Newsletter, 36, 39, 54, 65, 66; article clippings, 58, 61, 232n71; covers, 47, 233n96; mailing list database, 37, 61, 185, 190, 228n12; outreach strategy, 55–56, 58; pedagogical strategy, 59–60; printing techniques, 57, 60–61; sections and content, 56

lesbian history, 5, 13, 155, 160, 171; attachments to, 162–63; Black women in, 23, 120, 122; digital technologies and, 154, 204; indexes and bibliographies, 111, 113, 118, 121; information activism and, 2, 196; Instagram accounts, 4, 205–10; making of, 32; precarious access to, 59; research and studies, 37, 53, 54; revival of, 24–25, 207–8; role of networks in, 36

Lesbian Periodicals Index, The (1986), 116, 130, 227n110; cover, 107; finished product, 152; as an information interface, 129, 139; reason for creating, 133; reindexing of, 146; subject headings, 112, 121; success of, 114; work process and materials, 111, 112–13, 151–52. *See also* Circle of Lesbian Indexers

lesbian studies, 27, 34, 37, 113, 114, 121, 139

Lesbian Switchboard of New York: bisexual callers, 91; boredom experienced at, 102, 103, 104; call logs, 28–29, 67–68, 70–71, 72, 73, 74–82; conflicts and administrative frustrations, 99–100; decline and closure, 29, 75, 104; filing practices, 76; information retrieval, 26, 69, 98–99; infrastructure for basic support, 96–98; location, 70, 235n28; policies, 81, 87; training, 99; trans callers, 87–89, 95; volunteer availability, 91–92; volunteers/callers with disabilities, 90–91; women of color and, 89–90

LGBTQ, 23, 132, 199, 208, 224n71; archives, 4, 15, 20, 40, 76, 157, 159, 167, 191; historical materials, 157–58, 184; information hotlines, 29, 95, 239n96

libraries, 114, 150, 194, 243n68; card catalogues, 249n2; check-out cards, 128; gendered labor of, 132, 136, 173, 245n114; lesbian materials in, 105, 113, 127, 129

library hand, 136

Library of Congress (LOC), 7, 129, 135, 183

Licona, Adela C., 157

Light, Jennifer, 11

literature, 37, 83, 91, 105, 113, 122

London Gay and Lesbian Switchboard, 85

Lorde, Audre, 21, 118, 120, 223n69, 242n52; speeches and readings, 10, 175, 176, 253n68

Love, Heather, 98

mailing lists, 55, 58; computerized, 1–2, 37, 61, 185, 189–90

Malin, Brenton J., 22, 221n37

marginalized groups, 3, 20, 38, 120; community archives and, 15, 159, 182–83, 250n13; counterpublic formation and, 16–17, 18–19

masculinity, 14, 67, 100, 199, 257n152

Matrices: A Lesbian/Feminist Research Newsletter, 116; editorials and feedback, 54–55; end of, 66; founders, 26–27, 33–34; mastheads, *35*; network model, 35–37, 41–42, 46, 48–51, 62–65, 213; printing techniques, 60; publication frequency, 39, 66; regional editors, 49–50; requests for information, 53–54, 65, 137; research and researchers, 52–53, 63–65; role in outreach, 40; sections, 50, 53; stories, 39–40, 229n32; subscribers and contributors, 34, 38–39, 49, 54–55

McClain, Ronika, 165–66, 200, 249n4

McLeod, Don, 252n41

Medel, China, 210

media archaeology, 5, 192, 218n12, 252n47

media practices, 3, 10, 15, 77, 185, 214, 216; as archivable, 14, 29; digital, 16, 31, 177, 215; infrastructural approach to, 8–9; as *rememberable*, 69; of telephone hotlines, 69, 75, 86; in transition, 202

media studies, 3, 9, 128, 260n40; feminist, 11, 14, 52, 86, 227n111; queer, 80

media technologies, 3, 11–12, 22, 52, 169, 202; adoption of new, 185–86, 255n99; aesthetics of access with, 13, 176, 177; decisions about, 186–87; historicizing, 51, 70; information infrastructures and, 6–7, 84; online, 163

mediated encounters, 14, 128

Meeker, Martin, 44–45

memory, 140, 212

metadata, 13; descriptions, 146, 194, 196, 198–99, *201*, 201–2, 213; trans subjects and, 184, 197, 201, 257n157

Mills, Mara, 90

Montoya-Sloan, Colette Denali, 188, 203, 249n4; digitization projects, 153–54, 172, 174, 175, 177–79; identity, 165

Mulvin, Dylan, 12

Muñoz, José Esteban, 164

Musser, Amber Jamilla, 21, 120

Nakamura, Lisa, 11, 43, 129, 178, 258n160

Namaste, Viviane, 24

National Association of Gay and Lesbian Switchboards, 84

National Women's Mailing List, 1

Nestle, Joan, *46*, 159–60, *161*, 172, 189, 212, 257n152

network models, 41–43, *42*, 62. *See also* communication networks; support networks

neutrality of information, 12, 97–98; indexing and, 110, 131, 134

New Alexandria Lesbian Library, 39–40, 44

new media technologies, 3, 4, 11; introduction of, 140, 185, 255n99

newsletters: content sharing, 54; digitized, 157; feminist organizing and, 44–45, 227n110; as a genre, 60; importance to archives, 37–38; indexes and bibliographies for, 7, 106, 129; as networks, 27–28, 34–36, 41–46, 55, 230n45; sorting techniques, 45, *46*. See also *Matrices: A Lesbian/Feminist Research Newsletter*

Noble, Bobby, 85, 236n53

objects: analog/digital, 157, 184, 208, 216; scene of desire, 213; of study, 166

online access: to catalog databases, 31, 177, 194–95; digitization and, 158–59, 203; lesbian-feminist history and, 207–8; networks, 60, 66; permissions and agreements, 38, 174, 191–92, 198, 200, 214; photography collections, 198–99, 200; server space and, 169. *See also* Instagram

online public access catalog (OPAC), 11, 194–95

oral history, 38, 50, 70, 174, 177, 253n68; movement, 60, 153, *154*, 175

Otherwild, 205–9, 258n5

outreach strategies, 192, 195; of newsletters, 40, 55–56; of telephone hotlines, 83–84

paper glut, 126, 243n73

paper movement, 4–5. *See also* Women in Print Movement

paperwork, 75–77, *78*, 211

Paperwork Explosion (1967 film), 243n73

pathways, 109–10, 114–16, 138

patriarchy, 17, 19, 120, 163, 164, 207, 242n51

"Patriarchy Is a Pyramid Scheme" slogan, 205–6, *206*, 209

Peach, Imogen (pseud.), 173, 193–94, 195–96, 249n4
pedagogy of failure, 171
Penelope, Julia. *See* Stanley, Julia Penelope
Penthouse (magazine), 63–64
periodicals: access to, 40, 113–14; boom in, 105; collections, 138–39; early lesbian, 121, 128, 228n8; network imagery of, 42; reproduction of content, 54, 63; total publications, 34, 227n110, 227n5. See also *Lesbian Periodicals Index, The* (1986)
"phone-phobia," 95, 96
photographs: of audiocassette tapes, 157, *158*; digitization and metadata, 13, 169, 197–202; misinformation of, 208, 259n12. *See also* Instagram
politics, lesbian-feminist, 31, 33, 34, 36, 97; digital technologies and, 154, 193; LHA's, 155, 162–63, 202
pornography, 17, 64, 176
Potter, Clare, *107*, 122, 129, 131; collaboration with Roberts, 113–14, 116, 151; on creating subject headings, 130, 133–34, 146; formation of the Circle of Lesbian Indexers, 106, 115; on indexing's social role, 108; knowledge about indexing, 123, 132, 150; learning WYLBUR, 124, 139, 141–42, 149–50; managing the thesaurus, 143–46; periodical collections, *138*, 138–39; reflection on computers, 109, 151–52, 215; sense of feeling overwhelmed, 211, 212–13; training and coordination work, 111, 136, *137*, 140
Power, Lisa, 85
Pratt Institute, 156, 169, 174, 181, 253n68
precarity of information, 20, 24–25, 211, 227n110
preservation, *72*; cost-effective formats, 166; digitization and, 13, 154, 157, 169, 176, 179, 181, 202–3; of feminist networks, 40; obsolete formats and, 168; of old catalog records, 195–96, 214
print culture, 4–5, 14, 76; archives, 65, 75; feminist, 28, 30, 41, 51, 66, 69, 87, 231n64; indexes and, 125, 138; networks, 27, 36, 66
printing technologies, 36
privacy concerns: computer databases and, 2; and consent from donors, 182, 191–92; of gender and sexuality, 17, 63–64; networks and, 28, 64, 65

publics, lesbian, 29, 70, 155, 159, 163; indexes and, 111, 123, 129, 130, 132
publishing movement, 19–20, 209

queer history, 30, 166, 210; of information, 3, 25, 217n5
queerness, 15, 16, 25, 118; lesbian feminism and, 162, 163–64, 191, 198

race, 119–21, 127, 238n73; class and, 242n51; solidarity around, 18, 223n67; switchboard operators and, 89–90, 238n73
racism, 15, 23, 119, 207, 241n37. *See also* antiracism
Radicalesbians, 18
radical feminists, 3, 87, 182, 209
Radical Rose Recordings, 175
Rakow, Lana, 86, 98
RAND Corporation, 41, 124, 141, 142, 247n174
Rault, Jas, 182
Rawson, K. J., 39–40, 146, 256n136
Reagon, Bernice Johnson, 118, 241n37
referral information, 83–84, 88, 236n43, 238n73; for basic support of lesbianism, 97, 98; for lesbians with disabilities, 91; race considerations, 89–90, 238n73
relational databases, 124, 140–41
Rentschler, Carrie, 8, 186, 217n4, 255n102
Ridinger, Robert B. M., 243n68
Roberto, K. R., 197
Roberts, JR (pseud.): on *Black Lesbians*, 116, *117*, 118–19, 121–22, 127, 138, 212; Potter's comments on, 113–14, 132–33, 151; resignation from *Matrices*, 63
Robertson, Craig, 77
Robertson, Tara, 192
Rodriguez, Rio, 15
Rosenzweig, Roy, 51
Ross, Mirha-Soleil, 170, 252n50
Rowe, Aimee Carrillo, 119
Rubin, Gayle, 48–49
Ruhleder, Karen, 8
rural lesbians, 58, 232n70

safety, 18–19, 20, 64, 95, 131, 232n92
Salsa Soul Sisters, 90, 121